To LANDRUM —

WITH ~~~~~~~~~~~~ AND

WITH THE ASSURANCE
THAT I DO NOT EXPECT
HIM TO READ EVERY
WORD!

Roger

APRIL 20, 1991

Improving Compliance with International Law

Volume 14, Procedural Aspects of International Law Series

The Procedural Aspects of International Law Series
RICHARD B. LILLICH, *editor* (1964–1977)
ROBERT KOGOD GOLDMAN, *editor* (1977–)

Improving Compliance with International Law

Roger Fisher

University Press of Virginia
Charlottesville

THE UNIVERSITY PRESS OF VIRGINIA

Copyright © 1981 by the Procedural Aspects of
International Law Institute, Inc.
200 Park Avenue, New York, New York 10017

First published 1981

Library of Congress Cataloging in Publication Data

Fisher, Roger Dummer, 1922–
 Improving compliance with international law.

The Procedural aspects of international law
series; v. 14)
 Includes index.
 1. International law. 2. Pacific settlement of
international disputes. I. Title. II. Series:
Procedural aspects of international law series; v. 14.
JX4003.F53   341.5'2   80–14616
ISBN 0–8139–0859–0

Printed in the United States of America

Editor's Foreword

This book is the fourteenth volume in the Procedural Aspects of International Law Series and is published by the University Press of Virginia for the Procedural Aspects of International Law Institute. The author, Roger Fisher, Williston Professor at the Harvard Law School, is a prodigious international law scholar who, for more than a decade, has paid particular attention to questions relating to international disputes and the means for realizing their peaceful resolution.

Professor Fisher's basic argument is that existing methods of handling international conflict need improvement and that exploring and devising new techniques for achieving increased state compliance with international law could advance that goal. This book, he notes, is "*not* a general treatise on bringing about world peace" (p. 8), but "is concerned with the problem of bringing law to bear on governments, the problem of applying to nation states 'those wise restraints that make men free'" (p. 9). In this regard, the author's emphasis "is not on specific proposals of what should be done to make governments obey international law" (p. 4); rather, he shows "how governments may be induced to comply with legal and other norms on the basis of an analysis of their current behavior patterns" (p. 4). This is an imaginative, superbly analytical work which suggests credible alternatives to traditional notions of and techniques for enforcing international law.

I wish to acknowledge with thanks the assistance of Richard B. Lillich, Howard W. Smith Professor at the University of Virginia Law School and former PAIL Series editor, for arranging the publication of this book and of Barbara A. Pollack and Stephanie H. Klein, my Dean's Fellows, for their substantial contributions in the editing of this work.

ROBERT KOGOD GOLDMAN

Washington, D.C.

Acknowledgments

For more than a dozen years this book has been in gestation. During that time countless students have contributed in endless ways to the development of these ideas and these words. They know better than any recitation can recall the extent of my debt to them. To three in particular I owe special thanks. Peter Trooboff, friend, colleague, and now well-known Washington lawyer, helped reorganize the entire structure, contributed many examples, and saved me from many, if not all, mistakes. Dan Ciobanu, distinguished scholar of international law, reviewed the entire text and suggested scores of illustrations and improvements in the manuscript. Most recently, Paul Hauser has handled the difficult task of shepherding me and the manuscript until it reached the printer. To all of them I am most grateful.

Contents

Introductory Part

Law as a Means of
Making Governments Behave

CHAPTER I

General Approach

1. *The problem.* I am concerned with the process for coping
with international conflict. Like many others, I am disturbed by
the way nations carry on their disagreements. It usually is taken
for granted that thermonuclear war is an unsatisfactory way of
settling disputes.[1] Conventional war, generally conceded to be
better, is still far from being the best process one can hope for.
As a lawyer, I start with the hypothesis that law has something to
contribute. The central focus of this book is the process of fostering compliance of states with international law. The problem
is being examined for the purpose of attaining a better understanding of what ought to be done.

It is possible to examine international affairs from a more dis-
engaged point of view. Some of the best political scientists believe
that a scholar should be a detached observer — that accuracy of
perception comes from not being involved too closely. It often is
deemed bad form to corrupt one's analysis with personal notions
of what ought to be done. For some, international affairs is a
spectator sport. The commentator produces program notes explaining to the less skilled what is going on and predicting what
is likely to happen. He comments on the difficulties and dilem-
mas of the day without feeling any duty to explain what a particular official or government ought to do. Like an historian, he
can point out significant trends and forces. He thus can impart
some meaning to the chaos of facts.

An exchange I had with a French political critic illustrates this
approach. He had just been pointing out the fruitless nature of
his government's recent actions and policies when I asked him

---

[1]"In the Nuclear age there is no alternative to conducting . . . relations on the basis of
peaceful coexistence." *See Basic Principles of Relation Between the United States of America
and the Union of Soviet Socialist Republics,* 66 DEPT STATE BULL 898 1972 66 AM. J. INT'L L.
921 (1972). As early as 1959, Jessup suggested that in U.S.-Soviet relations there should
be adjustments "which politics tells us are impossible but which science tells us are essential." *See* P. JESSUP, THE USE OF INTERNATIONAL LAW 130, 139 (1959).

what *he* would have it do. I recall clearly the shocked expression on his face. I might just as well have suggested that a gourmet should not criticize a rotten egg unless he were able to lay a better one.

For myself, I would distinguish politics from cooking. While there may be objective standards of perfection in eggs, political conduct should be judged by the available alternatives that are better. The political analysis that imparts the most meaning to me is the one which calls attention to open choices.

With this bias by way of background, it is clear that this book is not intended simply as a description of the way in which governments currently behave. The following chapters are written with two basic assumptions in mind: (*a*) that people have choices; and (*b*) that the method for handling international conflict ought to be improved. I try to suggest considerations that may be useful to people whose choices can help move us in that direction. It seems to me that one advantage of looking at the world with the purpose of changing it in a particular direction is that problems come more clearly into focus. Then, there is a standard of relevance. Then, definitions and distinctions have value depending upon their utility; they are not simply questions of definition about which there can be unlimited debate.

2. *Which direction do we want to go?* My emphasis is not on specific proposals of what should be done to make governments obey international law. Rather, I intend to show how governments may be induced to comply with legal and other norms on the basis of an analysis of their current behavior patterns. At the present time, there are a great many widely held assumptions about how law works — and why it does not work — with respect to governments. Many of these assumptions are implicit rather than explicit. They underlie both day-to-day decisions of governments and proposals for future international arrangements. I want to examine such assumptions and put forward some alternative hypotheses. Most of my theories are not subject to proof, just as the assumptions upon which governments currently operate are not subject to proof. Their appeal will depend upon their apparent plausibility.

To the extent that the ideas and hypotheses are implausible or inadequate, they still may stimulate the development of more accurate theories of governmental control. Every political theory necessarily is an approximation. My approximations are cruder than most, due, in part, to an attempt to generalize about governments that differ widely. Some of these ideas, I like; with others, I am quite dissatisfied. In many respects, I have no doubt been busy, as my colleague Louis Sohn has told me, "unlocking doors that are already open." In extenuation, I would urge that the harm of rediscovering what others know is far less than that of becoming seduced by established patterns of thought and of failing to ask basic questions.

Specific suggestions and examples are useful primarily for illustrating a way of thinking. Like a lawyer arguing a case, I sometimes may get carried away with the merits of the position being urged. This posture does not trouble me. As a firm believer in the adversary system, I am convinced that wise decisions are more likely to result from having competing views advanced forcefully than from having everyone play the role of judge.

3. *The realm of the possible.* A book that is designed to suggest ways of improving the process for causing compliance with international law obviously assumes that change is possible. How *much* change is possible? What should be taken as given and what should be taken as subject to change? This question is probably the single most fundamental question in political discussion.

Almost all political differences can be explained, in the last analysis, by different assumptions or conclusions about what can and cannot be changed. These differing assumptions and conclusions deserve far more explicit consideration than they generally receive. More is involved than a disagreement about the facts. What one takes as "subject to change" is also a function of the time period being considered and of the effort being made to achieve change. More particularly, what can be changed is, within limits, a function of the operating assumption about what can be changed. In one sense, it may be unrealistic for an owner of a house to operate publicly on the assumption that he can sell his house for $80,000. In a more sophisticated sense, it may be highly realistic, for by so behaving one is likely to increase the price that one can obtain. Letting one's reach exceed his grasp may increase the amount within one's grasp.

One can choose what one wishes to consider within the realm

of the possible, depending upon one's purpose. A rough way of indicating what one has chosen is to identify the time period within which it is conceivable that a given change might be wrought. For purposes of this book, a period of roughly ten to twenty years has seemed useful. Looking a decade or so ahead enables one to take a bearing on where he or she wants to go, without being influenced unduly by immediate obstacles such as impending elections or the stubbornly held views of particular individuals. It enables one to be concerned with political strategy rather than tactics. To err on the side of designing a utopia for the distant future runs the risk of being irrelevant, but even such suggestions may have substantial impact. (The communist model of Karl Marx was highly unrealistic; yet defining that goal was one of the most effective political acts in the history of the world.)

If I assume that more is within the realm of the possible than the reader is prepared to concede, it is to some extent deliberate. We may not know what to grasp until we know which way to reach.

4. *Will it work?* Several points should be borne in mind when the reader considers the extent to which the general approach toward improving compliance with international law suggested here would work. First, we are seeking to understand the kind of international system that would be an improvement over the one we have now. In an important sense, the existing international system does not work. The domestic law enforcement scheme within the United States does not work in the sense of producing satisfactory compliance with laws of the United States. The legal system of the United States does not produce prompt compliance with the laws where, as in the civil rights area, there is strong and organized political opposition. Even within the United States, which is a cohesive community with a strong central government, existing and proposed enforcement techniques cannot be expected to work in all situations. But perhaps no better legal techniques exist. "Working" is not an either/ or matter.

The situation of the international community is not unlike that of a group of men in a boat in rough seas. If one man suggests that both stability and speed will be improved by raising a sail and shifting the ballast, an opposing prediction that the boat still will not weather anticipated storms is wholly irrelevant unless there is some more promising course of action.

Second, we are seeking to devise machinery that will both operate under and help bring about a steadily improving political climate. It perhaps is more realistic to assume that hostilities and working relationships among the major powers of the world will be quite different in the future[2] than to assume that the particular tensions which have dominated the recent past will continue. Interdependence and shared interests are becoming increasingly obvious. In such a world, the compliance problem may be less difficult than it now appears. In such a world, the techniques discussed here may operate more effectively than they could today.

5. *A note of caution about analogies.* Throughout the book, extensive use is made of analogies. By and large, they are intended as suggestive examples rather than proof. The very concept of "law" in the international community can be understood only by analogy to domestic law. Typically one thinks of the criminal law where compliance is achieved by fear of punishment. But constitutional law and administrative law are more relevant to the problem of controlling governments. Although there are significant differences between the problems of causing the state of West Virginia to pay a judgment of the United States Supreme Court[3] and causing the Government of Albania to pay a judgment of the International Court of Justice,[4] understanding the difficulties that even a strong central government has in collect-

---

[2]Changes in Soviet-American and Chinese-American relations since 1965 when this sentence first was written support this assumption.

[3]*See* Virginia v. West Virginia, 206 U.S. 290 (1907); 209 U.S. 514 (1908); 220 U.S. 1 (1911); 222 U.S. 17 (1911); 231 U.S. 89 (1913); 234 U.S. 117 (1914); 238 U.S. 202 (1915); 241 U.S. 531 (1916); 246 U.S. 565 (1918).

[4]*See* The Corfu Channel Case, [1949] I.C.J. 4. Despite the final judgment of Dec. 15, 1949, in which damages of £843,947 were awarded to the United Kingdom against Albania, the amount was never paid. Following discussions between the two governments, Albania offered to pay the sum of £40,000 in final settlement of the British claim; in January 1951, that offer, however, was rejected by the British Government as not worthy of consideration. Subsequently, the British Government endeavored to obtain Albanian monetary gold, which had been removed from Rome by the Germans in September 1943 and subsequently found in Germany by the Allied forces. *See* 1 S. ROSENNE, THE LAW AND PRACTICE OF THE INTERNATIONAL COURT 143–44 (1965).

ing debts from subordinate state governments may contribute to arriving at a solution of the international problem. Although no one would argue that whatever legal technique is successful within the United States in the 1970s would be equally successful within the international community in the 1980s, the fact that the international community will be quite different is not in itself a sound reason for rejecting the technique. On the other hand, the fact that some legal techniques do not work and could not be expected to work in controlling the behavior of the federal or state governments does suggest that those techniques should not be relied upon in seeking to control the behavior of governments in general.

Thus, the task at hand is to design legal machinery that appears to be more effective than what we now have — machinery that will produce as high a degree of compliance as can reasonably be expected, given the state of the international community. This study is designed to help identify improvements in legal techniques for causing compliance with international law. A separate question, which cannot be dealt with in the abstract and is not dealt with here, is whether, even with such enforcement techniques, the anticipated compliance with a particular proposed rule is so low that the rule should not be adopted. In considering a particular rule the risks of noncompliance must be weighed against the risks involved if there is no such rule at all.

6. *Location of the problem.* This book is *not* a general treatise on bringing about world peace. Law has a small, although necessary, role to play in securing peace and prosperity,[5] and complements the roles played by economics, education, science, agriculture, communication, travel, and so forth. Just as educational, economic, and social measures may be more significant than the enforcement of court decrees in overcoming the evils of governmentally imposed racial segregation, so such measures in the international community may be the most significant means of attaining the ends of law enforcement. Furthermore,

---

[5] In my view, law can play a somewhat larger role than that suggested by Brierly, who wrote: "Law never creates order; the most it can do is to help to sustain order when that has once been firmly established, for it sometimes acquires a prestige of its own which enables it to foster an atmosphere favourable to the continuance of orderly social relations when these are called upon to stand a strain." J. BRIERLY, THE OUTLOOK FOR INTERNATIONAL LAW 74 (1944).

the willingness of government leaders to tolerate the temporary setbacks involved in any law enforcement scheme depends upon such losses being outweighed by the benefits derived from participation in the international community.[6]

But not all such legal techniques are within our purview. Perhaps the greatest opportunity in international law lies in facilitating a cooperative attack on man's problems on an international basis. International organizations such as the Universal Postal Union, the World Health Organization, and the International Monetary Fund suggest how legal draftsmen can work with others in strengthening the fabric of the international community. Much more, however, remains to be done. In place after place, the world would benefit from the international equivalent of the TVA or the New York Port Authority. As Professor Hardy Dillard, later a member of the International Court of Justice, said in 1963 in his Presidential Address at the annual meeting of the American Society of International Law, "The *relationship* between what is national and what is international needs to be reexplored in light *not* of traditional doctrine but of emerging interests, demands, and expectations and *not* in terms of jural manipulation but of forging imaginative institutional arrangements operating under the umbrella of the United Nations."[7]

So the purpose of this book becomes much more limited than a general program for peace, and narrower even than an examination of the role law should play in bringing about world peace. This book is concerned with the problem of bringing law to bear on governments, the problem of applying to nation states "those wise restraints that make men free."

---

[6]In British-U.S. relations, legal techniques long have been used, but only on an ad hoc basis as a calculated way of reducing potential costs. "[I]n the repeated British-American clashes of important interests, arbitration or another form of peaceful adjustment was never taken for granted. The governments took their decisions only after earnest calculation of the values at stake, the minimum and maximum results to be anticipated from an arbitral or negotiated settlement, and the risk and probable cost of war." P. CORBETT, LAW IN DIPLOMACY 139 (1959). Corbett described the Alaska boundary arbitration as a "classic demonstration of the use of arbitral forms not for the purpose of obtaining an impartial decision on points of difference, but as a means of enabling one side to surrender without a politically costly loss of face." *Id.* at 156. For similar reasons, the two governments earlier had agreed to arbitrate the *Alabama* controversy. *See, e.g.,* G. SCHWARZENBERGER, POWER POLITICS: A STUDY OF WORLD SOCIETY 233 (3d ed. 1964).

[7]57 AM. SOCY INTL L. PROC 50, 66 (1963).

Even here the field is broader than the subject matter of this book. Basically, I am not concerned with improving the substantive rules of existing international law. From my point of view, consideration of what international law ought to be can be divided into three main problems. The first consists of devising wise rules — in answering the question: What ought the law to be? For example, discussion of the legality of high-level reconnaissance over another country,[8] of the testing of nuclear weapons,[9] and of providing aid to revolutionary movements[10] has been directed primarily at this question of what the substantive law on a point is or ought to be. The second problem is that of

---

[8] It is widely recognized that it is a violation of international law for one state to fly aircraft on hostile reconnaissance missions over another state. The U-2 incident powerfully reaffirmed this view. On the other hand, world praise (and the absence of protest) in response to the Soviet Sputnik satellite established that outer space was beyond the jurisdiction of any state. The legality of reconnaissance from outer space apparently is now recognized. Article XII of the Treaty with the Union of Soviet Socialist Republics on the Limitation of Anti-ballistic Missile Systems, May 26, 1972, United States–Union of Soviet Socialist Republics, 23 U.S.T. 3435, T.I.A.S. No. 7503, provides that "each party shall use national technical means of verification at its disposal in a manner consistent with generally recognized principles of international law" — a formula broad enough to include, if not devised primarily for, satellite surveillance. Since, however, there is no physical boundary between "air space" and "outer space," the substantive law remains subject to debate. *Cf.* Lissitzyn, *Some Legal Implications of the U-2 and RB-47 Incidents,* 56 AM. J. INTL L. 135, 137 (1962).

[9] For states party to the Treaty Banning Nuclear Weapon Tests in the Atmosphere, in Outer Space, and Under Water, Aug. 5, 1963, 14 U.S.T. 1313, T.I.A.S. No. 5433, 480 U.N.T.S. 43, nuclear tests therein prohibited are illegal. France, China, and others have declined to accede to the Treaty. But even in the absence of the Treaty, atmospheric tests that produce radioactive fallout in other states may be considered a violation of traditional international law. *Cf.* The Trail Smelter Arbitration (United States v. Canada), 3 R. Int'l Arb. Awards 1906 (1938 + 1941) (pursuant to which Canada paid for damage in the United States caused by fumes from a smelter in Canada); such was the contention of Australia and New Zealand in their dispute with France over the atmospheric testing of French nuclear devices in the territory of French Polynesia. [1973] I.C.J. 103, 109. The International Court of Justice declined the case on procedural grounds (Nuclear Test Case, [1974] I.C.J. 260, 272), leaving the issue of substantive law open.

[10] Traditionally, foreign aid to revolutionary regimes was considered unlawful, unless the fighting reached the conditions of belligerency recognized by the local government itself. The Institut de Droit International reaffirmed the traditional viewpoint in article 2 of its Règlement of Sept. 8, 1900, 18 ANNUAIRE DE L'INSTITUT DE DROIT INTERNATIONAL 277 (1900). The practice of states, especially since the end of World War II, has continuously eroded the traditional rule. Resolutions of the General Assembly of the United Nations have gradually affirmed the existence of an international right and perhaps even a duty to assist revolutionary movements, at least when they assume the form of wars of national liberation. The rule of international law obviously has become unclear.

the process for establishing a proposed rule as one which ought to be respected. How should the rule be adopted? Rules may be adopted by a comprehensive treaty, such as the 1958 Geneva Conventions on the Law of the Sea;[11] by a specific agreement on a narrow subject, such as the partial nuclear test ban treaty;[12] by a resolution of an international organization which is followed by general acquiescence of member states; or by practice which is pursued by states in the belief that they are complying with an international obligation, and so forth.[13] Different consequences flow from the use of such different "legislative" techniques.

The third problem in considering what international law ought to be is the problem of causing compliance with the prescribed norms of conduct once they have become rules of international law. This problem is the one to which this book is directed.

7. *Traditional approaches.* Most people hold a view of international law which runs somewhat as follows: There is a great difference between positive law — law with a policeman behind it — and so-called international law. International law is a body of vague rules for the attention of the political scientist and the amusement of the law student not much interested in law. It should not be confused with real law, which, as Justice Holmes pointed out, is "the articulate voice of some sovereign or quasi-sovereign that can be identified,"[14] and "does not exist without some definite authority behind it."[15] Law is the command of a sovereign backed by force. And however much it is hoped that nations will abide by acknowledged rules, they do not now; nor can they ever be compelled to do so, at least in the absence of world government. Only wooly thinking would confuse positive law enforced by our courts — our Constitution, our civil and

[11]Geneva Convention on the High Seas, Apr. 29, 1958, 13 U.S.T. 2312, T.I.A.S. No. 5200, 450 U.N.T.S. 82; Geneva Convention on the Continental Shelf, Apr. 29, 1958, 15 U.S.T. 471, T.I.A.S. No. 5578, 499 U.N.T.S. 311; Geneva Convention on the Territorial Sea and Contiguous Zone, Apr. 29, 1958, 15 U.S.T. 1606, T.I.A.S. No. 5639, 516 U.N.T.S. 205.

[12]Treaty Banning Nuclear Weapon Tests, note 9 *supra.*

[13]*See* Fisher, *Constructing Rules that Affect Governments,* in ARMS CONTROL, DISARMAMENT AND NATIONAL SECURITY 56 (D. Brennan ed. 1961).

[14]Southern Pacific, Co. v. Jensen, 244 U.S. 205, 222 (1917) (dissenting opinion).

[15]Black & White Taxicab & Transfer Co. v. Brown & Yellow Taxicab & Transfer Co., 276 U.S. 518, 533 (1928) (dissenting opinion).

criminal laws — with the moral directives that go by the name of international law. So runs the traditional party line of the legal profession.[16]

8. *The existing pattern of compliance.* Conflict and violence often obscure both the fact that international law is a significant factor in today's world and that there is a vast amount of routine compliance with it. Not only do countries daily respect the legal limits on the extent of their territorial jurisdiction and the authority of other governments, but there is also a mass of routine contact and intercourse among nations that is governed by norms which the governments call international law and to which they openly adhere. Thousands of times a day, ships defer to the rules of the high seas; foreign aircraft are allowed to enter and leave pursuant to legal arrangements; radio frequency allocations are respected; the mail is carried pursuant to international obligation; aliens are accorded the rights guaranteed to them by treaty and customary international law; governments honor their international financial commitments, and so forth. Even in areas of military and political concern, a legal commitment makes a difference. Having signed the Moscow Test Ban Treaty of 1963,[17] both the Soviet Union and the United States are more reluctant to conduct an atmospheric test of a nuclear weapon than they would be if they had not signed it. Governments which spend millions on propaganda and information programs know that their actions are noticed and that a country pays a price for a blatant violation of international law.[18]

Despite all the routine compliance, there is a good deal of noncompliance. Looking at these exceptions more closely, we find that there rarely is agreement on whether international law in fact is being violated. Almost invariably, the country whose conduct is in question denies the conduct, denies that it is responsible for what is taking place,[19] contends that the conduct is

[16]*See, e.g.,* H. Kelsen, Principles of International Law 19–20 (2d rev. ed. R. Tucker ed. 1966).

[17]Treaty Banning Nuclear Weapon Tests, note 9 *supra.*

[18]The Soviet invasion of Czechoslovakia in August 1968, for instance, was carried out at the cost of souring the Soviet relationship with Communist parties in Western Europe, as well as with other nongovernmental organizations which generally had been favorable to the foreign policy of the Soviet Union.

[19]Intelligence activities and foreign support for dissident groups provide, perhaps, the greatest number of examples. Even more conspicuous are the denials of violation of

permitted under international law,[20] or justifies the conduct on the ground of violations by another country.[21] Allegations of noncompliance are perhaps most frequent where international law is the least clear, as in the limits placed on aerial bombardment in time of war. On the other hand, conduct, such as American U-2 reconnaissance overflights of Cuba in 1964, which is contrary to what most countries would consider to be the unmistakable meaning of a rule of international law, is likely to occur only if substantial interests are at stake. Even here, conduct that is public and continuous almost always will be justified as legal. In exceptional cases, where no argument is made that the conduct is permitted by international law as such, a country often will assert that it has a sovereign "right" to engage in the conduct in order to protect vital national interests.[22]

It is fair to say that most reformers in the field of international law have accepted the notion that the basic way of enforcing law is by a policeman, and that the way to improve compliance with international law is to establish an international police force strong enough to impose the law upon any country.[23] A necessary corollary to the military superiority of the proposed police

territorial sovereignty of foreign states by those governments which seem to have been involved in political kidnappings, such as the kidnapping of Eichmann from Argentina. For a discussion of the Eichmann case, see Silving, *In Re Eichmann: A Dilemma of Law and Morality*, 55 AM. J. INT'L L. 307, 315–16 (1961).

[20]This seems to have been, for instance, the main line of reasoning of President Kennedy's Proclamation 3504. *Interdiction of the Delivery of Offensive Weapons to Cuba*, 47 DEPT STATE BULL. 717 (1962); 57 AM. J. INT'L. L. 512–13 (1963).

[21]President Johnson used the Tonkin incident as a justification for the bombardment of North Vietnam; in the Mayaguez case, President Ford justified his order for the military expedition within Cambodian territory by referring to the failure of the Cambodian authorities to release the ship which, he contended, had been seized unlawfully.

[22]An example is the Declaration of Santiago on the Maritime Zone, signed by Chile, Ecuador, and Peru, on Aug. 18, 1952. After declaring, *inter alia*, that it is the duty of each government to prevent natural "resources from being used outside the area of its jurisdiction so as to endanger their existence, integrity and conservation to the prejudice of peoples so situated geographically that their seas are irreplaceable sources of essential food and economic materials," the three governments proclaimed "as a principle of their international maritime policy that each of them possesses sole sovereignty and jurisdiction over the area of sea adjacent to the coast of its own country and extending not less than 200 nautical miles from the said coast." 4 M. WHITEMAN, DIGEST OF INTERNATIONAL LAW 1089–90 (1965).

[23]This was the conception advocated by President Roosevelt toward the end of World War II, and it underlies much of the system for the maintenance of international peace and security established by the Charter of the United Nations. During the visit of Mol-

force is that there must be substantial disarmament by the major powers.[24]

The best sustained consideration of the process by which governments could be caused to obey international rules is no doubt Grenville Clark and Louis Sohn's *World Peace Through World Law*.[25] That important and valuable book spells out what might be involved in enforcing respect for international rules against arms and violence. Part of the authors' theory is that of the policeman on a larger scale. As stated by Clark in the introduction,

> In short, our conception is that if police forces are necessary to maintain law and order even with a mature community or nation, similar forces will be required to guarantee the carrying out and maintenance of complete disarmament by each and every nation and to deter or suppress any attempted international violence.[26]

Although the Clark and Sohn proposals go far beyond the establishment of an international police force, they seem to share two premises with more traditional approaches. First, the necessary international machinery should be designed primarily with the big problems in mind — the problems of war, aggression, and deliberate violations of international law. Machinery capable of dealing with such problems will be adequate to deal with lesser problems. Second, the basic method of law enforcement is that of the criminal law. A major enforcement effort should be to deter any violations of the law. When deterrence has failed, force will be needed to stop the violation and to pun-

---

otov, Soviet Minister for Foreign Affairs, to Washington in May 1942, President Roosevelt took the position that it was the duty of the United Nations — Great Britain, the United States, the Soviet Union, and China — to act jointly as the "policemen of the world." *See also* 3 U.S. FOREIGN REL. 568 (1942); 2 C. HULL MEMOIRS OF CORDELL HULL 1642–43 (1948).

[24]In the system conceived by President Roosevelt, the four major powers were supposed to maintain sufficient armed forces to impose peace on a disarmed world. *See* 3 U.S. FOREIGN REL., *supra* note 23 at 568–69. Roosevelt's basic assumption was that the four policemen would and should act in concert as guarantors of international peace and security. The assumption was ill-founded. But that is not my objection. The very approach to the matter was erroneous: the system was based on a war model designed to deal with issues at a late stage in their development, instead of devising means for compliance with international law before international peace and security are endangered.

[25]G. CLARK & L. SOHN, WORLD PEACE THROUGH WORLD LAW (2d ed. 1960).

[26]*Id.* at xxix.

ish the violator. When violations of international law have been found, sanctions should be imposed against the guilty country, or, perhaps, punishment should be imposed upon the individual officials responsible for the conduct, as in the Nuremberg case.

Both premises seem questionable. The greatest talent of the law appears to be to deal with questions when they are small and to keep them small. Law enforcement, I believe, should be more than and quite different from internationally organized war. Without disputing the desirability of the United Nations' being able to put an army into the field to stop aggression, as in Korea in 1950, or to have the forces to maintain internal law and order where effective government has broken down, as in the Congo in 1960, this book starts at the other end of the problem. To use a medical analogy, one way to design a medical system would be to design the institutions and techniques needed to cope with a raging epidemic, and then to apply comparable techniques on a smaller scale to less serious instances of disease. An alternative technique is to focus on preventive medicine and the treatment of individual cases, and then to supplement the available services with the institutions and techniques needed to cope with epidemics. This latter approach is the one suggested here. Primary attention is directed here to the problem of "ordinary" violations of international law by governments and the ways of dealing with them. Supplemental consideration is given to the problems of coping with the epidemic proportions of problems like war, aggression, and anarchy.

These latter problems have received a great deal of attention elsewhere. Furthermore, it is patently impossible to design an international law enforcement system capable of dealing with the worst contingencies, for among such contingencies are various kinds of disloyalties and insurrections within the system itself. No one would think of designing a federal law enforcement agency in this country around the possibility that the Army could refuse to obey the President. We design enforcement machinery to meet more likely and less drastic possibilities, and should worse happen, we would expect the individuals in it to proceed in as nearly the routine way as circumstances permit — and hope for the best. The primary task of the law is to *avoid* a maximum confrontation, not to handle it — to deal with disorder in an orderly way which tends to dampen rather than inflame it.

Law is best understood not as an alternative to force or to politics but as a way of structuring political forces. In the world of the future, a balance of power — or a separation of powers — will remain desirable. Law and legal institutions can affect that balance or that separation. Perhaps they can so affect and control the form and content of issues within the international community that an accommodation between order and change can be maintained which is comparable to that within domestic communities. The notion of a balance of power should not offend those of us brought up on the checks and balances of the United States Constitution. Nor should the notion of limited central forces be anathema to those raised under a government which, for the first decades of its existence, had fewer forces at its command than did many of the subordinate states of the union.

The second premise here challenged is that the primary enforcement technique for international rules should be comparable to that of the criminal law — deterrence and the punishment of violations.

9. *The unique characteristic of governments.* The concept of law as the command of a sovereign buttressed by organized force was useful for distinguishing the law that *is* from the law that *ought to be*. John Austin's definition of law did not apply, however, to rules restraining the behavior of the state itself, which Austin referred to as rules of "positive morality." The "power of government," he said, "is incapable of *legal* limitation."[27] A large part of our legal experience, however — certainly in the United States — is with limitations upon government. Typically, more than half of the cases considered by the United States Supreme Court in a given year involve the adjudication of the rights and duties of the federal government. For all such cases — especially for all of those which the government loses — it is not useful to think of law as a command with superior force behind it. When it comes to enforcing law against governments, it turns out that governments and government officers are not like bank robbers.

[27]J. AUSTIN, THE PROVINCE OF JURISPRUDENCE DETERMINED AND THE USES OF THE STUDY OF JURISPRUDENCE 191–93, 346 (Noonday Press edition 1954).

A brief consideration of the differences suggests why somewhat different methods of producing compliance with the law might be appropriate.

In one sense, of course, there is no such thing as a "government"; it is a legal abstraction. There are simply human beings fulfilling certain roles and acting "officially." But the concept of a "government" is ingrained deeply and understood so well that it is far more useful to deal with governments as such than it is to assume them away and deal exclusively with the officers. It is well to remember, however, that in seeking to influence a government, we are seeking to influence the official conduct of one or more human beings acting pursuant to institutional arrangements.

Being an abstract term, a government, like a corporation, is less subject to the kinds of punishment that normally are used to enforce the criminal law. On the other hand, in contrast to an individual criminal, a government is involved so deeply with law that it will find it difficult, if not impossible, to adopt an antilaw posture. A government is a legal structure, operating pursuant to legal powers, administering a system of laws. Its power depends upon obedience to law by its subordinate officials and by the public at large. It uses the adoption and enforcement of laws as the basic means of governing.

The continued existence of any government depends not only upon respect for domestic law but also upon respect by all other governments for at least certain minimal provisions of international law. The very boundaries of a state are lines whose practical significance depends upon their legal significance. A government's existence, its independence, its right to govern and to speak for its people, are understandable only in terms of some form of international law. Max Huber emphasized this with convincing force in the *Island of Palmas* case:

> Sovereignty in the relations between States signifies independence. Independence in regard to a portion of the globe is the right to exercise therein, to the exclusion of any other State, the functions of a State. The development of the national organisation of States during the last few centuries and, as a corollary, the development of international law, have established this principle of the exclusive competence of the State in regard to its own ter-

ritory in such a way as to make it the point of departure in settling most questions that concern international relations.[28]

The public and many government officials have tended to have a view of law which distinguishes sharply between domestic and international legal obligations. Regardless of that view, the line between laws that are obeyed and laws that are broken does not correspond to the line between domestic law and international law. Many international rules, such as those establishing international boundaries and the rights of vessels on the high seas, are accorded greater respect by actions, if not by words, than corresponding domestic legal limitations on a government's power. This is particularly true of governments that do not have a strong tradition of respect for domestic limitations on their authority.

In some respects the task of obtaining compliance by governments is far more difficult than the task of controlling individuals. We are dealing with vast political enterprises invested with great power. In other respects, however, they may be more vulnerable to the law since they derive so much of their power from it. A government is reluctant to admit that it is doing an illegal act and generally will seek to justify its conduct. Big governments like the United States often comply with constitutional restraints and other rules without a bigger force to make them do so. A government is a gigantic and complex machine. As with other such machines, it may not be necessary to have a bigger or a stronger one to bring it to a stop. A brake (or a monkey wrench) may be enough. Law enforcement against governments is most likely to be successful if it makes maximum use of those techniques to which governments are uniquely susceptible.

10. *Acceptability.* A method of producing compliance with international law will not work unless it is generally acceptable to the international community. But that is not surprising; we are accustomed to government with the consent of the governed. Acceptability is critical. The task is to devise those methods which will produce the most compliance that one can expect to get from the international community, given the limitations imposed by durable ways of thinking.

[28]Island of Palmas Case (Netherlands v. United States), 2 R. Int'l Arb. Awards 829, 838 (1928).

What kind of arrangements would be acceptable to the world five, ten, or even twenty years hence is obviously a guess. There is little merit in quarreling over such predictions. Fortunately, I am not drafting a comprehensive treaty to be submitted on a take-it-or-leave-it basis. Nor am I speaking for the United States. This book suggests both a general approach and some particular variables that might be adjusted to meet problems of changing acceptability. Past experience indicates that the world is more likely to move toward improving the international law system by bits and pieces rather than by adopting at one time a comprehensive revision of the United Nations Charter. In light of this expectation, it seems more useful to explore the kind of forces that tend to cause governments to respect international law than to debate whether a particular scheme would be acceptable within ten years or might be acceptable within twenty-five.

CHAPTER II

The Multiple Objectives
of Compliance

1. *Framing the question.* The concept of compliance seems simple enough at first impression: if we want a government to comply with a rule of international law, we want its conduct to conform to the rule. In many situations, the concept of compliance is as simple as that. In others, however, either the rule or the facts, or both, may be unclear or disputed. In such cases, what is meant by compliance is not at all simple. And, even in instances where the facts and the rule have been cleared up, time has elapsed; the milk has been spilled. There remains the question of what ought to happen next. This chapter is devoted to exploring the kinds of compliance which an international law enforcement system ought to be designed to produce.

2. *Reasons for wanting more compliance.* Several different objectives are subsumed within the idea of compliance. Identifying them with some precision may illuminate the different means of attaining them. The first reason for wanting governments to respect a rule is to protect the interest that the rule is designed to serve. Just as we want a driver to stop his car at a red light in order to avoid a collision, so we want a government to respect the provision of the Antarctic Treaty[1] prohibiting arms in Antarctica in order to avoid that continent's becoming involved in military rivalries. We would like a country to respect the limit on the radio frequencies allocated to it in order to prevent its interfering with the use of other frequencies by other countries. In short, we want compliance with the rule for the same reason that we wanted the rule in the first place.

That, however, is not the only reason for which we want compliance. Once we have established a rule, we want that rule respected whether or not a violation would in fact cause the harm

[1] The Antarctic Treaty, Dec. 1, 1959, 12 U.S.T. 794, T.I.A.S. No. 4780, 402 U.N.T.S. 71.

that the rule was designed to avoid. We want the driver to stop
his car at a red light whether or not going through the red light
would result in a collision — in fact whether or not there is any
car at all on the intersecting street. We would like Argentina
scrupulously to respect the prohibition on armaments within
Antarctica even if a minor violation would cause no harm to any-
body.

Most rules are necessarily broader than the interest they are
designed to protect. Where a violation of the rule would not impinge on the interest protected, we nonetheless desire compliance, both to protect the rule and to protect the entire system of
rules. The problem is one of a precedent; we do not want the
rule to be broken a first time to avoid its violation in the future,
at which time protected interests may in fact be involved. If the
driver goes through the stop light when no cars are coming, he
is more likely, we fear, to go through it again when he would in
fact cause a collision. Looking at the precedent problem more
closely, we see that there are four separate ways in which one
violation may cause damage other than by impinging immediately upon the interest the rule was designed to protect. The
precedent may make it more likely that the violator will break
the same rule again, or it may increase the likelihood of his violating other rules. Or the precedent may affect others who know
of it, leading them to break either the same or some other rule.

These different reasons for wanting compliance — sometimes
to avoid actual injury and sometimes to protect the legal system
— lead to significant differences in the kind of compliance we
want. In cases in which the precedent is the only concern, it is
not too late to remedy the situation completely after a violation
has occurred. The driver who has gone through a red light
might be ordered to pay — and in fact pay — a fine of one
hundred dollars. The precedent of the violation has done no
harm. In fact, the net effect of the precedent is likely to be favorable to law enforcement. Before the violation, there was a
rule which neither the driver nor the community knew was
taken seriously; now they know differently. Similarly, if Argentina's implacement of arms in Antarctica were followed promptly
by its being required to remove them, the net effect of the precedent might be beneficial. It would lead to increased respect by

Argentina and other countries both for the Antarctic Treaty and for international law in general.

Even in cases in which a violation causes some actual and immediate injury, we are also concerned with the precedent that the violation may set. To the extent that the precedent is our concern, the problem can usually be dealt with after the fact. Both the lawbreaker and others who hear of the violation can be informed of subsequent events that turn the precedent of a violation into a precedent of law enforcement.

As discussed in Chapter V, some laws, both domestic and international, are purely precautionary in nature. Examples of such rules are ones that prohibit the carrying of concealed weapons, the storage of explosives in residential buildings, or the unauthorized entry of foreign ships into a country's internal waters. A simple violation of such a rule causes no immediate injury. For such precautionary rules, the reasons for which we want compliance will usually be better served by some harmless violations followed by appropriate action than by a fewer number of violations that are ignored.

3. *Compliance where there is a dispute.* If the discussion in Chapter I of the existing pattern of compliance is correct, the major area in which improved compliance is needed is where there is a dispute. Whether the dispute is a consequence of alleged noncompliance or whether the alleged noncompliance is a consequence of a dispute, the two go hand-in-hand. There is a real question about what is the appropriate compliance objective where there is a dispute about what is meant by compliance. (We will postpone until later the question of who can convert a situation into a dispute. The conduct of a government might, for example, be challenged as illegal by another government, by a United Nations official, by individuals or groups directly affected, or by an academic writer in the *American Journal of International Law.*)

On its face, a dispute may be either over a violation which has already occurred or over the future conduct of a government. The practical significance of every dispute, however, is wholly in the future. This is not always appreciated by the parties. They may concentrate a great deal of attention on disagreement over past facts without focusing on their relevance for the future.

What has happened has happened. What ought to happen may well depend upon the past; but what is important operationally is to decide on what ought to happen next. An objective is necessarily future-oriented.

At this point it becomes critical to identify *whose* objective we are considering.

4. *Compliance objectives of those outside the dispute.* From the standpoint of one with no specific stake in the dispute, the compliance objectives seem reasonably straightforward. Where there is a standing rule of international law, the plain meaning of which is generally understood, governments ought in general to conform their behavior to it. Aside from the possible educational benefits resulting from occasional violations being properly dealt with by the law, initial compliance with standing rules is one objective.

The more troublesome problem occurs when there is a genuine or plausible dispute. In the case of an international dispute, what is it that those seeking compliance with international law want to have happen? Consider the problems at any one time associated with Berlin, the Arab refugees, Kashmir, Cyprus, the Spanish Sahara, or the Aegean continental shelf. The legal rights and duties of the countries involved are far from clear. Laymen as well as lawyers know that there is no such thing as the objective "true" meaning of a law existing in the abstract and waiting to be found. Where the meaning of a rule of law is in dispute, a third country does not automatically know what conduct it wants — what conduct constitutes "compliance with the law."

There are several ways in which a state that is not a party to a given dispute might resolve the question of what conduct would constitute compliance with the law in that case. The third state might look at the two countries involved in the dispute, pick one of them as its friend, and conclude that whatever its friend said was right. Canada, for example, might conclude that in disputes between the United States and a communist country, the United States was always right, and that whatever the United States Government said with respect to the facts and the applicable international law would be accepted by Canada. Some governments do not support friends because they are right, but rather conclude they are right because they are friends.[2] No such standard, however, can be accepted as a reasonable compliance objective for an impartial member of the international community. In a disputed matter, compliance with the law cannot mean having one's friends prevail.

A second way of resolving the question is for every member of the international community to examine each problem and reach an independent judgment about the facts of the case and about the applicable law. There is a widespread tendency among governments to behave as though it were incumbent upon each one of them to decide for itself the merits of each dispute so that each will know what ought to happen — so that each will know what compliance with the law would be in that case. In most instances, more than one view could reasonably be taken. Any such process of independent determination by each state can lead only to more disputes;[3] it cannot identify a single, appropriate compliance objective for the community of states.

The third and, upon examination, the only acceptable means for defining the appropriate compliance objective for an uninvolved member of the community is that there be a fair procedure for determining in any dispute what ought to happen, and that whatever such procedure concludes should happen, should in fact happen. Such a determination might be reached through a variety of processes including negotiation, conciliation, arbitration, or adjudication. It might be anywhere along the scale that runs from a suggestion through a recommendation to a binding legal decision. For the concept of compliance with the law to be as clear as possible, the community would prefer that the process be capable of producing an authoritative determination as to what, in this case, would constitute compliance. A

[2] This often is true in regard to the stands taken by delegations during debates within the United Nations. For a description of this "group policy," see Hambro, *Some Notes on Parliamentary Diplomacy* in TRANSNATIONAL LAW IN A CHANGING SOCIETY: ESSAYS IN HONOUR OF PHILIP C. JESSUP 284–86 (W. Friedman, L. Henkin & O. Lissitzyn eds. 1972).

[3] Take, for instance, the contest for international recognition when two rival governments are fighting for power within one country (as happened in Cambodia after the coup of Lon Nol) or when factions of the same government are in conflict, such as the fight between the Lumumba and the Kassavubu factions in the Congo. In both cases, members of the United Nations were called upon to recognize the credentials of delegations representing the contending governments or factions. The original dispute assumed a new dimension among members of the United Nations.

court of law — or some comparable institution — is crucial to the very concept of compliance whenever its meaning is in dispute. Once a court has resolved a dispute and decided what ought to happen, the compliance objective of the community is clear: it wants its members to comply with that decision. The community thus wants a law enforcement scheme which produces compliance with standing rules (first-order compliance) when those rules are clearly understood, and compliance with an authoritative decision (second-order compliance) where there has been a dispute. This distinction between compliance with standing rules and compliance with particular decisions is absolutely fundamental. It underlies our entire consideration of the compliance problem.

5. *The inconsistent objectives of a disputant.* A government which is involved in an international legal dispute has a point of view quite different from that of governments which are not involved: it wants to win the dispute. The disputant has adopted a position as to the meaning of the relevant international rule. At one level, its compliance objective seems direct and simple. It wants its view of the law and facts to prevail and all governments to act accordingly.

The difficulty with this point of view is that each government is also a member of the international community. As such, it is interested in the establishment and maintenance of an orderly scheme of international law, including a fair system for settling disputes. Each government thus has the somewhat inconsistent objectives of winning disputes and having them settled. Neither objective can automatically be placed above the other. Although the United States would like to win each dispute, it is not seeking a world in which any one country wins every dispute. Internationally, as well as domestically, our government is interested simultaneously in winning each case that it argues in court and in promoting the rule of law — a regime in which the government does not always win.

The conflict between wanting to win disputes and wanting to settle them peacefully is genuine. It is not surprising that those who emphasize "victory" tend to pay less attention to "peace," and vice versa. Even within a well-functioning community, such as the United States, the more that the legal system decides for, and thus becomes identified with, one side of a major conflict (as the Supreme Court has tended to do on the issue of civil rights), the less able it becomes to act as an impartial arbiter whose decisions are readily respected.

Domestically, the dual interest of a government is well recognized, at least by government counsel. Particularly those in the Office of the Solicitor General, who argue regularly before the Supreme Court for the government, recognize that they are both counsel for an adversary and officers of the court. They recognize that the government has both an interest in winning a particular case as well as a pervasive long-term interest in furthering a legal system in which the government is often called to account and in which someone else's view of the law prevails.

Internationally, officers of a government tend to focus their attention almost exclusively on the interest which that government has in winning its disputes with other governments. We Americans are particularly ethnocentric; we tend to perceive the compliance problem as being how to make other governments comply with our views of the law. Of course, the United States and other governments will and should continue to press for the interpretation of a rule of law that they believe to be the correct one. (Even here, they should take long-term as well as short-term considerations into account.) A government should not, however, insist that it is always right. Each disputant government must somehow reconcile its inconsistent objectives. Perhaps the best way to do so is to pursue its general compliance objective as a member of the community by working toward an effective international law enforcement scheme, and by pursuing its particular interests *within* that scheme, thereby seeking to advance persuasively the legal positions for which it contends. The tendency of governments is to give too much attention to the short-term interest in winning a dispute and too little to the benefits of living in a law-abiding community.[4]

6. *Compliance with standing rules.* Some further refinements and qualifications on the law enforcement objective of causing com-

---

[4]Jessup has emphasized the enormous advantage of living in such a community, and has stressed the need "for political realization of the utility of a pattern of law-abidingness in the international issues," at least for those "which may appear to be less than crucial for the survival of civilization." P. JESSUP, THE USE OF IINTERNATIONAL LAW 28 (1959).

pliance with standing rules should be explored. Consider the case of an alleged past violation where the facts are in dispute. It is alleged, for example, that a driver went through a stop light or that saboteurs hired by one country were responsible for an explosion in another. At this point, the only way still possible to produce compliance with the standing rule is for the tribunal to find the facts to fit the rule. First-order compliance will have been produced if the court finds that in fact the light was green, or that in fact the explosion was caused by an accident. Are such findings a reasonable compliance objective?

Where facts are in dispute, there is no sure method of finding out what really happened. The best that we can do is to arrange the machinery so that those authorized to decide are as impartial as possible and so that the machinery does not have built-in factors tending to distort its objective judgment. To avoid such distortion, it is necessary, once facts have occurred which might or might not be in conformity with international law, that the enforcement scheme should no longer be seeking to produce first-order compliance in that instance. Little damage is done by such "retrospective compliance" provided that it is the result of an honest mistake. Any routine tendency to find the facts to fit the rules, however, undercuts respect for the system.[5]

A comparable problem exists where the facts are clear but the interpretation of the rule is in doubt. Here again, a court can find that disputed conduct was in fact in compliance with the law by so interpreting the law. In the case of *Reservations to the Con-*

[5] Experience shows that this happens when political considerations dictate a face-saving legal solution. One instance is the report submitted by the Lytton Commission to the League of Nations in regard to the Japanese acts of war against China. In the early 30s, the Japanese were engaged in a campaign of conquest for large areas of the northeastern part of China. However, as historian E. H. Carr observed, the members of the League were not prepared to resist an act of aggression committed by a powerful and well-armed state. E. Carr, INTERNATIONAL RELATIONS BETWEEN THE TWO WORLD WARS, 1919–1939, at 172 (1947). The Council decided to send to the Far East a League Commission (known as the Lytton Commission) to investigate on the spot "any circumstance which, affecting international relations, threatens to disturb peace between China and Japan." *Id.* at 167. Although the Commission rejected the various grounds upon which Japan had sought to justify its invasion of Manchuria, it carefully avoided any pronouncement which might have entailed the application of sanctions under article 16 of the League Covenant. *Id.* at 169–70. The Commission did its best to find the facts to fit the rules. It helped the League save face, but at the cost of undercutting respect for the system of collective security.

vention on the Prevention and Punishment of the Crime of Genocide, for instance, the International Court of Justice found that the principle of integrity of treaties was not applicable to that convention,[6] thereby implicitly recognizing the validity of the reservations made by the communist countries. Similarly, in its *Advisory Opinion on Legal Consequences for States of the Continued Presence of South Africa in Namibia (South West Africa) Notwithstanding Security Council Resolution 276 (1970)*, the Court held that the General Assembly of the United Nations had the power to terminate the mandate of South West Africa,[7] thereby dismissing the submission that the Assembly had acted ultra vires.[8] In such cases, a judicial "whitewash" poses a threat to the international community. It is more important that a tribunal be free from any special incentive to find that there was compliance when the question is one of law rather than one of fact. A decision as to the facts usually affects only the particular case. A decision interpreting a rule of law is likely to affect many cases in the future. Particularly where the international legislative process is as difficult and as cumbersome as it is now and is likely to remain in the future, international tribunals should be free to concentrate their attention on the wise articulation of the legal rule and free from undue concern over the consequences of finding a violation. If extremely harsh consequences were to be imposed upon the finding of a violation, the effect might be more to deter a court from reaching that conclusion than to deter a government from engaging in that activity.[9]

7. *Compliance with decisions as an objective.* If the first basic objective of a law enforcement system is to cause compliance with standing rules, its second objective is to cause compliance with decisions that "settle" disputes by interpreting those rules and

[6] Reservations to the Convention on the Prevention and Punishment of the Crime of Genocide, [1951] I.C.J. 22.

[7] Advisory Opinion on the Legal Consequences for States of the Continued Presence of South Africa in Namibia (South West Africa) Notwithstanding Security Council Resolution 276 (1970), [1971] I.C.J. 49–50.

[8] *Id.* at 45.

[9] This might have been the case with the judgment granted by the International Court of Justice in the second phase of the South West Africa cases. The Court cautiously dismissed the applications of Ethiopia and Liberia on procedural grounds. *See* [1966] I.C.J. 50. Presumably, it did so, at least in part, out of concern for the political implications of a request for enforcement by the Security Council of a judgment adverse to South Africa.

applying them to the facts of a case. The distinction between first-order compliance (causing respect for standing rules) and second-order compliance (causing respect for authoritative decisions) is frequently blurred; yet that distinction is of critical importance, particularly when one is seeking to enforce rules against governments and government officers.

One could generalize and say that in the international community the existing pattern of first-order compliance is fairly good. The critical problem is that there is no pattern of second-order compliance; there is no orderly process by which disputes lead to decisions that then are followed. Suggestions that violations of standing rules of international law demonstrate the inadequacies of international law miss the point. Tort law is not proven inadequate by the frequent occurrence of auto accidents, nor is contract law proven inadequate by the fact that contracts are broken. The weakness in the international legal system lies in its lack of an orderly and lawful way of coping with alleged departures from what the law provides. The system needs ways of obtaining authoritative determinations with respect to alleged noncompliance and a pattern of compliance with such determinations.

There are many kinds of international institutions and processes that could produce an authoritative determination. There also are many kinds of determinations. Different kinds of determinations and the compliance problems associated with them are discussed in Part II. In many cases, the character of the determination makes it easy to achieve compliance with it. Such cases include, for example, those in which an international tribunal finds that the conduct in question is permitted under international law.[10]

8. *The compliance expected of governments.* In considering the kind of compliance with international law that we should hope to obtain from governments, we have no better guide than to

[10] For example, in The Case of the S.S. *Lotus*, Collection of Judgments, [1927] P.C.I.J., ser. A, No. 10, at 23, the Permanent Court of International Justice held that no rule of international law precluded Turkey from applying its municipal law to persons within its jurisdiction for acts committed on the high seas. There was no difficulty in obtaining compliance with this decision, which simply approved past conduct to which France had strongly objected.

examine the kind of compliance that law-abiding governments give to their domestic law. International law is not unlike constitutional law in that it imposes legal obligations upon a government that in theory the government is not free to ignore or change. In the United States, we have had experience with trying to cause both the federal and state governments to comply with the Constitution and with federal law. Current efforts to enforce the fourteenth amendment and civil rights legislation provide a vivid lesson of the difficulties in enforcing law against governments. They also may illustrate the kind of compliance that international law enforcement should take as its objective.

In the international arena, the problem of law enforcement traditionally, and even recently by such modern scholars as Hans Kelsen and Myres McDougal,[11] has been discussed in terms of "sanctions." The problem is often seen as one of determining when a violation has occurred and imposing sanctions upon the violator. This would suggest that the basic objective is one of causing first-order compliance, compliance with the substantive rules of international law, and that the basic technique is that of the criminal law. The aim is to deter violations by imposing sanctions upon the guilty government.[12]

Successful domestic experience in controlling governments by law is wholly different. The term "sanctions" is unknown. Constitutions and laws limiting the conduct of governments are never treated as though they were criminal statutes for the violation of which a guilty government is to be punished. Compliance by governments, state or federal, is not sought through a method of deterrence and punishment. So far as the legal system goes, little of its energies are directed toward the objective

[11] H. KELSEN, PRINCIPLES OF INTERNATIONAL LAW 18–20 (2d rev. ed. R. Tucker ed. 1966); Kelsen, *Théories du droit international*, 84 RECUEIL DES COURS (Hague Academy of International Law) 5, 31 (1953–III); M. McDOUGAL & F. FELICIANO, LAW AND MINIMUM WORLD PUBLIC ORDER (THE LEGAL REGULATION OF INTERNATIONAL COERCION) 266 (1961).

[12] The possibility of an international criminal court to try governments for their past conduct and to impose such consequences as economic sanctions was considered thoroughly in the Institut de Droit International on the basis of a proposal by Donnedieu de Vabres. [1948] ANNUAIRE DE L'INSTITUT DE DROIT INTERNATIONAL 244 (Bruxelles); [1950] ANNUAIRE DE L'INSTITUT DE DROIT INTERNATIONAL 439–40 (Sienne).

of producing first-order compliance, even with our most basic provisions. Apparently in the United States, we neither seek nor expect a high degree of first-order compliance, even with the Constitution. Congress has often adopted unconstitutional statutes; on hundreds, if not thousands of occasions, the federal and state governments have violated rights of individuals guaranteed by the Constitution. In untold ways, officials acting for a government have exceeded their authority. But still we look to the United States as being an example of a law-abiding community, a model which the international community should emulate.

Because of the tendency of governments to justify their conduct, most, if not all, violations of standing rules first appear as disputes. The government whose conduct is in question may dispute the facts; it may dispute the interpretation or validity of the rule; or it may contend that despite the rule its conduct was justified because of some higher rule, or a prior violation by others, or because of changed conditions or some special circumstances. For some period of time, it usually is unclear whether or not there has been first-order compliance. Once the question is settled, however, the legal machinery does not turn its attention to the imposition of sanctions. On the contrary, domestic experience suggests that the proper objective is to decide what should take place now and to cause compliance with that decision. No one talks of punishing the United States Government for having unconstitutionally deprived a man of his passport. No one talks of punishing the state of Mississippi for having discriminated in the past in an unconstitutional fashion against blacks. No one even suggests the necessity of converting a violation of the Constitution into a lesson for the future. The typical compliance that we have come to expect our courts to exact from our governments is compliance with decisions rather than compliance with standing rules.

Within the field of second-order compliance experience with decisions prohibiting future illegal action has been longer and more successful than experience with decisions ordering governments to make amends for past violations of the law. A decision of the United States Supreme Court that the state of

Georgia should compensate a plaintiff as a result of Georgia's having failed to fulfill its legal obligations in the past[13] led to the prompt adoption of the eleventh amendment, which barred federal courts from entering any more such decisions. For the first seventy-five years of this country's existence, no court had competence to issue a decision that the United States Government should pay money for having failed to comply with a contract. It was not until 1946 that courts were authorized to order the government to pay compensation to those injured as a result of the government's tortious conduct. Even today, the scope of such remedial decisions is sharply limited. In most instances, neither the federal nor state governments will be ordered to make amends for their past illegal conduct, whether that conduct was improperly to bar a book from the mails or to send an innocent man to jail. The most that is usually ordered is that the government no longer engage in the particular action which now has been found to be unlawful.

Domestic experience therefore suggests that with respect to governments — as governments — the major objective of a law enforcement system should be compliance with determinations, rather than compliance with standing rules. Even in this limited area, however, we should expect more success in stopping illegal conduct from continuing than in trying to cause governments to redress wrongs already committed.

9. *The compliance expected of government officers.* When a domestic law enforcement system seeks to cause governmental compliance with law by proceeding against the government as such, it sometimes does adopt the techniques of the criminal law. The problems in implementing such a deterrent approach are discussed in Chapter IV. First-order compliance by officers may be noted here as a possible objective of a law enforcement scheme. Although criminal prosecutions of a government official are far rarer than suits seeking to enjoin an officer from continuing in what is alleged to be an illegal course of conduct, impeachment and other prosecutions are known. Generally, government officers in this country are not held criminally responsible for violations of the Constitution or other legal restraints on the

---

[13] Chisholm v. Georgia, 1 U.S. 16, 2 Dall. 419 (1793).

government's conduct. Criminal prosecution is usually reserved for illegal conduct that was undertaken for private ends.

Threats of criminal prosecution, in particular for contempt, are used to cause officers to comply with court decisions. Again, the objective here is second-order compliance. And again, the objective is limited most usually to enforcing an order that an official should stop engaging in the particular conduct. Indeed, the officer is rarely ordered to make amends for the wrong for which he was responsible. The judge who sent a man to jail contrary to the law, or the official whose public statement wrongfully ruined a woman's reputation, is not required to pay damages. We grant government officials a large measure of immunity to encourage them to exercise their discretion and their judgment freely. Domestic experience thus suggests that whether the proceeding is against governments or against government officers, the most promising of the numerous objectives in the enforcement of international law is to obtain determinations as to future conduct and then to seek compliance with those determinations.

Part I
First-Order Compliance: Causing Respect for Standing Rules

Introductory note. By now it should be clear that in my view an international law enforcement system should *primarily* seek to cause compliance not with the rules of law themselves but rather with decisions that apply the law to particular cases of alleged violations. Some effort, however, should be directed at causing governments and individuals to respect standing rules in the first place.

This part considers the problem of causing respect for standing rules — first-order compliance. Section A, consisting of Chapters III and IV, discusses and essentially rejects the conventional enforcement theory based on applying a system of deterrence as found in the criminal law to governments or to individuals accused of violating standing rules of international law. Section B, consisting of Chapters V, VI, and VII, treats three techniques other than deterrence that might promote first-order compliance. Both sections emphasize the limits on any international law enforcement system that relies primarily on gaining first-order compliance and that lacks an authoritative means for reaching decisions about alleged violations of standing rules.

A
Using Deterrence

CHAPTER III

Deterrence Against Governments

1. *The general theory.* Conventional enforcement theory would apply to governments the system of deterrence found in the criminal law. The international community would attempt to induce governments to comply with the rules of international law by establishing a way of punishing those governments which violated the law. Fear of such punishment would be counted on to deter some, if not all, illegal conduct by governments.

Before analyzing this enforcement technique, it should be clearly defined. We are concerned here with a system of preestablished threats for departures from established rules. For example, a treaty might establish that any country which used radio frequencies not allocated to it might be punished either by having the number of its radio frequencies reduced, or by being required to pay a fine to the United Nations, or by having its allocated frequencies jammed for a stated period of time. Also, it might be provided that any country launching an aggressive war would be punished to the extent authorized by the Security Council. This punishment might include the destruction of some of the aggressor's cities, the loss of some of its territory, or the boycott of its exporting industries. Although the actual punishment might be imposed by national action, it would be inflicted in implementation of an authoritative international decision that a country had violated the law and ought to be so punished.

Fighting by internationally authorized forces might be required in order to place these forces in a position where they could impose punishment. The punishment itself, however, should be distinguished from such fighting. A policeman's conduct in subduing a thief is quite different from the punishment that may later be imposed upon the thief. A private citizen, for example, is authorized to prevent a thief from stealing his property by such force as is reasonably necessary. Yet, the private citizen may not impose a penalty upon the thief in order to deter him and others from repeating such conduct. The punishment with which we are concerned comes after the thief is subdued and is designed to serve as a lesson to him and others not to break the laws against theft in the future.

A system designed to impose punishment must also be distinguished from one intended to frustrate wrongdoing. In one sense, a thief may be deterred from trying to rob a bank by the heavy steel doors of the vault or by the fear that the guards will prevent his being successful. He also may fear that the money will be taken back from him after he has stolen it. Efforts directed toward preventing successful law defiance do have a deterrent effect. A true deterrent system, however, is one designed to deter any violation by the standing threat that a violator runs the risk of punishment. In such a system, punishment is understood as an intentionally imposed hardship or unpleasant consequence beyond that involved in compensating the injured party or depriving the violator of the benefits of his wrongdoing. Punishment would be intended to serve as a lesson for the future. Although it may be clear in theory, this line between punishment intended to deter and other apparent forms of punishment is blurred in practice. For our purposes, we will consider the required forfeiture of counterfeit currency,[1] for example, as simply the frustration of the illegal endeavor. The forfeiture of automobiles, ships, or aircraft found to have been used for smuggling counterfeit currency will be regarded as the imposition of a deterrent penalty.[2]

2. *Considerations in favor of international deterrence.* At the present time, there is a vast network of national threats in support of various rules of international law. To move toward a system of internationally administered threats supporting international law need not involve a clear or dramatic break from the present. It is frequently suggested that international law, generally understood to be in a state of infancy with respect to causing compliance, should expect to use the primitive techniques of the criminal law rather than the more sophisticated methods of constitutional or administrative law. To work toward the gradual replacement of independent national or regional threats of

[1] *See* 18 U.S.C. § 492 (1970).
[2] *See, e.g.,* 49 U.S.C. §§ 781–84 (1970).

retaliation with an orderly system of prescribed international penalties imposed on governments found to have violated international law might seem to be a desirable and perhaps feasible extrapolation from the present political environment. The kinds of forces now operating would continue to operate, but they would be regularized and brought into a recognized system of law enforcement.

Not only would an international deterrent system build upon the system of national threats now in existence, but also it would appear to be a definite improvement. The threats would be standing rather than ad hoc, and they would be international rather than national. A penalty which has been defined and authorized before an issue is raised would appear to have greater legitimacy than one which is made at the last minute in an effort to deter a particular move. In the international community, threats that are "on the books" would be taken into account by the professional officers running the government. If the threat were credible and the probable costs of the proposed violation outweighed the anticipated benefits to the government, the deterrent might be effective. On the other hand, an ad hoc threat, particularly one made by another nation, tends to stir up political feelings among the less responsible elements within a country. One might contrast the effect of a criminal statute against robbery on a West Side gang with a threat from a rival gang to "get out of here or else." It is easier to defer to a fixed condition than to a special demand; it is easier to defer to a neutral authority than to an adversary. Even if the risks were the same, a group would seem somewhat less likely to back down to an ad hoc ultimatum than to a preexisting penalty provision. All these considerations suggest that, other things being equal, an international deterrent system in support of standing rules might operate more successfully than the present system of independent national threats.

Although the rules of international law, like other rules of law, necessarily are somewhat ambiguous, such ambiguity need not undercut a criminal law sort of deterrence. The concept of reckless driving is somewhat vague; yet criminal penalties for reckless driving do deter a driver from getting into the general area where a problem exists. And even though, as discussed below, there may be a temptation on the part of an international tribunal not to punish a government for conduct in the area where a rule is uncertain — and hence to construe the rule narrowly as not applying — the rule can be clarified, and enlarged if necessary, by agreement so that the net effect could be to strengthen the deterrent for the future.

Finally, the major argument in favor of a deterrent system of causing first-order compliance is that when it works it causes compliance before the rule is broken, rather than after. By tending to avoid the first violation, whether the rule is precautionary or not, it is "self-operating" on most occasions and avoids any injury whatever to the interest the rule is designed to protect.

3. *The contrary domestic experience.* A plausible case can thus be made in favor of using standing threats of punishment against governments as a means of deterring them from violating standing rules of law. Nevertheless, the successful experience of causing governments to respect the law is based almost exclusively on other methods. A quick survey of the means by which governments are kept under law indicates almost no use against governments as such of the deterrent technique of enforcement.

The experience of the United States is particularly informative because state governments are not mere branches of the federal government. While having an independent existence, state governments are legally bound by higher federal law, whether the Constitution, common law, or legislation. One might think that the way to cause the states to respect the higher federal law would be to have the federal government enact penalties to be imposed upon any state found guilty of violating it. Sanctions comparable to those suggested for the enforcement by threat of international law could readily be imposed upon a state convicted of violating the Constitution. The state might lose, for example, some of its territory; it might be isolated economically; it might be fined by the federal government; or its citizens might be taxed for one year at a higher federal income tax rate than the one imposed on citizens of other states. Other penalties could be devised, such as cutting the mail service to twice each week or denying the transmission of television programs to the state except on Sunday mornings.

The remarkable fact appears to be that rarely does the federal government in this country attempt to deter a state from violating the law by threatening the state with punishment. In fact, the reluctance to have either the central government or other states take action against a state either to cause compliance or to punish noncompliance has deep historical roots in the American system of government. The Articles of Confederation had provided for enforcement of the laws against the states and not against individual citizens. As Alexander Hamilton explained in *The Federalist*, complying states were unwilling, however, to use force to cause a noncomplying state to alter its conduct. The complying states preferred to join in the noncompliance so that "the guilt of all would thus become the security of all."[3] As a result of this early experience, the new Constitution gave the central government authority over individual citizens and not simply over the states.

The President was given authority to use force when needed to implement federal law. In 1792 Congress gave the President power to use federal forces whenever domestic disorder prevented the execution of the federal law through the ordinary course of judicial proceedings.[4] This statute was used to suppress violent interference with federal officials seeking to enforce federal laws. State officials whose inaction had often led to the need for federal forces were not required by the statute to cooperate with the federal forces. In fact, no special finding on the willingness or ability of local authorities to carry out federal law or protect federal officials was necessary before invoking the statute.[5] In the post–Civil War period, another statute by Congress was needed to permit the President to use federal forces whenever a class of persons was being deprived of a constitutional right because of public violence and the state authorities either had failed, had refused, or were unable to protect them.[6] Since 1957, three Presidents have invoked this statute to justify the use of federal forces to suppress racial uprisings in connection with school integration.

[3] THE FEDERALIST No. 16 (A. Hamilton ed. 1888) 149.
[4] *See* 10 U.S.C. § 332 (1970).
[5] U.S. COMMISSION ON CIVIL RIGHTS, LAW ENFORCEMENT: A REPORT OF EQUAL PROTECTION IN THE SOUTH 149 (1965).
[6] *See* 10 U.S.C. § 333 (1970).

Neither of the statutes authorizing the President to use force is intended to inflict on the state in which public violence occurs the kind of deterrent punishment that we have been examining. Both laws simply allow for the removal of the cause of noncompliance — usually public violence by individuals or groups. No matter how guilty the state in which the incident occurs may have been in allowing or even encouraging the incident to happen, the federal law does not authorize punishment of the state as such.[7] (We will consider in the next chapter what action may be taken by the federal authorities against individual state officials who interfere with the constitutional rights of citizens.)

A deterrent enforcement philosophy might appear to be the basis for the regulations of the Secretary of Health, Education, and Welfare providing for nondiscrimination in federally assisted programs as required by Title VI of the Civil Rights Act of 1964. These regulations establish a procedure leading to a decision by the Department to deny, suspend, or terminate grants and federal assistance programs under its jurisdiction because the recipient state has failed to comply or give an assurance that it will comply with Title VI of the Civil Rights Act of 1964.[8] In addition, the Commissioner of Education has issued a statement of policy outlining the procedure and the substantive requirements which a state's school system must follow and meet in or-

[7] In April 1963 the United States Civil Rights Commission suggested a deterrent system for enforcing the Constitution upon state governments. The Commission issued a special "interim report" in which it asked the President to explore his legal authority "to withhold Federal funds from the State of Mississippi, until the State of Mississippi demonstrates its compliance with the Constitution. . . ." At the same time, the report requested the Congress to "consider seriously" legislation implementing the suggestion to withhold funds. The Committee indicated that Mississippi received from the federal government each year approximately $650,000,000 including grant-in-aid programs, U.S. Corps of Engineers construction contracts, prime military contracts, redevelopment loans, small-business loans, and public works projects. If Mississippi was violating the Constitution, then the federal government should consider cutting off the state financially. U.S. COMMISSION ON CIVIL RIGHTS, INTERIM REPORT 3–5 (Apr. 16, 1963). This recommendation caused considerable controversy. When the Civil Rights Commission produced its third biennial report in October 1963, the recommendation for federal action had already been watered down. The suggestion to consider a total-deterrent enforcement system against a southern state was no longer included. The biennial report recommended cutting off federal funds for specific projects in "impacted areas" that were being operated or administered in a discriminatory manner. [1963] U.S. COMMISSION ON CIVIL RIGHTS, ANN. REPORT.

[8] See 45 C.F.R. §§ 80.1–80.13 (1976).

der to show that local desegregation plans, either voluntary or under court order, accomplish the purposes of the Civil Rights Act of 1964.[9] By denying a benefit to the noncomplying states or their school systems rather than demanding affirmative action, these regulations employ a useful enforcement technique which we shall consider at greater length in Chapter XIII. But it should be emphasized that this technique does not amount to the kind of deterrent punishment which we have recognized as part of the conventional enforcement theory of international law. Once a state complies with the federal regulations, there is no additional burden placed upon it. The purpose of this enforcement mechanism is to withhold federal funds so as to avoid their illegal use. The regulations do not attempt to punish a state for prior misuse of such funds. Moreover, the funds are withheld in order not to subsidize the state programs that support the institutions where discrimination occurs — schools. Funds are not, as the Civil Rights Commission suggested,[10] withheld from unrelated federally funded programs in a state until that state desegregates its schools.

State governments also appear to make little use of punishment as a means for gaining compliance by their cities and towns. At one time, towns were held collectively liable for criminal conduct occurring within their borders. But the extent of the penalty imposed was usually limited to some form of redress for the injury done. Rarely is the fear of a penalty used to control the conduct of a local government. An occasional statute does impose a financial penalty upon a municipality for its failure to comply with the law. Such penalties seem to be used primarily when the law imposes an affirmative obligation upon the local government, and where it might be easier to collect the penalty than to compel the action required by the law. Thus, Massachusetts requires each town of more than 3,000 inhabitants to provide and maintain a lockup. A town which fails to provide or maintain the required lockup is subject to a fine of ten dollars for each month it neglects this duty.[11] In a few cases, a city has been fined after prosecution by a state for failing to perform a

[9] *Id.* §§ 181.1–181.15.
[10] *See* note 7 and accompanying text *supra*.
[11] *See* MASS. ANN. LAWS ch. 40, § 34 (Michie / Law. Co-op, 1973).

duty, such as eliminating what constituted a criminal nuisance,[12] or for failing to complete a road which the city had itself decided was needed.[13]

One might almost stop here, for if there is no domestic experience of successfully applying a deterrent method of law for producing first-order compliance by governments, then this method should probably not be tried internationally. We could logically conclude that those legal techniques which have effectively caused governments to comply substantially with existing legal restrictions should be adapted to cause governments to comply with the additional legal requirements of international law. In fact, many of the existing restrictions upon the United States Government established by act of Congress are comparable to those accepted under international law. Some restrictions, such as the prohibitions against counterfeiting foreign currency or lending military support to a group seeking to overthrow a friendly foreign government, are identical. Here, domestic law and international law prohibit the very same conduct. Thus, it would seem more promising to use techniques that have generally caused a government to respect domestic limitations to enforce international ones, rather than to adopt a new, unproved technique. Although the existing obligations of domestic law are different in significant respects from the obligations of international law, the two problems of enforcement are more nearly analogous than either of them is to the problem of deterring a thief from robbing a bank. In both cases, we are seeking to gain compliance by a collective body which enjoys governmental powers and immunities and which acts by virtue of the decisions of individuals who control it. Unlike the case of the thief, we are not simply attempting to influence the conduct of an individual who is subject to the law. We are trying instead to gain compliance by groups of officials. Despite this similarity between enforcing domestic and international law against governments and the historical absence of deterrent techniques in the domestic setting, it may be worthwhile to try to analyze the pos-

[12] See, e.g., City of Ludlow v. Commonwealth, 147 Ky. 706, 145 S.W. 406 (1912).
[13] See, e.g., Commonwealth v. City of Boston, 33 Mass. (16 Pick.) 442 (1835).

sibility of using a deterrent technique as found in the criminal law against a government. We will attempt to discover, to the extent possible, where the difficulties are and such promise as this technique might have for enforcing international law.

4. *The twin problems of effectiveness and acceptability.* We could design a system which, in theory, would produce a high degree of first-order compliance. By definition, this system would be highly effective. But the governments whose consent would be necessary to bring about and maintain this system would probably find it unacceptable. On the other hand, a deterrent system acceptable to these governments would probably fail to produce much first-order compliance — it would be ineffective.

Each of these critical problems — effectiveness and acceptability — is not a matter for precise measurement but rather one of rough judgment. In addition, the possible variables in such a law enforcement system are so numerous that it is impossible to consider all the permutations and combinations. One such variable is obviously the kind of punishment that an international authority is authorized and prepared to impose. In our simplified analysis of the problems of effectiveness and then of acceptability, we will consider three general ranges of punishment that might be authorized:

1. thermonuclear bombing and other forms of violent destruction;

2. economic sanctions, loss of territory, and, comparable middle range sanctions; and

3. fines, forfeitures of particular property or rights, moral condemnation, and other modest but significant penalties.
These crude approximations of a scale of punishments should serve to illustrate the kinds of problems that would be encountered by a system of law imposing punishment upon governments.

5. *Effectiveness — the need for a credible threat.* If violations of a standing rule are to be deterred, the threat of punishment must be credible. It is not enough for the punishment to appear serious to the governments that we seek to deter. For a deterrent enforcement system to be effective, there must be a sufficiently high degree of probability that the punishment would be im-

posed if the law is violated. If we can now estimate that there would in fact be little chance of the penalty's being imposed, so can the government whose violation we are seeking to deter.

The credibility of threatened punishment depends on a number of factors. First, undiscovered conduct cannot be punished. Against a government which is confident that its conduct will remain secret, no deterrent will be credible.[14] Second, the credibility of a threat may be reduced if there is no one to raise the question of a violation in an appropriate tribunal.[15] Leaving aside these two points, the credibility of threatened punishment can be thought of as dependent upon the likelihood (*a*) of the authorized international tribunal's reaching a decision that a penalty ought to be imposed and (*b*) of that decision's being implemented. Even if the threatened punishment is credible, the deterrent will not be effective unless (*c*) the government is influenced by the threat. These three problems of effectiveness will be considered in this order before turning to the question of acceptability.

a. *Credibility: reaching a decision to punish*

(1) *In general.* At this point, we are considering how likely it would appear to a government contemplating a violation of international law that the Security Council, for example, upon having the matter come to its attention, would decide that a penalty should be imposed on that government for its wrongful act.[16] To some extent, this would depend on the nature of the violation and the nature of the penalty to be imposed. But there seems to be something both in the nature of international bodies and in the nature of governments to militate against the one's deciding that punishment should be imposed upon the other.

The Security Council feels some collective responsibility for what happens after its decision. A decision not to impose pun-

[14] The problems involved in acquiring information about dubious conduct through inspection or otherwise are dealt with in Chapter VII.

[15] Who should raise the question of a violation of international law is considered in Chapter VIII. What are appropriate tribunals is considered in Chapters IX and X.

[16] In form, the Security Council is not concerned currently with all violations of international law by states, but only with those which endanger international peace and security. The Council, however, has the discretionary power to determine the circumstances under which a violation of international law endangers international peace and security and to call for action accordingly. Moreover, the Council is the sole judge of its own competence. Again, one could argue that in the absence of an amendment to the

ishment will usually appear less likely to provoke an international crisis then would one condemning a government as a law violator and ordering it punished. There is a tendency to look to the immediate future; getting out of the present situation will now seem more important than imposing a punitive lesson for the more distant future.

Perhaps more important than the natural tendency of committees and committeelike organizations to avoid a punitive decision would be a commendable reluctance to impose punishment upon one group for action that was taken by another. The "government" that undertook the violation of law is an abstraction. One government official or, more likely, several of them made a decision presumably designed to benefit the country for which they were acting. The decision by India to seize the Portuguese territories of Goa, Damao, and Dio in December 1961, for example, is reported to have been taken without a formal cabinet meeting and, in part, for the political benefit of the then Defense Minister, Krishna Menon, who was running for reelection in Bombay.[17] To impose punishment in that case upon "the Government of India" or upon "the Indians" would have resulted in imposing pain and hardship upon innocent parties rather than upon those directly responsible for the violation of international law by virtue of the invasion. In domestic terms, it would be like imposing punishment for the misconduct of a trustee by assessing a fine against trust funds. The primary consequence of such punishment would be to injure the innocent beneficiary rather than to reach the real wrongdoer, the trustee.

Charter, the Security Council is not competent, strictly speaking, to impose penalties for violations of international law. It has, however, the power to order enforcement actions; one might contemplate a development of the powers of the Council on the basis of the principle stated by the International Court of Justice in the case of Reparation for Injuries Suffered in the Service of the United Nations: "Under international law, the Organization must be deemed to have those powers which, though not expressly provided in the Charter, are conferred upon it by necessary implication as being essential to the performance of its duties." See [1949] I.C.J. 182. See also the language of the opinion of the International Court of Justice in the case of Legal Consequences for States of the Continued Presence of South Africa in Namibia (South West Africa) Notwithstanding Security Council Resolution 276 (1970): "The reference in paragraph 2 of this Article to specific powers of the Security Council under certain chapters of the Charter does not exclude the existence of general powers to discharge the responsibilities conferred in paragraph 1." [1971] I.C.J. 52.

[17] Cf. Wright, The Goa Incident, 56 AM. J. INT'L. L. 617, 629 n.36 (1962).

To be sure, governments in the past have demonstrated no great reluctance to imposing hardship upon the people of a country for the misdeeds of their leaders. Much of the impact of postwar "reparations" fell on those whose guilt was only theoretical.[18] The tendency to think of a country in monolithic terms as a single entity which acts and suffers as a unit remains widespread. Governments today are willing to impose economic sanctions upon "Cuba," "South Africa," or "Southern Rhodesia" without distinguishing between those within each country who are responsible for the decisions and those who will suffer as a result of the sanction. Most actions imposing hardships on a people have not been justified as punishment. Some have been called "reparations" designed to make amends to those injured. The reduction in the Cuban sugar quota was said to be necessary because American officials had concluded that, in view of the Cuban agreement with the Soviet Union to barter goods for sugar, the United States could no longer depend on Cuba as a reliable supplier of sugar.[19] These measures against Cuba were said to be designed to induce future change in the policy of Fidel Castro's government, as were the British economic restrictions imposed against Rhodesia following the unilateral declaration of independence.

One notable exception to this reluctance to justify harsh action against a country as punishment was the behavior of the Israeli Government following the six-day war. According to the Israeli

[18] Perhaps the best example still remains article 231 of the Treaty of Versailles, which was conceived as a sort of philosophical foundation for the German "reparations" after World War I. That article reads: "The Allied and Associated Governments affirm and Germany accepts the responsibility of Germany and her allies for causing all the loss and damage to which the Allied and Associated Governments and their nationals have been subjected as a consequence of the war imposed upon them by the aggression of Germany and her allies." Treaty of Versailles, June 28, 1919, 2 C. BEVANS, TREATIES AND OTHER INTERNATIONAL AGREEMENTS OF THE UNITED STATES OF AMERICA 1776–1949, at 43, 137–38 (1969). It was Germany as a whole, and not its leaders, that was forced to admit the guilt and to accept the responsibility. Historian A. J. P. Taylor rightly contrasted the Versailles policy with that followed by the Allies in 1814, when they "made out that they had been fighting only Napoleon, not France." A. TAYLOR, A HISTORY OF THE FIRST WORLD WAR 171 (1966).

[19] THE FACTS CONCERNING RELATIONS BETWEEN CUBA AND THE UNITED STATES — A REPLY TO ALLEGATIONS MADE IN THE UNITED NATIONS AGAINST THE UNITED STATES BY PRIME MINISTER FIDEL CASTRO OF CUBA, AM. FOREIGN POLICY: CURRENT DOCS. 228 (1960).

Government, Egyptian commandos were crossing the Suez Canal cease-fire line during October 1968 in violation of the existing cease-fire agreement between Israel and Egypt and with the full knowledge and cooperation of the Egyptian Army. On November 1, 1968, Israeli commandos attacked a transformer station and two bridges on the Nile between Aswan and Cairo. Premier Levi Eshkol of Israel made clear that the purpose of the attack was to teach Egypt a lesson — to warn that country of the dangers of violating the cease-fire agreement.[20] On a nation-to-nation basis, punishment is not common, but it does happen.

(2) *Thermonuclear or other forms of violent punishment.* A threat of massive retaliation by an international authority as a means of deterring governments from violating rules of international law would be undercut by the relative confidence which any government would have that no international body would in fact ever decide to punish a government by inflicting violent destruction upon its country. International bodies take time to act, particularly when their purpose is to determine guilt and to order the infliction of punishment. The more time that passes between the violation and the time of decision about punishment, the less likely would be a decision to impose violent destruction. Sudden retaliation by one nation against another is highly credible as long as the justification is extremely serious and the reaction time extremely short. Whether or not retaliation fulfills any rational purpose once the deterrent has failed, it makes "emotional sense." Presumably, thermonuclear or other destructive punishment would be considered by an international body only for the most drastic forms of law violation, such as clear cases of direct armed attack by one powerful state against its neighbor. Even here, there are instinctive reservations about the international community's reaching a decision to inflict destruction as a lesson for the future.

Consider the case cited above, of the seizure of Goa and other Portuguese territories by India in 1962. Assuming, contrary to what actually happened, that the Security Council fairly deter-

---

[20] N. Y. Times, Nov. 1, 1968, at 1, cols. 2 & 3. Similarly, Israeli commandos infiltrated Jordanian territory in early December 1968 and blew up two bridges linking Amman and the port of Aqaba. The purpose of this attack too was to punish — in this case for the raids in Israel by terrorist groups based in Jordan.

mined that this was a case of unprovoked aggression in violation of international law; even so, it seems most unlikely that it would have concluded that as punishment for the violation one of India's cities should be destroyed. The reader who prefers may consider the likelihood that he, personally, as a member of the Security Council, having considered illegal the Soviet Union's conduct in Hungary in 1956 or in Czechoslovakia in 1968, would have voted to select a Soviet target for destruction as the appropriate punishment. Or would the reader have voted to select some other city or facility for destruction as punishment for Britain, France, or Israel, considering their conduct in Suez in 1956 to have been in clear violation of international law? The children and families involved in any such destruction quickly come to mind and would probably play a decisive role in the final decision.

Our experience in helping rebuild Germany and Japan after World War II suggests how inappropriate national punishment seems once some time has passed. The present credibility of national threats of nuclear retaliation rests in large part upon the fact that striking back would presumably be part of an ongoing military effort to gain victory in a war. Striking back would not be an after-the-fact infliction of agony designed "to teach them not to do that again."

Perhaps the fact that would make an international decision to impose violent and drastic destruction most unlikely is the more modest nature of most violations of international law. A threat of massive nuclear retaliation at times and places of our own choosing, the United States discovered, did not cause other governments to stop what we considered to be nibbling aggressive behavior. Fear of counter-retaliation does not seem an adequate explanation for the ineffectiveness of the threat; violent destructive retaliation, whether nuclear or not, is in fact so inappropriate for most situations with which the world is faced that not even a hostile national government is prepared to inflict it.

(3) *Economic or other middle-range sanctions.* Less drastic forms of punishment suggested have included loss of territory; embargoes and boycotts; and various forms of political isolation, such as the closing of foreign embassies and consulates. Experience suggests that an international authority would be more

likely to reach a decision that such punishment should be imposed in a particular case than it would be to decide upon military destruction. A closer examination indicates that the kind of sanction imposed as punishment for past misdeeds — as contrasted with that directed toward inducing a change in continuing behavior — is quite limited.

Loss of territory, inflicted in the past as punishment upon unsuccessful aggressors, is so out of keeping with the rapidly changing mores of international politics[21] that a threat to assign people from one government to another does not seem a plausible deterrent. A government's violation of international law in the past is hardly a persuasive reason for ordering citizens who happen to live in a particular corner of a country to be subject thereafter to a different government.[22] Apart from credibility, the history of adjustment of European boundaries after wars suggests that *punishing* a country by depriving it of some of its territory is more likely to cause future breaches of international law than to deter them. Thus, the German annexation of Alsace-Lorraine after the Franco-Prussian War of 1870 by the Treaty of Frankfurt led to the highly emotional French revanchist movement and, in part, contributed to the outbreak of World War I. Similarly, the fact that the Treaty of Versailles left compact German populations outside the borders of Germany contributed to the tension which preceded World War II and provided the Nazis with an appealing argument for German expansion.

Decisions to impose economic sanctions, such as embargoes and boycotts, upon a government which has violated international law, however, would appear quite likely. The willingness of national governments, such as the United States, to impose such restrictions in an ad hoc fashion upon governments that it considers to have violated international law would indicate that an international organization also might be willing to do so. The

---

[21]*But see* Schwebel, *What Weight to Conquest?*, 64 AM. J. INT'L L. 344–47 (1970).

[22]The formula of forced transfer of populations from territories assigned to foreign states that was devised by the Potsdam Conference (*see* 3 C. BEVANS, *supra* note 18, at 1220) does not appear more acceptable. It was considered at length by the Institut de Droit International during its session of Sienne (April 1952) (44/2 ANNUAIRE DE L'INSTITUT DE DROIT INTERNATIONAL 138 (1952)) from the point of view of its legality (*see, e.g.*, Scelle, *id.* at 176; Schatzel, *id.* at 183), rather than its political advisability (*see, e.g.*, Huber, *id.* at 163). *But see* Winiarski, *id.* at 191 (defending the Potsdam formula).

credibility of this threat would be particularly high if, as we are assuming here, the form of punishment were authorized by preexisting international arrangement.

In some instances, the United States itself has established preexisting rules about the imposition of economic sanctions. Both the Battle Act and the Hickenlooper Amendment to the Foreign Assistance Act are legal arrangements designed to deter other governments from engaging in particular international conduct by establishing a standing threat that economic assistance will be cut off in the event that the prohibited conduct occurs. Congress provided in the Battle Act for an embargo on the shipment from the United States of strategic goods to "any nation or combination of nations threatening the security of the United States, including the Union of Soviet Socialist Republics and all countries under its domination."[23] The Act then calls for the termination of "all military, economic or financial assistance to any nation" found to have shipped strategic goods to the Soviet Union or its satellite countries.[24] The Act also provides for the control of the shipment of nonembargoed goods to the same countries and requires similar cooperation in implementing these restrictions from countries receiving United States aid. The Hickenlooper Amendment requires the President to suspend aid to any country that has nationalized the property of or repudiated contracts with United States citizens or corporations if the country fails to take appropriate steps within six months to discharge its obligations by providing "speedy compensation" for such property in convertible currency equivalent to its full value or similar compensation for the damages arising from a repudiated contract.[25]

Neither the Battle Act nor the Hickenlooper Amendment, however, imposes the kind of true deterrent punishment that we have been considering. The Battle Act provides for the resumption of assistance when the President determines that "adequate measures have been taken by the nation concerned to assure full compliance with the provisions" of the Act restricting shipment of strategic goods. Similarly, the Hickenlooper Amendment al-

[23] See 22 U.S.C. § 1611 (1970).
[24] Id. at § 1611b(b).
[25] Id. at § 2370(e)(1).

lows the President to resume American aid payments when he is satisfied that "appropriate steps are being taken" to provide the compensation as required under that provision. Even in enacting these moderate sanctions, the Congress has stopped short of punishing governments for their conduct. The two laws merely seek to gain compliance. The sanctions terminate as soon as the governments comply. They do not remain in force to serve as a lesson to others to refrain from similar conduct.

Most economic sanctions have been undertaken with mixed motives. If the exclusive purpose of the sanctions is punishment, some difficult questions arise. In particular, how long should the embargo, boycott, or curtailment of economic assistance last? It would be possible to devise a scheme under which the Security Council, for example, having found that a country violated international law, could order that country to be punished by ordering other countries not to sell goods to it for a period of one year. Once an economic measure is thought of as punishment rather than as economic pressure toward better behavior, it loses much of its appeal. Depriving a country of some economic arrangement for an arbitrary period of time, not related to what that country is doing now but because of something it did in the past, would seem a less likely decision than if the economic measures are directed toward producing future change.

One further aspect of economic measures should be pointed out. It seems far easier to reach a decision to stop what can be considered a benefit than to impose an affirmative hardship. Cutting off economic aid, financial grants, or technical assistance is an easier decision to reach — and hence a more credible threat — than stopping trade. Any curtailment of trade not only affects the country being punished but also causes injury, often more serious, to the economic partner.[26] The curtailment of something that is considered a benefit is easier to administer and easier to justify intellectually. As a first measure of sanction, it was easier for the United States to curtail the domestic purchase

[26]The problem for Zambia created by United Nations sanctions against Rhodesia, with which Zambia had had strong economic ties, is a striking example. The participation of Zambia in the economic sanctions that were first recommended and then ordered by the Security Council against Rhodesia proved to be a hardly bearable burden for the fragile economy of the country. The matter was brought to the attention of the Security

of sugar from Cuba at higher than world prices than it was to cut off exports to that island republic. Similarly, reaching a decision to suspend United Nations technical assistance to a member for one year as punishment for violating international law would not be as difficult as a decision to double that country's United Nations assessment for the year. This would be true even if the doubled assessment represented a smaller dollar amount than the loss by virtue of the suspended technical assistance.

(4) *Fines and confiscations.* To a point, the more modest and appropriate the penalty, the more likely it is that an international body would decide to impose it, and hence, the more credible the threat. Should the international community establish a scheme of deterrent penalties to be imposed upon governments that were found to have committed "ordinary" violations of international law, it is quite likely that the International Court of Justice, or another body charged with the task of setting the penalty, would in fact decide that the penalty should be imposed. This kind of decision would seem quite probable if the tribunal were satisfied that it would be implemented rather than defied.

If a penalty called for confiscation of property, the more closely the property involved is related to the violation in question, the easier it would appear to be to require forfeiture. For example, a country might be found guilty of fishing illegally in the national waters of another country. A tribunal might be will-

Council, which, in paragraph 15 of its Resolution 253 (1968), requested "States Members of the United Nations, the United Nations Organization, the specialized agencies and other international organizations in the United Nations system to extend assistance to Zambia as a matter of priority with a view to helping it solve such special economic problems. . . ." S.C. Res. 253, 23 U.N. SCOR, Supp. (Jan.-June 1968) 5, U.N. Doc. S / INF / 23 / Rev. 1 (1968). The request was reaffirmed in Security Council Resolution 277, 25 U.N. SCOR, Supp. (Jan.-Dec. 1970) 5, U.N. Doc. S / INF / 25 (1970); but it soon became clear that practical measures rather than general appeals were necessary. To this effect, the Security Council decided in Resolution 327 (1973) to entrust a Special Mission "to assess the needs of Zambia, in maintaining alternative systems of road, air, rail, and sea communications for the normal flow of traffic." S.C. Res. 327, 28 U.N. SCOR, Spec. Supps. (1&2) 3, para. 3, U.N. Doc. S / INF / 29 (1973). Then, taking note of the urgent economic needs of Zambia as indicated in the report of the Special Mission and the annexes thereto, the Security Council appealed again "to all States for immediate technical, financial and material assistance to Zambia in accordance with resolutions 253 (1968) and 277 (1970) and the recommendations of the Special Mission, so that Zambia can maintain its normal flow of traffic and enhance its capacity to implement fully the mandatory sanctions policy." 28 U.N. SCOR, Spec. Supps. (1&2) 15, para. 67, U.N. Doc. S / 10896 / Rev. 1 (1973).

ing to decide not only that the fish illegally caught should be forfeited, but also that the ship used to catch those fish should be confiscated or impounded for a set period of time. The loss of the fish would not be punishment as much as deprivation of the fruits of illegal conduct, like the bank robber who must give up stolen money. But the loss of the ship would constitute a punishment aimed at deterring others from fishing illegally in the waters of the convicting state. The international law of contraband and prize recognized as early as 1798 that by the "ancient law of Europe" not only the contraband goods being smuggled through a blockade but also the ship itself is subject to legal forfeiture.[27] If a deterrent system of punishment were created today, comparable penalties might run to the benefit of some fund held by the United Nations, rather than to the benefit of the national government injured by a violation of international law.

The acceptability of penalties that are closely related by subject matter to the substance of the violation — penalties "that fit the crime" — is quite remarkable. In theory, there might seem little reason for the deterrent being more effective the more closely related in subject matter it is to the conduct one is trying to deter. The crude fairness, however, of depriving a country of a radio frequency for abuse of the radio waves, or of requiring the litterbug to pick up papers, appeals both to those imposing the penalty and to the community in general.

As we have already observed, arranging for a financial penalty to be a lost benefit rather than a fine makes the imposition more likely. Fining states that allowed advertising billboards along new interstate highways was both impractical and politically unacceptable. Rather than formulating the financial consequences in these terms, the Highway Beautification Act of 1965 provides that states which fail to make provisions for meeting federal standards, including exclusion of advertising billboards, will have their federal aid highway funds apportionment reduced by 10 percent. The state, however, begins to receive a full apportionment as soon as it does provide for compliance with the federal standards within its borders. Even this milder form of penalty is not aimed at deterring future violations by other states

---

[27] *See* The Ringende Jacob, 1 Chris, Rob. (Admr.) 89 (1798).

nor at punishing a state once compliance has been achieved.[28] As already noted, the penalties imposed on states for violating the Civil Rights Act of 1964 have been formulated in the regulations in the form of withholding federal funds from the programs in which segregation is still practiced.

b. *Credibility: implementing a decision to punish.* There is a second aspect of the credibility of a standing threat to punish a government for violation of international law. Assuming that the decision would be taken, how likely would it appear to us and to the threatened government that it would be carried out? From the point of view of understanding the kind of international law enforcement system toward which we should be working, the question concerns the type of international apparatus that would be necessary to increase the likelihood that various kinds of decisions to punish would be implemented. This raises such questions as whether the International Court of Justice should have a marshal or even an army to back up its decisions. Here, I am concerned simply with the credibility of implementing a decision to penalize a government, while deferring for the moment the question of whether such an international apparatus, even if it were a potentially effective one, would be acceptable to the international community.

(1) *Threats of thermonuclear or other forms of violent punishment.* In our earlier discussion, we concluded that the threat of an international decision to unleash massive nuclear retaliation is not credible as a means of deterring most violations of international law. As a result, little attention will be given here to the difficult problems of how an international force, capable of carrying out a decision to punish a country by destroying some area within it, might be established. As against many countries, all it might take would be a comparatively few airplanes with some high-explosive bombs. For major powers, however, the situation becomes far more difficult to calculate. Unless the United Nations had overwhelming forces — and seemingly, even if it did — there would be a risk that it would be counter-deterred from imposing any punishment.[29]

---

[28] *See* 23 U.S.C. § 131(b) (1970).

[29] As Schwarzenberger put it in another context, "even if in law security machinery of the United Nations could be made to work against these Powers, it could be hopelessly

Probably the easiest way to equip the United Nations with the power to implement a decision to inflict destructive punishment would be to authorize it to hire, deputize, or request one or more national governments to execute the sentence. Since an international force might be reluctant to carry out a harsh penalty, just as an international tribunal would be hesitant to impose the penalty in the first place, it might be advisable to use a national military contingent willing to perform the task of executioner. But this "solution" to the problem of carrying out a harsh sentence against a government might well create more problems than it would solve. It might generate new wars, rather than prevent them.

(2) *Economic and other middle-range sanctions.* The likelihood of implementing an international decision to impose economic punishment upon a country for violating international law is probably low. In one sense, the implementation of such sanctions is comparatively easy, for not much international machinery is required. But economic punishment, nevertheless, is difficult to inflict. With military sanctions, collective measures can be markedly painful even if some countries do not participate. But economic punishment is likely to be wholly ineffective if a handful of countries refuse to participate and allow their trade with the country being punished to continue or, in fact, to increase. In addition, punishing a country by refusing to sell or to buy goods is approximately as painful for the government inflicting the sanction as for the wrongdoer. Unless advance arrangements are made among participating governments for sharing equitably the economic costs of imposing such punishment, the burdens will inevitably fall unequally upon them.[30] The countries upon which the burdens fall most heavily are likely to question after-the-fact punishment that is basically unrelated to the wrong done. Furthermore, the profitability of trading with the punished country while others are abstaining will surely tempt some countries not to go along with any boycott or embargo ordered, or, at least, to wink at black-market trade.

Such reasons explain what happened in the two major cases

---

outclassed by the armed forces and weapons systems of the super-Leviathans." *See* G. SCHWARZENBERGER, POWER POLITICS: A STUDY OF WORLD SOCIETY 392 (3d ed. 1964).

[30] *See* note 26 and accompanying text *supra*.

of collective economic sanctions — against Italy in the period of October 1935–May 1936 and against Southern Rhodesia since 1965 — that were decided respectively by the Council of the League of Nations and the Security Council of the United Nations.[31] In the first case, the sanctions were approved by all European members of the League except Austria, Hungary, and Albania. The attitude of those three countries can be accounted for by the close economic and political ties that they had with Italy. Other members of the League were in an uncomfortable position because a long period of sanctions would have frustrated other objects of their foreign policy. France, for example, found itself "in the unhappy position of having to employ sanctions against the new ally whom she had gained less than a year ago."[32] It was not surprising, therefore, that the French Government tried to negotiate a solution to the Italian adventure in Ethiopia[33] rather than to strengthen the sanctions of the League of Nations. The episode ended in the League's lifting the sanctions and recognizing Italy's conquest of Ethiopia. Nothing could have been a clearer acknowledgment of failure.

Recent experience with the use of economic sanctions to punish governments or influence their actions does not alter significantly the conclusions drawn from the 1930s. The United Nations General Assembly and the Security Council both determined that the situation created by the white regime of Prime Minister Ian Smith, which declared unilaterally that Southern Rhodesia was independent, constituted a threat to international peace and security.[34] The Security Council passed resolutions calling first for voluntary and then mandatory sanctions.[35] The United States adopted regulations designed to cut Rhodesia off

[31] For an analysis of the policy of sanctions within the two international organizations and its effects upon international relations, see Taubenfeld & Taubenfeld, The "Economic Weapon": The League and the United Nations, 58 Proc. Am. Soc'y Int'l L. 183 (1964).

[32] See E. Carr, International Relations Between the Two World Wars 1919–1939, at 226 (1947).

[33] Id. at 227–28.

[34] But see Fenwick, When Is There A Threat To Peace? — Rhodesia, 61 Am. J. Int'l L. 753 (1967).

[35] The Security Council gradually implemented its policy of sanctions by moving from selected and optional to general and mandatory economic sanctions. In Resolution 217 (1965), the Council called upon "all States to refrain from any action which would assist and encourage the illegal regime and, in particular, to desist from providing it with arms, equipment and military material, and to do their utmost in order to break all eco-

economically and cause the Smith regime to renounce its declaration of independence.[36] Great Britain and a number of other
countries took similar action. Both Portugal and South Africa,
however, continued to trade with Southern Rhodesia,[37] and un-

nomic relations with Southern Rhodesia, including an embargo on oil and petroleum
products." S.C. Res. 217, 20 U.N. SCOR, Supp. (Jan.-Mar. 1965) 8, U.N. Doc. S / INF /
20 / Rev. 1 (1965). Resolution 232 (1966) was more categorical. First, the Council expressly mentioned articles 39 and 41 of the Charter as the legal basis of the Resolution.
Second, it reminded member states that the failure or refusal by any of them to implement the Resolution would constitute a violation of article 25 of the Charter. Third, the
Council specifically indicated the categories of economic activities that were prohibited.
Fourth, it requested the Secretary-General of the United Nations to report to the Council
on the progress of the implementation of the Resolution. S.C. Res. 232, 21 U.N. SCOR,
Supp. (Jan.-Dec. 1966) & Spec. Supp. (No. 1) 7, 8–9, U.N. Doc. S / INF / 21 / Rev. 1
(1966). Resolution 253 (1968) went further: (a) the sanctions indicated therein were
mandatory; (b) political sanctions were added to those of an economic character; (c) those
member states which had persisted in trading with Southern Rhodesia were censured;
and (d) a special committee of the Council was set up to supervise the implementation of
sanctions by member states and specialized agencies of the United Nations. S.C. Res.
253, 23 U.N. SCOR, Supp. (Jan.-June 1968) 5, U.N. Doc. S / INF / 23 / Rev. 1 (1968).
Resolution 277 (1970) gave expression to the policy of active nonrecognition, which, at
the suggestion of Secretary of State Stimson, had been applied successfully by the League
of Nations to Manchukuo. In the operative paragraph 3, the Security Council called
upon "member States to take appropriate measures, at the national level, to ensure that
any act performed by officials and institutions of the illegal regime of Southern Rhodesia
shall not be accorded any recognition, official or otherwise, including judicial notice, by
the competent organs of their State." S.C. Res. 277, 25 U.N. SCOR, Supp. (Jan.-Dec.
1970) 5, U.N. Doc. S / INF / 25 (1970). Last but not least, as a reaction to municipal acts,
such as the Byrd Amendment (see note 40 and accompanying text supra), Resolution 333
(1973) requested states with legislation permitting importation of minerals and other
products from Southern Rhodesia to repeal it immediately, and to impose severe penalties on their nationals evading or breaching the imposed sanctions. S.C. Res. 333, 28
U.N. SCOR, Spec. Supps. (1&2) 14, U.N. Doc. S / INF / 29 (1973).

[36] On Nov. 29, 1972, the Office of Export Control of the Department of Commerce
amended § 385.3 of the Export Control Regulations (15 C.F.R. § 11.1–11.6 & 31 C.F.R.
§ 521.101–525.805), dealing with the control of exports to Southern Rhodesia. The purpose of the amendment was to make it clear that the legal authority for the control of
such exports was derived from the United Nations Participation Act (59 Stat. 619 (1945),
as amended 63 Stat. 734 (1949), 74 Stat. 797 (1960), 79 Stat. 841 (1965)) as well as from
the Export Administration Act of 1966 (83 Stat. 841 (1969), as amended 86 Stat. 644
(1972)). The first sentence of § 385.3 was amended to read as follows: "Pursuant to the
authorities contained in § 5 of the United Nations Participation Act [22 U.S.C. § 287(c)]
as well as the authorities contained in the Export Administration Act of 1969, as
amended, and in conformity with the United Nations Security Council Resolutions of
1965, 1966, and 1968, the United States has imposed a virtually total embargo on exports
and re-exports of U.S.—origin commodities and technical data to Southern Rhodesia."
See also 67 AM. J. INT'L L. 332–33 (1973).

[37] That practice was objected to strongly by the Security Council. In Resolution 253
(1968), the Council "deplores the attitude of States that have not complied with their

der pressure from United States business interests, the United States Congress adopted the Byrd Amendment to the Strategic and Critical Materials Stock Piling Act of 1971,[38] permitting the importation of Rhodesian chrome "in blatant disregard of our treaty undertakings."[39] Even countries with regulations against trading with Rhodesia were unable to restrain merchants from taking advantage of the highly profitable sales possible in the Rhodesian territory. The combination of all these factors made the sanctions bearable for the Rhodesian economy. The political goal of undermining the regime was not attained by a decade of collective efforts.

(3) *Fines and minor penalties.* Even when a financial obligation is imposed for a civil debt found to be owing by an international tribunal, collecting from a defendent government can be a difficult task. In 1946 two British warships struck mines while passing through the Corfu Channel in Albanian territorial waters. Both ships were seriously damaged and a number of British sailors were injured and killed. The Security Council of the United Nations recommended on the basis of article 36, paragraph 3 of the Charter that the governments of the United Kingdom and Albania refer their dispute to the International Court of Justice for a final decision.[40] In *The Corfu Channel Case*, the Court held that Albania was liable to the United Kingdom for the damages caused by the mining of this international strait.[41] Once liability

---

obligations under Article 25 of the Charter, and censures in particular those States which have persisted in trading with the illegal regime in defiance of the resolutions of the Security Council, and as such have given active assistance to the regime." S.C. Res. 253, 23 U.N. SCOR, Supp. (Jan.-June 1968) 5, U.N. Doc. S / INF / 23 / Rev. 1 (1968). In Resolution 277 (1970), the Council was more specific. Its sixth operative paragraph "condemns the policies of the Governments of South Africa and Portugal, which continue to maintain political, economic, military, and other relations with the illegal regime in Southern Rhodesia in violation of the relevant resolutions of the United Nations." S.C. Res. 277, 25 U.N. SCOR, Supp. (Jan.-Dec. 1970) 5, U.N. Doc. S / INF / 25 (1970). The condemnation is reiterated in Resolution 333 (1973), where the persistent refusal of South Africa and Portugal to cooperate with the United Nations in the effective observance and implementation of sanctions against Southern Rhodesia is characterized as a clear violation of the Charter of the United Nations. S.C. Res. 333, 28 U.N. SCOR, Spec. Supp. (1&2) 14, U.N. Doc. S / INF / 29 (1973).

[38]*See* 67 AM. J. INT'L L. 548 (1973).

[39]Diggs v. Schultz, 470 F. 2d 461, 466 (D.C. Cir. 1972).

[40]The matter was brought before the Court only by the United Kingdom. The Court found that by appearing, Albania had submitted itself to the Court's jurisdiction. [1948–49] I.C.J. 32.

was established, Albania disputed the Court's right to assess damages for the incident and refused to participate in further proceedings. Nevertheless, in a second judgment, the Court awarded the United Kingdom £843,947 for the various damages to the destroyers and naval personnel.[42] Albania has never paid this judgment and refuses to do so.[43]

This unfavorable experience with a *civil* action against a government suggests that it would be even more difficult to collect the fine assessed when *criminal* liability is established. One device that might help to assure payment of fines would be to require governments to deposit a certain amount of gold in Geneva or at The Hague as security for payment of such penalties. At the time of the negotiations of the Moscow Test Ban Treaty,[44] American officials considered a suggestion that each nuclear power should deposit a certain number of tons of monetary gold with some neutral authority. In the event of a violation of the treaty, there would have been little difficulty with the application of the sanction: a fine of one ton of this gold, for instance, could have been forfeited to the United Nations. That prospective loss might have proved a significant deterrent against any violation, particularly if the gold had not already been irretrievably lost to a country.[45]

If a modest international constabularly force existed, a decision to confiscate designated contraband items or property in some way associated with them might be implemented with some degree of confidence. We shall postpone for now a discussion of the methods of enforcing such a judicial decision: that topic is considered in the part of this book on second-order compliance.

c. *Credibility and second-order compliance.* Before turning to the third aspect of effectiveness — influencing a government — no-

[41] [1949] I.C.J. 4.

[42] *Id.* at 221.

[43] *See* note 4, ch. 1, and accompanying text *supra.*

[44] Treaty Banning Nuclear Weapon Tests, Aug. 5, 1963, 14 U.S.T. 1313, T.I.A.S. No. 5433, 480 U.N.T.S. 43.

[45] For example, each of the depositing countries might have been allowed to get the gold back if the treaty were terminated with a year's notice. In the meantime, the depositing countries might have been free to receive interest on the deposited gold or to use it as security for international credit.

tice how the discussion has progressed. In considering the application of a criminal law deterrent method against governments as a way of causing governments to respect standing rules (first-order compliance), it appears that the credibility of the threatened punishment may be crucial. And, here, it turns out that the critical question may well be whether the international community has an adequate way of causing compliance with an international determination that, in this case, punishment should be imposed (second-order compliance). In short, the very deterrent method of seeking to cause first-order compliance assumes the existence of some method of causing second-order compliance — some method of making reasonably sure that an international decision that punishment ought to be imposed will in fact be implemented. The kind of threat that an international judicial system can credibly make in an effort to deter any violation of standing rules depends upon the kind of judicial decision with which it is capable of causing compliance.

The brief discussion above of the likelihood of threatened punishment's being implemented could thus be expanded to incorporate the entire subsequent discussion of the problems of causing compliance with determinations. One could well say that the first task is to understand the methods of enforcing judicial determinations and the probable limits upon them. Only thereafter can one adequately consider the limits upon the credibility of a deterrent threat imposed by the difficulty of ensuring that a decision that punishment should be imposed would be carried out. A system capable of producing second-order compliance is a prerequisite to a system capable of implementing threats to punish.

6. *Effectiveness: influencing a government by a credible threat.* Even where a threatened punishment is credible, the deterrent will not be effective unless the government is influenced by the threat. We do not have much experience with attempting to influence corporate abstractions, like a government, by a preexisting legal scheme involving established penalties for violations. In current international political practice, there is a general — and perhaps useful — blurring among various kinds of threats. On some occasions, threats by several major powers might reasonably be compared with reminders by an international authority that violators of international law will be dealt with

harshly,[46] much the way the Commissioner of Internal Revenue may remind taxpayers of the criminal penalties for tax evasion. On most occasions, intergovernmental threats are identified as the threat of an adversary, not of the community, and as in support of an ad hoc demand, not of a rule of law. Experience with such threats is difficult to compare with the kind of deterrent that a legal system imposing punishment upon governments would involve. Contemporary threats are probably more effective to the extent that they are more explicit as to the precise action or inaction that is required. They are less effective to the extent that they appear less legitimate and tend to occur later, after inconsistent action may already have been initiated.

We can perhaps draw some conclusions with respect to influencing large, abstract entities with threats by examining domestic experience with large corporations and the antitrust laws. In the United States, we have attempted to enforce the antitrust laws against corporations. Between July 1955 and December 1966, over eight hundred corporations were fined about $11.5 million under the Sherman Act, with the average fine being about $13,000. In that same period, nearly $1.4 million in fines was paid by over four hundred individual defendants, with an average fine of about $3,400.[47] This experience with corporations has hardly been conclusive. No doubt, some corporations consider the possibility of a fine, or the chance of a treble-damage action under the Clayton Act,[48] as one of the modest risks to be taken into account and weighed against possible gains. To

[46] National warnings were made more legitimate and more credible by Resolution 255 (1968) of the Security Council relating to measures to safeguard states that did not have nuclear weapons and that were parties to the Treaty on the Non-Proliferation of Nuclear Weapons. The Council recognized that "aggression with nuclear weapons or the threat of such aggression against a non-nuclear weapon State would create a situation in which the Security Council, and above all its nuclear-weapon State permanent members, would have to act immediately in accordance with their obligations under the United Nations Charter." Accordingly, the Council welcomed "the intention expressed by certain states that they will provide or support immediate assistance, in accordance with the Charter, to any non-nuclear-weapon state party to the Treaty on the Non-Proliferation of Nuclear Weapons that is a victim of an act or an object of a threat of aggression in which nuclear weapons are used." S.C. Res. 255, 23 U.N. SCOR, Supp. (Jan.-June 1968) 13, para. 2, U.N. Doc. S / INF / 23 / Rev. 1 (1968).

[47] ABA ANTITRUST SECTION, ANTITRUST DEVELOPMENTS, 1955–68, at 222, *Citing* J. CLABAULT & J. BURTON, SHERMAN ACT INDICTMENTS 40 (Supp. 1967).

[48] Clayton Act, ch. 323, § 7, 38 Stat. 730 (1914) (current version at 15 U.S.C. § 18 (1970)).

some corporations, however, the moral condemnation of the corporation as a "criminal" might be quite significant.[49] It is difficult to estimate what kind of a penalty is sufficient to deter a collective enterprise from engaging in illegal conduct in which it would otherwise engage. This difficulty is particularly evident in the case of a government. Violations of international law frequently are politically motivated and perhaps can be compared with crimes of passion rather than with the more deliberate type of action inherent in an antitrust violation. To that extent, international law violations, like crimes of passion, will not be deterred by threats of punishment for the wrong done.

There are four other distinctions between deterring normal criminal conduct and deterring governments. These distinctions help to explain the difficulty inherent in trying to influence governments with a credible threat.

a. *Perception.* Let us assume that appropriate penalties had been devised for violation of the international rule that a coastal state must not deny unjustifiably innocent passage through its territorial waters to a merchant ship. Moreover, we shall assume that these penalties were established so that objectively, as perceived by a being from Mars, the likelihood of the penalty's being imposed and its seriousness should outweigh the possible advantage to be gained for a country by violating this rule. Nevertheless, a government's perception of the comparative values involved in determining whether or not to violate this international rule may be quite different from an objective one. Governments, for a number of reasons, tend to be concerned much more with immediate problems than with the more distant future. In the Department of State, for example, most of the time of the top officials is devoted to the current crisis. Thus, in deciding whether to deny innocent passage to a merchant ship and

---

[49] An unusual attempt to apply criminal sanctions against a corporation occurred in 1978 when a county grand jury in Indiana indicted the Ford Motor Company for reckless homicide for designing, manufacturing, and failing to repair a 1973 Pinto automobile in which three teenage girls had died. The indictment named only the corporation, no individuals. Since no prison sentence would be possible and the maximum possible fine was $35,000, a major purpose of the indictment was presumably that of moral condemnation. A criminal conviction might also be of help to plaintiffs suing the corporation for damages. The indictments handed down on Sept. 13, 1978, were widely reported. *See, e.g.,* Boston Globe, Sept. 14, 1978, at 2, col. 2.

violate the international rule, a government is likely to be concerned much more with the advantages of taking this action now than with the possible penalties to be imposed in the future following some kind of international proceeding. Governments will tend to discount remote penalties more than pure logic would dictate.

b. *A group decision.* Deterring a government means persuading a group. In the process of reaching a group decision members of the group are frequently more concerned with the effects within the group of positions taken in the process of reaching a decision than with the effect on the country of the ultimate decision. This phenomenon is perhaps seen most clearly in a democracy during an election year. It is generally understood that during the six months before a presidential election in the United States, for example, the foreign policy decisions of the United States should not be expected to reflect a reasonable weighing of the pros and cons for the United States vis-à-vis the rest of the world. Even with President Johnson out of the political race, Republican supporters of Richard Nixon charged that the Administration's decision to halt the bombing of North Vietnam six days before the 1968 election was a "political trick" to help the Democratic nominee, Vice-President Humphrey.

A collective decision reached by a government thus is likely to be quite different from the decision that would have been reached by any one individual. Each member of a group is deeply concerned with his present and future status within the group. He may wish to appear firm, or brave or patriotic. The resulting collective decision, especially in response to a threat, is likely to be something other than an objective appraisal of national benefits and losses. Fortunately for international law, it is likely that extreme positions will be canceled out by the effect of group consideration. But, unfortunately, it is equally likely that present policy positions will be "hardened" in order to maintain the prestige of those proposing them.

Although most clearly demonstrated in the case of democracies, the same phenomenon is no doubt present in other governments as well. Foreign policy decisions of the Soviet Union, China, or Egypt, for example, are often explained after-the-fact by knowledgeable commentators as having been taken "for internal reasons." Some reports explained, for instance, that the decision by the Soviet Union and other Warsaw Pact countries to invade Czechoslovakia in August 1968 was the result of an internal struggle between so-called hardliners and supporters of "peaceful coexistence" within the Soviet Union. More recently, Harold Russell reported that Soviet diplomats had acknowledged that a substantial portion of the original Soviet rationale for the Conference on Security and Cooperation in Europe had disappeared before the signing of the Final Act of the Conference in Helsinki.[50] The Soviet Union, however, could not abandon the idea because of the personal prestige that General Secretary Brezhnev had invested in the Conference.[51]

Despite the plurality of people involved, there is a continuing tendency to treat another country as a unit and to expect it to react rationally by weighing the national advantages and disadvantages. The entire deterrent theory is valid only to the extent that a rational governmental decision is unaltered by the internal political process. On a drastic decision, such as one to launch thermonuclear war, the group distortion may not alter the decision that would be reached by a rational individual. On the other hand, over the vast range of intermediate foreign policy decisions into which would fall most of the "ordinary" violations of international law, domestic considerations play a significant and sometimes decisive role. Such internal forces would appear to have been in control at various times when United States policies toward China, Cuba, and Israel were determined. In the case of Israel, for example, the significant Jewish vote in New York City may have influenced the Democratic Administration's demand that Egypt end its blockade of the Straits of Tiran in June 1967 and may have tended to produce a markedly pro-Israeli stance among Democratic senatorial candidates in New York State.

---

[50] On Aug. 1, 1975, the chiefs of state and other high representatives of thirty-three European countries, the United States, and Canada signed the Final Act of the Conference on Security and Cooperation in Europe. The complete text is reproduced in 37 DEP'T STATE BULL. 323 (1976), 14 INT'L LEGAL MATERIALS 1293 (1975), 70 AM. J. INT'L L. 417 (1976).

[51] See Russell, The Helsinki Declaration: Brobdingnag or Lilliput? 70 AM. J. INT'L L. 246 (1970).

c. *Gap between the deciders and the sufferers.* The decision makers for any government are not only a group of individuals with rivalries and concerns that affect their collective decision. Even as a group, they are distinct from those upon whom the penalty would fall should it ever be imposed. An international threat to punish a country, whether by destroying a city, by depriving it of territory, by imposing an economic embargo, or by imposing a fine, is not a threat directed at the group responsible for governmental decisions. They may be affected as individuals, but others would be the primary sufferers. Furthermore, an external threat may strengthen, in some cases, the hand of the government, not weaken it. Some governments find external threats useful rather than harmful. When the League of Nations imposed economic sanctions against Italy, Mussolini used the action as an excuse for extending Fascist control over the national economy and rallying the Italian people behind his government. The threatened punishment became a reward rather than a deterrent.

The less genuinely concerned a government is about the welfare of its people, the less likely an international law enforcement scheme would be to influence the government by threatening a punishment which would fall primarily on its people. A threat to a country affects the decision makers only to the extent that they truly have the country's interests at heart and share the threatener's perception of what those interests are.

d. *Effectiveness of a credible threat — a domestic example.* Perhaps a fair surmise about the effectiveness of a credible deterrent penalty system on government behavior can be derived from considering various possible federal penalties imposed upon state governments. At one end of the scale, there would seem to be modest, routine penalties comparable to those which might be applied to private persons and organizations. For example, consider the obligation of state governments to withhold and forward to the federal government federal income taxes on the salaries paid to state employees. A special interest charge against the state for failure to forward such funds within a designated time might well be an effective deterrent. The state official responsible for sending the withholdings on to the federal government would understand that doing his job well for the state involved sending the funds promptly in order to avoid the penalty. This presumably would be true even though the penalty did not fall directly upon the official but upon the state treasury. At the other end of the scale, credible threats of drastic destruction — if they could be arranged — also would be likely to be effective. Should the federal government *credibly* establish that any town in which the public schools were not integrated racially by the following Monday would be destroyed by nuclear or high-explosive bombardment, one would guess that the schools might be integrated. Government officials can justify to themselves and others the necessity of surrendering to overwhelming military force.

Whether or not the threat of middle-range sanctions such as embargoes and boycotts would influence a state government is more problematic. The many objections to these sanctions, which already have been mentioned in discussing their use against other countries, would apply with equal or even greater force if the federal government tried to impose them against a state. Consider what would happen if Congress passed a statute requiring the federal government to cut off all shipments of selected goods into and out of a state and all travel to and from a state unless the state fully complied with the Civil Rights Act of 1964. Aside from the constitutional problems raised by the law, it would no doubt fail to achieve its purpose. Unlike their response to credible threats of massive destruction, the states would probably refuse to give in to this threat of economic isolation. The noncomplying states could be expected to ask their citizens to rally in defiance of the federal statute and to aid in the creation of a self-sufficient economy.

7. *Acceptability of the system.* A system of destructive punishment to be inflicted upon countries that broke the law in order to deter violations of international law does not seem within the realm of what is politically acceptable. The unwillingness of any government to agree that an international body should have the legal right to destroy part of its country if that body decided that the government had violated international law can probably be taken for granted. The problems of establishing an acceptably constituted body and the procedures to govern it would also seem insurmountable.

Although a scheme to deprive countries of their territory as punishment would appear unlikely to commend itself to the international community, the threatened imposition of economic sanctions might. Here, the sanction is one that has been imposed in the past and one that is imposed currently from time to time by various governments. Further, it has the great advantage, from the point of view of any government, that if at the time it did not wish to go along with any particular economic measure it would probably have the de facto power not to do so. It is difficult to say whether a system of economic sanctions imposed as punishment would be less attractive to countries asked to participate if the measures were imposed as "permanent" or if they were ordered to be imposed for one year or some other stated period of time. "Permanent" economic strangulation of a people because of some past departure from international law for which their government was responsible would seem far less likely to be acceptable to all those necessary to implement it. Sanctions for a short period of time might well seem futile.

If there were to be sanctions to enforce the sanctions — if, for example, an international police force were authorized to patrol the borders of the country being punished and to destroy all trucks, ships, aircraft, and trains attempting to cross the border either way — the acceptability of the system might go further down.

There would seem to be nothing inherently unacceptable about a scheme for imposing modest financial fines and confiscations, provided adequate limits were established. It would probably be easier to establish penalties in connection with particular rules than to set up broad general authorities to levy fines for any violation of international law.

8. *Conclusions.* From this analysis of the problem of seeking to cause governments to respect standing rules of international law by threatening their countries with punishment in the event of a violation, some hypotheses can be drawn. An international system which would issue threats of retaliatory destruction is unlikely to be acceptable. Even if it were acceptable, it is unlikely that its threats would be sufficiently credible to be an effective deterrent for most of the possible violations of international law, or perhaps for any of them.

Whatever merit economic embargoes and boycotts may have as a means of inducing a government to alter current behavior, they seem inappropriate as a punishment for past misconduct. The threat of imposing "permanent" economic isolation would not be sufficiently credible and the threat to impose a period of economic restraint as punishment would not be sufficiently impressive to act as an effective deterrent.

Modest financial penalties and authorized seizures might be both effective and acceptable as a deterrent to modest violations of international law. The critical question would seem to be the ability to implement the decision that the penalty should be imposed. The more closely related the penalty is to the offense for which it is being imposed, the more acceptable it is likely to be. Also, it is likely to fall more nearly upon the persons responsible for the decision and therefore to have a greater chance of affecting their decision. In the case of financial penalties, acceptability and ease of implementation will be increased if it can be structured as a loss of a benefit rather than as the imposition of a separate obligation to pay. In the case of the destruction or confiscation of property acceptability of the penalty will be increased if it is applied to property used in the commission of the offense which can thus be considered in some way to have become tainted by the illegality.

CHAPTER IV

Deterrence Against Individuals

Over the years, it has been recognized that international law will become increasingly effective the more it applies directly to individuals as well as to governments. Starting from this sound premise, it has usually been assumed that the central means of applying law to individuals is through the use of the criminal law.[1] Individuals cause governmental decisions. Applying a conventional enforcement theory, the hope has been to deter violations of standing rules of international law by threatening criminal punishment against the individuals responsible for a violation.

The theory of personal guilt for causing a government to violate international law was basic to the prosecution of war criminals at Nuremberg. The Tribunal emphatically stated: "Crimes against international law are committed by men, not by abstract entities, and only by punishing individuals who commit such crimes can the provisions of international law be enforced.[2] As a strong reaffirmation of the same policy, the United Nations

---

[1] This philosophy was expressed in article 277 of the Treaty of Versailles, according to which "the Allied and Associated Powers publicly arraign William II of Hohenzollern, formerly German Emperor, for a supreme offence against international morality and the sanctity of treaties," Treaty of Versailles, June 28, 1919, 2 C. BEVANS, TREATIES AND OTHER INTERNATIONAL AGREEMENTS OF THE UNITED STATES OF AMERICA 1776–1949, at 43, 136 (1969). That attempt to establish international criminal responsibility of individuals directly responsible for grave breaches of international law failed: "On November 10, 1918, William II had left his country and taken refuge in Doorn, Holland, where he spent the rest of his life. An attempt by the Allies in 1920 to persuade Holland to surrender him for trial was declined politely but firmly, the Netherlands government expressing doubts about the legality of the proposed procedure and a disinclination to withdraw their protection from one who had freely sought it." G. CRAIG, EUROPE SINCE 1815, at 534 (1961). See also S. GLUECK, WAR CRIMINALS: THEIR PROSECUTION & PUNISHMENT 126–28, 163–64 (1944). Of course, hanging the Kaiser in no way would have proven the philosophy a success.

[2] 41 AM. J. INT'L L. 221 (1947), Judgment of the Nuremberg Tribunal, 82 U.N.T.S. 285–86 (1951). Also, according to article 7, the official position of defendants, whether as heads-of-state or responsible officials in government departments, could not be considered as freeing them from responsibility or as mitigating their punishment. Id. at 286.

General Assembly unanimously affirmed at its first session in Resolution 95(I) "the principles of international law recognized by the Charter of the Nuremberg Tribunal and the judgments of the Tribunal."[3] Thus, an international system for seeking to deter certain kinds of violations of international law by threatening punishment against government officers already exists.

Over the years, there have been numerous proposals to use deterrent methods for enforcing international law against individuals. The four 1949 Geneva Conventions on humanitarian law applicable to armed conflicts represent a notable illustration. For example, article 49, paragraph 1 of the Geneva Convention for the Amelioration of the Condition of the Wounded and Sick in Armed Forces in the Field reads:[4] "The High Contracting Parties undertake to enact any legislation necessary to provide effective penal sanctions for persons committing, or ordering to be committed, any of the grave breaches of the present Convention defined in the following Article."[5] Although the 1963 Mos-

---

[3]G.A. Res. 95(1), U.N. Doc. A / 64 / Add. 1 at 188 (1947). In consequence of that resolution and the subsequent practice of states, one could presume safely that international criminal responsibility of individuals for grave breaches of international law has become a settled principle of general international law. In 1947 the General Assembly directed the International Law Commission to formulate the principles of international law recognized in the Charter of the Nuremberg Tribunal and in the judgment of the tribunal. The Commission undertook a preliminary consideration of the extent to which the principles contained in the Charter and in the judgment constituted principles of international law. They concluded that since the Nuremberg principles had been affirmed unanimously by the General Assembly in Resolution 95 (1) of Dec. 11, 1946, their task was not to express any appreciation of those principles as international law but merely to formulate them. THE WORK OF THE INTERNATIONAL LAW COMMISSION 21–22 (rev. ed. 1972).

[4]Geneva Convention for the Amelioration of the Condition of the Wounded and Sick in Armed Forces in the Field, Aug. 12, 1949, 6 U.S.T. 3114, T.I.A.S. No. 3362, 75 U.N.T.S. 31. *See also* article 50, ¶ 1 of the Convention for the Amelioration of the Condition of Wounded, Sick and Shipwrecked Members of Armed Forces at Sea, Aug. 12, 1949, 6 U.S.T. 3217, T.I.A.S. No. 3363, 75 U.N.T.S. 85; article 129, ¶ 1 of the Convention Relative to the Treatment of Prisoners of War, Aug. 12, 1949, 6 U.S.T. 3316, T.I.A.S. No. 3364, 75 U.N.T.S. 135; and article 146, ¶ 1 of the Convention Relative to the Protection of Civilian Persons in Time of War, Aug. 12, 1949, 6 U.S.T. 3516, T.I.A.S. No. 5365, 75 U.N.T.S. 287. In the opinion of Richard Falk, this rule actually is declaratory of a universal obligation that is incumbent upon belligerents under customary international law. *See* Falk, *Songmy: War Crimes and Individual Responsibility. A Legal Memorandum*, 17 REV. CONTEMP. L. 107, 112 (1970).

[5]Article 50 reads: "Grave breaches to which the preceding Article relates shall be those involving any of the following acts, if committed against persons or property pro-

cow Test Ban Treaty does not expressly require personal punishment, it does require each government to "prohibit" various kinds of nuclear tests. The treaty thus raises the possibility that signatory governments would adopt criminal legislation to enforce the test ban against their own officers.[6]

This chapter considers the value and appropriate direction of efforts to improve compliance with standing rules of international law through deterring individuals by national or international threats.

1. *The domestic experience and its relevance.* In considering how effective an international law enforcement scheme aimed at deterring officers might be, our major source of data will be existing experience. In the internal practice of nations, far more use has been made of the technique of punishing government officers than of the technique of punishing state or local governments as such. Obviously, there are significant differences between a system in which the courts of an officer's own country seek to deter him from exceeding the legal limits on the government's authority by threatening him with punishment and a system in which the threatened punishment would be determined and imposed by courts operating under international authority. In the present international atmosphere, it could be assumed that a judge would generally be more willing to order the punishment of a foreign officer than he would be to order the punishment of an officer of his own country. Presumably, this would be in part because of the greater natural hostility toward the foreign officer and in part because of the possible risks to the judge's own position in ordering the punishment of an officer of

---

tected by the Convention: willful killing, torture or inhuman treatment, including biological experiments, willfully causing great suffering or serious injury to body or health, and extensive destruction and appropriation of property, not justified by military necessity and carried out unlawfully and wantonly." Geneva Convention for the Amelioration of the Condition of the Wounded and Sick in Armed Forces in the Field, Aug. 12, 1949, *supra* note 4, at 43. *See also* similar provisions in the other three Geneva conventions, *supra* note 4, at 69, 131, 211.

[6]The Russians submitted a Draft International Agreement to Forbid the Production and Use of Weapons Based Upon the Use of Atomic Energy for the Purposes of Mass Destruction. Included in that Draft Convention was the following provision: "Article 3. The High contracting parties, within six months of the entry into force of the present agreement, shall pass legislation providing severe punishment for the violation of the terms of this agreement." N.Y. Times, June 20, 1946, at 4, col. 6.

his own government. Obviously, the problems of implementing a decision to punish would also be significantly different depending upon whether the punishment had been ordered by a national or an international authority. Nonetheless, existing data are the best thing that we have to go on in analyzing this problem. We will have to make allowances for the differences between the national systems that we have today and the international system that we might have in the future and draw such conclusions as we are able to draw.

Domestic experience may be a better model than it appears at first blush. If there are serious limits to the effectiveness within a well-organized national society of deterring officers by threats of punishment, one may well question whether we should adopt that method as a goal for a well-organized international society. To put it another way, one may well question any general use of the method if in today's international community there are not enough shared values for a court with criminal jurisdiction over government officers to operate successfully,[7] and if in today's national communities there are too many such values at work.

2. *Effectiveness and acceptability.* As with a deterrent scheme directed at governments, the effectiveness of a deterrent scheme

---

[7] The opposition of governments to setting up an international criminal court is manifest. On Dec. 9, 1948, the General Assembly of the United Nations requested in Resolution 260B, 3(1) U.N. GAOR, U.N. Doc. A / 810 at 177 (1948), the International Law Commission "to study the desirability and possibility of establishing an international judicial organ for the trial of persons charged with genocide or other crimes over which jurisdiction will be conferred upon that organ by international conventions." It also requested the Commission, in carrying out that task, "to pay attention to the possibility of establishing a Criminal Chamber of the International Court of Justice." THE WORK OF THE INTERNATIONAL LAW COMMISSION, *supra* note 3, at 22. The Commission concluded that the establishment of an international judicial organ for the trial of persons charged with genocide or other crimes was both desirable and possible. After giving consideration to the Commission's report, the General Assembly adopted Resolution 489 (V) of Dec. 12, 1950, establishing a committee composed of the representatives of seventeen member states for the purpose of preparing concrete proposals relating to the creation and the statute of an international criminal court. G.A. Res. 489, 5 U.N. GAOR, Supp. (No. 20) 77, U.N. Doc. A / 1775 (1950). The draft statute prepared by the Committee proposed that the court should have a permanent structure but should function only on the basis of the cases submitted to it. The report of the Committee, together with the draft statute, was communicated to governments for their observations, but only a few commented on the draft. *See* THE WORK OF THE INTERNATIONAL LAW COMMISSION, *supra* note 3, at 23. The General Assembly decided, however, in Resolution 687 (VII) to

aimed at governmental officers will depend upon the seriousness of a threat, its credibility, and the extent to which a government officer is influenced by threats. The credibility depends
upon the likelihood of the violation's being detected, the likelihood of the tribunal's reaching a decision that punishment
ought to be inflicted, and upon the likelihood of that decision's
being implemented. Again, we will postpone the question of obtaining knowledge of violations and deal in sequence with the
two credibility problems of reaching and implementing a decision to punish: the problem of influencing an officer by credible
threats and the acceptability of such a criminal law system.

3. *Credibility: reaching a decision to punish.* Looking at the process
by which the decision is made whether or not to punish a government officer for having gone beyond the legal limitations applicable to the government, one recognizes that there are at least
three quite different ways in which a reluctance to punish government officers can be demonstrated: in the decision to prose-

---

set up a new committee with the same composition. Its terms of reference were: (1) to
explore the implications and consequences of establishing an international criminal
court and of the various methods by which this might be done; (2) to study the relationship between such a court and the United Nations organs; and (3) to reexamine the draft
statute. G.A. Res. 687, 7 U.N. GAOR, Supp. (No. 20), U.N. Doc. A / 2361 (1952). The
new report of the Committee was placed before the Assembly at its 1954 session. The
Assembly decided, however, in Resolution 898 (IX) of Dec. 14, 1954, to postpone consideration of the report until it had taken up the report of the Special Committee on the
question of defining aggression, together with the draft code of offenses against the
peace and security of mankind. G.A. Res. 898, 9 U.N. GAOR, Supp. (No. 21), U.N. Doc.
A / 2890 (1954). The Assembly hoped to clarify the applicable law before establishing
the machinery for its enforcement. In 1968 the General Committee of the General Assembly clearly related consideration of the item to the agreement on the definition of
aggression. *See* THE WORK OF THE INTERNATIONAL LAW COMMISSION, *supra* note 3, at 24.
Although the Assembly adopted in Resolution 3314 (XXIX) the definition of aggression
(G.A. Res. 3314, 29 U.N. GAOR, Supp. (No. 31) 143–44, U.N. Doc. A / 9631 (1974)),
the discussion of the 1953 report on the establishment of an international criminal court
was not resumed. Consideration by the General Assembly of the punishment of war
criminals and of persons who had committed crimes against humanity provided a good
opportunity to reconsider the matter of international criminal jurisdiction. In the Convention on the Non-Applicability of Statutory Limitations to War Crimes and Crimes
against Humanity, the Assembly adopted, however, the principle of national jurisdiction
(23 U.N. GAOR, Supp. (No. 18) 40–41, U.N. Doc. A / 7218 (1968). Furthermore, the
General Assembly decided, at its 1676th plenary meeting, not to include the item entitled
"International Criminal Jurisdiction" in the agenda of its twenty-third session but to defer the item to a later session. *See* 23 U.N. GAOR, Supp. (No. 18) 41, U.N. Doc. A / 7218
(1968). The discussion of the item does not appear to have been resumed.

cute, in the way the law has been interpreted, and in the way the facts have been found.

a. *Discretion against prosecution.* In this country the ineffectiveness of criminal prosecution as a means of controlling the police is well recognized. If a police officer searches without a warrant or illegally arrests a criminal outside the jurisdiction of his authority and "kidnaps" him back into the state, there is little chance indeed that he will be prosecuted. Justice Murphy, dissenting in *Wolf v. Colorado*, pointed to one difficulty:

> Little need be said concerning the possibilities of criminal prosecution. Self-scrutiny is a lofty ideal, but its exaltation reaches new heights if we expect a District Attorney to prosecute himself or his associates for well-meaning violations of the search and seizure clause during a raid the District Attorney . . . has ordered.[8]

Justice Douglas, dissenting in *Irvine v. California*, thought federal prosecution of state officials little more likely: "An already overburdened Department of Justice . . . cannot be expected to devote its energies to supervising local police activities and prosecuting police officers, except in rare and occasional instances. . . ."[9] One student of the problem of how to keep the police in line pointed out:

> Since 1921 there has been a federal statute making it a misdemeanor for a federal officer to participate in an unlawful search and seizure. [—18 U.S.C. 2236.] In the intervening 34 years, however, there have been no reported prosecutions under the act, although there have been innumerable cases in the federal courts in which convictions have been reversed because of unlawful search and seizure. No criminal trespass actions arising out of illegal search and seizure have been found.[10]

It is no wonder the author concluded that criminal remedies were ineffective. In the years following the appearance of his article, the Supreme Court showed increasing concern for illegal

---

[8] 338 U.S. 25, 42 (1949).

[9] 347 U.S. 128, 151–52 (1953).

[10] Foote, *Tort Remedies for Police Violations of Individual Rights*, 39 MINN. L. REV. 493, 494 (1955). The successful prosecution of President Nixon's assistant John Ehrlichman for illegally breaking into the office of Daniel Ellsberg's psychiatrist is one of the few cases of criminal conviction of a government officer for breaking and entering that has been justified as official action.

searches and seizures, eventually announcing the "exclusionary rule" in *Mapp v. Ohio*.[11] Yet, despite this trend in the Supreme Court decisions, the statute making participation by a federal officer in an illegal search or seizure a misdemeanor remains a dead letter.

The popular reluctance to prosecute officers for doing their duty as they saw it, no matter what the law might have been, apparently covers all conduct short of that which offends natural law notions of morality. Although few states have statutes on illegal searches and seizures comparable to the federal statute discussed above, a number of states do provide for the punishment of one *maliciously* procuring a search warrant or *willfully* exceeding his authority in exercising it.[12] For such conduct as brutal third-degree tactics by police or the participation by concentration camp officials in programs of human slaughter, there is far less reluctance to prosecute whether or not the conduct was in the performance of official duty. An early New York decision involving wiretapping illustrates this widely felt distinction between doing what may be improper for the sake of the public good and doing the same thing for personal gain. The New York County District Attorney filed an information charging the police commissioner "with wrongfully obtaining knowledge of telephonic messages passing over the wires rented to and used by certain labor organizations." The committing magistrate dismissed the information, and the District Attorney appealed. On appeal, the dismissal was affirmed

> for the all-sufficient reason that it was conclusively established that he [the police commissioner] had committed no crime, but on the contrary, the knowledge of conversations conducted over the telephone wires in question was acquired solely in his official capacity as police commissioner for the purpose of detecting crime, and which in fact, resulted in the conviction of a number of individuals, and that knowledge of such conversations was only utilized for the purpose of detecting suspected criminality.[13]

To some extent the likelihood of prosecution is increased if

[11] 367 U.S. 643 (1961).
[12] *See* the statutes cited in Mr. Justice Frankfurter's opinion in Wolf v. Colorado, 338 U.S. 25, 30n.1 (1949).
[13] People v. Hebbard, 96 Misc. 617, 162 N.Y.S. 80 (1916).

the job is given to a different organization from that of the officer who committed the offense. Today, a prosecutor from one country might be quite willing to initiate prosecution of an officer in another country.[14] In general, the more widely distributed the function of starting a case, the greater the likelihood that someone with the right to initiate a proceeding will want to do so. At the same time, one can expect that as a sense of international community develops, a reluctance to prosecute even officers of other countries will increase. In this country, we find that not only are state officers unwilling to prosecute each other, but federal prosecutions of state officers, even for civil rights violations, are rare indeed. A collegiate feeling could be expected to develop among officials of different governments, leading to a reluctance to prosecute each other.

b. *Interpreting the law.* Within a single national government, a decision to punish an official for exceeding his authority involves no international problems. There certainly is recognized authority and power to impose punishment. Nevertheless, those responsible for reaching a decision to punish either a federal or state officer are often tempted to find that, when properly construed, the law was not violated. Every standing rule is ambiguous with respect to some applications. Where a government official is being prosecuted for having acted in his official capacity contrary to law, and where he can plausibly contend that the rule permitted his conduct, it is not likely that a court will disagree with his interpretation. A few examples will illustrate the problem.

The Postmaster General of the United States interpreted his authority as authorizing or requiring him to stop *Lady Chatterley's Lover* from going through the mail because it was an "obscene,

---

[14] The Application Instituting Proceedings in the Case of Trial of Pakistani Prisoners of War, [1973] I.C.J. 10, supports this proposition. In that case, following the 1971 war between India and Pakistan which resulted in the creation of Bangladesh, Bangladesh claimed the right to bring to trial on charges of genocide 195 Pakistani prisoners of war at the time in captivity in India. The evidence submitted by Pakistan in support of its application to the International Court of Justice (*id.* at 22) and the protracted negotiation between India and Pakistan made it abundantly clear that the authorities of India and Bangladesh were not only willing but eager to prosecute officers of another country. They ultimately abandoned the idea, but only after obtaining political concessions from Pakistan. For details of the case and the facts surrounding it, see Levie, *The Indo-Pakistani Agreement of August 28, 1973*, 68 AM. J. INT'L L. 95–97 (1974).

lewd, lascivious, indecent, filthy or vile article."[15] In a civil suit to enjoin the Postmaster General from continuing with his interference, the courts might well have disagreed with his interpretation of what is "obscene and non-mailable," as in fact they did.[16] On the other hand, it seems certain that a court would have been far more willing to find that the Postmaster General acted within the broad area of discretion given him by Congress if the only alternative had been to convict the Postmaster General as a criminal. So long as the Postmaster General was acting "governmentally" and not for personal gain, a court would be most reluctant to treat a mistake of judgment, no matter how erroneous, as criminal conduct.

Again, one can sense intuitively the forces on a court to interpret a rule liberally so as to avoid punishing a well-motivated government official if one imagines a law designed to enforce the first amendment by establishing criminal penalties against any Senator or Congressman who voted for a statute which unconstitutionally restricted free speech. It is almost inconceivable that the constitutionality of such a statute would even be litigated if it required a massive criminal prosecution of a majority of both houses of Congress. If such a case were brought, the Supreme Court would be far less likely to hold the statute unconstitutional. It would tend to interpret the government's powers broadly to avoid having to order the infliction of punishment upon public officials.

An international tribunal would presumably be somewhat more willing to find a violation of international law by a government official. How much more, it is difficult to say. The temptation to interpret such a statute so as not to create a major political dispute between governments would be strong. Moreover, international criminal standards are likely to be vague, particularly for crimes that contain a political element. For example, the General Assembly asked the International Law Commission in Resolution 177(II) of 21 November 1947[17] to prepare a draft code of offenses against the peace and security of mankind, indicating clearly the place to be accorded to the principles of in-

---

[15] 18 U.S.C. § 1461 (1970).
[16] Grove Press, Inc. v. Christenberry, 276 F.2d 433 (1960).
[17] G.A. Res. 177, 2 U.N. GAOR, U.N. Doc. A / 519 at 111 (1947).

ternational law recognized in the Charter of the Nuremberg Tribunal and in the judgment of the Tribunal. In the "crimes under international law for which the responsible individuals shall be punishable" article 2, paragraph 5 of the Commission's Draft Code of Offenses against the Peace and Security of Mankind includes "[t]he undertaking or encouragement by the authorities of a State of activities calculated to foment civil strife in another State, or the toleration by the authorities of a State of organized activities calculated to foment civil strife in another State."[18] The Commission's comments on this provision, however, give no indication of what is meant by "toleration" or what constitutes "activities calculated to foment civil strife in the territory of another State." The article of the Draft Code, like so many of the other articles, leaves substantial scope for interpretation by a tribunal which might want to avoid imposing criminal sanctions against an accused government official.

c. *Legal defenses.* An international agreement establishing a court with jurisdiction to order the imposition of criminal penalties upon an individual officer who is responsible for a violation of international law could, presumably, limit sharply or even abolish the legal defenses that might otherwise be available. Nonetheless, it is useful to consider the numerous defenses that domestic courts have developed to protect persons in the situation of an accused government officer. These defenses demonstrate a strong reluctance on the part of courts to order the punishment of officials acting from public motive unless their conduct amounted to a blatant defiance of a clear rule. Experience suggests that a legal defense of some kind would be found often enough to preclude criminal prosecution from becoming a credible threat.

Underlying the whole notion of a deterrent system is the idea that an individual at some point has a choice: a threat of punishment causes him or her to make the "good" rather than the "bad" choice. Punishment is imposed upon the person who culpably makes the wrong choice in order to deter him and others from making that choice in the future. The unwillingness of courts to inflict punishment upon anyone who did not know that he or she was acting improperly has frequently been reflected by an acquittal for lack of mens rea — a guilty state of mind. This

---

[18] THE WORK OF THE INTERNATIONAL LAW COMMISSION, *supra* note 3, at 21.

is a broad legal defense stemming from an opposition to punishing anyone who did not know he was at fault — an opposition to punishing one who could not have been deterred from doing wrong because he thought he was doing right.

A number of more specific defenses might be found to be available to the government officer charged with being a criminal on account of official action that violated international law. Although ignorance of the law is classically no defense to a criminal prosecution, the rule dates from a time when most crimes related to conduct that was morally reprehensible in itself. In recent years the trend of opinion has been toward changing the rule. In 1957 the United States Supreme Court held that the due process clause precluded punishing a woman for failing to register as a "convicted person" under a Los Angeles ordinance of which she offered to prove she neither knew nor would probably have known.[19] Perhaps the most thoughtful conclusions that have been drawn from experience with the criminal law are those contained in the Model Penal Code developed by the American Law Institute. Section 2.04(3)(a) of the Code would allow a broad defense of ignorance of the law where such ignorance demonstrated lack of the requisite criminal intent or, even if it did not, where the enactment defining the offenses is "not known to the actor and has not been published or otherwise reasonably made available prior to the conduct alleged."[20]

American authorities hold that a public servant or a private citizen who has acted pursuant to an express or implied representation of law made by a public authority may have a defense to a criminal prosecution no matter how mistaken that representation was. This view has been adopted in the Model Penal Code; section 2.04(3)(b) provides a defense to a prosecution when the defendant "acts in reasonable reliance upon an official statement of the law, afterwards determined to be invalid or erroneous, contained in . . . an official interpretation of the public officer or body charged by law with the responsibility for the interpretation, administration or enforcement of the law defining the [alleged] offense."[21] Although no official has the authority to change the criminal law or to grant amnesty in advance

[19] Lambert v. California, 355 U.S. 225 (1957).
[20] ALI MODEL PENAL CODE § 2.04(3) (2) (Proposed Official Draft, 1962).
[21] *Id.* § 2.04(3) (b).

by approving criminal conduct, courts have been quick to establish a defense for individuals, even private citizens, who acted under an erroneous interpretation of the law.[22]

Although the order of a superior, like ignorance of the law, is not recognized in modern international law as a valid defense, the amount of discussion on the subject demonstrates the strength of the feeling that a man should not be punished for doing what he has been officially ordered to do. Traditionally, at least for war crimes, orders from a superior constituted a defense. L. F. L. Oppenheim, in the first edition of his *International Law* in 1906, under the influence of the military codes of the time, stated:

> Violations of rules regarding warfare are war crimes only when committed without an order of the belligerent Government concerned. If members of the armed forces commit violations by order of their Government, they are not war criminals and cannot be punished by the enemy; the latter can, however, resort to reprisals.[23]

In the 1940 edition of *International Law* Hersh Lauterpacht changed this section by removing superior orders as a defense. Recognizing the difficulties created by this change, Lauterpacht explained:

> Undoubtedly, a Court confronted with the plea of superior orders adduced in justification of a war crime is bound to take into consideration the fact that obedience to military orders, not obviously unlawful, is the duty of every member of the armed forces and that the latter cannot, in conditions of war discipline, be expected to weigh scrupulously the legal merits of the order received, that rules of warfare are often controversial, and that an act otherwise amounting to a war crime may have been executed in obedience to orders conceived as a measure of reprisals. Such circumstances are probably in themselves sufficient to divest the act of the stigma of a war crime.[24]

Until 1944 the British Manual of Military Law recognized superior orders as a defense for war crimes.

The Charter of the Nuremberg Tribunal explicitly rejected

---

[22] *See* Hall & Seligman, *Mistake of Law and Mens Rea*, 8 U. CHI. L. REV. 641, 675 (1941).

[23] 2 L. OPPENHEIM, INTERNATIONAL LAW § 253 (1st ed. 1906).

[24] 2 L. OPPENHEIM, INTERNATIONAL LAW § 253 (6th ed. H. Lauterpacht ed. 1940).

superior orders as a legal defense. Article 8 provided: "The fact that the defendant acted pursuant to the order of his Government or of a superior shall not free him from responsibility, but may be considered in mitigation of punishment if the Tribunal determines that justice so requires."[25] Although superior orders, as such, did not constitute a defense, the orders could both mitigate punishment and demonstrate that the defendant was coerced. In the opinion of the Tribunal, the true test was not the existence of the order "but whether moral choice was in fact possible."[26] The practice of mitigating the punishment of officers who were acting under superior orders, although not as effective as the practice of finding such officers innocent, would tend to undercut the deterrent effect of a criminal statute.

The experience of the Soviet Union in applying criminal restraints on officials acting for governmental reasons is illuminating. The 1926 Criminal Code of the Russian Soviet Federative Socialist Republic (the RSFSR — the state within the Soviet Union that encompasses more than half the area and population of the country) dealt with abuse of authority or official position. Article 109 provided that an official would be criminally liable if he acted systematically in a manner not required by his duties so as to upset the operation of his agency, to cause harm to it, or to create a breach either of public order or of individual rights. Under this provision, an official was also responsible if he abused his authority with knowledge that serious consequences might result. Both of these offenses were committed even if the official acted for governmental purposes. There was a provision punishing abuses of authority for mercenary motives, but such personal interest was not an essential element of the crime as defined under the two other branches of the statute.

[25] 82 U.N.T.S. 286, 41 AM. J. INT'L L. 221 (1947). Principle IV of the Principles of International Law Recognized in the Charter of the Nuremberg Tribunal and in the Judgment of the Tribunal, which were prepared by the International Law Commission, deleted the words "but may be considered in mitigation of punishment if the Tribunal determines that justice so requires." In its commentary to Principle IV, the International Law Commission explained that "the question of mitigating punishment is a matter for the competent Court to decide." [1950] 2 Y.B. INT'L L. COMM'N 375, U.N. Doc. A / CN.4 / Ser. A / 1950.

[26] 41 AM. J. INT'L L. 172, 221 (1947). See also decision of the Federal Supreme Court of the Federal Republic of Germany in the case of the killing of Russian slave laborers in 56 AM. J. INT'L L. 139–40 (1963).

Experience with this attempt to deter officials by threats of criminal punishment was unsatisfactory. The law was changed in 1960. The new provision about abuse of authority or of official position makes an official criminally liable only when his action was "committed for mercenary or any other personal interest."[27] To be convicted now, the official must have acted for personal gain. If one acts for what he or she believes are valid governmental purposes, abuse of authority apparently does not result in criminal liability. The largest republic of the Soviet Union has thus tried and abandoned its attempt to prevent abuse of authority or official position for governmental motives by threats of criminal punishment. One can guess that such threats were as incredible there as would be comparable threats here.

One example in this country of the persistent failure of the criminal law as a means of controlling officers has been the federal statute prohibiting wiretapping.[28] Police disregard of this criminal statute, which has significant popular support, demonstrates how much credibility it lacks and hence how ineffective a deterrent may become when, as a matter of course, it is not imposed. The "legal" reluctance to impose punishment on officers appears to be limited largely to cases in which the law is unclear or in which the officer was acting under a mistaken view of the law. The wiretapping situation suggests that the "political" or practical reluctance both to prosecute and to convict goes further. In recent years civil and criminal litigation has removed all ambiguity about the scope of section 605 of the Federal Communications Act.[29] It bars the tapping of telephones by federal agents[30] or by state law enforcement officers and makes all evidence so obtained inadmissible in federal courts.[31] Even though a New York State statute purports to permit a telephone tap under an ex parte order issued by a state court judge, the Supreme Court ruled in *Benanti* that the state agents, in committing a wiretap under such an order, were violating federal law. Yet, de-

---

[27] Criminal Code of the RSFSR, art. 170 (1960).
[28] *See, e.g.*, Westin, *The Wire-Tapping Problem*, 52 COLUM. L. REV. 165 (1952).
[29] *See* 47 U.S.C. § 605 (1970).
[30] Nardone v. United States, 302 U.S. 379 (1937).
[31] Benanti v. United States, 355 U.S. 96 (1957).

spite the clarity of the rule, the tapping of telephone lines by public officers continues undeterred. Apparently, the officers are reasonably confident that even if a prosecution is brought, a jury will not convict them. A comparable confidence in de facto immunity from punishment must help explain the burglaries and other crimes committed by officers of the Federal Bureau of Investigation and the Central Intelligence Agency revealed since 1974.

d. *Freedom in finding the facts.* In establishing a rule of international law by treaty, it should be possible to circumscribe markedly the freedom of a tribunal to interpret the rule loosely and to find that as a matter of law certain defenses were available. This could be done by making the rule as clear as possible and by providing explicitly that the defenses listed above would not be legally available to an accused officer. The domestic experience suggests, however, that this would not be enough to cause a tribunal to order punishment. In a criminal trial, there are almost of necessity issues of fact; for example, whether the act was committed "intentionally" or "knowingly." The famous trial of Peter Zenger in New York in 1775 for printing a libel about the Colonial Governor demonstrates that at least a jury will find facts so as to acquit a man for conduct for which they believe he should not be punished.

Our domestic experience with reaching a decision to punish a government official reveals the many difficulties with this approach. Even where criminal statutes purport to apply to government officers and their official actions, convictions are rare for a number of reasons: the failure to prosecute, the interpretation of the law, the existence of defenses, and the freedom in finding facts. The latter suggests that for most international offenses, the threat of criminal punishment would not be credible because an international authority would be unlikely to reach a decision that punishment should be imposed.

4. *Credibility: implementing a decision to punish.* As in the case of creating credible threats against a government, the ability of an international scheme to cause first-order compliance by threats of punishment will depend, inter alia, upon its ability to cause second-order compliance — compliance with its decision, the subject dealt with in Part II of this book.

There is a serious problem in making any threat of criminal punishment under international authority credible, even if it could be assumed that, upon knowing of evidence warranting a finding of guilt, an international court would order punishment to be imposed. As mentioned above,[32] in 1950 the General Assembly appointed a Committee on International Criminal Jurisdiction to prepare a draft convention for the establishment of "an international judicial organ for the trial of persons charged with genocide or other crimes over which jurisdiction will be conferred upon that organ by international conventions."[33] Because of the political aspects of most of the cases that would be heard before such a court, the Committee's "prevailing sentiment" was that the possibility of trials in absentia "should not be envisaged."[34] The Committee gave the Secretary General of the United Nations the responsibility for executing sentence in the absence of a convention on sentencing.[35] The Committee, however, decided that "no State should, under the statute, be obliged to carry out warrants of arrest or other similar decisions of the court."[36] As a result, even if the court had jurisdiction under the Convention to hear a case against someone accused of violating international criminal law, getting the defendant before the court would depend upon the cooperation of the state in which he was located. Moreover, states would have no obligation to assist the court in carrying out either the warrants of arrest or the execution of sentences unless they had previously agreed to do so.[37]

Short of military defeat, governments might be unwilling to allow their officers to be punished by an international au-

[32] See note 7 and accompanying text *supra*.

[33] G.A. Res. 489, 5 U.N. GAOR, Supp. (No. 20) 77, U.N. Doc. A / 1755 (1950).

[34] Report of the Comm. on International Criminal Jurisdiction, 7 U.N. GAOR, Supp. (No. 11) 12, U.N. Doc. A /2163 (1952).

[35] Article 52 of Draft Statute for an International Criminal Court, 7 U.N. GAOR, Supp. (No. 11) 25, U.N. Doc. A / 2163 (1952).

[36] Report of the Comm. on International Criminal Jurisdiction, *supra* note 34, at 19.

[37] Article 31 of the Draft Statute for an International Criminal Court, 7 U.N. GAOR, Supp. (No. 11) 23, U.N. Doc. A / 2163 (1952). For detailed discussion, see the contributions by Wright, Liang, & Finch in 46 AM. J. INT'L L. 60, 73, 89 (1952). *See also* Klein & Wilkes, *United Nations Draft Statute for an International Criminal Court: An American Evaluation*, in INTERNATIONAL CRIMINAL LAW 526 (G. Mueller & E. Wise eds. 1965).

thority.[38] At least an officer might be likely to so conclude. One suggested means of overcoming this problem would be to devise unusual forms of punishment that could be imposed upon an officer from other countries. Such punishment might include various sorts of moral condemnation, a prohibition on travel, and the refusal by other governments to deal in any way with the officer in question. All such devices, while increasing the credibility of the threat, would tend to decrease its seriousness. They would thus seem to weaken the probable fear of a deterrent threat while increasing the likelihood of its imposition. One could also consider the idea of eventual punishment, as at Nuremberg, when conditions have so changed as to permit the international authority to capture the individual concerned, and the idea of legalizing international kidnapping ventures from abroad to bring a suspect before a competent court.[39]

5. *Influencing an officer by credible threats.* Beyond the fact that a government officer would probably consider the threat of criminal punishment for breaking a rule of international law as a threat which had a small chance of being carried out, there is a serious question of how influential such a threat would be even if there appeared to be a major chance of its being carried out. For a number of reasons even credible threats are likely to be less effective in influencing the decisions of government officials than in influencing the conduct of most other people.

a. *Many officials may not know the facts.* One factor limiting the influence of a deterrent threat on the decisions of government officials is the fact that some of those involved in governmental violations would not realize it and could not be deterred. Wholly apart from any ambiguity of the rules, many officers and government employees, particularly in subordinate positions, could be deceived or kept in ignorance about the true purpose of the activity in which they were engaged.

In most private companies, an employee who is told not to ask

---

[38] *See* comments by Sir Gerald Fitzmaurice on Donnedieu de Vabres's *Projet d'institution d'une Cour penale internationale*, in 44/1 ANNUAIRE DE L'INSTITUT DE DROIT INTERNATIONAL 423 (Sienne, 1952). *See also* the observations by Badawi Pasha, *id.* at 401. The Case of Trial of Pakistani Prisoners of War, note 14 *supra*, further substantiates this point.

[39] For a brief discussion of several famous cases of abduction, see Cardozo, *When Extradition Fails, Is Abduction the Solution?*, 55 AM. J. INT'L L. 127 (1961).

too many questions and is ordered to do such-and-such a thing will suspect that something improper is involved. He will be on notice and may begin to worry about the personal risk of punishment. In the government, on the other hand, particularly in the military and intelligence establishments that presumably would be involved in many of the more serious violations of international law, secrecy is common. Many people participating in a violation could do so without any reason to suspect that that was the case, and for them any deterrent would be ineffective. Some kinds of arms control provisions would be particularly vulnerable to this problem of lack of information among subordinates. Quantitative limitations on the number of men or weapons could be violated with only the top officials knowing of it. Those persons in command of a given number of men or in charge of a particular number of weapons might properly be kept wholly in the dark about the number of men or weapons that were located in other areas. Only those few people who knew the total number of men or weapons would be aware of the violation and would be in a position to be influenced by a deterrent.

One can even conceive of situations in which no one was aware that an international limitation was being broken. For example, if the United States were openly to decide to reduce its inventory of a given weapon below the number permitted in a treaty, several different commanders might decide independently to retain secretly enough additional weapons to bring the United States up from its stated inventory to its internationally permitted quota. Although violating internal orders, each commander might honestly believe that his conduct did not result in a violation of the treaty.

b. *Duty may be more influential than threats.* In activities that are regulated by standard criminal statutes, there is reason to believe that estimates of personal gain and loss are controlling. The man who is thinking of embezzling funds, robbing a store, or exceeding the speed limit will consider the risks. If it is quite likely that he will be arrested and punished, he will probably not undertake the activity. The prevailing ethic among thieves and speeders is that it is not smart to get caught. The activity envisaged is being undertaken for personal benefit. If instead of personal benefit there is to be personal loss, the incentive for breaking the law does not exist. If punishment can be made sufficiently likely and sufficiently serious, there is good reason to believe that crimes rationally committed for reasons of personal gain will be deterred. (Among individuals who commit crimes for personal motives, however, irrationality could make a deterrent ineffective; then again, it might make the deterrent more effective than it rationally should be.)

To the extent that a government is caused to violate international law by an individual's seeking to make a personal gain, a credible threat of criminal punishment would be expected to deter the violation. Private citizens, for example, might be hired to build a prohibited weapon and might undertake the work because of especially high compensation. For such persons, a high risk of being caught and punished would presumably be an effective deterrent. As to most violations of international law, however, the person responsible will be a government official and the motivation will not be one of personal gain. The timid bureaucrat who is thinking primarily of himself, his career, and his gains and losses would not seem to be the typical initiator of a violation.[40] The incentive for violating a treaty or other recognized legal limitation upon a government is not likely to be personal gain but perceived national interest or other public interest. And, for a public official who is acting in the national interest as he sees it, the threat of possible personal punishment is not likely to be decisive.

The prevailing ethic among political leaders and public servants is quite unlike the prevailing ethic among professional criminals. Among public officials, one type of hero is the man who does his duty as he sees it without regard to the personal consequences. The fact that he risks personal punishment makes his conduct all the more laudable.[41] Another type is the organization man, who does what he is supposed to do without

[40] "Bureaucratic decision-making is by its nature rule-governed. A bureaucrat called upon to act on behalf of the state normally would not even consider that the commission of a violation to promote national policy was an option open to him." Falk, *New Approaches to the Study of International Law*, 61 AM. J. INT'L L. 480 (1967).

[41] Considering the problems posed by the elaboration of international criminal law, Sir John Fisher Williams stressed this idea: "But it is surely a mistake to suppose that the individual mind will effectively be restrained by the possiblity—necessarily remote—of

sticking his neck out. Either one is primarily moved by one perception or another of his duty.

In the military establishment particularly, officers and soldiers
are brought up to risk almost certain death rather than fail in
their duty to their country. As long as a soldier is confident where
his duty lies, he is quite likely to undertake extremely hazardous
activity even though there is no compensating chance of personal gain. National leaders risk thermonuclear war in pursuit
of the national interest, recognizing that they personally would
stand a serious risk of being killed. One can guess that of all the
factors affecting President Kennedy and his advisers during the
October 1962 Cuban missile crisis, fear of possible punishment
before a future Nuremberg Tribunal for having violated international law was not considered and, had it been raised, would
have been dismissed out of hand.[42] Governments apparently
find little difficulty in recruiting patriotic men and women to
gather intelligence from foreign countries, despite the fact that
as spies they face a highly credible threat of serious personal
punishment.

As a class, government officials in this respect are like consci-
entious objectors, civil rights demonstrators, Jehovah's Witnesses, revolutionaries, and the Buddhists who protested in
Vietnam in 1963. They perceive their acts to be in the furtherance of a duty. Like political heroes of all time, they are prepared
to undergo personal sacrifice in the pursuit of public ends. The
higher the official and the more important his decision, the less
likely he is to be affected by a petty calculation of personal consequences. These officials, however, are motivated by a strong
desire to maintain both a good public image and their personal

having to answer before an international tribunal for the performance, as a general rule,
in war-time of an act which the municipal tribunal in fact does not punish and which
therefore the general tone of surrounding society does not condemn. When national
passions conceived in their effect on the individual to be altruistic, not egotistical, are
aroused, the fear of individual punishment in a remote future is singularly weak as a
motive, if indeed it operates at all." J. WILLIAMS, CHAPTERS ON CURRENT INTERNATIONAL
LAW AND THE LEAGUE OF NATIONS 251 (1929).

[42] Robert Kennedy did not mention any concern of this kind by the President or his
advisers, but rather national, military, and humanitarian considerations. This appears
particularly clear during the crucial discussion that occurred on the morning of Oct. 27,
1962. See R. KENNEDY, THIRTEEN DAYS. A MEMOIR OF THE CUBAN MISSILE CRISIS 93–99
(1969).

position. Public understanding that conduct is wrongful is significant.

c. *Offsetting threats*. For an officer who is motivated by a sense of fear, the fear of the immediate reaction of a national superior is likely to outweigh fear of the more remote possibility of punishment under international authority.[43] In examining the deterrent effect of criminal prosecution, it is probably useful to distinguish between a "cooperator" in a government program and the superior who is responsible for the original decision. If, as suggested above, higher officials tend to be influenced more by a perception of the national interest than by a calculation of personal consequences, it does not follow that subordinate officials can be counted on to frustrate the violation. To be effective, a deterrent should operate not only on the official who is considering a given illegal program of action but also on those who may be told to carry it out. Underlying the Nuremberg trials was the idea that subordinates should have known that they might be punished for going along with Hitler's outrageous programs and that that fear should have played a part in causing them to refuse to cooperate.

It is difficult to generalize here because so much depends upon the particular circumstances of each case. Nonetheless, a subordinate caught between the immediate dictates of his superior and the standing dictates of the law is subject to conflicting pressures that can be analyzed. To some extent, as suggested above, he will be influenced by notions of where his duty lies. To the extent that his decision will be controlled by his calculation of the personal consequences to him of following one course of action or the other, the fear of punishment for an anticipated

[43] The judgment of the Nuremberg Tribunal cites, for instance, the regulations of Sept. 8, 1941, for the treatment of Soviet prisoners of war that were issued by the German High Command. They read, *inter alia*: "Anyone carrying out the order who does not use his weapons, or does so with insufficient energy, is punishable. . . . Prisoners of war attempting escape are to be fired on without previous challenge. No warning shot must ever be fired. . . . The use of arms against prisoners of war is as a rule legal" (41 Am. J. Int'l L. 227). It is true that the Geneva Convention did not prohibit all use of arms against prisoners of war, but apparently it did so under the circumstances described in the Nazi order. Nonetheless, German officers and soldiers were ordered, under the immediate threat of punishment, to execute the provisions of the regulations. The fear of such punishment obviously was likely to outweigh the fear of the remote possibility of punishment under international authority for breaches of international law.

violation of international law will be offset by the fear of punishment for failing to follow his superior's instructions. In such a calculation, the relative ambiguity of the two commands is crucial. For example, every enlisted man in the Armed Forces of the United States is told at the time of entrance on active duty and again after six months of active duty that violation of or failure to obey a "lawful general order or regulation" is punishable as a court-martial may direct.[44] Consider the choices open to an Air Force pilot who receives an order to drop napalm on North Vietnam — an order which he might regard as unlawful under the generally accepted principles of international law.[45] He can disobey the order and risk immediate punishment imposed by a court-martial. Or he can obey the order and risk punishment at some unspecified date by an undetermined tribunal for violation of a standard of international law which is ambiguous and disputed. To the extent that a pilot's choice is motivated by fear of personal punishment, the risk of a future Nuremberg will be outweighed by the risk of an immediate court-martial. Whatever may be his view of the international rule, unless the Air Force pilot feels absolutely certain that he is right, he is likely to go along with his commander. The commander's instructions of what to do—bomb a specified territory at a given time—are more explicit than the standing rule of international law and hence more compelling. Similarly, the threat of a court-martial backing up the commander's order is more immediate, personal, and explicit than the fear of being called before a hypothetical international tribunal.

[44]*See* 10 U.S.C. §§ 892, 937 (1970).

[45]There is a basic principle of international humanitarian law that "the right of belligerents to adopt means of injuring the enemy is not unlimited." *See* article 22 of the Hague Regulations on Laws and Customs of War on Land, Oct. 18, 1907, 36 Stat. 2277, T.S. No. 539, 1 BEVANS 631. Also, it is forbidden to employ arms, projectiles, or material calculated to cause unnecessary suffering. *See* Hague Regulations, *id.* at art. 23, ¶ 1(e). The question of incendiary weapons was discussed by government experts at the request of the Diplomatic Conference on the Reaffirmation and Development of International Humanitarian Law Applicable in Armed Conflicts (U.N. Doc. CDDH / 47, at 7). The discussion focused on the question of whether incendiary weapons should be prohibited completely or partially. *See* I.C.R.C. CONFERENCE OF GOVERNMENT EXPERTS ON THE USE OF CERTAIN CONVENTIONAL WEAPONS, *Lucerne* 24.9–18.10 1974, at 31–35 (1975). It allowed the inference that presently the use of incendiary weapons is permitted. For a survey of the subject, see Cassese, *Weapons Causing Unnecessary Suffering: Are They Prohibited?* 58 RIV. DIR. INT'LE 12 (1975).

6. *Acceptability of an individual-deterrent system.* It appears from the above discussion that an international system which threatens individuals responsible for violations of international law with criminal punishment would be effective in producing first-order compliance with respect to only limited categories of rules. Aside from an extremely limited area of effectiveness, the system of threatening individuals — in most cases government officials — with criminal punishment for being responsible for the government's exceeding the limits on its authority suffers from defects that might make attempts to strengthen it unacceptable to most governments.

a. *It would tend to deter disclosure.* Although a government official might not be deterred from engaging in activity that he thought the circumstances required, fear of personal punishment might deter him from public disclosure of what he was doing. Because of the vagueness or ambiguity of a rule, an official could believe that he was behaving properly. Even so, he could be expected to keep the facts as concealed as possible, since a mistake in his judgment could conceivably result in criminal punishment. In some areas, particularly in the enforcement of arms control or disarmament provisions, secrecy will be a critical problem. In such areas, disclosure should be encouraged rather than deterred. As in the case of income tax, inducing a pattern of first-order compliance as well as coping with alleged noncompliance depends upon having available the necessary facts. The income tax analogy suggests that if punishment were to be used, it might be wise to make the explicit provision that no one would be punished for conduct found to be in violation of the treaty if the facts had been fully and promptly disclosed. Or, perhaps, heavy additional punishment could be meted out for nondisclosure.

b. *Fear of personal consequences warps an officer's judgment.* Whatever deterrent effect an international criminal law system might have would tend to spill over and affect conduct on the permitted side of the various rules of international law. Officials might be influenced by personal concern to err on the side of caution. Compliance is not the only interest. Governments also wish public officials to make wise choices among those courses of conduct which are permitted. The United States and any other government would properly fear that an effective deterrent system would also deter officers from exercising wise judgement in the area in which a rule was in doubt. Within our national legal system, the reluctance to punish government officials discussed above reflects more than soft-hearted sympathy. Courts have recognized the unfortunate pressure toward a timid do-nothing policy which could be produced by punishing a government official in the one case in which he happened to step across a legal line.

To encourage the free exercise of an officer's judgment, the practical immunity from criminal prosecution is supplemented in many cases by a legal immunity from civil liability. Judges cannot be held liable for damages caused by their illegal or unconstitutional decisions.[46] Legislators are immune from suits for what they may say on the legislative floor, as are administrative officials for most of their official statements. In *Gregoire v. Biddle*,[47] the plaintiff, a Frenchman, sued two successive Attorneys General of the United States, two successive Directors of the Enemy Alien Control Unit of the Department of Justice, and the District Director of Immigration at Ellis Island. He alleged that the defendants had "conspired together and maliciously and willfully entered into a scheme to deprive the plaintiff . . . of his liberty contrary to law." He also alleged that they had deprived him of the equal protection of the laws in violation of sections 43 and 47 of the Civil Rights Act of 1871.[48] The plaintiff had been held in custody for nearly five years during World War II, despite a ruling by the Enemy Alien Hearing Board that he was not German as the defendants had believed. Upholding the lower court's dismissal of plaintiff's complaint for failing to state a claim, Judge Learned Hand explained the reasons for allowing nearly absolute civil immunity to officials even in these circumstances:

> It does indeed go without saying that an official, who is in fact guilty of using his powers to vent his spleen upon others, or for any other personal motive not connected with the public good,

[46] *See* Stump v. Sparkman, 435 U.S. 349 (1978).
[47] 177 F.2d 579 (1949).
[48] Civil Rights Act, ch. 22, §§ 1, 6, 17 Stat. 13, 15 (1871) (current version at 42 U.S.C. §§ 1983, 1986 (1970)).

should not escape liability for the injuries he may so cause; and, if it were possible in practice to confine such complaints to the guilty, it would be monstrous to deny recovery. The justification for doing so is that it is impossible to know whether the claim is well-founded until the case has been tried, and that to submit all officials, the innocent as well as the guilty, to the burden of a trial and to the inevitable danger of its outcome, would dampen the ardor of all but the most resolute, or the most irresponsible, in the unflinching discharge of their duties. Again and again the public interest calls for action which may turn out to be founded on a mistake, in the face of which an official may later find himself hard put to it to satisfy a jury of his good faith. . . . In this instance it has been thought in the end better to leave unredressed the wrongs done by dishonest officers than to subject those who try to do their duty to the constant dread of retaliation.[49]

In an international setting, we are not concerned so much with interpretations of the motives for official action as with an incorrect view of the applicable international rule by a government officer. But the problem of deterring the free exercise of an official's judgment by threatening personal liability remains the same as that Judge Hand identified in the domestic situation. The theory of deterring an official's acting illegally by threatening him with punishment is wholly inconsistent with the theory of granting an official civil immunity in order to encourage the wise exercise of his discretion.

In the case of private conduct, the necessity of enforcement is felt to justify such excess deterrence as may occur, although there are strong traditions to the effect that criminal statutes must not be vague. In the case of government employees, however, the public interest is on both sides of the rule. Criminal enforcement of international prohibitions against weapons research, for example, might deter valuable and actually lawful scientific research that fell within the shadow of the rule. This drawback would appear to be a direct function of the ambiguity of the rule. A threat of punishment for violation of a clear and sharply defined rule would not have a deleterious effect on an officer's judgment among permitted courses of action.

[49] 177 F.2d 579, 581 (1949).

c. *Warping the judgment of the courts.* The reluctance of a court to punish a man for doing what he thought was his duty results not only in an ineffective deterrent but also in a badly construed rule. A court which is focusing on the question of whether a particular well-motivated official should be punished for the conduct in which he or she was engaged is likely to find that conduct permissible. The same court considering the same provision in a proceeding for a civil injunction would focus on the question of what is the wisest interpretation of the rule for the future. In such a context, the court might well find that the conduct should be deemed barred. As discussed above, the very tendency of courts to construe rules favorably to publicly motivated defendants in order to avoid their being punished "unfairly" could be expected to result in a whittling away of the rules. Even injunctions, by altering expectations, will sometimes seem unfair, a fact which may unduly affect an interpretation, but the problem will usually be greater in the case of punishment. Although a further treaty or possibly an administrative interpretation could fix up the rule for the future, such corrective action is often politically difficult, if not impossible, to accomplish. In the international arena the rules about amending treaties make it even more difficult than amending the United States Constitution.

d. *Disrespect for the law.* Extending a system which would have those public officials punished who acted from public motives in an area in which the law was less than certain would tend to weaken respect for the law. If such persons should in fact be punished, substantial elements of the community could be expected to object and to criticize the law. Even the conviction of Lieutenant Calley for committing multiple murders of women and children at My Lai in Vietnam produced a storm of protest. On the other hand, if law violaters are not punished, there is a risk of undermining respect for the law. The failure to prosecute and convict police officers for violating the prohibition on wiretapping undoubtedly weakens public respect for the law, although it is impossible to estimate how much. The experience in this country with Prohibition suggests that even where the laws themselves do not command public support, the failure to enforce them has a damaging effect on public regard for law.

The harmful effect on law enforcement of providing punishment for men who acted with "good" motives may go further. One of the strongest sanctions that a society has available to it is the formal determination that someone is blameworthy and deserving of punishment. Although this may not be true in the case of hardened criminals, it certainly is true in the case of public officials. Having been convicted as a criminal and, in particular, having been found deserving of a prison sentence, a public officer has received a severe blow whether or not he actually goes to prison or is required to pay a fine. But every time such formal condemnation is imposed upon a man whom the community believes is not in fact deserving of moral blame, the sanction is weakened. As Professor Henry M. Hart, Jr., wrote, the indiscriminate use of the criminal law "dilutes the force of the threat of community condemnation as a means of influencing conduct in other situations where the basis of moral condemnation is clear."[50]

The above considerations would form a rational basis for a government's concluding that a comprehensive system designed to deter individuals from violating every rule of international law would be unwise and hence unacceptable. There would be other doubts stemming from a fear that the international system might go wrong and might try to punish a government's own officers for doing what, in the opinion of the government, they really ought to be doing.[51] The fact that the principles of the Nuremberg trials were unanimously accepted by the members of the United Nations in 1946 suggests that most governments find the notion of personal responsibility and punishment for violating international law acceptable, provided that the conduct was awful enough. The political reluctance to accept an international scheme which in fact might routinely impose punishment for violations of international law would seem to depend upon the vagueness of the rules being enforced, the degree of confidence in the tribunal interpreting the rules and deciding upon punishment, and upon the means established for implementing the decisions reached.

Certainly, one can expect that a criminal law system would not

---

[50] Hart, *The Aims of Criminal Law*, 28 LAW & CONTEMP. PROB. 421 (1928).

[51] Under present international law, each state retains the right to give its own interpretation of international law. *See* Gross, *States as Organs of International Law and the Prob-*

be acceptable to most governments as a means of causing first-order compliance with international law in general. The general system of international law would include both vague provisions, such as that against one state's interfering with the sovereignty of another, and customary rules about which there is current controversy, such as those governing the compensation due aliens affected by general land-reform measures. Criminal law techniques would seem most acceptable when applied to knowing and deliberate violations of specific rules established by treaty and supported by a widespread moral consensus.[52]

The willingness of a government to accept the jurisdiction of a court with authority to decide that one of its officials ought to be punished as well as to accept a scheme for implementing such a decision is probably best considered in connection with the problem of causing governments to accept a scheme of producing second-order compliance. The problem is one of accepting international determinations of what ought to happen in a specific case and accepting the means of causing it to happen. In general, a government's fear is not so much of what an international court will probably decide, but rather of what it might conceivably decide. Governments might be more willing to submit their officers to trial by an international authority if the maximum punishment that could be imposed were drastically limited, such as a six-month or, even, a thirty-day confinement. The acceptability of the jurisdiction of the tribunal would also be increased if a government could see that if the worst should happen — if an international court were about to order the government's head-of-state seized and punished at the insistence of an adversary for what was in fact legitimate conduct — the government would have some way of frustrating either the

---

lem of Auto-interpretation, in LAW AND POLITICS IN THE WORLD COMMUNITY 76–77 (G. Lipsky ed. 1953). There is no evidence that states are prepared to grant to any international criminal court the power to determine what international law is.

[52] Even for that category of treaties, states are reluctant to accept the criminal jurisdiction of an international tribunal. Article VI of the Convention of the Prevention and Punishment of the Crime of Genocide, *entry into force* Jan. 12, 1951, 78 U.N.T.S. 277, for instance, provides that persons charged with genocide or any other act related to it shall be tried either by a competent tribunal of the state in the territory where the act was committed or by such international penal tribunal as may have jurisdiction. Twenty-five years have elapsed from the entry into force of the Convention, but the contemplated international penal tribunal has not yet been established.

reaching of the decision or its implementation. Some kind of last-ditch veto power, as will be discussed in Chapter XI, might well be essential, depending on how broad the international criminal jurdisdiction was to which they were being asked to commit themselves.

7. *Conclusion.* With the precedent of the Nuremberg trials and the unanimous acceptance by the General Assembly of the principles upon which they were based, the rudimentary framework of an international criminal law system for deterring individuals from violating international law is already in existence. The analogous experience of domestic legal systems suggests that such deterrence of individuals is a promising method of law enforcement only for certain limited violations of limited kinds of rules. The area for the effective use of criminal law techniques against government officers centers on conduct, such as torture or poisoning, which is widely and deeply held to be morally reprehensible. It also includes illegal conduct undertaken for private gain. Beyond such offenses, the technique has potential effectiveness for deliberate and knowingly wrongful violations of clear-cut rules, as might be demonstrated by their being committed clandestinely. Judging from experience with governments, such instances comprise a small portion of the problem of enforcing international law.

It would be difficult to devise a system which would produce credible threats of punishment for violating international law generally, and even if one could, it might be both ineffective and unacceptable. Government officers, who are the individuals primarily concerned with violations by governments of international law, apparently are motivated more by their perception of what they ought to do and by specific instructions directed to them by those in authority than by general rules and by general threats of personal punishment should they violate those rules. The next three chapters consider techniques other than deterrence for causing respect for standing rules. They consider what can be done to arrange matters so that it appears to a government that it ought to comply with the law and so that it also appears so to the individual officers concerned.

B
Nondeterrent Techniques for
Causing Respect for Standing Rules

Introductory note. The two previous chapters have suggested that in most cases a system of threatening punishment either of governments or of individuals in order to gain compliance with standing rules of international law will be neither effective nor acceptable. International deterrent machinery is not the only technique available to cause increased respect for standing rules of international law. Chapter V discusses what the draftsman of an international rule can do toward increasing first-order compliance. Chapter VI considers altering the forces toward compliance by affecting the general international reaction to noncompliance. Chapter VII, the final chapter in this part, considers the compliance that may be produced by weaving an international rule into the fabric of a government's domestic arrangements.

CHAPTER V

Compliance as a
Function of the Rule

1. *The effect of content on compliance.* It is obvious that from the point of view of a government, the content of a rule is all important. The incentive to break a rule of international law or to respect it depends overwhelmingly upon the particular subject matter of the rule. But the negotiator or draftsman concerned with a particular subject matter is looking for guidance on what he might do to make a rule on which he is working as durable as possible. With or without international punishment machinery, what can be done at the time a rule is being considered to maximize the forces that will tend to cause governments to respect it?

a. *Conforming the rule to common sense.* A rule draws strength in proportion to the extent to which it makes sense to those to whom it applies. Other things being equal, a limitation should be articulated and drawn in such a way that the public believes the line is not purely arbitrary, but rather that things are different on one side of the line from what they are on the other.

There is now an international rule, perhaps of no legal effect but nonetheless a rule to be contended with, that it is permissible to use conventional weapons but not to use nuclear weapons.[1]

---

[1]Whether the rule is a rule of international law is a subject of controversy. In the Shimoda Case, a Japanese court held that the use of atomic bombs in 1945 had been illegal. *See* 58 AM. J. INT'L L. 1016 (1964). *See also* Falk, *The Shimoda Case: A Legal Appraisal of the Atomic Attacks upon Hiroshima and Nagasaki*, 59 AM. J. INT'L L. 759, 791–93 (1965). A recent statement by the United States in the United Nations was prompted by the adoption by the General Assembly of Resolution 2936 (XXVII), Non-use of force in international relations and permanent prohibition of the use of nuclear weapons. After recalling its prior Declaration on the Prohibition of the Use of Nuclear and Thermo-nuclear Weapons contained in Resolution 1653 (XVI), the Assembly stated in the first operative paragraph of Resolution 2936 (XXVII) that it "*solemnly declares*, on behalf of the States Members of the Organization their renunciation of the use or threat of force in all its forms and manifestations in international relations, in accordance with the Charter of the United Nations, and the permanent prohibition of the use of nuclear weapons." G.A. Res. 2936, 27 U.N. GAOR, Supp. (No. 30) 5–6, U.N. Doc. A / 8730

Although some conventional weapons are more destructive than the smaller nuclear weapons, the line between conventional and nuclear weapons conforms to public understanding, and in a rough way, it does divide the worst weapons from the less dangerous ones. A rule permitting nuclear weapons up to four kilotons but prohibiting larger ones would not have the strength implicit in a rule drawn along the nuclear/conventional line that has preexisting significance in the minds of so many people.

Similarly, the Antarctic Treaty provision that there shall be no military installations on that continent has a greater appeal to common sense, and one can guess is less likely to be broken, than would a more arbitrary provision listing specific kinds of weapons that would be permitted and others that would not. A rule such as that once adopted by the Communist Chinese with respect to Quemoy, not to shell the island on even days of the month, lacks the raison d'être that gives a rule internal strength. The Chinese were therefore freer to abandon this rule than they would have been to abandon other forms of unilateral restraint, such as limiting bombing to rural areas or to military installations.

Involved in the idea of having a rule appeal to common sense is the proposition that it should follow some readily discernible or natural line. The three-mile limit on the breadth of a coastal state's territorial sea gained support in the eighteenth century because, as one author stated, "it was the rule that the sea should salute the land and the range of guns determined the limit within which the salute ought to be rendered."[2] Shore guns in the eighteenth century could reach about one marine league (somewhere between 2.4 and 4.6 land miles). But as the range of

---

(1972). Explaining the United States abstention to Resolution 2936 (XXVII), Ambassador Christopher H. Phillips stated: "I also wish to point out that the United States and many other members voted against General Assembly Resolution 1653 (XVI), the Declaration on the Prohibition of the Use of Nuclear Weapons. We continue to regard that resolution, which asserts that the use of nuclear weapons at any time and under any circumstances is *ipso facto* a violation of the Charter and a crime against humanity, as without any legal basis. The draft resolution before us today refers to this earlier resolution, and appears to assert that nuclear weapons have been prohibited. However laudable the goals of the proponents of this resolution, we are, of course, unable to support such a proposition which so clearly flies in the face of reality and law." *See* 67 AM. J. INT'L L. 330 (1973). For the viewpoint advocating maintaining the legality of nuclear weapons, see M. McDOUGAL & F. FELICIANO, LAW AND MINIMUM WORLD PUBLIC ORDER 659 (1961).

[2]C. COLOMBOS, THE INTERNATIONAL LAW OF THE SEA 79 (4th rev. ed. 1959).

guns on shore increased, the three-mile limit began to appear as an arbitrary distance and was no longer accepted as a rule of international law.[3] The problem of finding natural boundaries has also been considered in connection with establishing and maintaining limits on limited war. It goes beyond the matter of having the line understood. A rule which can be made to coincide with a sharp break or natural discontinuity is likely to produce more compliance than an equally understood rule which simply draws a line. A rule against drinking could be expected to produce more inherent compliance than a rule against having a third drink. One difficulty with the rule of international law once suggested by the Soviet Union prohibiting the taking of photographs from satellites for the purpose of military intelligence was the blurred nature of the line. There is no sharp discontinuity between photographs taken for research or meteorological purposes and those taken for military purposes. Article IV of the Outer Space Treaty tries to draw a line which conforms to common sense: The parties undertake not to place nuclear weapons or other weapons of mass destruction in space or on celestial bodies and also to use the moon and other celestial bodies exclusively for peaceful purposes.[4] It was not possible, however, to follow a sharp discontinuity as there is a fuzzy line between peaceful purposes and other purposes.[5] There also may turn out to be some ambiguity about what is a weapon of mass destruction. Finally, the distinction between firing a nuclear missile through space (which is not prohibited) and "placing" a nuclear warhead in space (which is prohibited) may lack some of the common-sense appeal that was sought.

[3] See Baty, The 3-Mile Limit, 22 AM. J. INT'L L. 515–16 (1928); Kent, The Historical Origins of the Three-Mile Limit, 48 AM. J. INT'L L. 537 (1954).

[4] Treaty on Principles Governing the Activities of States in the Exploration and Use of Outer Space, Jan. 27, 1967, 18 U.S.T. 2410, T.I.A.S. No. 6347, 610 U.N.T.S. 205.

[5] Some states have proposed another line that hardly conforms to common sense. They suggested that remote sensing of the earth's environment and natural resources constitutes a space activity which is fundamentally different from any of those envisaged by the Outer Space Treaty (id.) because it is characterized as "earth-looking" rather than "outward-looking." See 68 AM. J. INT'L L. 517–18 (1974). For the United States objections to such a distinction, see the statements by Leonard Jaffe to the combined session of the Working Group on Remote Sensing of the Earth by Satellites and the Task Force of the Working Group (id. at 517–19), and by Ronald F. Stowe before the Legal Subcommittee of the U.N. Committee on the Peaceful Uses of Outer Space (69 AM. J. INT'L L. 645–48 (1975)). See also note 34 and accompanying text infra.

b. *Conforming the rule to notions of fairness and morality.* An international rule which is supported by natural law notions of what is fair and right would seem to have far more chance of being durable and better respected than one which is contrived. The distinction between conduct that is *malum in se* (bad in itself) and conduct that is only *malum prohibitum* (bad because it is prohibited) is recognized in domestic law. In general, a rule will have a better chance of being respected if it is against killing or stealing than if, for example, it requires persons to inform on their friends.

An international limitation will usually appear to be fairer if it is *stated* in reciprocal or general terms, rather than as binding upon only one or certain countries. The impact of a treaty on each country will necessarily be different since no two countries are in exactly the same circumstance. Yet compliance is likely to be increased if the obligation is defined in such a way that by its terms it falls equally upon both countries. Two examples illustrate this point.

In the 1946 Trade Agreement between the Republic of the Philippines and the United States, American citizens and businesses were accorded broad rights to develop and utilize natural resources and to operate public utilities in the Philippines.[6] To give effect to this so-called parity provision, the Phillipines had to amend their constitution. Philippine leaders particularly resented this provision; many of them regarded it as an infringement of their sovereignty. When the 1946 Trade Agreement was revised, the Filipinos asked for "either complete termination of this provision, or alternatively, a satisfactory reciprocal formula."[7] As a result, the 1955 Revised Trade Agreement provides that citizens of either country have the right to exploit the natural resources and to operate public utilities in the territory of the other on the same basis as nationals of that territory.[8] As a matter

[6] Agreement with the Republic of the Philippines on Trade and Related Matters, July 4 & Oct. 22, 1946, United States–Republic of the Philippines, art. VII, paras. 1 & 2, 61 Stat. 2611, T.I.A.S. No. 1588.

[7] Salans & Belman, *An Appraisal of the United States–Philippines' Special Relationship*, 40 WASH. L. REV. 403 (1965).

[8] Agreement with the Republic of the Philippines Concerning Trade and Related Matters, July 4, 1946, *as revised* Sept. 6, 1955, United States–Republic of the Philippines, art. VI, 6 U.S.T. 2981, T.I.A.S. 3348 (effective Jan. 1, 1956).

COMPLIANCE AS A FUNCTION OF THE RULE   109

of legal theory, the rights granted are fully reciprocal in the new agreement. The facts apparently are that Filipinos neither have wished to undertake substantial investments in natural resources or public utilities in the United States nor have encountered difficulty in doing so. By stating the "parity" rights in reciprocal terms, however, the negotiators assured, or at least encouraged, continued respect for these rights in the Philippines until their expiration in 1974.

Perhaps a more striking example occurred when India and Pakistan were seeking to negotiate a treaty through the good offices of the World Bank over the withdrawal of irrigation water from the Indus River system. The two countries agreed that as long as the talks continued "neither side would take any action to diminish the supplies available to the other side for existing uses."[9] India is upstream and Pakistan is downstream. Pakistan had no opportunity to diminish the water available to India. The impact of this particular restraint was wholly on India, but its legitimacy was increased by the use of language that applied equally to the two countries.

Making a rule congruent with religious, moral, or psychological notions of what is right can be accomplished not only in formulating the rule. Once a rule has been formulated, the moral content can be emphasized. For example, article I of the Nuclear Test Ban Treaty provides that each of the parties "undertakes to prohibit, to prevent, and not to carry out any nuclear weapon test explosion, or any other nuclear explosion, at any place under its jurisdiction or control . . . if such explosion causes radioactive debris to be present outside the territorial limits of the State under whose jurisdiction or control such explosion is conducted."[10] Better compliance with this Treaty is likely to the extent that public attention is drawn to this prohibition on poisoning with radioactive fallout the air breathed by all the people of the world.[11] Any short-term gains that a government

[9] Letter from President Black of the World Bank to the Prime Ministers of India and Pakistan (March 13, 1952), Government of Pakistan, Canal Waters Dispute (1958); cf. Laylin, *The Indus River System*, 54 Am. Soc'y Int'l L. Proc. 144 (1960).

[10] Treaty Banning Nuclear Weapon Tests in the Atmosphere, in Outer Space and Under Water, *done* Aug. 5, 1963, 14 U.S.T. 1313, T.I.A.S. No. 5433, 480 U.N.T.S. 43.

[11] This is what the General Assembly did in Resolution 3257 (XXIX), Urgent need for cessation of nuclear and thermonuclear tests and conclusion of a treaty designed to

might think it would realize by carrying out a nuclear test which involved substantial radioactive debris outside its territory could be outweighed by the negative public reaction because of the prior emphasis on the moral content of the international rule.

   c. *The choice between first-order compliance and precautionary rules.* Assuming that governments, like people, are less likely to violate a rule which has a high moral content than they are to commit a "technical" violation of a "technical" rule which does not immediately cause any real injury to anyone, those working on the formulation of international rules have a difficult choice to make. Hoping to induce maximum compliance, they can formulate a rule so that it falls as closely as possible along a discontinuity on the far side of which is conduct that almost everyone will recognize as evil. Examples from domestic and international law would include rules against attacking people with switchblade knives, going through a red light when to do so would cause a collision, parking one's car in front of a hydrant when the hydrant is needed for fighting a fire, arresting an ambassador on a petty offense when he is engaged in important inter-

---

achieve a comprehensive test ban, adopted on Dec. 9, 1974. After recalling its prior resolutions expressing the same idea, the Assembly declared that "cessation of nuclear weapon testing would be in the supreme interest of mankind, . . . to relieve the deep apprehension concerning the harmful consequences of radio-active contamination for the health of present and future generations." *See* 29 U.N. GAOR, Supp. (No. 31) 20, U.N. Doc. A / 9631 (1974). Similarly, in their separate applications instituting proceedings in the Nuclear Tests Case, Australia and New Zealand stressed the same danger and claimed the infringement of the same right. The former claimed that "the right of Australia and its people, in common with other States and their peoples, to be free from atmospheric nuclear weapon tests by any country is and will be violated." *See* [1973] I.C.J. 103. New Zealand maintained that the nuclear testing undertaken by the French Government in the South Pacific "violates the rights of all members of the international community including New Zealand, to the preservation from unjustified artificial radioactive contamination of the terrestrial, maritime and aerial environment and, in particular, of the environment of the region in which the tests are conducted." *See id.* at 139. Without deciding upon the merits of the case, the Court on June 22, 1973, ordered as a provisional measure that "the French Government should avoid nuclear tests causing the deposit of radio-active fall-out on Australian territory" (*id.* at 106) and "on the territory of New Zealand, the Cook Islands, Nive, or the Tokelau Islands" (*id.* at 142). In 1973 the French Government disregarded the order of the Court (*id.* at 448) and maintained its position that France had the right to test nuclear weapons in the atmosphere. (For the French legal position, see the separate opinion of Judge Gros, *id.* at 277, 279, 286–88.) In 1974, however, apparently deferring to public concern, France stated that the atmospheric tests of that summer would "in the normal course of events, be the last of this type" (*id.* at 266).

national business, bombing cities with thermonuclear bombs, and so forth. Such rules are minimal rules, prohibiting no more conduct than is necessary to preserve the readily understandable interest at stake. Because of the fact that any violation of the rule would cause injury, one could expect a high degree of first-order compliance. On most occasions, the rules would be respected.

On the other hand, any violation is likely to cause serious injury. To reduce the chance of such injury, legal rules are frequently formulated further back from the edge. New York has a law against possessing switchblade knives.[12] It is made an offense to go through a red light even if no cars are coming, and to park in front of a hydrant even when to do so does not interfere with its use. There is a treaty against *testing* nuclear weapons. Ambassadors are immune from arrest at all times. Most rules prohibit somewhat more conduct than absolutely necessary to protect the interest the rule is designed to serve. Sometimes this is done to make the law easy to understand. Other rules are purely precautionary in order to reduce the chance of actual injury. Although a rule against carrying switchblade knives may result in fewer stabbings than would a rule against stabbing with switchblade knives, there are likely to be more violations of the first rule than of the second. Many people who would not commit stabbings are likely to feel that it is all right to carry such a knife for protection, and do so. On the other hand, quite a few violations of a precautionary rule can occur without there being any real injury.

There is thus a fairly basic choice for those working on the formulation of a rule of international law. Other things being equal, the more elemental the rules are, the more inherent moral content there is and hence the more first-order compliance that can be expected. The further back the rules are from the brink — the more they deal with conduct that is *malum prohibitum* rather than *malum in se* — the less first-order compliance should be expected. Precautionary rules are designed not so much with the objective of causing initial respect (for we expect violations) but rather with the objectives of protecting the ulti-

---

[12] N.Y. PENAL LAW § 265 (McKinney 1976).

mate interest and of simplifying administration and enforcement.

d. *Including a termination clause.* As contradictory as it may seem, continued compliance with a treaty obligation is likely to be increased by including in the treaty a defined right of termination. Although a legal right to terminate an obligation simply confirms in large part a practical power of termination which exists already, the legal provision nonetheless affects the practical power. An explicit right of termination will in some cases make termination easier politically. On the other hand, granting an express right which is substantively and procedurally circumscribed will in other cases make repudiation more difficult.

The 1963 Moscow Test Ban Treaty[13] suggests that authorizing termination with notice and under stated conditions makes it more difficult to repudiate a treaty without notice or under other conditions. Article IV of the Test Ban Treaty reads:

> This Treaty shall be of unlimited duration. Each Party shall in exercising its national sovereignty have the right to withdraw from the Treaty if it decides that extraordinary events, related to the subject matter of this Treaty, have jeopardized the supreme interests of its country. It shall give notice of such withdrawal to all other Parties to the Treaty three months in advance.[14]

Without such a clause, a party might feel that changed circumstances justified its repudiation or withdrawal. It could then present the world with a fait accompli by resuming atmospheric testing. Now, with a right to terminate upon three months' notice, a country would have a slightly more difficult task in justifying termination without notice. Defining what a party may do in the exercise of its national sovereignty makes it more difficult to justify exercising "sovereign rights" inconsistent with the treaty. Giving notice precludes termination by the more painless method of fait accompli. During the three months' notice period, a withdrawing country could expect to receive from numerous countries urgent pleas not to withdraw, pleas that it would have to ignore to continue its chosen course.

The Vienna Conference on the Law of Treaties seems to have

---

[13] Treaty Banning Nuclear Weapons Tests, note 10 *supra.*
[14] *Id.* at art. IV.

reached a similar conclusion about the value of defining the procedure leading to the termination of a treaty. Article 56 of the Vienna Convention on the Law of Treaties, dealing with the denunciation of a treaty containing no provision regarding termination, provides:

> 1. A treaty which contains no provision regarding its termination and which does not provide for denunciation or withdrawal is not subject to denunciation or withdrawal unless: a) it is established that the parties intended to admit the possibility of denunciation or withdrawal; or b) a right of denunciation or withdrawal may be implied in the nature of the treaty.
>
> 2. A party shall give not less than twelve months' notice of its intention to denounce or withdraw from a treaty under paragraph 1.[15]

Unlike the Moscow Test Ban Treaty, this provision does not limit the reasons for which a country can terminate a treaty which has no denunciation clause. The Vienna Convention, however, does allow for a "breathing period" similar to the one required by the Moscow Treaty.

In addition to complete termination, it might be wise to provide a range of alternative forms of possible action such as the temporary suspension of one particular provision, if performance was found to be impossible, or the termination of certain clauses. The International Convention for the Safety of Life at Sea[16] provides in article VI that a Party may in the case of war or other hostilities that affect it either as a belligerent or a neutral "suspend the operation of the whole or any part of the" detailed regulations contained in that treaty. The article also allows the suspending Party to terminate its suspension at any time. Coastal states that adhere to the Convention on the Territorial Sea and the Contiguous Zone[17] may, according to article 16, paragraph 3, "without discrimination amongst foreign ships, suspend temporarily in specified areas of its territorial sea the innocent pas-

[15] U.N. Conference on the Law of Treaties (1st & 2d Sessions, 26 March–24 May 1968 & 9 April–22 May 1969), U.N. Doc. A / CONF. 39 / 11.

[16] International Convention for the Safety of Life at Sea, June 17, 1960, 16 U.S.T. 185, T.I.A.S. No. 5780, 536 U.N.T.S. 27.

[17] Convention on the Territorial Sea and the Contiguous Zone, Apr. 29, 1958, 15 U.S.T. 1606, T.I.A.S. No. 5639, 516 U.N.T.S. 205.

sage of foreign ships if such suspension is essential for the protection of its security."[18] By offering parties to a convention something less than total denunciation when temporary national difficulties prevent respecting a particular undertaking, these provisions encourage continued respect for the remainder of the treaty.

Although one should not exaggerate the importance of such clauses, it seems fair to conclude that they do make treaties a little more realistic and a little more durable — especially when the provision and the basis for termination or lesser action are explicitly included in the treaty itself.[19]

2. *How the rule is established.* A tendency toward first-order compliance rather than noncompliance can be affected not only by the content of the rule but also by the way in which it is established as a rule to be respected. Without exploring here the general problem of establishing international law, we can look at those factors in the establishment process which tend to increase initial respect for standing rules.

a. *Fair procedure.* International law has necessarily recognized that treaties imposed upon a defeated power after a war are as legally binding as treaties concluded between states of equal strength in time of peace. No one would suggest, however, that a defeated government in fact felt as obliged to continue to respect an imposed treaty as one into which it had entered voluntarily. In 1848 France announced that "the treaties of 1815 are no longer valid in the eyes of the French Republic." In 1871 Russia repudiated the 1856 Straits Convention placing restrictions on the passage of its warships that had been imposed on Russia at the conclusion of the Crimean War.[20] Bolshevik Russia de-

---

[18]Coastal states may not exercise this right of suspension in straits used for international navigation between two parts of the high seas. This was the point of contention between the United States and the Soviet Union in the Vilkitsky Straits case. *See* 62 AM. J. INT'L L. 150–51 (1967).

[19]Such clauses also serve to strengthen the principle of respect for law by providing a legal framework for the exercise of the de facto power of a state to free itself from treaty obligations. *Cf.* Fitzmaurice, *Law of Treaties*, [1957] 2 Y.B. INT'L L. COMM'N 16, 69: "The attitude of the *terminator*, whether justified or not, is to claim to have grounds on which there is a right to terminate the treaty. But the *repudiator* says in effect that the treaty has no existence for him, and he refuses to be bound by it any longer. The terminator recognizes the obligation, though purporting to be entitled to put an end to it. The repudiator rejects it altogether."

[20]E. CARR, THE TWENTY YEARS' CRISIS, 1919–1939, at 182 (1964).

nounced the 1918 Treaty of Brest-Litovsk. Hitler's first demands in Europe were phrased in terms of correcting the "injustices" imposed on the German people by the Treaty of Versailles at the close of World War I.[21] Treaties entered into between countries grossly unequal in bargaining power are also subject to later attack. The former French and Belgian colonies associated with the Common Market, for instance, demanded substantial revisions of the trade agreement that they had signed with the European Economic Community shortly after their independence when they were considerably weaker.[22]

When a rule is being agreed upon between large and small nations, it seems wise to get as much of an imprimatur of fairness stamped upon it as possible. One way to accomplish this result is to have negotiations held under the auspices of an international agency, such as the World Bank. Another method is to have some kind of international endorsement, as when the General Assembly commends by resolution draft treaties to be concluded by states under the auspices of the United Nations.[23] Still another technique is to include representatives of countries of all sizes and political persuasions in the treaty-making process, even if their immediate concern with the subject matter of a treaty is limited. The Outer Space Treaty,[24] for instance, concerns primarily the United States and the Soviet Union, at least for the present. The negotiations of that treaty, however, were conducted in the twenty-four-member Legal Sub-Committee of the Committee on the Peaceful Uses of Outer Space, whose chairman at that time was Manfred Lachs of Poland, a country with little technological capability or political ambition in outer space.

Where a country is seeking to establish a rule of international law by acquiescence in a course of conduct, it should pay atten-

[21] G. CRAIG, EUROPE SINCE 1815, at 685 (1962).

[22] Convention of Association between the European Economic Community and the African and Malagasy States with this Community, Dec. 19, 1962, 2 J.O. COMM. EUR. 1429 (1964).

[23] See, e.g., Resolution 2222 (XXI) approving the draft Treaty on Principles Governing the Activities of States in the Exploration and Use of Outer Space, including the Moon and Other Celestial Bodies, 21 U.N. GAOR, Supp. (No. 16) 13, U.N. Doc. A / 6316 (1966), and Resolution 2345 (XXII) approving the draft Agreement on the Rescue of Astronauts, the Return of Astronauts and the Return of Objects Launched into Outer Space, 22 U.N. GAOR, Supp. (No. 16) 5–6, U.N. Doc. A / 6717 (1967).

[24] See notes 4 & 23 and accompanying text supra.

tion to the general principles of equitable estoppel. There would seem to be no unfairness in the way in which the international rule that satellites are permitted to overfly any country was established. Satellites were flown with great publicity over all parts of the world and no protest was made.[25] On the other hand, there is a little more difficulty with the rule that general international law permits "spy" satellites — satellites placed in orbit for the purpose of gathering military intelligence from countries over which they pass. The lack of publicity given such satellites would make it far easier for a country to dispute the existence of any rule permitting them. Similarly, countries in the United Nations, which have had an opportunity to engage in debate, find its resolutions somewhat more compelling than do countries like Communist China which were excluded from the United Nations for a long period of time.

b. *As clarification of existing law.* One of the most important techniques of inducing respect for a rule is to have it reasonably identified not as a new rule but as a clarification of a preexisting rule of law. Much of the power of a judicial decision stems from the understanding that the judge is finding law rather than making it. Others can increase the strength of the rules they formulate by operating under comparable restraints. The rules embodied in the Geneva Convention on the High Seas will tend to have greater respect to the extent that they are, as stated in the Preamble of the Convention, "generally declaratory of established principles of international law."[26] One cost of improving the law may be decreased respect for it. In the case of a treaty purporting to be declaratory of existing law, the increased effectiveness is applicable both to those who adhere to the treaty and to those who do not. A general multilateral treaty, such as the Vienna Convention on the Law of Treaties, which is accepted by many nations as a clarification of existing law, tends to be binding even on countries that do not adhere to it.[27] To the extent that the treaty reflects a community judgment as to what the law is, no

---

[25] *See* Lachs, *The International Law of Outer Space*, 113 RECUEIL DES COURS (Hague Academy of International Law) 99 (1964–III).

[26] Geneva Convention on the High Seas, Apr. 29, 1958, 13 U.S.T. 2312, T.I.A.S. No. 5200, 450 U.N.T.S. 82.

[27] Vienna Convention on the Law of Treaties, note 15 *supra*.

country can wholly escape it. As Professor Milan Bartoš stated in the International Law Commission:

> If learned authors were able to state what were customary rules of law, *a fortiori* a decision by a large number of States had even greater authority. The world has moved beyond the nineteenth-century ideal of codification by scientific bodies; in modern times the process was taking place in the name of the international community, and even when states did not assume treaty obliga-tions, as members of that community they were bound to respect the rules confirmed by it.[28]

Furthermore, a country which has adhered to such a treaty will find it difficult to justify noncompliance with the rule even by repudiating the treaty.[29]

The General Assembly would be well advised to recognize the significant power that it has to reflect a community judgment as to existing international law,[30] contrasted with the drastically limited power it has to establish what are admittedly new rules.

---

[28][1961] 1 Y.B. INT'L L. COMM'N 254 (Mr. Bartoš's comment, para. 6).

[29] Article 43 of the Vienna Convention on the Law of Treaties, *supra* note 15, at 295, makes it unmistakably clear: "The validity, termination or denunciation of a treaty, the withdrawal of a party from it, or the suspension of its operation, as a result of the appli-cation of the present Convention or of the provisions of the treaty, shall not in any way impair the duty of any state to fulfill any obligation embodied in the treaty to which it would be subject under international law independently of the treaty." Commenting upon the draft of this rule, the International Law Commission "considered, that al-though the point might be regarded as axiomatic, it was desirable to underline that the termination of a treaty would not release the parties from obligations embodied in the treaty to which they were also subject under any other rule of international law." *Id.* at 57.

[30] Among the resolutions of the General Assembly reflecting a community view as to existing international law, at least three have assumed prominence in the practice of states and of the organs of the United Nations. The first, Resolution 1514 (XV), contains the Declaration on the Granting of Independence to Colonial Countries and Peoples; G.A. Res. 1514, 15 U.N. GAOR, Supp. (No. 16), U.N. Doc. A / 4684 (1960). The second, Resolution 1803 (XVII), pertains to Permanent Sovereignty over Natural Resources; G.A. Res. 1803, 17 U.N. GAOR, Supp. (No. 17), U.N. Doc. A / 5217 (1962). The third, Resolution 2625 (XXV), contains the Declaration on Principles of International Law con-cerning Friendly Relations and Co-operation among States in accordance with the Charter of the United Nations. The latter expressly provides in one of its final para-graphs that "the principles of the Charter which are embodied in the Declaration con-stitute basic principles of international law." *See* 25 U.N. GAOR, Supp. (No. 28) 121, 124, U.N. Doc. A / 8038 (1970). *See also* Sohn, *The Development of the Charter of the United Na-tions: The Present State*, in INTERNATIONAL LAW ASSOCIATION: 1873–1973, at 52 (Kluwer ed. 1973).

By distinguishing more sharply than it has those occasions when it is recommending action that countries are not obliged to undertake from those occasions when it is reflecting a sound community judgment on what is required by the existing state of international law, additional strength could be given to the latter recommendations. This is not simply a question of words. It requires that the content of a resolution be comparable to that which could be reached by a judge acting within the normal limits upon the judicial function.

An example may illustrate the point. In Resolution 1762(XVII), the General Assembly of the United Nations condemned all nuclear weapon tests and urged the United States and the Soviet Union to complete negotiation of a test ban treaty.[31] A year later, in Resolution 1910(XVIII), the General Assembly called upon "all States to become parties to the Treaty banning nuclear weapon tests in the atmosphere, in outer space and under water, and to abide by its spirit and provisions. . . ."[32] Rather than simply calling on France, China, and other nonsignatories to sign the test ban treaty — a recommendation which has little impact — the General Assembly might reexamine the legality of atmospheric testing in the light of present knowledge about radioactive fallout and the widespread community acceptance of the test ban treaty.[33] For example, in March 1964 the Asian-African Legal Consultative Committee unanimously approved a resolution on the illegality of nuclear tests which included the following conclusions, which do not apply to underground tests because there the scientific data are still unclear:

> 2. Scientific evidence examined by the Committee shows that every test explosion of nuclear weapons results in wide-spread damage, immediate or delayed, or is capable of resulting in such damage; the present state of scientific knowledge does not indicate that the harmful effects of such test explosions can reasonably be eliminated. Such test explosions not only cause direct

---

[31]G.A. Res. 1762, 17 U.N. GAOR, Supp. (No. 17) 3, U.N. Doc. A / 5217 (1962).

[32]G.A. Res. 1910, 18 U.N. GAOR, Supp. (No. 28) 14, U.N. Doc. A / 5515 (1963).

[33]In the Nuclear Tests Case, Barwick, the Australian judge ad hoc wrote: "I think it must be considered that it is legally possible that at some stage the testing of nuclear weapons could become, or could have become, prohibited by the customary international law. Treaties, resolutions, expressions of opinion and international practice, may all combine to produce evidence of that customary law." [1974] I.C.J. 142,435.

damage, but pollute the atmosphere and cause fall out of radio-active material and also increase atomic radiation, which are detrimental to the well-being of man and also affect future generations.

3. Having regard to its harmful effects, as shown by scientific data, a test explosion of nuclear weapons constitutes an international wrong. Even if such tests are carried out within the territory of the testing State, they are liable to be regarded as an abuse of rights (abus de droit).

4. The principle of absolute liability for harbouring dangerous substances or carrying on dangerous activities is recognized in International Law. A State carrying out test explosions of nuclear weapons is therefore absolutely liable for the damage caused by such test explosions .

5. Test explosions of nuclear weapons are also contrary to the principles contained in the United Nations Charter and the Declaration of Human Rights.

6. Test explosions of nuclear weapons carried out in the high seas and in the airspace thereabove also violate the principle of the freedom of flying above the high seas, as such test explosions interfere with the freedom of navigation and of flying above the high seas and result in pollution of the water and destruction of the living and other resources of the sea.

7. Test explosions of nuclear weapons carried out in trust territories and self-governing territories also violate Articles 73 and 74 of the United Nations Charter.[34]

A General Assembly resolution declaring nuclear tests illegal could include many of the same conclusions and could also refer to the ruling of the Arbitral Tribunal in the *Trail Smelter Case* that

> under principles of international law, as well as of the law of the United States, no State has the right to use or permit the use of its territory in such a manner as to cause injury by fumes in or to the territory of another or the properties or persons therein, when the case is of serious consequence and the injury is established by clear and convincing evidence.[35]

A General Assembly finding that nuclear tests currently are illegal, unlike previous exhortations on the subject, might have

---

[34] Asian-African Legal Consultative Committee Res., U.N. Doc. A / CN. 4/172 (1964).
[35] Trail Smelter Case (United States v. Canada), 3 R. Int'l Arb. Awards 1906, 1965 (1938 & 1941).

a significant impact. It would provide a valid ground for a limited use of force, allowing countries, which might choose to do so, to organize blockade measures with a view to preventing particular islands from being used for the purpose of violating international law in this way. Even a secret expedition to sabotage a mainland test site would take on a good deal of protective political coloration as a law enforcement measure.

c. *Identifying a rule as "law."* In the international community today, the forces that tend to cause a government to respect international law are of the same general character as those which cause a government to respect "understandings," "rules of comity," "international practice," "custom," and so forth. Nonetheless, converting an understanding into a "legal" rule tends to increase the political costs of breaking it. It is easier to abandon a tacit agreement, a practice, or a moratorium than to break a legal obligation. The United States and the Soviet Union each adopted a moratorium on nuclear testing toward the end of 1958 when the Geneva Disarmament talks began. The moratorium had no legal basis. It was simply the result of a unilateral offer by the United States to suspend testing which the Soviet Union appeared to accept by suspending its testing shortly after the disarmament negotiations began. On August 31, 1961, the Soviet Union announced that it would end the three-year moratorium and would resume testing. The Russian leaders justified their action by citing the crisis over Berlin, the growing aggression of NATO powers, the French nuclear tests, and the rejection of the Soviet "troika" in the United Nations. The United States itself then resumed testing, on September 5, 1961.[36] Now the Moscow Test Ban Treaty of 1963 makes nuclear testing by its signatories in the atmosphere, in outer space, and under water a violation of international law.[37] The Soviet Union and the United States, as signatories, would certainly have a

[36] For a brief description of the sequence of the events, see A. CHAYES, T. EHRLICH & A. LOWENFELD, 2 INT'L LEGAL PROCESS 966–68 (1969).

[37] The United States and the Soviet Union assumed, on a bilateral basis, new obligations in the Treaty on the Limitation of Underground Nuclear Weapons Tests, which was done in Moscow on July 3, 1974. According to article 1 of the Treaty, each party undertakes to prohibit, to prevent, and not to carry out any underground nuclear-weapon test having a yield exceeding 150 kilotons at any place under its jurisdiction or control, beginning March 31, 1976. Furthermore, each party commits itself to limiting

much more difficult task in justifying a violation of the international obligation contained in the treaty than they did in the case of the informal moratorium.

With the establishment and strengthening of international legal machinery, the difference between law and nonlaw in the international community will increase. To a judge, the distinction is necessarily important, and as the role of judges increases, the distinction becomes one of increasing importance to others. But, even in the absence of judges, calling something a legal obligation makes a difference. When a rule is being established, calling it "law" may tend to decrease flexibility but will tend to increase compliance.

d. *A rule that is bargained for.* Domestically, we distinguish almost intuitively between the kind of legal obligation that results from a contract and the kind that results from a statute, whether it is civil or criminal. In international law, the distinction between normative and contractual obligations becomes blurred because treaties, the one form of lawmaking that is universally recognized, may include rules of different kinds.[38] As indicated above, to identify a rule as a clarification of general preexisting international law tends to make the rule more durable and more deserving of compliance. Such a rule tends to be more difficult to break than one which can be identified as inherently temporary and of limited application, comparable to the day-to-day contracts and undertakings made by private persons.

Among the latter arrangements, an obligation will tend to be more difficult to break if it is bargained for rather than if it has been unilaterally assumed. In international relations there appears to be something comparable to the common-law notion of consideration; a gratuitous promise, even if it is couched in

the number of its underground nuclear weapon tests to a minimum, and to continuing negotiations with a view toward achieving a solution to the problem of the cessation of all underground nuclear-weapon tests. *See Union of Soviet Socialist Republics–United States Treaty On The Limitation Of Underground Nuclear Weapons Tests,* 71 DEP'T STATE BULL. 216, 68 AM. J. INT'L L. 805 (1974). As of December 1979, this treaty had yet not been ratified.

[38] As Rosenne pointed out in the case of Reservations to the Convention on the Prevention and Punishment of the Crime of Genocide, the contracting parties, in one and the same treaty, can establish authoritative standards and impose reciprocal rights and obligations. *See* Reservations to the Convention on the Prevention and Punishment of the Crime of Genocide, [1951] I.C.J. 334. As to many articles, it is often difficult to say whether they are normative or contractual. *Id.* at 403.

terms of a legally binding obligation,[39] may be terminated far more freely than can a promise given in exchange for some consideration.

e. *A present change of status.* One of the most effective and remarkable ways of causing compliance with an international obligation is to identify what an agreement is doing in terms of a present change of status rather than in terms of a promise of future conduct. The general legal rights that flow from certain established concepts like ownership and territory are so well recognized that any attempt to alter the rules in one case would raise broad and fundamental opposition.

Consider, for example, a treaty under which the United States agreed to pay Russia $7.2 million if Russia would promise not to engage in any military or other activities without our consent in a designated area of half a million square miles of Russian territory. Once the fee had been paid, the restraint would be wholly on the Russian side. One can guess that, if this had been the form as well as the substance of the agreement we made with the Russian Czar in 1867, it might well have been repudiated long ago. In fact, although that was the substance of the agreement we made with Russia, it was put in the form of a "cession" in which the land in question, Alaska, was transferred from the status of being Russian territory to the status of being American territory.[40] By putting the treaty in this latter form and by having the United States pay the Emperor of all the Russians $7.2 million in consideration for the cession, there was far less of a tendency to break the obligation to refrain from action in the area.

The increased deference that tends to be accorded to an executed change of status may be particularly crucial in a treaty where a present change of status is accepted in exchange for a promise of future behavior. For example, Country *A* might

[39] For a discussion of the difference between a promise which gives rise to a moral obligation and a promise which legally binds the promisor, see Nuclear Tests Case, [1974] I.C.J. 373–75 (dissenting opinion of Judge de Castro); Frank, *Word Made Law: The Decision of the International Court of Justice in the Nuclear Tests Cases*, 69 AM. J. INT'L L. 612 (1975).

[40] Treaty Concerning the Cession of the Russian Possessions in North America, March 30, 1867, United States–Russia, 15 Stat. 539, 11 C. BEVANS, TREATIES AND OTHER INTERNATIONAL AGREEMENTS OF THE UNITED STATES OF AMERICA, 1776–1949, at 1216 (1974).

agree to accept a particular boundary provided that Country *B* undertook to provide designated amounts of irrigation water for each month in the future. Country *A* is likely to find that the boundary (based on status) is far more durable than the water supply (based on promise). A divorce remains final whether or not the alimony is paid. A country which grants independence to a territory in exchange for various undertakings is likely to find that it feels more compelled to respect the independence than the new country does to respect the executory promises.

f. *Degree of formality.* The importance for compliance of the way in which an obligation is undertaken or a rule is established is seen perhaps nowhere so clearly as in the degree of formality employed. The more formal pomp and ceremony is exhibited, the more deeply committed a government becomes to the rule that is being established. In theory, the oral undertaking of a foreign minister is as legally binding under international law as an obligation assumed in a written treaty,[41] but the practical political difference is enormous. Such matters as handling an agreement by treaty or by executive agreement, the level of the officials who sign the undertaking, and the ceremony involved all affect the degree of embarrassment that a government would suffer if it broke the agreement, and hence affect the tendency toward compliance.[42]

g. *Explicit consent.* In most of the discussion above, it is assumed that a legal obligation is being undertaken by agreement. This, however, is not necessarily so. A country which does not adhere to a multilateral treaty may find that, in some respects, it is nonetheless bound to the treaty as a practical matter. Widely accepted agreements establishing rules for ships at sea or diplomatic immunities, for example, are going to affect the legal rights of states that do not sign.

[41] "[T]here does not seem to be any rule of international law requiring that agreements of this kind must necessarily be in writing, in order to be valid." Opinion of Judge Anzilotti in the case of the Legal Status of Eastern Greenland, [1933] P.C.I.J., ser. A/B, No. 53, at 91.

[42] In recent years the United States, in its treaty relations with the Soviet Union, has paid less attention to the rule that agreements should be signed by state officials and has accepted, if not desired, the signature of the First Secretary of the Communist party. *But see* the criticism lodged from a formal point of view by Schroder, *Supremacy of the Communist Party of the Soviet Union Recognized in International Law?*, 70 AM. J. INT'L L. 322–28 (1976).

The legal force of treaties creating objective regimes or situations, such as the Antarctic Treaty,[43] rests largely on the acquiescence by third states to their provisions. Lord McNair explained the process:

> Strictly speaking, a treaty of this kind (which may or may not contain an accession clause) binds at first the parties thereto and no other States. But it is undeniable that after a period of time, to which no fixed duration can be attributed, the mere lapse of time and the acquiescence of other States in the arrangement thus made have the effect of reinforcing the essential juridical element of the treaty and of converting what may at first have been a partly *de facto* situation into a *de jure* one.[44]

It is improbable that any state not a party to the Antarctic Treaty would freely violate the principle of demilitarization of Antarctica set forth by the contracting parties.

Although the express agreement of a government to a rule established in a general multilateral treaty is not necessary, a government's respect for a rule of international law is likely to increase if the government can be induced to accept it explicitly and publicly, rather than simply to acquiesce in its application.

3. *Keeping a rule fresh.* The passage of time has two quite different effects on the tendency to comply with a rule. With time,[45] established practice may turn into international law; a course of conduct may become obligatory. Some rules seem to get their strength by being considered old and well established. That process appears to be the origin of the three-mile limit on a coastal state's claim of territorial waters and the privileges and immunities of diplomats (later codified in the Vienna Convention on Diplomatic Relations).[46]

On the other hand, the passage of time may make a rule out-

[43] The Antarctic Treaty, Dec. 1, 1959, 12 U.S.T. 794, T.I.A.S. No. 4780, 402 U.N.T.S. 71.

[44] A. McNAIR, THE LAW OF TREATIES 259 (1961).

[45] "In the contemporary age of highly developed techniques of communication and information, the formation of a custom through the medium of international organizations is greatly facilitated and accelerated; the establishment of such a custom would require no more than one generation or even less than that." [1966] I.C.J. 291. *See also* Lachs, *supra* note 25, at 99.

[46] Vienna Convention on Diplomatic Relations, Apr. 18, 1961, 23 U.S.T. 3227, T.I.A.S. No. 7502, 500 U.N.T.S. 95.

of-date. Changed circumstances may undercut the assumptions upon which a treaty was based or a customary rule established. The three-mile limit on territorial waters, established in the days of primitive cannon, has lost its rationale in the days of missiles, submarines, and aircraft. Many nineteenth-century rules of international law have been wholly undercut by the contemporary principle of self-determination.

There is a tendency on the part of governments to rely unduly on theoretical rights contained in ancient agreements and to underestimate the political vigor that can be instilled in a rule by bringing it up-to-date and reestablishing it as one to which an opposing government is freshly committed as of a recent date. The doctrine of *rebus sic stantibus*, under which it is presumed that every agreement contains an implied condition that it is to remain in effect only as long as the basic underlying conditions remain more or less the same, reflects more than an argument for an irresponsible country's getting out of its debts. Whatever our contentions may be, it may be wiser to agree to a new conference leading to a revised agreement than to rely on an old agreement. The difficulties encountered by the United States in 1964 in the Panama Canal Zone arose, in part, from a failure to recognize a need to revise the 1903 Convention with Panama for the Construction of a Ship Canal.[47] In the Canal Zone, as well as elsewhere, the extent to which our rights under a revised agreement[48] are less than under the old agreement may be more than offset by a higher degree of compliance — for the time being — with the new one.

4. *Conclusion.* In the absence of international deterrent machinery, governments may be induced to respect standing obligations of international law by the political price paid abroad and at home for noncompliance. The content of a rule and the manner by which it is established can, to some extent, affect the forces tending toward compliance or noncompliance. The next

[47] Construction Of A Ship Canal To Connect The Waters Of The Atlantic And Pacific Oceans, United States–Panama, Nov. 18, 1908, 33 Stat. 2234, T.S. No. 431. *See also* Hoyt, *Law and Politics in the Revision of Treaties Affecting the Panama Canal*, 6 VA. J. INT'L L. 289 (1966); Statement by the President of the United States on areas of agreement in the negotiations with Panama (Sept. 24, 1965), 60 AM. J. INT'L L. 397–98 (1966).

[48] The new Panama Canal Treaty was ratified in April 1978, S. 5796, 95th Cong., 2d Sess., 124 CONG. REC. (daily ed. Apr. 13, 1978).

two chapters, looking not at the rule but rather at the government, consider more closely these international and domestic forces, and what might be done to strengthen those that tend in the direction of causing a government to respect a standing obligation.

CHAPTER VI

Reciprocity and Enlightened Self-Interest

Without much in the way of international legal machinery, there is substantial respect for a great many standing rules of international law. To some extent, this is for internal domestic reasons within each country, which will be discussed in the next chapter. To a large extent, however, a government finds it in the national interest to comply with international law. This chapter considers the external factors that may now cause a government to respect rules of international law and the opportunities that may exist for altering these factors so as to increase first-order compliance.

1. *Automatic self-interest.* Some rules are practically self-enforcing, at least for those acting rationally. Compliance brings with it its own reward; noncompliance its own punishment. A rule that persons going to the top floor of an office building should ride the express elevator is complied with by most persons because of their immediate self-interest. Englishmen drive on the left even though there appears to be no statutory requirement to do so. It is simply in the interest of the driver to go with the traffic rather than against it. He will get to where he is going in less time and with less risk of collision if he complies with the rule.

Some rules of international law are directly comparable. In *Politics Among Nations*, Hans Morgenthau pointed out that "[m]ost rules in international law formulate in legal terms such identical or complementary interests. It is for this reason that they generally enforce themselves, as it were, and that there is generally no need for a specific enforcement action."[1] It is in the interest of a government to respect the rules of the road at sea and the rules regulating the altitudes and flight patterns of aircraft in order to avoid collisions. In most cases, it is in the immediate self-interest of a country to broadcast on a radio

[1] H. MORGENTHAU, POLITICS AMONG NATIONS 283 (3d ed. 1960).

frequency allocated to it rather than one allocated to a neighboring country if it wishes to have its broadcasts received without interference.

This immediate self-interest in a government's own compliance with some of the rules of international law is quite different from an appreciation of the interest that a government may have in having governments in general comply with a rule. A government, recognizing its interest in avoiding oil pollution of the sea, may desire a rule prohibiting it and may believe it to be in its interest to have general compliance with the rule. On the other hand, the same government might permit its ships, when on the far side of the globe, to flush their tanks in violation of the rule when it would save money to do so. The kind of direct self-interest here being considered would tend to cause compliance with the antipollution rule only when a country's ship was anchored off its own public beaches.

It might be possible to take limited steps to increase the operative effect of the self-interest in not violating international rules. Ingenuity in devising rules might result in more rules of this type. The self-interest involved, however, seems to depend more on the nature of the problem than on the formulation of the rule. Apparently more promising would be educational efforts to demonstrate an immediate self-interest which exists but which may be overlooked. Trade agreements, tariff concessions, the "hot line" agreement establishing a direct link between Washington and Moscow,[2] agreed reductions in the military forces, and numerous other international obligations may well be such that a government has an interest in its own compliance apart from the interest which it has in having everyone comply. Compliance with arms control agreements might avoid substantial military expenditures; tariff concessions might offer an economic stimulus to more efficient internal production.

Self-interest in fulfilling international commitments and in respecting established legal rules may be so strong that even sour

[2]Memorandum of Understanding Regarding the Establishment of a Direct Communications Link, *signed* on June 20, 1963, 49 DEP'T STATE BULL. 50 (1963); *supplemented* Sept. 30, 1971, by the Agreement With the Union of Soviet Socialist Republics on Measures to Improve the USA-USSR Direct Communications Link, Sept. 30, 1971, 10 INT'L LEGAL MATERIALS 1174–75 (1971).

relations between the states concerned would not undercut them. One example is the Memorandum of Understanding between the United States and Cuba on Hijacking of Aircraft and Vessels and Other Offenses.[3] Despite strong and long-lasting political differences between these two countries, it became in the self-interest of both Cuba and the United States to act together to reduce aircraft hijacking.

2. *Reputation and public opinion.* A country's conduct today affects its reputation, and its reputation affects its ability to accomplish desired objectives tomorrow. Even where a country's immediate interest may seem to be to violate a standing rule, the difference in reputation that can result from compliance or noncompliance may outweigh any immediate gain. For rough purposes, a country's reputation may be divided between a specific reputation for particular conduct and its general reputation.

a. *Specific reputation.* A member of the New York Stock Exchange keeps his promises so that his future promises will be valuable. As with an individual, a government's credit rating may be a liability or an asset. Routinely complying with a particular kind of obligation gives a government a reputation which it may be able to use to good advantage in the future. For example, Finland was able to borrow considerable sums abroad after World War II because it had paid its debts after World War I. Routinely failing to respect treaties or to pay debts tends to deprive a government of its ability to negotiate new treaties and to obtain new credit.

In an English case in which the Portuguese Government had successfully pleaded sovereign immunity to a claim for services rendered by three Liverpool tugboat owners who had pulled its ship when it ran aground, L. J. Scrutton referred to the problem of governments that fail to honor their legal obligations:

> If ships of the state find themselves left on the mud because no one will salve them when the State refuses any legal remedy for salvage, their owners will be apt to change their views. If the owners of cargoes on national ships find that the ship runs away and leaves them to bear all the expenses of salvage, as has been done

[3]Concluded by Exchange of Notes at Washington and Havana, Feb. 15, 1973, 67 Am. J. Int'l L. 619–20 (1973).

in this case, there may be found a difficulty in getting cargoes for national ships.[4]

Governments have, however, a remarkable ability to compartmentalize their reputations. A government is able to distinguish between a category of cases in which it routinely respects its legal obligations from other categories in which respecting its legal obligations may be a problem. It thus develops highly specialized reputations. The refusal of the Soviet Union to pay United Nations assessments for peacekeeping operations[5] did not affect its ability to obtain credit for commercial purchases abroad, since it routinely continued to pay commercial debts as they became due. The Cuban Government under Castro has managed to distinguish between its nonpayment of amounts owing as compensation for property taken from the problem of future payments for purchases of new buses and other equipment.

A government is also often able to distinguish between violations of international law committed under prior administrations and its successors. No doubt some governments have such a reputation of international irresponsibility that it handicaps their ability to work out new treaties in any area whatsoever. The greatest impact, however, of a government's concern for its reputation would appear to be in special areas such as commercial credit. Here, there are a large number of transactions of a closely similar nature. One study of these problems concludes:

> Any state that wishes to continue peaceful economic relations with the rest of the world and that, in particular, wishes to keep open the possibility of financing by foreign and international institutions, such as the United States Export-Import Bank or the World Bank, will be very careful to honor promises specifically

---

[4] The Porto Alexandre, [1918–19] All E.R. 615, 619.

[5] The Russians disputed the legality of the expenses incurred by the United Nations in regard to the United Nations Emergency Force (UNEF) and Opérations des Nations Unies au Congo (ONUC). For their legal stand on the issue, see Letter from the Acting Permanent Representative of the Union of Soviet Socialist Republics addressed to the Secretary-General (dated Sept. 11, 1964), transmitting a Memorandum entitled The Question on the Financial Situation of the United Nations, 19 U.N. GAOR, 2 Annexes (Agenda Item 21) 9, U.N. Doc. A / 5729 (1964). *But see* the reply of the United States Government in Letter from the Permanent Representative of the United States to the United Nations addressed to the Secretary General (dated Oct. 8, 1964), transmitting a Memorandum entitled The United Nations Financial Crisis, *id.* at 16.

given, even though the breach would not entail any legal sanctions in the strict sense.[6]

The short-run advantage of refusing to pay one debt is likely to be outweighed by the almost immediate inability to get credit in a larger amount.

In considering what might be done to strengthen this force for compliance, the analogy with a private credit rating suggests that some form of international Dun & Bradstreet might help. There are so few governments, however, that at least the commercial credit rating of each of them must be well known among those whose views count most. With respect to other kinds of legal obligations, however, it might conceivably be useful to establish a respected international office which would keep tabs on alleged violations of treaties or other rules of international law. Although in many cases either the facts or the law would be in dispute, a responsible judgment about the circumstances and the degree to which they reflect favorably or adversely on a country's law-abidingness might be given some weight by others in future dealings, and hence would be taken into account by governments themselves. The unwillingness of most international bodies to impose any kind of punishment after the fact would suggest that any such role as here suggested might best be filled by an independent body comparable to the International Commission of Jurists, a nongovernmental organization composed of about thirty well-known and respected international lawyers and judges. In cases of "especial gravity or importance," the Commission members and staff have initiated inquiries on an international scale and have issued reports, such as ones on Hungary and Liberia.[7] Any office to study violations of international law should also have the authority to study disputes or situations on its own initiative, rather than having to await a request from the parties or from an international body.

Attempts to increase the deterrent effect of a bad reputation about some kinds of noncompliance might well not be worth the effort. The circumstances of noncompliance and the justifica-

[6] W. FRIEDMANN & R. PUGH, LEGAL ASPECTS OF FOREIGN INVESTMENT 782 (1959).

[7] INTERNATIONAL COMMISSION OF JURISTS, THE HUNGARIAN SITUATION AND THE RULE OF LAW (1957); INTERNATIONAL COMMISSION OF JURISTS, THE CASSELL CASE: CONTEMPT IN LIBERIA (1961).

tions that will be advanced are extremely varied. It is difficult to generalize even on such a narrow field as a government's record on the payment of its foreign-held bonds. It may be better to direct this technique toward producing second-order compliance — here, toward causing a government to accept and abide by an appropriate way of dealing with its nonpayment, rather than toward deterring nonpayment in the first place. The Foreign Bondholders Protective Council, Inc., in New York operates on this general principle. The Council was formed in 1933 at the suggestion of the United States Government that such an organization was needed for the protection of American holders of foreign securities. Although it tries to convince governments not to default on their bonds, when default does occur, the Council "endeavors to bring about proposals or offers providing for fair and equitable treatment of holders of such bonds as are in default." The organization does not "blacklist" a government for having defaulted on its bonds. It, however, does have strong words in its annual report, which lists all outstanding dollar-bond obligations for any foreign government that has refused to work out or has failed to adhere to a settlement recommended by the Council. Since the report is widely distributed among potential bondholders, governments interested in maintaining their "international credit rating" are usually persuaded to adhere to whatever compromise emerges from negotiations with the Council. The emphasis of the Council is on compliance with the authoritative, negotiated settlement once an original default has occurred — *i.e.*, on second-order compliance.

b. *General reputation.* Fairly distinct from the "credit-rating" kind of reputation that a country has, which affects its ability to enter into new arrangements, is the general esteem in which it is held. It is often said that governments comply with international law because of world public opinion. A good deal of attention has been given by experts to the role of public opinion abroad as it affects a government's decisions in international affairs. It is quite certain that governments regard how they are viewed abroad as important. Both the Soviet Union and the United States, for example, spend a great deal of money and expend a great deal of governmental effort in establishing information and propaganda programs abroad. Many of these programs are directed toward establishing a favorable attitude toward the government that is making the effort. At the same time, governments realize that actions often speak louder than words. A government which is engaged in an expensive effort to create a favorable opinion will not violate international law lightly, if to do so would create a generally unfavorable opinion.

On hundreds of modest questions in which a particular course of conduct might subject a government to a charge of having violated international law, the officials concerned are quite likely to decide not to engage in the particular conduct because of the anticipated adverse effect on world public opinion — without defining either whose opinion would be involved or what the nature of the adverse opinion would be. Top government leaders invariably are politicians, and politicians care about what people think. Where the incentive to violate international law is only slight, fear of a hostile world public opinion may be decisive.

For conduct that a government considers important, however, fear of an adverse public reaction is unlikely to be decisive. Where the issue was keeping Czechoslovakia within the communist orbit, Soviet troops occupied that country in August 1968 despite a major and adverse effect on world public opinion. The arguable ambiguities in international law tend to weaken the deterrent effect of an adverse public opinion which results from a violation. The fear of being branded an aggressor after the fact by newspapers and public speakers, all of whom may be subject to a hostile bias in any event, is likely to be less important than the other stakes involved in any violation which would stir up that much opinion. In addition, while particular actions of a government may be regretted abroad, it may not be difficult to persuade those elites whose opinions are of greatest concern that the action was required — or was deemed required — by the circumstances. Furthermore, information services and other officials of a government can frequently be shifted for the time being to the task of demonstrating that the conduct in question was not a violation of international law. Thus, two days after the disastrous Bay of Pigs invasion of Cuba, the United States representative to the United Nations, Adlai E. Stevenson, argued that "[t]he United States has committed no aggression against Cuba, and no offensive has been launched from Florida or from any other part of the United States."[8] He also accused Castro of denying to the Cuban people the right of self-determination and of seeking to export his revolution illegally throughout Latin America.

Even if the public reaction abroad to a breach of an international rule is "adverse," that reaction is not always seen as inconsistent with the interest of the government that violated the rule. A government may prefer to be thought of as strong, or tough,[9] or as one which stands up to an opponent, or as one which sticks by its allies, rather than as one which respects international law no matter what the consequences.

Increasing the effectiveness of the sanction of world public opinion in support of observing standing rules seems difficult. Here, again, the force should be more effective for causing second-order compliance. Public opinion will get upset more easily over a government's violating a specific decision directed to it by an international authority than over its violating a standing rule about which it can argue. In July 1962 the International Court of Justice determined in its advisory opinion on Certain Expenses of the United Nations that expenses incurred by the United Nations for peacekeeping operations in the Middle East and the Congo constituted expenses of the organization.[10] Even though a small group of states including the Soviet Union and France refused to abide by that ruling and to make their contributions accordingly,[11] nearly thirty other countries, both large

[8] 42 DEP'T STATE BULL. 668 (1961).

[9] On May 15, 1975, President Ford in announcing the action of the U.S. expeditionary force that had been sent to Cambodia to rescue the *Mayaguez* and its crew stated: "At my direction, United States forces tonight boarded the American merchant ship *SS Mayaguez* and landed on the Island of Koh Tang for the purpose of rescuing the crew and the ship, which had been illegally seized by Cambodian forces. They also conducted supporting strikes against nearby military installations." *See* 69 AM. J. INT'L L. 878 (1975). The statement described a classic action of armed self-help, which had been condemned by the International Court of Justice in The Corfu Channel Case, [1949] I.C.J. 35. The American Government almost certainly violated the commands of international law, but in the political climate of South East Asia in the spring of 1975, one month after the fall of Saigon, the U.S. Government placed a higher value on the short-term benefits of looking tough than on the long-term benefits flowing from respect for international law.

[10] Advisory Opinion on Certain Expenses of the United Nations, [1962] I.C.J. 180.

[11] They stressed the advisory character of the Court's opinion and the illegality of the expenses incurred. For details, see [1962] U.N.Y.B. 541–49.

and small, did pay their assessments, which had been withheld until the Court's decision. Once a specific pronouncement by the Court had clarified the standing rule, those nations felt obliged to comply.

3. *Concern with consequential action by other countries.* The respect of governments for norms of international behavior is explained most frequently in terms of "reciprocity." The international community is so structured that even in the absence of any international institutions or central mechanism for decreeing awards and punishments, a government is often induced to comply with international law because the anticipated conduct of one or more other governments if it complies is deemed preferable to their anticipated conduct if it does not. The force of reciprocity is often taken for granted. Yet, it is not at all clear what determines the scope of reciprocal treatment — the unit of reciprocity. Explaining the basis of diplomatic immunity, for instance, the Second Restatement of the Foreign Relations Law of the United States comments that "states recognize that immunity of their diplomatic personnel in other states may be conditional upon a reciprocal grant of immunity to such personnel of the other states."[12] If the law of diplomatic immunity works because of reciprocity, why does international law as a whole not operate in the same way? If a government knew that if it should commit one violation of international law all other governments would violate all of its international rights, the original violation would be most unlikely. No one breach of international law could result in a benefit which would be sufficiently large to outweigh the detriment of having all other countries violate all of a nation's other rights protected by international law. Therefore, the problem of increasing compliance with international law might be looked upon as a problem of broadening the unit of reciprocity from narrow subjects of international law, such as the treatment of diplomats, to international law as a whole.

For present purposes, reciprocity can be considered by looking at the different kinds of responses by other governments that might induce one government to respect a standing rule.

a. *Gaining reciprocal compliance by setting a good example.* In some

[12] RESTATEMENT (SECOND) OF FOREIGN RELATIONS LAW OF THE UNITED STATES § 573, comment *a* at 229 (1965).

instances, the foremost consideration affecting a government's decision to respect an international obligation is setting a good example for other governments. Rather than being motivated by fear of reciprocal noncompliance, a government may be hoping to induce others to do what it is doing. The United States pays its United Nations assessments as much to set an example for other countries as for the fear that, if it does not pay, other countries will not either.

In thinking about what might be done to make better use of this affirmative force for compliance, the idea of an internationally instituted credit-rating system might be explored further, looking here for ways of rewarding good performances rather than for ways of penalizing bad ones. Perhaps the United Nations could induce countries to follow good examples by giving them maximum publicity. Governments concerned with propaganda and image-building might well be affected if there was an international megaphone amplifying their good deeds as well as a hostile press to amplify their misdeeds.

b. *Fear of adverse military or other national reaction.* The existing national deterrent system is undoubtedly important. Rather than representing a model for future expansion, it exemplifies the problem for which the approach to international enforcement, discussed in Part II of this book, is considered to be a substitute.

One point, however, is worth exploring. The hostile political reaction that may be anticipated from breaking a rule of international law often outweighs any incentive to break the rule. A government's dominant interest may be to stay out of trouble. One way to stay out of trouble is to follow the book. The case of the *Santa Maria* is particularly relevant in this regard. A few days after President Kennedy's inauguration, about twenty-five Portuguese revolutionaries boarded the Portuguese liner *Santa Maria* in Venezuela and Curaçao disguised as passengers. When these revolutionaries later seized the ship on the high seas and threatened to take it to Angola or elsewhere, the United States was caught between opposing political forces. American passengers were on board and United States officials were concerned about their health and safety. Portugal identified those who seized the ship as pirates and called on the United States and other maritime powers to do their duty under international law — *i.e.*, to aid the Portuguese Government in recapturing the ship and bringing the rebels to justice. At this point, any step the United States took would be likely to offend either the Portuguese Government or the rebel movement and its political supporters — unless a particular course of American action was required by international law. The Navy first believed that such a course of action was required and announced that it was sending ships from Puerto Rico to intercept the *Santa Maria* "under well-defined terms of international law governing piracy and insurrection aboard ship." Here, international law, like a seniority system or the rules of diplomatic protocol, provided an answer to a troublesome problem. The law, however, was not as the Navy first thought it. The *Santa Maria's* capture was an act of political insurrection against the regime of Portuguese dictator, Premier Salazar, and not a seizure of property for private ends. And, it is clear that under international law action taken for political purposes is not piracy.[13] The United States had no obligation to seize the ship, which eventually surrendered itself — to be dealt with according to international law — at a Brazilian port. When there is not strong incentive toward one course of action or another, as it appeared in this case, following the book will often seem the wisest course of action.

c. *Fear of reciprocal noncompliance with the same obligation.* In the existing international community, there are some generally understood but quite vague rules about what the law is when the law gets broken. At one extreme is the case of a bilateral treaty which sets up some special obligations understood to be reciprocal. For example, France has granted American nationals the right to engage in "all types of commercial, industrial, financial and other activities" within French territory on the same basis as French nationals, and the United States has granted French na-

---

[13] Article 15, ¶ 1 of the Geneva Convention on the High Seas, April 29, 1958, 13 U.S.T. 2312, T.I.A.S. No. 5200, 450 U.N.T.S. 82, provides: "Piracy consists of any of the following acts: (1) Any illegal acts of violence, detention or any act of depredation, committed for private ends by the crew or the passengers of a private ship or a private aircraft, and directed: (a) On the high seas, against another ship or aircraft, or against persons or property on board such ship or aircraft; (b) Against a ship, aircraft, persons or property in a place outside the jurisdiction of any State." For a legal analysis of the case of the *Santa Maria*, see Green, *The* Santa Maria: *Rebels or Pirates*, 27 BRIT. Y.B. INT'L L. 496 (1961).

tionals similar rights.[14] Such a treaty might be compared with a sales contract in domestic law. If one of the parties violates the treaty in a substantial way — *e.g.*, French officials systematically refuse to permit American nationals to open stores in Paris — the other party is "allowed" to rescind the treaty and call the whole thing off. At the other extreme are universal rules of international law. In such a case, a violation by one country ought not to justify other countries' breaking the same rule. If Country *A* commits an aggression against its neighbors, this aggression does not justify Country *B*'s committing an aggression against its neighbors. (The first aggression might justify some countries' resorting to arms in self-defense.)

There is no doubt that the general cloak of legitimacy which surrounds reciprocal noncompliance makes the implied threat of it quite likely. And there is no doubt that where conduct will become known to other countries, a government which wishes a rule to stay in effect may be caused to respect a rule by fear of reciprocal noncompliance. This is probably true in regard to compliance with the international humanitarian law of armed conflicts. But, for many rules, this threat is insignificant. In a domestic setting, the threat that if one litters the roadside others will follow suit is likely to be an ineffective deterrent, even though it is believed to be true. Similarly, oil tankers might ignore the International Convention for the Prevention of Pollution of the Seas by Oil and discharge oily ballast in prohibited zones.[15] The short-run benefit from littering or getting rid of oily ballast outweighs, at least for the violator, the marginal contribution of his illegal act toward long-range damage.

Further, for the country that wants a rule abolished or drastically changed, the threat of tit for tat will be as ineffective as the threat of throwing Br'er Rabbit into the briar patch. If such a country can persuade others to disregard a rule by disregarding it itself, it will find its conduct being rewarded rather than punished. Thus, the Declaration of Santiago on the Maritime Zone signed in August 1952 by Chile, Ecuador, and Peru assert-

[14]Convention of Establishment with France, Nov. 28, 1959, United States–France, art. 5 (1), 3 U.S.T. 2398, T.I.A.S. No. 4625.

[15]International Convention for the Prevention of Pollution of the Seas by Oil, May 12, 1954, 3 U.S.T. 2989, T.I.A.S. No. 4900, 327 U.N.T.S. 3.

ing "exclusive sovereignty and jurisdiction . . . over the ocean adjacent to the coasts of their respective countries up to a minimum distance of 200 maritime miles"[16] was, at that time, a blatant violation of the customary law of the sea. It created the risk — which since then has materialized — that other countries also would violate the customary law of the sea and exercise their own national power over large adjacent parts of the ocean. This risk of reciprocal noncompliance was not a deterrent to Chile, Ecuador, and Peru, which wanted the old law changed.

Another example is provided by the formal notice of the denunciation of the Warsaw Convention by the United States on November 15, 1965, because, in the view of the United States, the Convention unduly limited liability arising from air accidents.[17] Satisfied with a substantial increase (from \$8,300 to \$75,000 per person) of the limits of international carrier liability, the United States Government decided to continue its adherence to the Warsaw Convention.[18] If the denunciation had gone into effect, there is no doubt that United States officials would have welcomed other countries' joining its refusal to participate in the Convention's restrictive provisions. One of the major difficulties with the threat of reciprocal noncompliance is that it tends to be destructive of the rules. Often, instead of open repudiation, the first "violation" is in fact a dispute. It is a unilateral determination by one adversary that certain conduct justifies its own noncompliance. The response of noncompliance is frequently more serious than the alleged violation and often results in an escalating series of breaches of the disputed provisions. The Arab-Israeli conflict has provided examples of this action-reaction cycle.[19] An impartial determination in such cases would be a major step forward. An authoritative decision by someone

[16] Declaration of Santiago on the Maritime Zone, Aug. 1952, *reprinted in Hearings on H. R. 9584 Before the Comm. on Merchant Marine and Fisheries*, 83d Cong., 2d Sess. 33 (1954). *Cf.* 4 M. WHITEMAN, DIGEST OF INTERNATIONAL LAW 69 (1965).

[17] *See* in relevant part, the press release issued by the Department of State, 60 AM. J. INT'L L. 395–96 (1966).

[18] *See* the State Department Announcement of May 13, 1966, *id.* at 824–26. For details, see Lowenfeld & Mendelsohn, *The United States and the Warsaw Convention*, 80 HARV. L. REV. 497 (1967).

[19] *See, e.g.*, Falk, *The Beirut Raid and International Law of Retaliation*, 63 AM. J. INT'L L. 415 (1969).

would help eliminate those cases in which one country's alleged noncompliance is used by another to excuse even greater noncompliance.

d. *Fear of general disregard of law.* A government may be induced to comply with international law by fear of the consequences of a general breakdown of law and order. If one country breaks some rules, other countries may break other rules, and the situation may go from bad to worse.

The effect of this kind of reciprocal breakdown of law and order is difficult to measure. It quite likely plays a role in the thinking of government officials but, probably, rarely deters a particular breach of law which otherwise seems desirable. The threat is too remote and uncertain. A government's ability to obscure the facts or argue about the law is such that no one instance of alleged noncompliance with a standing rule of international law would be likely to trigger any general breakdown of law. The international game might get a little rougher, but such a foreseeable consequence is neither so serious nor so likely that it can be counted on to affect the conduct of many governments.

In considering how the existing pressure of reciprocity might be improved to produce even greater compliance with international law, one again shifts to the objective of second-order compliance. Where the standing rules are subject to argument, where the original "violation" may in fact be compliance, and where each country is the judge of how much noncompliance would be reciprocal and how much would be justified, reciprocity has built-in limits. Also, the rules affect different countries so unequally that disregard of the "same" rule may or may not be an effective threat.

If reciprocity could be shifted from reciprocal respect for each substantive rule to reciprocal respect for international decisions, then the force of reciprocity might be effectively marshaled in support of compliance. Each government might respect the decisions of the International Court of Justice, for example, because it would lose less in the particular case than it could expect to gain from reciprocal respect for such decisions by other countries.

CHAPTER VII

Internal Forces for
First-Order Compliance

1. *A general approach.* The most important steps that can be taken to cause governments to respect standing rules of international law are those which can be taken within each country. International agreements when supplemented by domestic legislation are more effective than any such agreement standing alone.[1] Just as a government has an interest in entering into a treaty, it similarly has an interest in implementing its own compliance. The kinds of measures discussed in this chapter might be undertaken unilaterally, by agreement with other countries, or as part of a general program of strengthening the forces for compliance with international law. The general approach should be politically acceptable since most governments would rather tie their own hands than have them tied in an equally effective manner by someone else. The willingness of a government to tie its own hands in a particular case is likely to depend primarily upon the substance of the rule and somewhat upon similar activity by other governments. The ability of a government to tie its own hands effectively will vary greatly from government to government, depending upon its domestic institutions and upon the degree to which that government is restrained by legal limits.

Two problems of definition should be identified. One problem results from a deliberate blurring of any distinction between international and domestic rules. This chapter suggests that one of the best ways of causing respect for international law is to make it indistinguishable from domestic law. Rules that may be adopted because of their effect on the international relations of governments — or that may exist already as public international law — ought, I believe, to be incorporated in domestic legislation

---

[1] Furthermore, this avoids the problem of determining which treaties are self-executing and which require implementing legislation.

so that they in fact become domestic law. If diplomats are to be exempt from domestic taxation, not only should an international treaty say so, but the tax code also should so stipulate. A conscious effort to blur the distinction between international rules and domestic rules makes it difficult to speak precisely of an "international" rule as contrasted with a "domestic" one.[2] Since we are primarily concerned with the practical results that legal and other techniques have on governmental behavior and not on preserving a theoretical distinction between different levels of authority, the definitional problem will not bother us so long as confusion can be avoided about the practical measures that might be undertaken.

If the distinction between international rules and domestic rules is blurred, it becomes necessary to define the concept of first-order compliance to fit both kinds of rules. In international law theory there has always been a problem of whether a government which improperly injured an alien and then compensated him adequately had or had not violated international law. Would the careless running over of a Frenchman by a United States Post Office truck, for example, constitute a violation of international law? According to traditional theory, there would be no violation unless the United States refused the victim access to its courts or unless the court rendered an evidently unjust decision because of corruption, threats, unwarrantable delay, or some similar abuse of the judicial process — a "denial of justice."[3] Similarly, if a country expropriates the property of aliens and fails to pay just compensation, international lawyers usually maintain that the wrong, if there is one, arises from the failure to make amends, not from the act of expropriation. In both situations, the claim by the alien's government of an international wrong is conditional on the alien's having first attempted to gain satisfaction through the local courts or administrative bodies of the expropriating state, that is, upon having exhausted local remedies.[4]

[2] This practical suggestion is made regardless of the philosophical explanation given the relationship between international and internal law by the "monistic" and "dualistic" schools of thought.

[3] *See, e.g.,* J. BRIERLY, THE LAW OF NATIONS 281 (6th ed. H. Waldock 1963).

[4] Giving the rationale of this rule in the Interhandel Case, the International Court of Justice held that "[b]efore resort may be had to an international court in such a situation,

To avoid confusion, the concept of "first-order compliance" is used here to refer to initial governmental respect for a standing rule of law, whether that rule be domestic (*e.g.*, postal trucks must not drive negligently) or international (*e.g.*, aliens must receive compensation for expropriated property).

In examining the domestic aspects of causing first-order compliance, it may be useful to look first at what may be done to alter an individual's internal motivation, such as his attitude, values, conscience, and sense of duty. We can then consider what might be done within a country to affect a rational calculation of the advantages and disadvantages of compliance both for the government and for individuals, and, finally, what might be done within a country to make noncompliance more diffcult.

2. *Affecting what people want to do.* Basic perceptions of the world, of what is right and wrong, of what is desirable and of what is undesirable, are shaped primarily for any given government by considerations other than the law. Family, schools, cultural attitudes, and the implicit assumptions of any society are subject to change, but not primarily through legal tinkering. Education, television, advertising, newspapers, and magazines can affect a country's goals and its ideas about how to attain them. An overall approach to the problem of improving governmental compliance with international law would have to examine seriously what could be done in these nonlegal areas to change the perceptions and the motivations of decision makers and those of the world in general. Here, however, I am concerned principally with legal techniques.

In a consideration of legal and quasi-legal techniques, the basic values of a national society can be taken pretty much as given. The problem of changing what people want to do is largely one of identifying the objectives of international law enforcement with motivations that already exist.

3. *Adopting international rules as ones to be respected.* Law can be used to sharpen and clarify obligations. Where rules are vague or are thought to be ones of "comity" rather than of law, the fuzziness can be removed. More particularly, where existing rules

---

it has been considered necessary that the State where the violation occurred should have an opportunity to redress it by its own means, within the framework of its own domestic legal system." [1959] I.C.J. 6, 27.

of international law are considered as binding only on governments and not on individuals, steps can be taken to change that understanding.

It is as an educational device that international criminal provisions might be most effective. Although, as discussed earlier, a threat of international criminal prosecution is unlikely to cause a government officer to act contrary to his duty as he sees it, the identification of certain conduct as an international crime may well affect an officer's perception of where his duty lies. Assume, for example, that an officer is thinking about organizing a program to train armed bands to infiltrate and to upset the internal order of a hostile country. The officer will probably think differently of this plan if he knows that the United Nations Draft Code on Offences against the Peace and Security of Mankind, based on the Nuremberg Principles, recognizes as a crime "under international law for which the responsible individuals shall be punished . . . [t]he undertaking or encouragement by the authorities of a state of activities calculated to foment civil strife in another State. . . ."[5]

So long as one is not relying upon them as an effective method of deterring violations, treaties and other methods of identifying violations of international law as crimes for which an individual officer is liable to severe punishment can fulfill a valuable educational role. To avoid some of the problems previously discussed, it would seem wise to have the criminal provisions apply explicitly to government officers and define the proscribed conduct as precisely as possible. It would also seem wise to have the offenses limited to those that were committed "deliberately" by persons who knew, or believed, that the conduct in which they were engaging was illegal. Defenses also should be drawn narrowly and should emphasize the defendant's intent and freedom to make a moral choice. By so doing, government officers would have a better idea of the circumstances under which their compliance with a superior order would entail greater personal responsibility. In addition, such narrowly drafted provisions would serve to identify deliberate, knowing violations of international law as morally reprehensible, without having the prob-

[5] United Nations Draft Code of Offences Against the Peace and Security of Mankind, *reprinted in* THE WORK OF THE INTERNATIONAL LAW COMMISSION 83 (rev. ed. 1972).

able failure of prosecutions for such violations undercut respect for the law. Presumably most, if not all, of those violations which occurred would be justified on the ground that the individual concerned thought for some reason that his conduct was lawful. In such a context, seeking civil relief for future conduct, rather than criminal punishment for past conduct, would be generally accepted as appropriate.

Although treaties are the obvious method of identifying violations of designated international rules as "bad" conduct in which an officer should not engage, other international means are available. In the case of Nazi war crimes, the four major Allied powers signed in August 1945 the London Agreement,[6] which established the International Military Tribunal and gave it jurisdiction over "existing" international crimes — i.e., crimes against peace, war crimes, and crimes against humanity.[7] This precedent lays the foundation on the international level for further clarification or progressive development of "existing " law under which an individual is subject to criminal penalties for failing to comply with international rules, whatever might be the domestic law in his country. Although the movement in this direction would probably be centered in the International Law Commission and the General Assembly of the United Nations, this activity could also take place in ad hoc conferences attended by both governmental and perhaps even nongovernmental representatives.[8]

Sharpening and clarifying international rules and emphasizing that such rules are directly applicable to individuals tend to produce compliance both by identifying noncompliance as "bad" and by providing ready-made answers to problems that arise. For example, a typical bureaucrat (like the rest of us) looks for a course of conduct which he may justifiably adopt without having to make an independent decision himself. Decisions tend

[6] The London Agreement, Aug. 8, 1945, 59 Stat. 1544, E.A.S. No. 472, 82 U.N.T.S. 279.

[7] See INT'L MIL. TRIBUNAL CHARTER art. 6, reprinted in 3 C. BEVANS, TREATIES AND OTHER INTERNATIONAL AGREEMENTS OF THE UNITED STATES OF AMERICA 1240–47 (1969).

[8] Other measures also deserve special attention. See, e.g., Technical assistance to promote the teaching, study, dissemination and wider appreciation of international law, G.A. Res. 2099, 20 U.N. GAOR, Supp. (No. 14) 89, U.N. Doc. A / 6014 (1965).

to be painful. Bureaucracy thrives on standing operating procedures. By taking these attitudes into account, international
rules that deal clearly and explicitly with designated situations
will tend to produce complicance automatically. Indeed, the War
Office (now Ministry of Defence) of the United Kingdom appears to have recognized this point, at least with respect to a
rather unique bureaucracy — the army. Part III of its Manual of
Military Law is entitled "The Law of War on Land"[9] and was
written by Hersch Lauterpacht while he was still a well-known
professor of international law and before he became a judge of
the International Court of Justice. In six hundred and ninety-
four paragraphs, ranging from "The Opening of Hostilities" to
"Rights and Duties of Neutral States and Persons," Lauterpacht
stated the international rules of war on land in a simple and direct manner. The Manual begins by explaining in paragraph I
that the laws of war "are binding not only upon States as such
but also upon their nationals, and, in particular, upon the individual members of their armed forces."[10] The Ministry of Defence has distributed this manual widely and supplies looseleaf
supplements with new international conventions and rules to be
followed. By providing clear-cut answers to some of the difficult
questions facing military officers as well as the text of numerous
international conventions, the Manual promotes compliance
with these particular international rules. When a British army
officer needs an answer to a specific problem relating to the conduct of war, he knows where to look and will be more likely to
follow the international standard because it is readily available
to him.

4. *Blending international rules into the domestic legal fabric.* As
stated above, the force of an international legal norm upon a
government officer is greatly increased if that rule becomes one
of domestic law. Government officers, in general, are not certain
that they ought to comply with international law. They apparently operate on the assumption that it is frequently right for a
government to take international law into its own hands. But a

---

[9]COMMAND OF THE ARMY COUNCIL: THE WAR OFFICE, THE LAW OF WAR ON LAND (3
MANUAL OF MILITARY LAW) (1958).
[10]*Id.* at para. 1.

government officer rarely believes that he ought to take domestic law into his own hands. Converting an international legal obligation into a domestic one drastically increases the forces toward first-order compliance.

Some governments on the domestic level are more law-abiding than others, but every sizable government operates according to rules. The functions of government cannot be carried on in a state of anarchy, nor by a wholly ad hoc series of decisions. A major technique of producing respect for standing rules of international law is to weave those rules into each government's domestic legal system. Every government office acts according to some book; the goal of the promoter of international law should be to have his rules written in *that* book. In some countries, these rules may be found in the constitution or the statutes at large. In other countries, they may be the precepts of the party constitution as elaborated by the current party line. But, wherever the rules are that are considered authoritative and binding by government officials, as well as by the man in the street, that is the place where the international rules should be incorporated to obtain the highest probability of initial compliance. To the extent that "international" obligations become indistinguishable from "domestic" ones, an officer's perception of his duty — of what ought to be done and what ought not to be done — will apply indiscriminately to both. The international rules will have been placed in a general category where initial compliance tends to be automatic. Patriotism and national loyalty will be aligned on the side of compliance.

A large number of international rules have already been written into the domestic law of the United States and of other countries as well. Many of these rules, as international obligations, are unwritten. Writing international rules into domestic law lets people know that these obligations are ones which ought to be respected. Great Britain, for example, implemented the Convention on the Privileges and Immunities of the United Nations[11] and the International Court of Justice by issuing an Order in Council making that Convention a part of domestic

---

[11] Convention on the Privileges and Immunities of the United Nations, Feb. 13, 1946, 21 U.S.T. 1418, T.I.A.S. No. 6900.

law.[12] Also, in the Geneva Conventions Act, 1957,[13] it is provided that "grave breaches" of the international rules contained in the four Geneva Conventions of 1949[14] are punishable as domestic offenses by the British courts.

In the case of the United States, examples of making international norms part of domestic law include provisions against the counterfeiting of foreign obligations or securities[15] or postage or revenue stamps;[16] against launching an expedition against a friendly nation[17] or other violations of neutrality;[18] and against the export of narcotics to any country that is not a party to the International Opium Convention.[19] Anyone committing on the high seas "the crimes of piracy as defined by the law of nations" is subject to the punishment if he is afterwards brought into or found in the United States.[20] The United States also makes it an offense for anyone

> being the owner, master or person in charge or command of any private vessel, foreign or domestic, or a member of the crew or other person, within the territorial waters of the United States ... [to] knowingly ... [permit] said vessel to be used as a place of resort for any person conspiring with another or preparing to commit any offense ... in violation of the treaties of the United

[12] The Diplomatic Privileges (United Nations and International Court of Justice) Order in Council, 1947, 1 STAT. R & O & STAT. INST. REV. 520 (No. 1772).

[13] Geneva Conventions Act, 1957, 5 & 6 Eliz. 2, c. 52, § 1.

[14] Geneva Convention for the Amelioration of the Condition of the Wounded and Sick in Armed Forces in the Field, Aug. 12, 1949, 6 U.S.T. 3114, T.I.A.S. No. 3362, 75 U.N.T.S. 31; Geneva Convention for the Amelioration of the Condition of Wounded, Sick and Shipwrecked Members of Armed Forces at Sea, Aug. 12, 1949, 6 U.S.T. 3217, T.I.A.S. No. 3363, 75 U.N.T.S. 85; Geneva Convention Relative to the Treatment of Prisoners of War, Aug. 12, 1949, 6 U.S.T. 3316, T.I.A.S. No. 3364, 75 U.N.T.S. 135; Geneva Convention Relative to the Protection of Civilian Persons in Time of War, Aug. 12, 1949, 6 U.S.T. 3516, T.I.A.S. No. 3365, 75 U.N.T.S. 287 [hereinafter cited as Geneva Conventions].

[15] 18 U.S.C. § 478 (1970).

[16] 18 U.S.C. § 502 (1970).

[17] 18 U.S.C. § 960 (1970).

[18] 22 U.S.C. §§ 461–65 (1970).

[19] 21 U.S.C. § 953(a) (1) (A) (1970). See also International Opium Convention, Jan. 23, 1912, 38 Stat. 1912, T.S. No. 612, 8 L.N.T.S. 187; Protocol Amending Agreements, Conventions, and Protocols on Narcotic Drugs, Dec. 11, 1946, 61 Stat. 2230, 72 Stat. 1796, T.I.A.S. No. 1671, 1859, 12 U.N.T.S. 179.

[20] 18 U.S.C. § 1651 (1970).

States or of the obligations of the United States under the law of nations. . . .[21]

In addition, the Uniform Code of Military Justice contains a number of the rules of international law, such as the one forbidding looting or pillaging.[22] In 1975 President Ford signed Public Law 94–131, "To carry into effect certain provisions of the Patent Cooperation Treaty, and for other purposes."[23] By identifying an obligation as coming from one's own government, there is a greater chance to exploit the instinctive desire to comply on the part of those officers who have the power to cause a governmental violation.

5. *Taking rules seriously.* To define an international rule as one which ought to be respected by individual officers and even to incorporate that rule into domestic law may not be enough to convince an officer that the particular rule is one with which he really wants to comply. There is so much legal window dressing in existence that most of us, particularly government officers, can readily distinguish rules that are important and ought to be respected from those which are nominal. A rule will have a greater educational role if it has the indicia of being taken seriously.

The most important mark of taking a rule seriously is that there is some governmental agency or office charged with administering and implementing the law. Active people concerned with producing first-order compliance will tend to educate others to the fact that this rule is one with which they want to comply. Questionnaires, explanatory pamphlets, interviews, and periodic reports all tend to prevent a rule's becoming a dead letter. Where the provisions of a particular law, such as the Geneva Conventions on the rules of war,[24] are complex and detailed, training programs on the content of those rules might be both desirable and effective. Professor Richard R. Baxter has suggested having periodic internationally administered tests, on a

---

[21] 18 U.S.C. § 2274 (1970).

[22] Uniform Code of Military Justice, Articles of War, art. 103, 10 U.S.C. § 903 (1970).

[23] Patent Cooperation Act, Pub. L. No. 94–131, 89 Stat. 685 (codified in scattered sections of 35 U.S.C. (1970)).

[24] Geneva Conventions, note 14 *supra.*

random basis, to determine how well the soldiers of different countries know the Geneva Conventions, pointing out that "[t]he man who is well schooled in the conventions will find it harder to violate them, even though he is told to do so, than the man who has only a shaky knowledge of their contents."[25] Supplemental devices that might be considered would be special oaths to comply with certain rules, sworn reports that to the best of one's knowledge no violation had occurred, requests to the officers concerned for their recommendations regarding any change in the rules, and so forth. Such actions tend to show that one's own government is taking the rule seriously and is desirous of having the rule respected. When schooled on the need for such first-order compliance, most officers probably will accept such rules as governmental policy and will identify those rules as what they want.

6. *Making noncompliance unreasonable.* Just as a government and an official may be induced to comply with a rule by a rational calculation of the *international* consequences of compliance and noncompliance, so may they be persuaded by the *domestic* consequences of such actions. There are four variables to be taken into account in calculating the consequences of compliance and noncompliance with a legal rule: (1) the advantages and (2) the offsetting disadvantages anticipated if the rule is respected, weighed against (3) the advantages and (4) the offsetting disadvantages if the rule is not respected. Although it may be possible to improve compliance by affecting any one of these variables, legal techniques tend to concentrate on the side of noncompliance, seeking to frustrate the anticipated advantages and increase the disadvantages. Methods of frustrating the anticpated advantages are discussed in Part II, which considers what can be done after a violation has occurred. We have already considered in Chapters III and IV the weaknesses of a system which seeks to deter noncompliance by threats of formal punishment of either governments or individual officials. Chapter VI considered the technique by which automatic costs of noncompliance can be built into the *international* system. We here consider what kinds of automatic costs might be built into the *domestic* frame-

[25] Baxter, *Forces for Compliance with the Law of War,* 58 AM. SOC'Y INT'L L. PROC. 82, 86 (1964).

work, both from the point of view of the government as a unit and from that of an individual officer.

a. *Increasing the domestic costs to a government of noncompliance.* A government pays a price domestically for reversing a policy and for breaking the law. It may be possible to identify an international rule so strongly with governmental policy or with domestic law as to make these internal costs a significant deterrent in support of international law.

Anyone who has worked in a government can vouch for the attention that is given to prior statements of policy. When a government becomes committed to an existing policy, it usually believes that a reversal of that policy will cost it something with its own constituency. The government will be criticized; it will lose popular support; it will have to admit that its prior policy was wrong; and so forth. Although these fears are often exaggerated, they certainly exist and generally appear to be quite strong. To be most effective, a government must have popular support which, in turn, depends upon some understanding, at least among elite groups, of what the government is trying to do. It is not coincidence that political organizations have platforms, policies, and programs. Nor is it coincidence that a great deal of effort is spent to demonstrate the continuity and consistency over time of the policies being pursued. The political successors of Lincoln, of Franklin D. Roosevelt, and of Lenin insisted that in each case they were carrying on with the same basic policies. Foreign policies, such as Atlantic unity or support for the United Nations, develop domestic constituencies. Governments and other political bodies believe that they would lose support or pay some other domestic political price if they announced that on a matter of policy which previously was firmly held they had changed their mind and were going off in a new direction.[26] Even where a change in policy is necessary, governments will usually prefer to present the new policy as simply an "updating" or minor modification of the old one.

To the extent that this is so, a government's tendency to comply with an international rule will be increased by identifying

[26] Witness the difficulty the United States has had in considering the Peking government rather than the Taipei government as the Government of China.

that rule as being in furtherance of a policy to which the government is strongly committed. The rhetoric of "peaceful coexistence" may be sufficiently vague so as not to impose a significant restraint on the conduct of those governments which have professed the policy. Explicit international engagements that get tied up in governmental policy become more difficult to escape. The Moscow Test Ban Treaty of 1963[27] and the Non-Proliferation Treaty of 1968,[28] for instance, have been hailed loudly and publicly by both the United States and the Soviet Union. We can sense in this country that domestic political considerations would be a major factor tending to deter an administration from violating either of these treaties. Having convinced the majority of the people that the treaties represent stepping-stones on the road toward peace and essential elements in furtherance of major policies, the government would pay a significant price domestically in breaking them.

Any government that devotes as much attention to doctrine and propaganda as does the Soviet Union must also become, to some extent, the prisoner of its own words. The government buys popular enthusiasm, conviction, and support for present policies at the cost of limiting the freedom with which it can change them. The importance of doctrine to the Soviet Union is demonstrated by the fact that the current Sino-Soviet controversy in the communist world is not exclusively nor even primarily over proposals for immediate action, but rather over doctrine as such. The strength of the necessity felt by China and the Soviet Union to conform to prior policies is suggested by their repeated efforts to demonstrate that their current actions are consistent with those policies.

Not every rule of international law can be made of such domestic political importance that a government will be deterred from breaking it. On a limited number of important restrictions, however, governments often can inadvertently tie their own hands by domestic political commitment. One government also can affect, to some degree, the domestic political commitment of another government. For example, having the Test Ban

[27] Treaty Banning Nuclear Weapon Tests, Aug. 5, 1963, 14 U.S.T. 1313, T.I.A.S. No. 5433, 480 U.N.T.S. 43.
[28] Non-Proliferation Treaty, July 1, 1968, 21 U.S.T. 483, T.I.A.S. No. 6839.

Treaty signed in Moscow, rather than in a Western capital, built in a modest, additional Soviet commitment to the treaty. Publicly recognizing the important role that another government has played in proposing and negotiating a treaty, or identifying the treaty as demonstrating the success of one of their policies, is likely to promote additional political commitment to that treaty. One can surmise that if a large granite monument to the Test Ban Treaty were built in Red Square, with quotations of Soviet military and political leaders in support of the treaty chiseled into the stone, the domestic political embarrassment of breaking the treaty might be increased further. To be sure, policies can be changed. Stalin's body can be removed from Red Square; monuments, like pictures, can be taken down. The domestic political commitment to an international rule is nonetheless significant. It would seem worth exploring other ways of strengthening such commitment.

The political cost to a government of reversing a policy is quite different from the cost that results from a government's demonstrating its own lack of respect for domestic law. If international legal obligations are woven into the fabric of domestic law, a government cannot disregard them without worrying about the problem of inducing defiance of the law in other areas by other people. A government needs internal rules to be effective. Its strength depends upon a rule-abiding tradition and attitude. It becomes risky for a government to let rule compliance erode too far. If a government decides that its officers should violate certain statutes and legal restrictions in one case, it then runs the risk that they and others will decide to violate the same or other rules in other cases. International obligations are not inherently different from domestic ones. Once an international obligation is incorporated into our domestic law, it becomes a domestic obligation. We tend to comply with it, no matter who benefits directly and no matter how remote might be the indirect benefit to this country. The international obligation that the United States must pay just compensation to aliens if it takes their property is written into the fifth amendment of our Constitution. An administrative decision by the government to violate this obligation, for example, by seizing houses owned by aliens without paying them anything, would entail domestic costs to the government. The same would be true if government officers decided to counterfeit foreign currency in contravention of the criminal statute prohibiting this activity[29] or to ignore the statute and regulations establishing procedures to assure that livestock exported from the United States is free from communicable diseases.[30] These costs involve eroding the fabric of compliance with law on which the government's own effectiveness rests. If a parent tells his child to answer the phone and say that he is not at home, he risks undermining the child's belief in honesty. If he tells the child to violate secretly rules laid down by the other parent, he is undercutting his own ability to make rules that should not be broken.

If governments tend to exaggerate the political costs of changing a policy, they appear to underestimate the costs involved in governmental illegality. Unlike the political criticism to which a government may become immediately subject upon reversing a policy, the erosion of respect for law, induced by the government's having broken the law, tends to be quiet, delayed, and difficult to prove. If the official illegality can be confined to a designated group, as may frequently be the case with the United States Central Intelligence Agency, a government is likely to pay little or no attention to the intangible cost of inducing disrespect for law. If, however, noncompliance by the government requires the affirmative cooperation of those outside the government, the deterrent effect of this consideration may be more important. The government might well be reluctant to teach business firms to keep two sets of books in order to frustrate international inspectors. The desire to show American governmental respect for statutory law no doubt led to the indictment in October 1968 of nine Cuban exiles charged with violations of the neutrality of the United States by making war against another nation from United States soil.[31]

b. *Increasing the domestic costs to an officer of noncompliance.* As discussed in Chapter IV, it is difficult by threats of criminal punishment to deter an officer who is acting for a public purpose

[29] 18 U.S.C. § 478 (1970).

[30] 21 U.S.C. § 113 (1970). *See also* 9 C.F.R. § 91.4 (1977).

[31] 18 U.S.C. § 960 (1970); N.Y. Times, Oct. 12, 1968, at 8, col. 3. The exiles had fired on a Polish freighter in Miami and had threatened attacks on the ships and planes of other countries continuing to trade with Cuba.

from exceeding his legal authority. On the other hand, like the government as a whole, the individual officer must calculate the consequences of his suggesting or deciding to change an established policy or to engage in prohibited conduct. He may not worry about being prosecuted and convicted, but he is likely to worry about the effect that his suggestion or action might have on his own career.

A government cannot reconsider every question every day. To be effective, the government must proceed in an orderly way and act consistently over a period of time. Other things being equal, a suggestion to change a policy is far more likely to be rejected than accepted. There is also a tendency to identify an individual officer with the position he advanced. A subordinate runs the risk of being considered not only mistaken but incompetent if he frequently makes proposals that are rejected. By suggesting that an existing policy is wrong or that a statute should be violated, an officer subjects himself to being considered odd, unsound, or disloyal. The more firmly imbedded an international rule is in the policies and domestic laws of a country, the greater will be the political risks to any officer who suggests departing from that rule.

Rigidities of governmental policy can be built into the system. The substantial pressures toward conformity of expressed opinion that exist in all governments, even the most talkative, can be focused in support of particular policies or commitments. The adherence of the United States to the North Atlantic Treaty Organization might be strengthened by a congressional enactment prohibiting the use of any federal funds for studying problems involving our withdrawal from NATO. Such an action would be comparable to the congressional rider that prohibited the disbursement of any federal funds for either private or governmental study of "surrender by the Government of the United States of this country and its people to any foreign power in any event or under any circumstances."[32]

Security procedures also remain a potent weapon. A statute or regulation barring from government service as a security risk any person who belonged to an organization which favored

---

[32] 50 U.S.C. § 407 (1970). *See also* 104 CONG. REC. 17516 (1958) (remarks of Senator Russell).

withdrawal from the United Nations or who personally advocated such a position would tend to make it less reasonable for an official to suggest that the United States break its legal commitments to the United Nations. Even an informal policy of promoting "internationally minded" officials rather than those with an "America-First" bias might have a substantial effect over a period of time in deterring officials from suggesting repudiation of international commitments. Building such rigidities into a government's policy may not be wise in a particular case, just as it may not be wise to enter into a particular treaty or to respect a speed limit. In general, seeking to cause governmental compliance with standing rules by deterring officers from speaking freely against existing policies would seem to be one of the *least* wise methods of law enforcement.

7. *Making noncompliance difficult.* Beyond seeking to make noncompliance undesirable and unreasonable, one can seek to make it difficult. This technique of inducing respect for rules by making it difficult to break them is frequently used in addition to the technique of deterrence. We not only punish thieves, but we also use locks and safes. A no-parking rule may be enforced in a given area by so designing it that nobody desires to park there, by threatening to impose a five-dollar fine upon anyone who does park there, or by placing concrete pillars in such a way that it is difficult, if not impossible, to park within the prohibited area. We may seek to control a horse by a judicious use of the carrot and the stick — or we may build a fence. And there is much to be said in favor of fences.

One basic limitation on the preventive technique should be noted. The difference between preventing a bad action and requiring a good action is significant. If the rule is that the horse should not leave the pasture, we can enforce it with a fence. But if the rule is that the horse should pull the wagon to market, we must rely on the carrot or the stick. Inaction may be made unreasonable, but it can rarely be made difficult. If the rule is one that requires affirmative action, such as reporting to a draft board or building a dam, the technique of making noncompliance difficult is almost invariably inapplicable.

a. *Making noncompliance difficult for governments.* Governments are legally bound by many provisions of domestic and international law. In general, governments comply with these provisions. Certainly, one important factor tending to cause compliance is that noncompliance by a government is often difficult to bring about.

In some instances, this difficulty is a physical one, comparable to the fence that restrains the horse. In fact, the rule of international law protecting the territory of one country from incursion from its neighboring countries is often enforced by barbed-wire fences and fortifications that make a violation physically difficult. But, such cases are few.

Precautionary rules frequently are intended to make it physically difficult for a government to violate a more basic legal provision. If a country did not have military weapons it would be physically difficult to violate article 2, paragraph 4 of the United Nations Charter prohibiting the use of armed force against another country.[33] Thus, all measures of physical disarmament are designed to make it physically more difficult for a country to wage a large-scale war in violation of the purposes and principles of the United Nations Charter. However, in most instances a government may find that the difficulty in breaking a rule stems from forces which are not international but domestic; not physical but institutional.

The most interesting institutional method of making noncompliance difficult is to construct a situation which requires the cooperation of two or more people to break the rule. Assuming that the rule is made to run to individuals, we might seek to induce each individual to comply with this standing rule by the various techniques previously discussed, such as altering his perception of his duty and making it unreasonable for him to attempt to break the rule. However, the situation might, in addition, be so arranged that it will take joint and simultaneous illegal action to succeed in breaking the rule.

The simplest example of such a situation is that of the grocery-store safe which requires two keys to open it; each key being given to a different employee who is supposed to keep it with him at all times. Compliance with the rule against embezzling funds is thus made increasingly likely. To embezzle the money

---

[33] U.N. CHARTER art. 2, para. 4.

will require the joint, illegal conduct of two trusted employees. Either employee, in suggesting embezzlement to the other, runs a substantial risk. Neither has it in his power to break the rule alone.

A government is a collective enterprise. Affirmative action usually requires the participation of several different persons. By dividing responsibility and establishing procedural hurdles, the affirmative participation of a large number of individuals is required for governmental action. Institutional methods of making noncompliance difficult for a government thus tend to supplement those forces which make noncompliance unreasonable. In order to foster maximum compliance with an international rule, that rule should be so woven into domestic legal arrangements that it would be an insurmountable task to take the steps necessary to change the domestic law or to get the proper authorizations for the particular activity. Then, for one officer or a handful to undertake an "illegal" violation of the rules would be both difficult and costly.

Every country has its own constitutional limitations and divisions of power that can affect the manner and degree to which it can be effectively tied up by an agreement. For example, in the United States, the President can repudiate a treaty, but not a statute. To maximize the durability of an international agreement to which the United States is a party, other governments would be well advised to ask that the treaty not be considered self-executing but instead be supplemented by full congressional legislation. For this country to disentangle itself from the legal engagement would then require new action by both the House and the Senate with innumerable chances for delay in committee. The procedural steps required to pass an act of Congress provide an opportunity for those who have an interest in the continued respect for the rule to be heard and to become effective.

As suggested above, we already have a number of international rules incorporated in domestic legislation, such as those in the Neutrality Act. Each of these statutes not only makes it embarrassing for the government to violate the rule but tends to make it difficult for the government to reach a decision to do so.

The domestic constitutional requirement that only the Congress can declare war provides an institutional hurdle which, in the past, may have impeded the United States from having engaged in some kinds of aggressive activity.[34] Currently, internal institutional arrangements within our military to prevent the unauthorized use of nuclear weapons may be more significant restrictions than any legal requirements. Other governments today are keenly interested in ensuring that it is difficult for the United States to attack another country, except under certain contingencies. However, the domestic rule that is enforced by institutional hurdles does not correspond precisely to the rule of international law. The American "fail-safe" system assures that nuclear weapons will be used only on explicit command from the President. These weapons would presumably be used even if the President's command were in violation of international law. Nevertheless, command and control techniques do help to prevent "ordinary" governmental violations of international law. The system of requiring two keys for the grocery-store safe has been highly refined and elaborated. As a result, the carrying out of a violation of international law within the governmental bureaucracy has become more difficult and somewhat less likely.

In this country, and in others, the substantive provisions of an international rule can be incorporated not only in constitutions, statutes, and military regulations but also in local legislation. An interesting example of how an international rule can survive its repudiation by the federal government occurred in connection with the Treaty of 1911 between the United States and Japan.[35] A subsequent California statute provided that aliens ineligible for citizenship should be allowed to acquire land only to the extent required by the Treaty, but not otherwise. The Supreme Court of California held that the substantive rule defined by the Treaty continued to be effective in the state even after the Treaty

[34] That requirement was reinforced by the adoption, on Nov. 7, 1973, of Joint Resolution 542 Concerning the War Powers of Congress and the President: H. R. J. Res. 542, 93d Cong., 1st Sess., 87 Stat. 555 (1973). *See Official Documents*, 68 AM. J. INT'L L. 372–76 (1974).

[35] Treaty of Commerce and Navigation, *proclaimed* Apr. 5, 1911, United States–Japan, 37 Stat. 1504, T.S. No. 558.

was repudiated by the United States in 1940. The Treaty rule was unaffected because it had become incorporated in the state's law, and that law was not altered by the subsequent federal repudiation.[36]

b. *Making noncompliance difficult for individuals.* The same division of functions that tends to make a violation of a standing rule difficult for a government also makes it difficult for an individual to do so on his own. As we have already noted, governments are not abstract entities; they are made up of individuals responsible for making and carrying out policy. Much governmental action is such that it automatically requires the cooperation of superiors and subordinates. In a relatively few cases, such as in some military situations, one individual is understood to have the right to make a decision which his subordinates are not to question regardless of how illegal it might seem to them. In these instances, domestic considerations will usually dictate that safeguards be established to prevent abuse. Command and control techniques are designed not only to prevent "governmental" violations of the rule against launching nuclear attack, absent a presidential decision, but also to prevent an individual officer, sane or insane, from making a reality of Peter Bryan George's novel *Red Alert.*[37]

c. *Acceptability of techniques making noncompliance difficult.* An obvious question is whether domestication of international obligations would be acceptable — whether governments would incorporate international rules into their domestic legal systems in such a way as to make it both more unreasonable and more difficult for governments to violate them. Undoubtedly, the leaders of governments themselves will not know the answer to that question until they are confronted with particular proposals in a specific context. In general, most governments would seem to prefer such self-enforcement over the various kinds of international military forces that have been proposed.

With respect to any one government, a limit on the potential effectiveness of weaving international rules into the domestic legal system is the effectiveness of that system. To the extent that a dictator's personal appeal allows him to govern with freedom

---

[36] Palermo v. Stockton Theatres, Inc., 32 Cal.2d 53, 195 P.2d 1 (1948).

[37] *Red Alert* provided the basis for the movie *Dr. Strangelove.*

to change constitutional or legislative provisions, or to ignore them, little compliance with international rules would be provided by according them the same status as domestic law. With skill and luck, the domestication of international rules might, at best, produce compliance comparable to that which governments gives their domestic law. The bigger the country, the more difficult it becomes to run as a one-man show, and the more its rulers must rely on some rules. It seems likely, therefore, that in the larger countries, whose compliance with standing rules is most important for the world, the domestication of international rules would be a significant factor working toward compliance.

To move toward that goal, it would seem possible to have both public and private international groups draft and promote the adoption of international conventions, uniform clauses, and uniform laws dealing with particular subjects. Indeed, two public international bodies have gained recognition for their useful efforts toward the unification of laws and state practices: the Hague Conference of Private International Law[38] and the International Institute for Unification of Private Law (Unidroit).[39] At least three private international bodies could be added: the Institut de Droit International, the International Law Association, and the International Bar Association. The Institut de Droit International has elaborated an impressive number of resolutions on various subjects of public and private international law;[40] the International Law Association also may be credited with commendable achievements.[41] The sustained activity

[38] For details, see Hoogstraten, *La Codification par traités en droit international privé dans le cadre de la Conférence de La Haye*, 133 RECUEIL DES COURS (Hague Academy of International Law) 337 (1967).

[39] For details, see Matteucci, *Introduction a l'étude systématique du droit uniforme*, 91 RECUEIL DES COURS (Hague Academy of International Law) 383 (1957).

[40] A table of those resolutions up to 1973 is published in 55 ANNUAIRE DE L'INSTITUT DE DROIT INTERNATIONAL at LXXXVIII (Session de Centenaire, Rome, 1973). Certain resolutions such as those on nationality, double-taxation matters in which uniform legislation is desirable, proof of foreign laws before national tribunals, renvoi, and extradition have had a significant impact upon the practice of states. For an examination of this problem in a broader context see De Visscher, *La contribution de l'Institut de Droit International au développement du droit international*, INSTITUT DE DROIT INTERNATIONAL, LIVRE DU CENTENAIRE 1873–1973, at 128, especially at 148 (1973).

[41] For an examination of its activity during a century of existence, see Munch, *L'influence de L'International Law Association sur la doctrine et la pratique du droit international*, in THE PRESENT STATE OF INTERNATIONAL LAW 23 (M. Bas ed. 1973).

of the International Bar Association has helped produce the Draft Convention for Taking Evidence and Serving Documents Abroad, the Draft Convention for the Unification of Certain Rules relating to Registration of Ships under Construction, and the Draft Convention on Damage Caused by Foreign Flight Craft to Third Parties on the Surface.

We are still far behind on the unification of national laws and state practices, but there is interest in this approach. Several provinces of Canada, for instance, have enacted the Reciprocal Enforcement of Judgments Act, recommended by the Canadian Commissioners on Uniformity of Legislation.[42] This Canadian legislation is substantially similar to the Uniform Foreign Money-Judgments Recognition Act, which four states in this country enacted after it was adopted by the National Conference of Commissioners on Uniform State Laws.[43] During the process of drafting and adopting their model laws on recognition of foreign money-judgments, the Commissioners of the two countries coordinated their efforts. This example in uniform legislation would seem a promising step not only toward improving and clarifying the law but also toward producing compliance with it. Domestication of international rules helps promote compliance with these rules here and abroad.

[42] *See, e.g.,* Reciprocal Enforcement of Judgments Act, IV 3 G. Rev. Stat. ch. 331 (1960).

[43] *See, e.g.,* Ill. Ann. Stat. ch. 77, §§ 121–29 (Smith-Hurd 1956).

Part II
Second-Order Compliance: Coping with Apparent Noncompliance

Introductory note. As indicated in the introduction to Part I, my view is that an international law enforcement system should concentrate on gaining maximum compliance with decisions that apply the law to particular cases of alleged violations, rather than on causing compliance with the rules of law themselves. Part I has examined the legal and quasi-legal techniques that would tend to cause governments to respect standing rules of international law in the first place and the limitations on those techniques. This part considers the problem of how we should cope with apparent noncompliance with rules of international law — how to produce second-order compliance.

Chapter II, which considered the objectives of compliance, pointed out that when dealing with governments domestic law enforcement machinery has directed its primary effort not toward causing initial respect for standing rules but rather toward coping with instances of noncompliance after they have occurred. The general method has been to obtain an authoritative determination of what should happen next, and to seek compliance with that specific determination. A system which successfully pursues this objective of second-order compliance does reduce the incentive for the initial violation and thereby tends to cause some increased respect for standing rules. Some first-order compliance is thus a fortunate by-product of a system designed as if its sole objective were to cause second-order compliance.

Traditionally, the judicial function has been thought of as separate from the enforcement function. The appropriate tribunal or administrative agency decides what the law is, and then the sheriff or the police see that it is carried out. It would appear, however, that compliance with a decision depends to a large extent — in the case of a government, almost exclusively — on the nature of the decision and how it was reached. If we seek to cause second-order compliance, a great deal of attention must be paid to the process that results in the decision with which we want governments and government officers to comply.

At the outset, it is worth questioning whether the determination is about something that happened in the past or about something that ought not to happen in the future. International enforcement machinery will not be called into play unless something has already happened: a violation of law, an alleged violation, or some conduct that appears to demonstrate an immediate threat. A court is usually called upon to decide an existing dispute arising from facts that have already occurred. On the other hand, second-order compliance, which is our objective, relates to future conduct. At any given time, what has already happened is water over the dam. We are concerned only with what happens hereafter. Once a determination has been reached, the compliance sought is compliance with the express or implied rule for future conduct embodied in that determination. The legitimacy of a determination for the future may well rest on a determination about what happened in the past. Thus, much attention is properly devoted to past conduct. But Part II, as a whole, is concerned with the role that determinations play in affecting future conduct.

The first step in gaining second-order compliance is to obtain an authoritative determination that a violation of international law has, or has not, taken place. Chapter VIII demonstrates that to obtain that determination it is necessary to have both knowledge of governmental conduct and someone to raise the issue of an alleged infringement. Once an appropriate plaintiff with proper "standing" is identified, we consider where his complaint should be brought. Chapter IX explains why the appropriate starting point for pursuing an alleged violation of international law is usually the domestic courts and examines how their procedures could be used. Chapter X explores the relationship that should exist between the domestic courts and current or newly created international institutions. Chapter XI concludes this section by suggesting what could be done to make international institutions acceptable to governments as a means for reaching authoritative determinations on breaches of the rules of international law.

In Chapter XII, we turn from questions of plaintiff and forum to consideration of the choice of defendant. Who should be the object of the proceedings following an alleged infringement of international law? Should decisions be made against no one in particular, against a government, or against an individual officer of a government?

Chapter XIII considers what the content should be of a decision that a violation has, or has not, occurred. Given the kinds of decisions that a tribunal can produce, and the techniques available for framing those decisions, how do we best ensure that a decision will tend to produce compliance?

Finally, we examine in Chapter XIV how a decision should be followed up, and what should be done in the event of noncompliance. Again, each instance of and reason for noncompliance should be treated as a new dispute for judicial consideration and determination.

As elsewhere, I am seeking to articulate the general features of an international law enforcement system toward which we might reasonably be striving. Without trying to prepare a precise blueprint of any one scheme, we shall be exploring the kind of tasks international machinery should be able to perform and the ways by which it might do so.

CHAPTER VIII

Who Raises the Question?

1. *The problem of information.* The legality of a government's conduct cannot be determined until somebody raises a question about it. And, before he can question conduct, he must have some knowledge of it. In recent years, two factors have tended to exaggerate the importance of information-gathering activities to the general problem of causing respect for international law. One factor has been the prominence that discussion of disarmament has assumed among those seeking to improve world order. Disarmament and the strengthening of international law are so frequently discussed together that it is often assumed that they must go hand-in-hand. The second factor has been the general reluctance of the Soviet Union to accept inspection and verification measures and its continued concern for secrecy. We should begin by putting these two considerations in perspective.

Desirable as they each may be, the level of arms and improved methods of causing governments to respect international law are quite independent of each other. Drastic reduction in military forces, such as that by the United States after World War II, may occur for reasons quite unrelated to improvement in methods for making international law effective. On the other hand, the existence of dangerous weapons in large quantitites may make governments more willing to accept international legal machinery than they would be if the situation appeared less critical.

Merging discussion of these distinct problems—disarmament and improving effectiveness of international law — has caused confusion. Emphasis on inspection and verification of disarmament and arms control measures has tended to suggest that comparable agreed inspection methods are needed for any international law enforcement. This is not so, as the subsequent discussion should demonstrate. The factual verification necessary for improved compliance with existing rules of international law is not the same as the information-gathering activities necessary for certain proposed reductions in arms.

The Soviet attitude toward inspection has also given undue importance to the issue of information. Lack of information and a corresponding lack of confidence in compliance have been a stumbling block on many occasions. This, in turn, has fostered the notion that if only there were adequate means of getting information, then there would be adequate compliance. In addition, public and governmental discussion has often assumed that an adequate scheme of verification was not only necessary before accepting various proposed agreements but, if obtained, would be sufficient to cause compliance with them.

a. *Information and first-order compliance.* In Part I we postponed the discussion of the role which information-gathering plays in conventional enforcement theory. Since most discussion of compliance has been directed toward producing initial respect for standing rules, the information problem has been thought of in the same terms. The question frequently has been viewed as one of gathering enough information so that (1) other countries will be assured that compliance with standing rules is taking place, and (2) each government will be deterred from committing any violation by the likelihood of detection. To meet these criteria, the inspection requirements must, in general, be extremely high. One can appreciate the amount of inspection that would be required in the enforcement of international rules by considering what the requirements would be if we sought comparable verification of governmental compliance with domestic legal restrictions. Imagine how much inspection would be necessary to assure us that the Post Office delivered every letter, that no government officer discriminated in hiring practices on the basis of race, that jury lists were fairly drawn, and that the Central Intelligence Agency did no more than it was legally authorized to do.

Further, when information is sought to produce first-order compliance by a deterrent method, the information should be sufficient to persuade not only the prosecutor who initiates the action but also those who must impose the punishment. In the context of an American criminal proceeding, the evidence must be such as to persuade twelve men to reach a unanimous decision to convict "beyond a reasonable doubt." In Chapters III and IV, we considered the difficulties of getting an international imposer of punishment to act following a determination that either a government or an individual violated international law. The amount of evidence necessary to persuade the international punishment-imposer to act is likely to be great indeed.[1]

Even if we assumed that complete information — 100 percent verification of first-order compliance — were possible, and we know that it is not, there are a number of other limitations on the conventional approach to the problem of inspection. Inspection does not equal control. Almost every known violation of the standing rules of international law has been undertaken with full appreciation that the violation would become known. For the government that is willing to engage in known violations, inspection is no deterrent. The problem is not so much one of knowing about violations of standing rules as it is one of failing, as discussed in Chapters V–VIII, to arrange those rules so as to cause maximum compliance with them. In addition, total inspection is not desirable. Absolute freedom for information collection by international or national officials is wholly inconsistent with our notions of privacy and the right to be left alone. The greater the freedom *for* the police, the less the freedom *from* the police. Unlimited inspection to enforce international rules would mean that inspectors, without cause, without a search warrant, and without even a knock on the door, would be free to enter any house or building at any time of day or night. Within the United States, we have recognized that there are things more important than looking for possible violations of the law.

These inherent restrictions on the amount of factual data that a law enforcement system is capable of gathering and on the amount that we would like it to be able to gather limit the effectiveness of the deterrent method of law enforcement. Chapters III and IV suggested that, in most cases, a threat of punishment would be incredible and ineffective, even if there were full knowledge of the facts alleged to constitute a violation. To the extent that those charged with inflicting punishment have less knowledge of those facts, the credibility of the threat is further

[1] For a discussion of the problem from a different perspective see Iklé, *After Detection—What?*, 39 FOREIGN AFF. 208 (1961).

weakened. Thus, informational problems are one more reason to adopt the objective of second-order compliance.

b. *Information and second-order compliance.* We turn now to the specific question with which we are primarily concerned—second-order compliance. To what extent is knowledge about noncompliance required? In one sense, knowledge of facts constituting possible noncompliance is essential to any scheme designed to produce second-order compliance. If no one knows the facts, then no question will be raised, and hence there will be no determination with which to seek compliance. On the other hand, a second-order compliance scheme is designed to deal successfully with instances of alleged noncompliance. Where there are no such instances, the machinery will have no problem with which to deal.

A scheme designed to produce second-order compliance is thus not dependent on the amount of available knowledge about first-order violations. By adopting a more limited objective, we have narrowed the problem to one of settling disputes where disputes exist. In so far as an international law enforcement system adopts the techniques of the civil law, rather than those of criminal law, the law waits for someone to make a complaint. The objective of this enforcement system has become not one of creating more disputes by digging up information about unreported violations but rather one of settling existing disputes. The success of the system will depend upon how well it copes with those complaints and disputes that exist, not on the number of secret violations that are uncovered.

There is no magic in thus doing away with the most difficult aspects of inspection and verification. Rather than reaching the optimistic conclusion that the information is not needed, we are reaching the pessimistic conclusion that the more limited objective of second-order compliance is the one on which an international law enforcement scheme should concentrate, and that the general nature of this scheme is independent of the amount of inspection that takes place. The enforcement system's basic task is to settle disputes and to make its decisions stick. Its services can be supplemented by as much, or as little, inspection as can be arranged. Depending upon how much information is likely to be available, various new restraints may, or may not, be acceptable to governments.

2. *International standing to seek a determination.* Once an alleged violation of international law becomes known, the question arises of who should seek an authoritative determination about what has happened and about what ought to be done. In domestic law, the problem is frequently thought of in terms of who should have legal "standing" to raise questions of various kinds. In an international setting, the issue of standing is partly a question of the institutions that ought to be available and partly a question of the rules about access to those institutions.

When there is an alleged violation of international law, we need to know who should be able to initiate a legal proceeding against a government, a government agency, or a government officer to seek an authoritative determination concerning the conduct. In view of the suggested blending of international and domestic law discussed in Chapter VII and of international and domestic courts discussed in Chapter IX below, the initial challenge may occur in a domestic court for an alleged violation of domestic law.[2] The concept of standing, as discussed here, also includes the right of a party who is dissatisfied with a domestic legal decision to appeal that decision to an international tribunal for a final and authoritative determination.

The conduct in question is assumed to be that of a government or a government officer, referred to here as the defendant. As noted later in Chapter XII, there might in fact be no defendant if the action were one for an advisory opinion or declaratory relief. Even in such cases, the conduct in question is usually that of a particular government or its officers. To avoid confusion, we shall refer to them as defendants.

Before considering the extent to which governments, international agencies, and individuals each should be free to initiate a proceeding, we should consider the objectives that standing should be designed to secure and the drawbacks that may exist by having too-ready access to the courts.

3. *General objectives in allocating standing.* For a number of reasons, the goal of second-order compliance would appear to be further advanced if there were free and open access to anyone

---

[2] In several of the so-called Vietnam cases, the plaintiff challenged the constitutionality of the acknowledged but undeclared war that the United States was waging in Vietnam. *See, e.g.,* Berk v. Laird, 429 F.2d 302 (2d Cir. 1970), and Sarnoff v. Connally, 457 F.2d 809 (9th Cir. 1972).

who wanted to raise a question about alleged noncompliance with international rules. In the first place, we would like disputes dealt with. Whenever anyone has a dispute with a government or with a government officer over conduct that is thought to be in violation of international rules, we would prefer an international system which was empowered to hear that dispute and to cope with it. Unless there is a legal outlet for hearing disagreement, one side or the other to the dispute might seek to resolve it by more violent means. Thus, it would seem desirable to have legal standing follow emotional involvement. That is, if someone *thinks* he has rights that are being violated, we would like him to be able to raise the question and have it decided, whether he is right or wrong.

More significantly perhaps, the theory of pursuing second-order compliance rests on the assumption that once a rule has been broken, the question will be promptly raised, a determination reached, and compliance with that determination obtained. Settling for second-order compliance as a more obtainable and realistic objective than that of first-order compliance means that a certain amount of noncompliance with rules must be anticipated and tolerated. Obviously, it would be desirable to minimize such noncompliance. To do so would require us to maximize the chance that an instance of alleged noncompliance will be brought before a tribunal. This objective again points toward free access. This, in turn, suggests that unless the drawbacks discussed below prove overwhelming, not only should we provide ready access to anyone who both knows and cares enough about such noncompliance to raise the question, but that we also might want to impose a duty on some people to start litigation.

Litigation is often thought of as a technique of last resort. And while generally it is desirable to have a negotiated settlement where practicable, there is much to suggest that international litigation should not be avoided or delayed. As a rule, small disputes are easier to settle than large ones. Major international disputes have generally grown from small ones. It will tend to be easier to obtain ultimate compliance with a determination which settles a small dispute than with a determination which requires the losing government to give up a lot. This would suggest that, as soon as a dispute arises, someone, if he chooses, should be entitled to seek a determination of the dispute. The action should be brought before the dispute has escalated into a larger one in which emotional interests have intensified, political positions have been taken, and governmental attitudes have become entrenched.[3]

It generally would seem desirable, however, to have a question of law raised and a case handled by someone who, in fact, cares about that particular case. For example, in domestic law it is thought desirable to have cases handled by "the real party in interest." He generally will be concerned with *this* case and press for its determination. Further, he will be interested in advancing all the considerations that might cause a tribunal to sustain his position, thereby making it easier for the tribunal to decide the matter well.

4. *Dangers in giving too many people standing.* While the objectives discussed above would argue for permitting almost anyone who wished to do so to begin a proceeding which questioned whether a government or a government officer was acting contrary to international law, there are competing considerations. Before considering the extent to which different categories of plaintiffs ought to be entitled to seek a determination, we should look at the various interests that might be injured if access to tribunals were too free and open.

It sometimes has been stated that individuals should not be able to initiate an action based on an alleged violation of international law because only states are the subjects of international law.[4] If the only danger in allowing individuals to bring actions is that some ancient theories underlying international law would have to be further reconsidered, so much the better.[5] Leaving

---

[3] For example, the escalation of retaliatory measures by Cuba and the United States might have been prevented if a third-party determination had been made in what was originally a small dispute concerning the expropriation of two American refineries, in consequence of their refusal to refine crude oil imported by the Cuban Government from the Soviet Union.

[4] *See, e.g.,* Phillimore, *Droits et devoirs fondamentaux des États,* 1 RECUEIL DES COURS (Hague Academy of International Law) 63 (1923). *See also,* 1 L. OPPENHEIM, INTERNATIONAL LAW 21, 519 (4th ed. 1928).

[5] For early pleas for such reconsideration, see Politis, *Le probleème des limitations de la souveraineté et la théorie de l'abus des droits dans les rapports internationaux,* 6 RECUEIL DES COURS (Hague Academy of International Law) 1, 8–10 (1925); Brierly, *Règles générales du droit de la paix,* 58 RECUEIL DES COURS (Hague Academy of International Law) 1, 42

aside such doctrinal thinking, rules limiting access to a tribunal which could consider an international law question might be needed to protect the court from excessive litigation, to protect the defendant from undue harassment, or to protect the plaintiff from improper representation. Each of these possible reasons for limiting access to tribunals merits some consideration.

a. *Protecting the court.* Fears have been expressed that if any individual could sue a foreign government (for example, in the International Court of Justice) then the floodgates would be opened. The Court would be overwhelmed with a great many cases with which it would be unable to cope. The limited time available to a court should be devoted to those cases that most deserve its attention. Article 34 of the Statute of the International Court of Justice provides that "[o]nly States may be parties in cases before the Court."[6] One justification for this rule is that it protects the Court from being overwhelmed by more cases than it can handle. Similarly, the constitutional and statutory limits on the original jurisdiction of the United States Supreme Court—one state can begin an action against another in the Supreme Court but most lawsuits must begin in lower courts—in part are designed to protect the Court's docket.

Limitations on who can raise a question might be aimed not only at saving a court from having to hear certain cases but also at requiring consolidation of a number of cases raising identical

---

(1936); Spiropoulos, *L'individu et le droit international*, 30 RECUEIL DES COURS (Hague Academy of International Law) 191, 210 (1929); Séfériadès, *Le problème de l'accès des particuliers à des juridictions internationales*, 51 RECUEIL DES COURS (Hague Academy of International Law) 1, 43 (1935). More importantly, the Institut de Droit International adopted at its session of New York, *Résolution concernant le problème de l'accès des particuliers à des juridictions internationales*, in which it expressed the opinion "qu'il y a des cas dans lesquels il peut être désirable que le droit soit reconnu aux particuliers de saisir directement, sous des conditions à déterminer, une instance de justice internationale de leurs différends avec des Etats," 35/2 ANNUAIRE DE L'INSTITUT DE DROIT INTERNATIONAL 311 (Session of New York, 1929). *See also* the observations made at a more recent date by Bastid and Salvioli on the report, Wengler, *Recours judiciaire à instituer contre les décisions d'organes internationaux*, 44/1 ANNUAIRE DE L'INSTITUTE DE INTERNATIONAL 224, 296, 348 (Sienne, 1952), and by Lauterpacht on the report, Huber, *Etude des amendements à apporter au Statut de la Cour internationale de Justice* 45/2 ANNUAIRE DE L'INSTITUT DE DROIT INTERNATIONAL 63 (Aix-en-Provence, 1954); Heydte, *L'individu et les tribunaux internationaux*, 107 RECUEIL DES COURS (Hague Institute of International Law) 287 (1962).

[6]Statute of the International Court of Justice, Oct. 24, 1945, art. 34, 59 Stat. 1055, T.S. No. 993.

or similar questions. If every American citizen who had some property taken by Cuba in the 1960s were able to bring a separate action against Cuba in the International Court of Justice, the burden on the Court surely would be far greater than if the United States, acting on behalf of all such citizens, brought a single case.

The limited capacity of any existing court to hear cases may impose a serious limitation on the work that it should be given. However, the problem is quite different when the goal is to identify the kind of international law enforcement system we would like to have in the future. Here, we should design courts capable of doing the work that ought to be done, rather than limiting the work to fit the assumed capacity of a court. If, for other reasons, it would be desirable to permit a person to raise a question about a government's noncompliance with international law, the burden on a court of having to hear the case should not be a valid ground for barring the case. On the contrary, our goal should be to establish enough courts to carry the work load.

With regard to the desirability of consolidating similar cases, the adoption of rules of procedure by international tribunals comparable to those domestic law provisions for joinder and class actions should be adequate to deal with the problem. For instance, in the United States we have discovered that there is no need to bar an individual black from having access to the courts simply because there may be many other blacks with similar grievances.

b. *Protecting the individual defendant.* Some actions may be brought seeking a determination that an individual government officer should stop engaging in certain conduct that allegedly violates international law. To protect such a government officer from harassment, is there a need to limit the number of persons who could question the legality of his activities? Under article 31 of the Vienna Convention on Diplomatic Relations,[7] diplomatic agents enjoy absolute immunity from criminal jurisdiction. They also have immunity in civil and administrative cases arising from their official conduct,[8] and existing United States statutes

[7] Vienna Convention on Diplomatic Relations, Apr. 18, 1961, art. 31, 500 U.N.T.S. 95.

[8] *Id.*

grant substantially the same immunity to diplomatic agents as does the Convention.[9] The principle underlying immunity here is that the legality of the official actions of diplomatic agents cannot be challenged in a foreign court in the absence of a waiver by their government, a waiver which is unlikely to be given.[10] The argument for immunity is that it would be difficult, if not impossible, for responsible diplomatic officials to carry on their important work if they could be dragged into a domestic court by anyone who wished to challenge the legality of their actions. As Cecil Hurst put it: "On no other terms would it have been possible for foreign diplomatic representatives to fulfill the tasks allotted to them."[11]

Our experience in a domestic setting is quite the contrary. So long as an official is being proceeded against civilly rather than criminally—that is, so long as he is not physically arrested and detained—he may continue his work while the case is being heard. Where the conduct in question is official conduct, those defending him will presumably be government lawyers retained for that purpose. In the United States, all government officers, except the President, are subject to suit by anyone for their official action. The Postmaster General, the Secretary of Defense,[12] and other cabinet officers are frequently sued by persons seeking to enjoin them from continuing in some allegedly illegal course of action. Attorneys from the Department of Justice regularly defend these actions. Such litigation constitutes one of the basic techniques for maintaining our government as a government under law. And it rarely interferes with the normal work of the officers concerned. Certainly, being subject to suit for exceeding legal limits interferes with the work of those officials far less than their being subject to call by congressional committees.

[9] 22 U.S.C. §§ 252–54 (1970).

[10] *But cf.* United States v. Arizti, 229 F. Supp. 53 (S.D.N.Y. 1964), one of the few cases in which a national government (in that case, the Government of Uruguay) waived the immunity of a diplomat accused of breaking the federal narcotic laws of the host country (United States). *See also* 59 AM. J. INT'L L. 162 (1965).

[11] Hurst, *Modern Origin of Permanent Diplomatic Missions,* in INTERNATIONAL LAW: COLLECTED PAPERS 171, 174 (1950). *See also* Giuliano, *Les relations et immunités diplomatiques,* 100 RECUEIL DES COURS (Hague Institute of International Law) 75, 88 (1960).

[12] *See, e.g.,* note 2 *supra.*

We frequently want our officials to have broad discretion and to exercise it free from concern over whether their action might subject the government or themselves to liability. That freedom, however, can be well secured by substantive rules of law, such as those which protect both a judge and his government from liability for the judge's decision which, on appeal, turns out to have been illegal. We bestow nearly absolute immunity on government officials from civil suit for the reasons stated by Judge Learned Hand in *Gregoire v. Biddle*.[13] However, the protection of government officials does not justify a procedural bar which denies certain categories of persons access to a tribunal.

c. *Protecting the defendant government.* The whole concept of sovereign immunity relates to protecting a government from being told by a court of law what it should and should not do. The fact that the United States Government and the governments of most of its constituent states today remain unwilling in their own courts to eliminate the defense of sovereign immunity should be enough to raise doubts about their willingness to eliminate that defense in foreign and international courts. The problem of sovereign immunity is discussed primarily in Chapter XIII. Here, we are concerned solely with the question of whether, in order to protect a defendant government, certain classes of persons should be precluded from bringing an action which could be brought by others to challenge the legality of the government's action.

There is precedent in domestic law for such discrimination. Our Constitution made each state subject to suit by other states and by the federal government. But the eleventh amendment was quickly adopted to preclude suits against a state in the federal courts by citizens of another state or by citizens or subjects of any foreign state.[14] Here, to protect a defendant state, jurisdiction is denied because of the character of the plaintiff, not because of the subject matter of the litigation. This limitation, however, has been weakened. Judicial interpretations of the eleventh amendment, culminating in *Ex Parte Young*,[15] have permitted suits to enjoin a state officer from acting pursuant to an

[13] 177 F.2d 579 (2d Cir. 1949). *See also* Chapter IV n. 47 *supra* and accompanying text.
[14] U.S. CONST. amend. XI.
[15] 209 U.S. 123 (1908).

invalid statute on the ground that the suit in theory is not against the state.[16]

The Securities and Exchange Commission successfully persuaded an appellate court in 1962 that a Canadian corporation, because it was an alien with no property in the United States, had "no standing" to challenge the legality of the Commission's action that injured the corporation.[17] On the law, the court's decision in that case seems clearly wrong.[18] In principle, it is equally incorrect. The federal government, one of limited powers, has no authority to treat anyone illegally. The courts generally are open to citizens and aliens alike; there is no statutory bar to suit by an alien corporation; and to the extent that aliens are willing to bring their grievances to our domestic courts for settlement rather than asking their governments for diplomatic protection, they should be encouraged to do so.

Two other interests of defendant governments that justify restrictions on the class of persons eligible to sue governments also fail to convince. Some have suggested that it would be beneath a government's dignity to be hailed into court by a mere individual. This reasoning seems several centuries out of date. To have a court determine a legal question between a government and an individual is no more demeaning when the individual is the plaintiff than when the government takes the initiative as in a suit for taxes or a criminal prosecution.

Although the traditional view that only states are the proper subjects of international law is on the wane, the older dogma barring suits by individuals against governments remains. For example, since the early 1950s the Convention for the Protection of Human Rights and Fundamental Freedoms has allowed the European Commission on Human Rights to receive petitions from individuals claiming to be victims of violations of the Convention by signatory governments (article 25).[19] Yet, individuals are not permitted to bring cases before the European Human

[16] See generally Note, *Sovereign Immunity in Suits to Enjoin the Enforcement of Unconstitutional Legislation*, 50 HARV. L. REV. 956 (1937).

[17] Kukatush Mining Corp. v. SEC, 309 F.2d 647 (D.C. Cir. 1962).

[18] See 77 HARV. L. REV. 351 (1963).

[19] European Convention for the Protection of Human Rights and Fundamental Freedoms, Nov. 4, 1950, art. 25, 213 U.N.T.S. 221 [hereinafter cited as European Convention on Human Rights].

Rights Court if they fail to receive satisfaction in the Commission's report on their claim or if a violating government refuses to comply with the Commission's recommendation. Only the Commission and governments may bring a case before the Court (article 48).[20] The Court has ruled that individuals may make their views known to the Court only by appearing as witnesses, if they are called, or by having the Commission present their case.[21] Even in this relatively advanced Convention, the outmoded belief that cases between individuals, as plaintiffs, and governments, as defendants, should not be permitted still persists.

A similar screening procedure was established in article 11 of the Statute of the Administrative Tribunal of the United Nations.[22] In addition to member states and the Secretary General, the person about whom a judgment has been rendered by the Tribunal has the right to object to that judgment by asking the Committee on Applications for Review of Administrative Tribunal Judgments (the so-called screening committee) to request an advisory opinion of the International Court of Justice on the matter.[23] However, that Committee has the discretionary power to decide whether or not there is a substantial basis for the application, and there is no appeal against its decision.[24]

There is, apparently, an increasing willingness to give individuals access to international organs in disputes concerning acts performed by other governments, particularly in the human rights area. Resolution 1503(XLVIII) of the Economic and Social Council allows communications on alleged violations of human rights that are sent to the United Nations by individuals or groups of individuals to be considered on their merits by the political organs of the organization.[25] Although the procedure

[20] *Id.* at art. 48.
[21] The Lawless Case, [1960] Y.B.EUR. CONV. ON HUMAN RIGHTS 492 (Eur. Comm. on Human Rights) (preliminary objections and questions of procedure).
[22] G.A. Res. 957, 10 U.N. GAOR, Supp. (No. 19) 31, U.N. Doc. A / 3116 (1955).
[23] *Id.* at art. 11.
[24] G.A. Res. 957, 10 U.N. GAOR, Supp. (No. 19) 31, U.N. Doc. A / 3116 (1955). *See also* Advisory Opinion on Application for Review of Judgement No. 158 of the United Nations Administrative Tribunal, [1973] I.C.J. 166, 170–71.
[25] E.S.C. Res. 1503, 48 U.N. ESCOR, Supp. (No. 1A) 8–9, U.N. Doc. E / 4832 / Add. 1 (1970). *See also* para. 2(a) of Resolution 1 (XXIV) in Report of the Sub-Commission on Prevention of Discrimination and Protection of Minorities for 1971, 24 U.N. ESCOR,

provided for in the Resolution has not yet been seriously tested, it nonetheless represents a significant step toward increasing the participation of individuals in improving compliance with international law.

The other interest of defendant governments that is supposed to justify restrictions on the class of persons eligible to sue governments is that of protecting defendant governments from being harassed with unjustifiable suits. Again, the courts could employ various techniques to dismiss frivolous claims. For example, security bonds could be required. The practice currently followed by British courts of requiring an unsuccessful plaintiff to reimburse the defendant for legal expenses, if adopted internationally, would discourage spurious claims and protect a government from needless expense. Further, an authoritative determination that a case is without merit is likely to be less time-consuming for a government than determining the case administratively, with the possibility of almost endless requests. A government usually has to defend an administrative decision on the ground that it was right; a judicial decision can be defended on the simple ground that, whether rightly or wrongly, the matter has been decided conclusively.

d. *Protecting the individual plaintiff.* At times the rights of an individual will be better protected if he is *not* entitled to initiate an action on his own behalf. In order to protect the interests of a child or a mentally incompetent adult, the law precludes him from going to court on his own; a guardian must act in his behalf. Without special leave of court, a man may not argue his own case but must have a lawyer, admitted to the bar of that court, pursue his interests.

A comparable position was taken in 1920 before the Advisory Committee of Jurists when it was considering whether individuals should be allowed to have direct access to the Permanent Court of International Justice. The Advisory Committee adopted

U.N. Doc. E / CN.4 / 1070 (1970) *reprinted in* 66 AM. J. INT'L L. 240 (1972). For details of the established procedure see Ruzié, *De droit de pétition individuelle en matière de droits de l'homme. A propos de la résolution 1503 (XLVIII) du Conseil economique et social des Nations-Unies*, 4 HUMAN RIGHTS J. 89 (1971); Carey, *Progress on Human Rights at the United Nations*, 66 AM J. INT'L L. 107 (1972); Humphrey, *The Right of Petition in the United Nations*, 4 HUMAN RIGHTS J. 463 (1971); Cassese, *The New United Nations Procedure for Handling Gross Violations of Human Rights*, 30 LA COMMUNITA INTERNAZIONALE 49 (1975).

the traditional view of international law that only states could institute international proceedings.[26] One argument for this position was that it would benefit the individual having a claim against a government. The American member of the Advisory Committee, former Secretary of State Elihu Root, explained this policy of protecting the individual plaintiff by contending, according to the summary records of the discussion, that

> the present system gave to individuals a means of protecting their rights superior to that which would be given them if they had the right to summon a State before an international tribunal. . . . Mr. Root did not think that a private individual would gain any advantage by taking before the International Court a case which his Government did not consider justified.[27]

Root also maintained that in "99 cases out of 100" the individual would be successful when his government thought that his case was justified and tried to settle the matter through diplomatic channels.[28]

Whatever the sentiment was at the time when Root spoke, and no doubt some of his contemporaries would have disagreed with him, the position taken by the Advisory Committee of Jurists would not command much support today. Indeed, almost every aggrieved individual would prefer a right of direct access to a court or other tribunal over the right to be protected from his own poor judgment by first having to persuade his government to espouse his claim. The 1965 Convention on the Settlement of Investment Disputes was adopted specifically with the view to creating a procedure for arbitration of disputes between states and nationals of other states.[29] It encourages nationals to take

---

[26] P.C.I.J. Advisory Committee of Jurists, Proces-Verbaux of the Proceedings of the Committee (June 16–July 24, 1920), at 205–17.

[27] Id. at 207.

[28] Id.

[29] Convention on the Settlement of Investment Disputes between States and Nationals of Other States, approved March 18, 1965, 17 U.S.T. 1270, T.I.A.S. No. 6090, 575 U.N.T.S. 159. See the Report of the Executive Directors on the Convention on the Settlement of Investment Disputes, in II / 2 DOCUMENTS CONCERNING THE ORIGIN AND THE FORMULATION OF THE CONVENTION 1070 (1968). See also Broches, The Convention on the Settlement of Investment Disputes Between States and Nationals of Other States, 136 RECUEIL DES COURS (Hague Academy of International Law) 331 (1972); G. SCHWARZENBERGER, FOREIGN INVESTMENT AND INTERNATIONAL LAW 135–53 (1969).

the initiative and to refrain from seeking diplomatic protection. Conversely, it prevents states from granting such protection. Article 27, paragraph 1 of the Convention provides:

> No Contracting State shall give diplomatic protection, or bring an international claim, in respect of a dispute which one of its nationals and another Contracting State shall have consented to submit or shall have submitted to arbitration under this Convention, unless such other Contracting State shall have failed to abide by and comply with the award rendered in such dispute.[30]

However judicious protective measures for children and the mentally incompetent may be, there is little justification for protecting competent adults by precluding them from acting for themselves.

e. *Protecting the plaintiff government.* A final reason for limiting an individual's access to a tribunal to raise a question about the legality of a government's behavior is that governments, particularly the government of the complaining individual, may prefer not to have the dispute litigated. For example, the State Department might object if an American citizen on his own could hail Cuba, or Canada, or the Soviet Union into an international court, particularly if the dispute related to a matter then under negotiation between the two governments. The interest of an individual in winning his case might be quite distinct from the interest the government would have. His government might prefer to have an international or domestic tribunal interpret a rule in such a way as to be in that government's long-run advantage, even though that interpretation might result in the individual's losing his case.

There is no doubt that governments currently give significant weight to such a concern. Executive officials do fear that action by an individual citizen or by a court might result in tying their hands. The extent of this fear was illustrated when in 1963 the

[30]Convention on the Settlement of Investment Disputes between States and Nationals of Other States, *supra* note 29, at para. 1, art. 27. Informal diplomatic exchanges for the sole purpose of facilitating a settlement of the dispute are permitted. To date, several disputes have been submitted for arbitration to the Centre: Holiday Inns / Occidental Petroleum v. Government of Morocco; Adriano Gardella Spa v. Government of Ivory Coast; Alcoa Minerals of Jamaica, Inc. v. Government of Jamaica; Kaiser Bauxite Company v. Government of Jamaica; Reynolds Jamaica Mines and Reynolds Metals Company v. Government of Jamaica. *See generally* ICSID, NINTH ANN. REP. (1974/1975).

State Department and the Department of Justice successfully argued that an American citizen should not be able to raise in an American court the question of the legality under international law of the taking of his property by another government, despite the fact that the property in question was now in the United States.[31] Fears do exist. If accepted as unchangeable, these fears set a limit on what can be done in opening up international questions for judicial determination. On the other hand, the legitimacy of these fears is far from clear. In connection with the various categories of persons and institutions that might raise a question of noncompliance with international law, we shall examine these fears and how they might be assuaged.

5. *Categories of parties plaintiff.* Having identified the general desirability of allowing practically anyone to raise a question concerning a government's compliance with international law and the interests with which such a policy might collide, we now turn to consider particular categories of question-raisers. The party, or plaintiff, initiating a case against a government might be:

1. a foreign government,
2. an agency or officer of the same government as the defendant,
3. a private citizen of the same country as the defendant,
4. an individual or group from a foreign country, or
5. an international agency of some kind.

Other kinds of plaintiffs are conceivable, such as a private international committee like the International Commission of Jurists. However, the discussion of these five categories of plaintiffs should help identify the kinds of institutions and rules about standing that would seem desirable in an international law enforcement scheme. Accordingly, each category of plaintiff will be considered separately.

a. *Suits by a foreign government.* An international system designed to cause compliance with international law through obtaining determinations with respect to international disputes and causing compliance with those determinations should certainly permit one government to challenge the legality of the ac-

---

[31] Banco Nacional de Cuba v. Sabbatino, 376 U.S. 398 (1964).

tion of another government. There seems to be no question about this where the matter in dispute involves an interest which is clearly and directly identified as governmental. Where an alleged violation of international law impinges upon government property, government officers, or national boundaries, for example, the injured government is without question an appropriate plaintiff. Thus, in *The Corfu Channel Case*,[32] the Government of the United Kingdom was the proper party to complain after two of its warships were damaged by mines in Albanian territorial waters.

Where a government's interests are more intangible, such as "national honor," the government still would seem to be an appropriate party plaintiff. Here, however, a limitation on the government's standing to bring an action might be studied as a desirable way of reducing the attention which is given to such ephemeral interests. In 1929 a United States Coast Guard vessel intentionally sank the *I'm Alone*, a schooner which was registered in Canada, was owned by a Canadian corporation, and was engaged in smuggling intoxicating liquors into the United States.[33] The two commissioners to whom the governments submitted the dispute found the intentional sinking was illegal and "as a material amend in respect of the wrong" ordered the United States to pay Canada $25,000. This amount was in addition to compensation that the United States paid for the actual damage done to the Canadian sailors on the ship.[34] Moreover, the United States was called upon by the commissioners "to formally acknowledge its illegality, and to apologize to His Majesty's Canadian Government therefore. . . ."[35]

The contrast between international recognition of an "insult to the flag" as an actionable wrong in the *I'm Alone* case and domestic nonrecognition of such a wrong is striking. If a private automobile "flying" New Hampshire license plates were wrong-

[32] *See* Corfu Channel Case, *supra* note 4, at Chapter I.

[33] The *I'm Alone* (United States v. Canada), U.S. Arb. Ser. No. 2, 3 Int'l Arb. Awards 1609 (1935). *See also* the distinction made between this case and Trail Smelter Case by the Arbitral Tribunal deciding the latter, *id.* at 1905, 1932.

[34] The *I'm Alone*, note 33 *supra*.

[35] *See* Note of Jan. 19, 1935, from the Secretary of State of the United States to the Minister of the Dominion of Canada, U.S. Arb. Ser. No. 2 (7), at 4.

fully fired upon by Massachusetts police, domestic law would not recognize any injury done to the state of New Hampshire. This nonrecognition tends to eliminate a source of dispute among the states. We might seek to reduce one sort of international conflict by adopting a similar policy of nonrecognition. One way to assure nonrecognition of such a claim would be to deny standing to a government which seeks to raise such an issue in either a domestic or an international court. However, this nonrecognition might be better accomplished by judicial or other development of substantive law, rather than by thinking of the problem in the procedural terms of who can raise the question.

The conduct of one country that has an injurious impact within the territory of another country may be another category of dispute where a government is an appropriate plaintiff. This category would include such cases as the *Trail Smelter Case*, where noxious fumes from Canada were damaging farms in the United States,[36] or the case where a piece of satellite launched by one country falls and causes injury within another country's territory.[37] In these cases, if only one person were injured and if he had an adequate remedy that he himself could pursue, there might be little necessity for his government to act in his behalf. However, the territorial aspect of this kind of dispute is likely to upset a government.[38] If it does, the government should have available a legal channel through which it can pursue its griev-

[36] 3 R. Int'l Arb. Awards 1905, 1962–66 (1935).

[37] *See generally* Treaty on Principles Governing the Activities of States in the Exploration and Use of Outer Space, including the Moon and Other Celestial Bodies, Jan. 27, 1967, 18 U.S.T. 2410, T.I.A.S. No. 6347, 610 U.N.T.S. 205.

"Each State Party to the Treaty that launches or procures the launching of an object into outer space, including the moon and other celestial bodies, and each State Party from whose territory or facility an object is launched, is internationally liable for damage to another State Party to the Treaty or to its natural or juridical persons by such object or its component parts on the Earth, in air space or in outer space, including the moon and other celestial bodies." *Id.* at art. VII.

The Canadian Government requested more than $1,000,000 from the Government of the Soviet Union as compensation for the search and clean-up operation of the radioactive debris from the Soviet satellite that disintegrated over northern Canada on Jan. 24, 1978. N.Y. Times, Feb. 14, 1978, at 11, col. 1.

[38] In the Trail Smelter Case, for instance, the United States pleaded not only the material damage of the crop in the state of Washington but equally the violation of its territorial sovereignty. *See* 3 R. Int'l Arb. Awards 1905, 1932 (1935). Australia and New Zealand asserted similar claims in the Nuclear Tests Case, [1973] I.C.J. 103, 139.

ance. Where, as in an international river dispute, there are a great many individuals affected, it makes sense to have their interests protected by their government.[39] When the state of Missouri sought to enjoin Illinois and the Chicago Sanitary District from polluting the Mississippi River, which flows into Missouri, the Supreme Court held that "if the health and the comfort of the inhabitants of a State are threatened, the State is the proper party to represent and defend them."[40] A government is a particularly appropriate party plaintiff when what is sought is a determination about future conduct, rather than compensation for past injury.[41] A government would also have a special concern if nationality were a significant factor in the mistreatment of one of its citizens abroad. In July 1917 Byron Everett Janes, an American citizen, was shot and killed in Mexico by a Mexican.[42] Although there were a number of witnesses and the authorities knew where to locate the killer, the Mexican officials delayed their investigation, and the murderer escaped. A number of Americans had been killed in Mexico under similar circumstances, and American officials feared that the Mexican Government's failure to prosecute the perpetrators was an implied invitation to attack other United States citizens. An arbitration commission confirmed the United States' charge that Mexico had failed to provide adequate protection to American citizens in that country and in awarding damages allowed "a reasonable and substantial redress . . . for the mistrust and lack of safety, resulting from the [Mexican] Government's attitude."[43] Even though the damages were ultimately (and somewhat irrationally) turned over to Janes's widow by the United States, the

[39]This was, for instance, the case with the Indus River dispute when the government of the downstream country—Pakistan—protected the interests of farmers who had been affected by action taken by the government of the upstream country—India. For the settlement of that dispute, see the Indus Basin Development Fund agreement, Sept. 19, 1960, 12 U.S.T. 19, T.I.A.S. No. 4671, 444 U.N.T.S. 259, *reprinted in* 55 AM. J. INT'L L. 797 (1961).

[40]Missouri v. Illinois and the Sanitary Dist. of Chicago, 180 U.S. 208, 241 (1901).

[41]This was, for instance, the intent of the Dutch Government in the case of The Diversion of Water from the Meuse, [1937] P.C.I.J., ser. A/B, No. 70, at 4–5.

[42]Laura M. B. Janes v. United Mexican States (United States v. Mexico) General Claims Commission Arbitration, 4 R. Int'l Arb. Awards 82 (1925).

[43]*Id.* at 89.

proper plaintiff to protect the interests of Americans traveling or working in Mexico in the future was the United States Government.

Traditional international law has long recognized the right of a government to espouse the purely private claims of its citizens against a foreign government. As the Permanent Court of International Justice held in the case of *The Mavrommatis Palestine Concessions*, "[i]t is an elementary principle of international law that a State is entitled to protect its subjects, when injured by acts contrary to international law committed by another State, from whom they have been unable to obtain satisfaction through the ordinary channels."[44] Where a large number of similar claims have arisen, such as through the Cuban Government's nationalization of private property held in Cuba by American citizens, there are practical reasons for allowing the United States Government to proceed in their behalf. The United States Government has performed a similar function in domestic litigation. In *United States v. Minnesota*,[45] the Supreme Court held that the government had standing to sue on behalf of the Chippewa Indians, who were "under the guardianship of the United States and entitled to its aid and protection."[46] In these situations, the government is serving as a kind of trustee for a group of individual claims, some of which by themselves might be so small as not to justify the effort required for collection and others of which could be pursued more vigorously by the Justice Department than by each claimant.

Espousal of individual claims does have its limits. United States courts have sometimes refused to allow a state to act on behalf of a group of its citizens. For example, Oklahoma was precluded from starting an action in the Supreme Court on behalf of a group of depositors in a defaulted bank. The Supreme Court stated that "the State must show a direct interest of its own and not merely seek recovery for the benefit of individuals who are the real parties in interest."[47] This decision can be justified as

---

[44] Mavrommatis Palestine Concessions, [1924] P.C.I.J., ser. A, No. 2, at 12.
[45] 270 U.S. 181 (1926).
[46] *Id.* at 193–94.
[47] Oklahoma *ex rel.* Johnson, Bank Comm'r v. Cook, 304 U.S. 387, 396 (1938).

a way of protecting the original jurisdiction of the Supreme Court. It may be proper that in seeking recovery on behalf of private depositors, a state should begin its action in a lower court. However, a government which wishes to act on behalf of a group of injured individuals should have standing to do so in some forum.

The rule for our domestic courts enunciated by the Supreme Court in *Massachusetts v. Mellon*[48] seems inconsistent with the international rule that would be desirable. In that case, the state of Massachusetts believed that the federal government was acting with respect to state citizens on a matter reserved by the Constitution to the states and was, by offering financial aid to states if they complied with certain conditions, "inducing the States to yield a portion of their sovereign rights."[49] The Supreme Court found "[n]o rights of the State falling within the scope of the judicial power" were involved and that Massachusetts had no right to sue on its own behalf.[50] The Court did recognize that a state could sometimes sue for the protection of its citizens but held that Massachusetts could not represent its citizens against the federal government, which was itself the proper party to represent citizens with respect to their federal rights. Internationally, we would want a different rule. We would want a national government to be considered an appropriate representative to vindicate rights of a group of its injured citizens, whether that government was proceeding against another national government or against the United Nations or one of that organization's agencies. This representation would be permissible even if, as we shall discuss later, another national government or the United Nations or one of its agencies would also be able to represent the rights of that same group of citizens. Unlike the situation in the United States where the federal government can be expected to act on behalf of a group of injured citizens, the international system cannot be relied upon to produce this kind of representation. Because we seek to create a system which provides an authoritative decision when a dispute exists, we should permit national governments to represent the cause of a group

[48] 262 U.S. 447 (1923).
[49] *Id.* at 479.
[50] *Id.* at 485.

of their citizens even if there are other governments[51] or international agencies[52] that also might act on their behalf.

Under traditional international law, a government may espouse not only the claim of a group of its citizens but also the purely personal claim of a single citizen against a foreign government. After a citizen has exhausted the available local remedies, his government may take the matter up with a foreign government diplomatically or through such judicial or arbitral procedures as may have been previously agreed upon by the two governments. Within the United States, we do not recognize a comparable right of a state to initiate an action on behalf of one of its citizens against another state. When the eleventh amendment barred a New Hampshire citizen from suing Louisiana to recover on one of that state's bonds, the state of New Hampshire sued on behalf of its citizen. In *New Hampshire v. Louisiana* the Supreme Court dismissed the New Hampshire suit and stated that "in our opinion, one State cannot create a controversy with another State, within the meaning of that term as used in the judicial clauses of the Constitution, by assuming the prosecution of debts owing by the other State to its citizens."[53]

By and large, we have been looking to successful domestic experience for guidance in bringing law to bear on governments

[51] Currently, under international law a government cannot protect the interests of its citiens who: (*a*) are shareholders in a company which has another nationality (Case Concerning the Barcelona Traction, Light and Power Company, Ltd., [1970] I.C.J. 47); or (*b*) are at the same time citizens of the state against which the diplomatic protection is exercised (Pinson Case (France v. Mexico), 5 R. Int'l Arb. Awards 381 (1928)), unless one nationality is proved to prevail over the other because of the existence of a genuine link between the protected citizen and the state (Merge Case (Italy v. United States), 14 R. Int'l Arb. Awards 246–47; Case Concerning the Barcelona Traction, Light and Power Company, Ltd., [1970] I.C.J. 50). *See also* article 4 of Resolution *The National Character of an International Claim Presented by a State for Injury Suffered by an Individual adopted by the Institut de Droit International*, 51/2 ANNUAIRE DE L'INSTITUT DE DROIT INTERNATIONAL 270–71 (1965); *compare* Fitzmaurice, *The Law and Procedure of the International Court of Justice: International Organizations and Tribunals*, 29 BRIT. Y.B.INT'L L. 1, 19 (1952).

[52] In the case of Reparation for Injuries Suffered in the Service of the United Nations, the International Court of Justice admitted the possibility of concurrence between the diplomatic protection by the national state of the international civil servant and the United Nations, though the Court refrained from establishing any order of precedence between them. [1949] I.C.J. 49. There may be concurrence between diplomatic protection by states and functional protection by an international body whose international personality has been recognized.

[53] 108 U.S. 76, 91 (1883).

in the international arena. That experience suggests that it might be wise to revise the international practice of governmental espousal of private claims. The decision of the International Court of Justice in the *Nottebohm* case indicates that presently under international law, a nation is not unfettered in its ability to espouse the claim of one of its nationals.[54] In that case, Liechtenstein instituted proceedings against Guatemala on behalf of one of its nationals, Nottebohm. The Court held that Liechtenstein lacked standing to bring the action because the connection of Nottebohm with that country was "lacking in . . . genuineness" and was not sufficient to permit the espousal of his claim. The fact that Liechtenstein regarded Nottebohm as its national and was concerned enough to proceed on his behalf[55] was not determinative or sufficient to give that country standing to espouse his claim before the Court.

The Court's reluctance to have a government act as a collection agency for whomsoever it chooses probably resulted from a desire to save the defendant government from having to litigate its case — a seemingly inadequate consideration. Had Nottebohm been able to proceed in his own behalf, there would have been sound reasons for requiring him to do so, rather than allowing him to raise the level of the dispute to the more political, and generally more dangerous, level of state to state. But, there is no international forum available to someone like Nottebohm.[56] As long as that remains true, a government sufficiently interested in espousing his claim should be permitted to seek an authoritative determination of whether his rights under international law have been violated.

Rather than seeking to deprive a government of its existing legal right to proceed internationally in behalf of one of its nationals, a preferable method of keeping disputes at a lower political level would be to establish an international forum in which the aggrieved individual himself could proceed. The existing in-

---

[54] Nottebohm Case, [1955] I.C.J. 4.

[55] *Id.* at 26. The decision of the Court was not an innovation in international law. *See, e.g.*, Canevaro Case (Italy v. Peru), 11 R. Int'l Arb. Awards 406 (1912); Pinson Case (France v. Mexico), 5 R. Int'l Arb. Awards 381; Merge Case (Italy v. United States), 14 R. Int'l Arb. Awards 246–47; Flegenheimer Case, 14 R. Int'l Arb. Awards 376; Graniero Case, 14 R. Int'l Arb. Awards 395.

[56] *See* Jones, *The Nottebohm Case*, 5 INT'L & COMP. L. Q. 230 (1956).

ternational law rule requiring an individual to exhaust available local remedies could easily be extended to require him also to exhaust any international remedy made available to him by the defendant government. If the complainant's country and the country with which he had a dispute were parties to the World Bank's Convention for the Settlement of Investment Disputes,[57] the individual might be required to pursue the conciliation or arbitration procedures under that agreement.[58] After these avenues had been exhausted, the plaintiff's government could have a right to espouse his claim, but only if the prior judicial, arbitral, or conciliatory proceedings had in some way been so unfair as to constitute a "denial of justice." Thus, the government's theoretical right to espouse an individual's claim could be preserved. Presumably, most cases would be settled conclusively by the prior proceedings in which the individual pressed his own claim.

A final question about a government's standing arises when the defendant government allegedly is violating a general international rule which does not cause any specific injury to the plaintiff nation or to any of its nationals. This question of standing was decisive to the outcome of the *South West Africa Cases*, in which Ethiopia and Liberia sought in the International Court of Justice to cause South Africa to comply with the terms of the League of Nations' mandate for South West Africa.[59] Neither Ethiopia nor Liberia was suffering any particular injury from South Africa's noncompliance. For a number of laudable reasons, they were interested in having South Africa comply with its international obligations. Ethiopia's and Liberia's membership in the League of Nations provided a technical argument for sustaining their standing to bring an action. And there seemed little reason to arrive at a different result for Ethiopia or Liberia than for a non-League member, such as Zambia or Uganda. However, in its controversial 1966 opinion in these cases, the Court refused to recognize the standing of Ethiopia or Liberia as former members of the League.[60] The Court also rejected the

---

[57]Convention for the Settlement of Investment Disputes between States and Nationals of Other States, note 29 *supra*.

[58]*See id.* at 8–21.

[59]Judgement on Second Phase, South West Africa Cases, [1966] I.C.J. 6.

[60]*Id.* at 32–33.

argument that those countries had a general standing to challenge South Africa's conduct because of their "interest" as members of the international community in the alleged violations of the mandate. In a pronouncement which produced much dissent and controversy, the Court held:

> Looked at in another way moreover, the argument amounts to a plea that the Court should allow the equivalent of an "actio popularis", or right resident in any member of a community to take legal action in vindication of a public interest. But although a right of this kind may be known to certain municipal systems of law, it is not known to international law as it stands at present: nor is the Court able to regard it as imported by the "general principles of law" referred to in Article 38, paragraph 1(c), of the Statute.[61]

The contention here is that the Court's holding is not what the law ought to be. It seems desirable that international rules for the general welfare be complied with even if their violation does not cause a discrete, identifiable injury to any particular individual or government. In the *Case Concerning the Barcelona Traction, Light and Power Company, Limited* the Court recognized that all states have an interest in there being compliance with some kinds of rules:

> In particular, an essential distinction should be drawn between the obligations of a State towards the international community as a whole, and those arising vis-à-vis another State in the field of diplomatic protection. By their very nature the former are the concern of all States. In view of the importance of the rights involved, all States can be held to have legal interest in their protection; they are obligations *erga omnes*.
>
> Such obligations derive, for example, in contemporary international law, from the outlawing of acts of aggression, and of genocide, as also from the principles and rules concerning the basic rights of the human person, including protection from slavery and racial discrimination.[62]

---

[61] *Id.* at 47.

[62] Case Concerning the Barcelona Traction, Light and Power Company, Ltd., [1970] I.C.J. 32. The Court greatly qualified this statement of principle by holding: "However, on the universal level, the instruments which embody human rights do not confer on States the capacity to protect the victims of infringements of such rights irrespective of their nationality." *Id.* at 47.

In the absence of an international agency specifically charged with enforcement responsibility, another government would seem an appropriate party plaintiff.[63] Although it is true that claims might be brought because of political hostility, a judicial means may be the best method of coping with the symptoms of such hostility. Even with an international enforcement agency, it also would seem desirable to let other states take the initiative in seeking a determination. Where the issue is what ought to be done in the future, rather than punishment, there seems less necessity for having a public prosecutor in charge. In shaping its decision, the tribunal itself can exercise more discretion than a prosecutor can in a case where the choice is between guilty and not guilty. The general desirability of providing a legal forum to which a government can proceed, if it so chooses, would seem to outweigh the advantages of requiring cases to be brought only by those particularly affected by the matter in dispute.

This question of general standing is of manifest practical importance and interest, as the *Nuclear Tests Case*[64] abundantly demonstrated. In that case, Australia claimed before the International Court of Justice to have a right "in common with other States and their peoples, to be free from atmospheric nuclear weapon tests by any country."[65] Judges Onyeama, Dillard, Jiménez de Aréchaga, and Waldock took judicial notice of that contention in their joint dissenting opinion, which states in pertinent part:

> With regard to the right to be free from atmospheric tests, said to be possessed by Australia in common with other States, the question of "legal interest" again appears to us to be part of the general legal merits of the case. If the materials adduced by Australia were to convince the Court of the existence of a general rule of international law, prohibiting atmospheric nuclear tests,

[63] In his separate opinion in the South West Africa Cases, Judge Jessup pointed out that there are "established situations in which States are given a right of action without any showing of individual prejudice or individual substantive interest as distinguished from the general interest," South West Africa Cases, [1966] I.C.J. 388. *See also* his individual opinion in the same cases (preliminary objections), [1962] I.C.J. 387.

[64] Nuclear Tests Case, [1973] I.C.J. 99.

[65] *Id.* at 103. New Zealand maintained that the French nuclear test "violates the rights of all members of the international community including New Zealand, that no nuclear tests that give rise to radio-active fall-out be conducted." *Id.* at 139.

the Court would at the same time have to determine what is the precise character and context of the rule and, in particular, whether it confers a right on every State individually to prosecute a claim to secure respect for the rule. In short, the question of "legal interest" cannot be separated from the substantive legal issue of the existence and the scope of the alleged rule of customary international law. Although we recognize that the existence of the so-called *actio popularis* in international law is a matter of controversy, the observations of this Court in the *Barcelona Traction, Light and Power Company, Limited* case suffice to show that the question is one that may be considered as capable of rational legal argument and a proper subject of litigation before this Court.[66]

A change of the Court's ruling in the *South West Africa Cases*[67] is all the more desirable as recent developments in international law show an increasing recognition of the interests of *mankind*. In this regard, principle 5 of the Declaration of the United Nations Conference on the Human Environment affirms the interest of mankind, rather than that of states, in the conservation of nonrenewable resources,[68] and the first principle of Resolution 2749(XXV) declares: "The sea-bed and ocean floor, and the subsoil thereof, beyond the limits of national jurisdiction (hereinafter referred to as the area), as well as the resources of the area, are the common heritage of mankind."[69] Commenting upon this Resolution, René-Jean Dupuy noted the existence of "a movement towards the implicit recognition of mankind as a subject of international law, for the interest of mankind is not simply that of the concertation of all States; it is a notion integrating the State, the collectivities and the individual."[70] "Mankind" cannot initiate a proceeding. Where the subject of a claim is the infringement of a right possessed by mankind, any state should be recognized as having both a legal interest in securing the protection of that right and the standing necessary to do so.

b. *Suit by an agency or officer of a defendant's government.* To the

[66] Joint Dissenting Opinion in the Nuclear Tests Case, [1974] I.C.J. 369–70.

[67] *See* notes 59 through 61 and accompanying text *supra.*

[68] *See* Report of the United Nations Conference on the Human Environment (Stockholm, 5–16 June 1972), at 4.

[69] Declaration of Principles Governing the Sea-Bed and the Ocean Floor, and the Subsoil Thereof, beyond the Limits of National Jurisdiction, G.A. Res. 2749, 25 U.N. GAOR, Supp. (No. 28) 24, U.N. Doc. A / 8028 (1970).

[70] R.-J. DUPUY, THE LAW OF THE SEA 52 n.19 (1974).

extent that international law rules become rules of domestic law and are made directly applicable to officers of every government (see Chapter VII *supra*), as much enforcement action as possible should be taken within the domestic legal system. For example, in the United States the Comptroller General, the Attorney General, officials of the regulatory agencies, and the Inspector General in the military services should be charged with the enforcement of international rules. These officials should be expected to initiate action questioning the conduct of their own officers as well as that of officers of other branches or agencies of the government where these officers apparently have violated existing law. It also would seem desirable to give the Comptroller General the authority to seek a court order restraining certain categories of future disbursements. Within the Soviet Union's military, as within our own, there is an office which receives complaints from individuals with respect to possible violations of law by officials. The Procuracy General there, like the Inspector General of the Army here, may investigate such claims and then suggest what should be done.[71] There seems no reason why the Attorney General might not be empowered to seek an injunction against a federal officer just as he can now seek an injunction against a state officer. For special fields, such as arms control, it might be wise to set up special enforcement agencies within each government, which would be charged with enforcing rules against other officers in the government. Government agencies might be established both at the federal and the state level with responsibility for implementing a treaty and working out appropriate administrative regulations — getting Parkinson's law on the side of compliance.

Domestic challenges to the legality of an officer's conduct would presumably occur within the domestic legal system. In addition, such challenges might conceivably be taken to an international court. Article 117 of the Treaty of March 25, 1957, establishing the European Economic Community (EEC) provides that when a question concerning interpretation of that Treaty "is raised in a case pending before a court or tribunal of a Member State, from whose decisions there is no possibility of appeal under internal law, that court or tribunal shall be bound

---

[71] *See generally* H. BERMAN, JUSTICE IN THE USSR (rev. ed. 1963).

to bring the matter before the [European] Court of Justice."[72] In
the Federal Republic of Germany, one of the states may refer a
dispute involving a question of public law between itself and the
federal government to the Federal Constitutional Court.[73] If the
issue in such a dispute turned on an interpretation of the EEC
Treaty, the Federal Constitutional Court would be obliged, under article 177 of the Treaty, to refer that issue to the European
Court of Justice.[74] In a manner analogous to this EEC procedure, international courts might be created to hear cases involving rules of international law in disputes where the plaintiff and
the defendant were agencies or branches of the same government. For the United States, referring such cases to an international court hardly would be more anomalous than the Supreme
Court's hearing the occasional case today in which different
agencies of the federal government are on opposing sides.

    c. *Suits by a citizen against his own government.* With the exception
of the European Convention on Human Rights,[75] there is little
international experience with remedies for a citizen against his
own government. The bulk of the available experience from
which we must draw conclusions is wholly domestic.

    Professor Louis Jaffe has given extensive consideration to the
standing of a private citizen to secure judicial scrutiny of governmental action where the individual is not particularly affected.[76]
In England and the United States, this has been done either

    [72]Treaty establishing the European Economic Community, March 25, 1957, art. 177,
298 U.N.T.S. 11. In its judgment in the case of Hessische Knappschaft v. Maison Singer
et Fils, [1965] C. J. Comm. E. Rec. 1191, [1965] COMM. MKT. REP. (CCH) ¶ 8042, the
European Court of Justice gave its own interpretation to article 177. For details, see H.
STEINER & D. VAGTS, TRANSNATIONAL LEGAL PROBLEMS 1186 (1968).

    [73]Article 93, paragraph 4, of the Basic Law of the Federal Republic of Germany. The
decision given by the Federal Constitutional Court, on July 31, 1973, represents a recent
use of this legal rule. The Bavarian State Government had applied to the Federal Constitutional Court for a declaratory judgment that the federal law concerning the Treaty
of December 21, 1972, between the Federal Republic of Germany (FRG) and the German Democratic Republic (GDR) on the Bases of the Relations between the FRG and the
GDR was not compatible with the Basic Law of the FRG and was therefore void. The
federal government then applied to the Court for a declaratory judgment that the law
was compatible with the Basic Law: The Court decided in favor of the federal government. For details, see 70 AM. J. INT'L L. 147 (1976).

    [74]Treaty establishing the European Economic Community, *supra* note 72, at art. 177.
    [75]*See* European Convention on Human Rights, note 19 *supra.*
    [76]Jaffe, *Standing to Secure Judicial Review: Public Actions* (pts. 1–2), 74 HARV. L. REV.
1265; 75 HARV. L. REV. 255 (1961).

through mandamus, in which a court orders an official to do that which the law requires him to do, or through a taxpayer's or citizen's suit in equity to enjoin officials from exceeding their authority. In England, apparently, a private citizen may not have standing to question governmental action that does not peculiarly affect him either in an action for mandamus or in a suit in equity. In the United States, particularly in state courts, there is extensive authority for allowing an individual not peculiarly affected to initiate an action challenging the public conduct of a public official. In his article, Professor Jaffe summarizes these authorities:

> There are, then, approximately forty states in which at the suit of a citizen or taxpayer it is possible to test the legality of local official conduct, be it negative or positive in character, and whether or not it has an impact on the expenditure of funds. There are at least twenty-seven states where the same is clearly true of state action, and another nine or more where it may be true. Though, as we know, the Supreme Court has rejected suits by federal taxpayers, the federal courts have entertained suits by territorial and District of Columbia taxpayers. The Supreme Court has adjudicated appeals from state judgments in local and state taxpayer suits.[77]

Professor Jaffe would urge judges to exercise caution in granting relief in suits involving federal action. But, with respect to state and local actions, he would eliminate technical restrictions on standing and would consider "the attenuated character of the particular impact on the plaintiff" as relevant, but not conclusive, against jurisdiction:

> The conclusion thus emerges that there should be a single form of citizen action — one which is competent to test state and local official conduct whether or not involving the expenditure of funds and whether negative or positive in form. The citizen, as the prime political unit of the democracy, should be the plaintiff.[78]

As noted, Professor Jaffe would confine the right of a citizen to challenge federal action in this country since he finds that judi-

[77]74 HARV. L. REV. 1265, 1280–81 (1961) (footnotes omitted).
[78]*Id.* at 1296.

cial review here is neither so appropriate nor so urgent as in challenges to state or local actions. A larger part of the federal government's business is in the areas of defense and foreign affairs where there is thought to be "a greater need that discretion be free of judicial control."[79] At the same time, he believes that in the case of the central government, public opinion and administrative controls are more effective than they are on the state level, at least as against gross dereliction, and hence make judicial review less desirable.

These are the conclusions reached by a distinguished student of domestic experience with citizens' suits challenging the public conduct of public officials. What do these conclusions suggest for those seeking increased governmental compliance with international obligations? Professor Jaffe has argued that standing to challenge federal action on "foreign affairs" issues would be inappropriate since many of these issues are better left for determination by the executive or the legislature. He reaches this conclusion because in foreign affairs the issue involved is often

> one for the decision of which there are no well-developed principles, or the issue is felt to be so closely related to a complex of decisions not within [a] court's jurisdiction that its resolution by [a] court would either be poor in itself or would jeopardize sound decisions in the larger complex.[80]

Despite these cautions, I reach a contrary conclusion. I think it desirable to recognize a right for the citizen of a country to challenge the legality of the conduct of officials of his own government, even though he is not particularly affected by that conduct and even though the question raised involves foreign affairs. At present, a United States citizen can challenge such action only if he is particularly affected by the official conduct. Thus, a serviceman's civilian dependent who has been tried abroad for murder by court-martial pursuant to a United States treaty with the country where the killing took place can challenge successfully the validity of that treaty despite its importance in the conduct of foreign affairs.[81] An American soldier

[79] *Id.* at 1312.
[80] *Id.* at 1304.
[81] Reid v. Covert, 354 U.S. 1 (1957).

has standing to attempt to enjoin the Secretary of Defense from turning him over to a foreign power for trial.[82] The survivors of an American killed in the crash of an airliner traveling from Hong Kong to Tokyo successfully challenged the constitutionality of the United States' adherence to the Warsaw Convention, which places limitations on both venue and liability for such accidents.[83] Finally, citizens have challenged the denial of a passport by the Secretary of State[84] and the Secretary's refusal to validate a passport for travel to restricted areas.[85] In such cases, a court properly may exercise caution in finding that the legal powers of the government or those of an executive official are being executed. A court is likely to find that the law gives a good deal of discretion to the executive and that the executive's interpretation of its own authority should be accorded great weight. For example, in *Zemel v. Rusk*,[86] the Supreme Court held that the Secretary of State was authorized to impose area restrictions on travel by the Passport Act of 1926 and, consequently, he could refuse to validate passports for travel to Cuba. But such judicial restraint in setting aside executive action is quite different from barring the plaintiff at the courthouse door.

If a private citizen were allowed to challenge government action that did not affect him particularly, comparable judicial restraint could adequately protect executive discretion. There appears to be no significant legitimate interest in saving the government from the time and the expense of defending its actions in court. Should the government be acting legally, a judicial decision upholding the government's position should help dispel doubts about the legality of its conduct and, thus, would be well worth the effort. The "general" injury to which a citizen may become subject because of the conduct of his government in the

[82] Wilson v. Girard, 354 U.S. 524 (1957).

[83] Burdell v. Can. Pac. Airlines Ltd., 10 Av. Cas. 18,151 (Ill. Cir. Ct. 1968), *withdrawn and revised*, 11 Av. Cas. 17,351 (1969). On rehearing, the Illinois Circuit Court declined to rule on the constitutional question in light of its holding that the Warsaw Convention did not apply to the facts of this case. For a discussion of the original *Burdell* decision and the constitutional issues it raises, see Hay, *Comments on Burdell v. Canadian Pacific Airlines and the Constitutionality of the Warsaw Convention*, 58 ILL. B.J. 26 (1969); Lowenfeld, *Some Comments on Burdell v. Canadian Pacific Airlines*, 3 VAND. J. TRANSNAT'L L. 47, 52 (1969).

[84] *See, e.g.*, Kent v. Dulles, 357 U.S. 116 (1958).

[85] *See* Zemel v. Rusk, 381 U.S. 1 (1965).

[86] *Id.*

international arena may, in fact, be far more serious than a particular injury to him such as a limitation on his passport.

The theory of allowing an individual standing only in cases where he is affected particularly is based not on the relative magnitude of the injury to him but rather on the idea that political avenues of correction are open to him if the public at large is affected. Yet, domestic political processes tend not to pressure a government toward compliance with the standards of international law unless there is a forum in which the particular conduct can be questioned. The long-term interest that is served by observing the rules of international law is not the kind of interest to which national political processes respond. The assumption that a government's illegal conduct in the international arena will tend to be corrected by internal political processes simply cannot be made.

One particular virtue of permitting citizens of a country to question whether their own government officers are complying with their international legal obligations is that the question can be considered by a court with citizens of the same country on both sides of the case. A case in this posture is less likely to inflame an international conflict than were it one between nations. A court also may be better able to deal with the matter free from national bias. The nationality of the plaintiff helps remind everyone that a country has interests on both sides of the question.

Under the European Convention on Human Rights,[87] eleven governments have recognized the optional competence of the European Commission of Human Rights to receive individual applications under article 25 of the Convention. As explained above,[88] individuals are not permitted to bring their cases before the European Court of Human Rights if they are dissatisfied with the Commission's decision. Moreover, challenges to governmental action are limited to "any person . . . claiming to be the victim of a violation by one of the High Contracting Parties of the rights set forth in [the] Convention."[89] Thus, an individual not particularly affected by executive action may not contest its

[87] Note 19 *supra.*
[88] *Supra* at 178–79.
[89] European Convention on Human Rights, *supra* note 19, at art. 25.

legality under the Convention. Only the governments that adhere to the Convention have the broad power to challenge any
alleged breach of the Convention. Despite these limitations,
however, a number of individual challenges to executive action
under the European Convention on Human Rights have resulted in corrective action extending beyond the particular injury suffered by the complaining party. For example, in the
Pataki case[90] the plaintiff, an Austrian citizen, challenged an appeal taken by the Austrian Public Prosecutor because the appeal
proceedings were in camera and neither the plaintiff nor his
counsel was permitted to be present. The Commission's report
on the appeal under the Austrian Code of Criminal Procedure
found that the appeal proceedings violated the Convention's requirements of a right to a fair trial and a right to counsel. As a
result, the Austrian Government amended its Code to change
this procedure and gave Pataki, as well as sixteen similarly situated plaintiffs before the Commission, another appeal under the
new provision.[91] The Commission has not decided a case involving an individual citizen's complaint challenging executive action on an issue relating to foreign affairs. However, the
Convention is sufficiently broad that it is not difficult to imagine
such a complaint being made in the future.

d. *Suits by foreign citizens.* Another category of potential plaintiffs consists of citizens of one country who wish to challenge the
legality of the conduct of another government or its officials. Is
it desirable to open domestic courts and, presumably on appeal,
international courts to suits by foreign individuals?

In general, providing for such actions seems advisable. An individual may wish to raise a question regarding the conduct of
another government in circumstances where his own government is reluctant to do so. As those who have sought to persuade
the State Department to espouse a claim against a foreign government know, the Department often is unwilling to act for reasons wholly apart from the merits of the case. It has been
suggested, with some truth, that the State Department has two
standard reasons for its reluctance to act: either relations with
the government in question are so bad at the moment that it

90[1960] Y.B. EUR. CONV. ON HUMAN RIGHTS 356 (Eur. Comm. on Human Rights).
91*Id.*

would be unwise to worsen them by raising the matter; or relations with that government are so good at the moment that it would be unwise to upset them by raising the matter. Allowing an individual to raise a question on his own not only increases the chances of the problem's getting to court but also tends to make the issue less political and reduces the risk of the dispute's resulting in a state-to-state confrontation. Thus, no particular fuss occurred when one French, one German, one Canadian, seven Japanese, and four British citizens joined two United States citizens in seeking to enjoin the Secretary of Defense and the Atomic Energy Commission from authorizing and carrying out further testing of nuclear weapons.[92] In the *Pauling* case, the Supreme Court held that the plaintiffs had no standing because they failed to allege a specific threatened injury to themselves.[93] In addition, the Court did not make any distinction between the United States and foreign plaintiffs. This limitation on standing is, of course, contrary to the argument above in favor of permitting a citizen to challenge public action by governmental officials even if that citizen is not particularly affected.

Two experiences with suits by a foreign individual against a government official in an international forum demonstrate how such suits help to reduce the political content of the dispute. In one case before the European Commission, a Pakistani and his son contested the refusal of British immigration authorities to admit them to the United Kingdom. The plaintiffs alleged that the 1962 Commonwealth Immigrants Act of the United Kingdom[94] under which they were denied entry violated their right to family life guaranteed by article 8 of the European Convention on Human Rights[95] and their right to receive a fair and public hearing by an independent and impartial tribunal in determination of their civil rights.[96] Raising objections to the 1962 British legislation in this manner has caused far less politi-

---

[92] Pauling v. McElroy, 278 F.2d 252 (D.C. Cir. 1960).

[93] *Id.* at 254.

[94] Commonwealth Immigrants Act of the United Kingdom, 10 & 11 Eliz. 2, c. 21 (1962).

[95] European Convention on Human Rights, note 19 *supra*.

[96] Alam v. UK, [1967] Y.B. EUR. CONV. ON HUMAN RIGHTS 478 (Eur. Comm. on Human Rights) No. 2991 / 66, July 15, 1967.

cal controversy and ultimately may achieve more results than if the complaint had been espoused by the Pakistani Ambassador in London or the Pakistani Prime Minster at the Commonwealth Conference of Ministers.

The other example of a foreign individual's suit against a government is provided for us in the European Coal and Steel Community (ECSC).[97] Under the ECSC Treaty, individual enterprises and associations may challenge "general decisions" and "recommendations" of the High Authority even though those decisions are not directed specifically at the complaining enterprise or association. These challenges to the High Authority's actions, in effect, may be a complaint that an ECSC member state is not fulfilling its obligations under the Treaty. However, the only ground for these challenges can be misuse of power (*détournement de pouvoir*), and the misuse must affect the particular enterprise or association making the complaint.[98] In examining experience under the ECSC Treaty, Professor Thomas Buergenthal has pointed out the value of allowing private interests abroad to raise questions about the legality of state activity in view of the political and bureaucratic impediments to one government's asserting the illegality of another government's activity.[99] The advantages of providing a forum where an allegation of illegality can be heard and authoritatively determined should more than offset any disadvantage either to the government of the plaintiff or to the government whose action is being challenged.

The traditional opposition of the United States to having its citizens deal directly with a foreign government on a matter in dispute is embodied in the Logan Act.[100] Adopted in 1799, the Act arose out of congressional opposition to the engaging of Dr. George Logan, a private citizen, in direct negotiations with

[97] Treaty establishing the European Coal and Steel Community, Apr. 18, 1951, art. 33, 261 U.N.T.S. 140. For details see D. VALENTINE, THE COURT OF JUSTICE OF THE EUROPEAN COAL AND STEEL COMMUNITY 71 (1955).

[98] *See* Stein & Hay, *Legal Remedies of Enterprises in the European Economic Community*, 9 AM. J. COMP. L. 325 (1960).

[99] Buergenthal, *The Private Appeal Against Illegal State Activity in the European Coal and Steel Community*, 11 AM. J. COMP. L. 325 (1962).

[100] The Logan Act, 18 U.S.C. § 953 (1976).

France over political differences between France and the United States.[101] In its current form, the Act reads:

> Any citizen of the United States, wherever he may be, who, without authority of the United States, directly or indirectly commences or carries on any correspondence or intercourse with any foreign government or any officer or agent thereof, with intent to influence the measures or conduct of any foreign government or of any officer or agent thereof, in relation to any disputes or controversies with the United States, or to defeat the measures of the United States, shall be fined not more than $5,000 or imprisoned not more than three years, or both.
>
> This section shall not abridge the right of a citizen to apply, himself or his agent, to any foreign government or the agents thereof for redress of any injury which he may have sustained from such government or any of its agents or subjects.[102]

While permitting an individual citizen to proceed against a foreign government on a personal claim, this statute reflects a policy quite contrary to the one which would permit a citizen to hail a foreign government or its officers into an international court on an international dispute which did not uniquely affect him. But this statute, it is submitted, is both unwise and contrary to the interests of either the United States or foreign governments. Although no one has been convicted under the Logan Act, there has been one indictment and there have been threats of prosecution on a few occasions.[103] At the same time, American citizens on numerous occasions, without special authority from the government, have discussed international matters with officials of foreign governments and have sought to influence these officials on outstanding disputes. The United States Government generally has recognized that it is wise to have foreign governments appreciate not only how it feels but also how its citizens feel about various matters. The Pugwash conferences at which American and other scientists have met with scientists and officials from the Soviet Union to discuss arms control and disarmament problems constitute a case in point. At these meetings, informed Americans have sought to influence the conduct

---

[101] For the origins and subsequent history of the Act, see Vagts, *The Logan Act: Paper Tiger or Sleeping Giant?*, 60 AM. J. INT'L L. 268 (1966).

[102] 18 U.S.C. § 953 (1976).

[103] *See* Vagts, *supra* note 101, at 271–81.

of the Soviet Government on matters in dispute between the two governments, but about which there is a large area of common interest.[104] Allowing differences to be discussed and dealt with at a number of levels makes a situation less precarious. Plurality of contact lends an element of stability.

Critics of the proposal that a citizen should be allowed to proceed directly against a foreign government in an international forum argue that such an action would "embarrass" the citizen's government. In many instances an editorial in the *New York Times* or a letter by a leading citizen attacking the foreign policy of this government is likely to be more "embarrassing" than having an unknown, private citizen seek to enjoin the conduct of a foreign government. The premise that on matters of foreign affairs this country must speak with one voice has not been accepted, whatever may be the current political myths. As we seek to bring to the international community ways of dealing with problems that have been used successfully within law-abiding countries, we should remember the virtues of having private individuals do what they think ought to be done without having to wait for their government's special permission.

There is also a distinct advantage for a government to have one of its own citizens free to question the conduct of another government. By so permitting, the government could have the legality of the disputed conduct raised and settled without having to take a position on the question. A government frequently tries to act unofficially. It may use private channels to launch a "trial balloon." Having its citizens question the conduct of a foreign government has many of the same advantages. The government has less at stake. If the citizen loses the case, the government loses little or nothing.

The embarrassment argument is frequently advanced on behalf of the defendant government as well. Yet a government should be no worse off being sued by a foreign individual than by a foreign government. In fact, from the point of view of the defendant it would seem better to be sued by an individual than by a government. In addition, such a suit would be no great change from present practice. The United States regularly

---

[104] For an account of the Pugwash movement, see J. ROTBLAT, PUGWASH — THE FIRST TEN YEARS (1967).

opens its courts to aliens who are free to challenge the legality of the action of a government officer that directly affects them. Suits for injunction and for mandamus can be brought by alien and citizen alike. The United States has permitted suits in the Court of Claims to be brought against it by those aliens whose governments permit comparable suits in their courts by citizens of the United States.[105] This provision, designed to encourage reciprocity by other governments, reflects a policy which favors cases brought by aliens, not a policy against such suits.

e. *Suits by an international organization or agency.* In the case of *Reparation for Injuries Suffered in the Service of the United Nations*,[106] the International Court of Justice was asked to decide whether the United Nations had the capacity to bring a claim for injury caused by the negligence of the defendant government to a United Nations agent while he was performing his duties. The Court held that the United Nations was an appropriate party to bring an action both for its own injury and on behalf of the United Nations agent suffering damages. In its opinion, the Court stated that the United Nations is "an international person" and is "capable of possessing international rights and duties, and . . . has capacity to maintain its rights by bringing international claims."[107] Where there is information available indicating noncompliance with a standing rule, respect for the international legal system tends to require that something be done. Where the wrong is a public wrong, not particularly impinging upon any one government or individual, it seems desirable to have an international organ charged with the duty of bringing the matter before a tribunal for determination.

One could conceive of a general international law enforcement agency to be established within the system of the United Nations and charged with considering all possible violations of international law. Where appropriate, that agency would seek a cease-and-desist order against a given government or officer. It seems unlikely, however, that such a broad and vaguely defined

[105] 28 U.S.C. § 2502 (1970).

[106] [1949] I.C.J. 1.

[107] Advisory Opinion on Reparation for Injuries Suffered in the Service of the United Nations, *id.* at 179. The Court — constrained by its own statute — refrained from recognizing the standing of the United Nations in its judicial proceedings (*id.*, at 178), but this deficiency can be corrected by an amendment to the statute.

jurisdiction would be acceptable. A more promising proposal would be for specific treaties to confer upon speclalized agencies, such as, for example, the World Health Organization, the International Civil Aviation Organization, or agencies specially established in connection with particular fishing treaties, the duty and the power to initiate an action to restrain governments from continuing conduct that was deemed to be violative of a particular treaty commitment. Furthermore, initiating judicial action might be limited to instances where a government refused to accept an administrative determination.

6. *Opening up the International Court of Justice: automatic espousal.* One way to promote greater use of the International Court of Justice and to permit individuals as well as states to initiate action would be to allow an individual to proceed in the name of his state. This could be accomplished in a number of ways and to varying degrees that should make it possible to find a politically acceptable way of giving individuals an increased ability to raise questions of international law.

At the present time, an American citizen who has suffered a particular injury at the hands of a foreign government carries in fact a major part of the burden of pressing his claim, even if the State Department agrees to espouse that claim. The citizen himself is expected to do much of the work in gathering evidence and preparing the claim for litigation. In this regard, a State Department instruction sheet explains: "It should be clearly understood that the responsibility for preparing their claims and obtaining appropriate evidence in support of allegations rests entirely with the claimants."[108]

As a step toward reducing the political, intergovernmental confrontation aspect of use of the International Court of Justice, the United States, either on its own or in conjunction with other governments, might adopt a policy of automatically espousing the claims of its citizens against foreign governments.[109] The

[108] U.S. DEP'T OF STATE, SUGGESTIONS FOR PREPARING CLAIMS FOR LOSS OF OR DAMAGE TO REAL OR PERSONAL PROPERTY (March 1, 1961), *reprinted in* R. LILLICH & G. CHRISTENSON, INTERNATIONAL CLAIMS: THEIR PREPARATION AND PRESENTATION 134 (1962).

[109] Under international law, governments have complete discretion in whether or not to espouse the claims of their nationals against foreign governments. As the International Court of Justice stated, "The state must be viewed as the sole judge to decide whether its protection will be granted, to what extent it is granted, and when it will cease."

theory underlying such a policy would be that the International Court or the arbitral tribunal itself could pass on the merits of the claims, and that there was little benefit in a preliminary administrative screening by the government concerned. Once it were understood that espousal was automatic, it would be recognized that bringing a suit did not indicate any particular involvement or hostility on the part of the plaintiff government. For example, the United States might have a permanent agent at The Hague who could review and sign the pleadings and other papers in order for the suit to conform to the rule that only states can bring actions in the International Court of Justice. After some experience with this procedure, members of the United Nations perhaps could be persuaded to amend the Court's Statute to allow individuals to bring certain kinds of actions against states in the International Court.

Domestic law suggests that this might be a promising way of proceeding. In the common law designed to question public conduct there are many actions that can be brought only in the name of the King, the Attorney-General, or the people, but which, in fact, are instituted and handled by a private litigant. The writs of quo warranto and mandamus, for example, were nominally brought by the King on the relation of a private party. For instance, federal habeas corpus actions today are in the form: United States on the relation of the prisoner versus the warden. The United States Government, nominally on the plaintiff's side of the case, in fact, defends the warden. The prisoner, however, is allowed to institute action in the name of the United States to challenge the legality of his detention. The myth that such action can be brought only by the government is preserved in form, but not in substance.

In beginning to move toward such automatic espousal, a government initially might limit its espousal to those actions in which the private citizen had a particular interest. The government might require the citizen to give advance notice of his intended action and reserve the right to object and to stop his action if unusual reasons appeared to make it desirable to do so. Alternatively, a government might require its affirmative consent for such an action to proceed but grant such consent as a

Case Concerning the Barcelona Traction, Light and Power Company, Ltd., [1970] I.C.J. 44. *See also* United States *ex rel.* Keefe v. Dulles, 222 F.2d 390 (D.C. Cir. 1954).

matter of course, whether the action was basically private or public. In Great Britain, the Attorney-General has broad power to sue for injunctions against a breach of statutory duty, public nuisance, and waste of public funds. A private person who is unable to allege an injury peculiarly to himself may proceed against a public authority only if the Attorney-General will permit the action to be brought in his name. Although the Attorney-General's discretion on this matter is absolute, it is said that in suits for an injunction "[h]e invariably permits the use of his name. . . ."[110]

Another variable which could be altered to make privately initiated challenges to international illegality more or less likely would be to shift the financial costs of such actions. At one extreme, a government might require not only that all counsel fees and out-of-pocket expenses be borne by the individual instigator but also that he post bond to cover the costs and expenses of the defendant should the court find that the suit was frivolous or wholly unjustified. At the other end of the scale, a government might provide the litigant free counsel at public expense, at least for cases that were not frivolous.

7. *Problems of settlement and waiver.* When a national of one country has initiated an action in the name of his government against a foreign government or one of its officers, the situation is not unlike that in domestic law where a shareholder brings a derivative suit in the name of his corporation against a third party. In such actions, there is often a difficult question about who should have the legal right to settle the case, on what terms, and with what effect.

When a government is espousing the interests of one of its citizens, no violation of international law requiring redress occurs unless the rights of the individual continue to be affected adversely. In principle, an individual may settle his case or waive his rights, thereby removing any basis for the government to continue to seek relief.[111] On the other hand, the government

---

[110] H. FINER, ENGLISH LOCAL GOVERNMENT 220 (4th ed. 1950).

[111] This proposition is not free from doubt. The General Claims Commission (Mexico, United States), in the case of Melczer Mining Company (U.S.A.) v. United Mexican States, said that "[i]t may be assumed that it would be very unusual for a government to press a claim in the absence of any desire on the part of the claimant. . . ." (4 R. Int'l Arb. Awards 481, 484 [1929]). But once the national government of a claimant has espoused the claim, the individual may not be able to waive his rights or to compromise it. Citing

also has the power to settle the case. Under current theories of international law, except for that area dealing with internationally protected human or minority rights, a government by international agreement may waive or settle the claims of its citizens, leaving them only such rights as they may have under domestic law to proceed against their own government.[112]

At the present time there is in United States law a subtle but important distinction between the government's simply refusing to espouse a claim of a national (in which case he has no remedy against the government) and a government's taking by eminent domain a claim against a foreign government and making a gift of that claim to the foreign government (in which case the national is entitled to just compensation from the United States Government).[113] In either case, the practical effect of the gov-

---

the Cayuga Indians Case, the same Commission mentioned "a recorded precedent in which the claimant undertook to withdraw a case presented by Great Britain to an international tribunal, which held, however, that the claimant had no power to do so so long as the government espoused the claim. The tribunal in its opinion said that Great Britain derived its 'authority to present' a claim not from the claimant or its representatives 'but from the principles of international law' and presented the claim 'not as the agent' of the claimant 'subject to having its authority revoked, but as a sovereign, legally authorized and morally bound to assert and maintain the interests of those subject to its authority.' . . . " (*id.* at 484). Further, a claimant may not be able to renounce in advance the diplomatic protection of his government. The question is raised by the so-called Calvo clause. In the case of North American Dredging Company of Texas (U.S.A.) v. United Mexican States, the General Claims Commission held that the individual "can not deprive the government of his nation of its undoubted right of applying international remedies to violations of international law committed to his damage. Such government frequently has a larger interest in maintaining the principles of international law than in recovering damage for one of its citizens in a particular case, and manifestly such citizen cannot by contract tie in this respect the hands of his Government" (4 R. Int'l Arb. Awards, 29). By focusing on the remedy, one can best sort out that part of a claim that an individual should be able to settle.

[112] In compromising a claim, the protecting government may or may not affect the cause of action that the aggrieved individual has toward the foreign government. Commenting upon the provisions contained in the "lump sum agreements" with Bulgaria and Rumania, the State Department made it clear in its letter of Sept. 14, 1966, to the Chairman of the Subcommittee on Europe of the House Committee on Foreign Affairs: "These provisions do not constitute a waiver of rights which claimants may have to seek additional claims payment by other remedies; they merely obligate the United States Government not to present the claims again on the diplomatic level." 61 AM J. INT'L L. 107 (1967).

[113] For a discussion of the status of the case law on this distinction, see RESTATEMENT (SECOND) OF THE FOREIGN RELATIONS LAW OF THE UNITED STATES § 213, and Reporter's Note at 629 (1965).

ernment's action on the international level is identical. The United States Government for foreign policy reasons may decide to waive or to settle a claim on the grounds that the particular interests of its national should be subservient to broader governmental objectives. In such cases where the financial or other interests of an individual are being sacrificed for the benefit of the country as a whole, it would seem that the proper thing for the government to do would be to take over its national's interests by eminent domain and to compensate him.

If an individual were given standing to initiate a suit in an international court to question the legality of the action of another government, the question arises whether his own government should be given the legal right to step in and drop the suit. Certainly the government should have that right in some cases and should not in other cases. Presumably, the wisest course would be to give the court the duty to decide whether the claim was one which the executive branch of a government had the legal discretion to waive or settle, or whether the plaintiff's claim raised an international legal issue which the court must decide and which his own government should not have the right to bury.

CHAPTER IX

Use of Domestic Courts and Procedures

It was suggested in Chapter VII that one of the best ways to increase initial respect by a government for the rules of international law is to weave those substantive rules into the fabric of the domestic law so that, in most cases, there is little or no difference between an international obligation and a domestic one. Similarly, in pursuing the objective of second-order compliance, it is desirable to make the maximum possible use of domestic procedures. Given information about possible noncompliance, anyone with standing who wishes to seek an authoritative determination as to what ought to be done should, if feasible, proceed first to a domestic court or administrative agency.

We should seek to build on what we have, rather than trying to design and to establish a wholly new legal system to be put into effect full-blown. Within every country, there are established means of reviewing governmental conduct. These means vary drastically, from country to country, as should our estimates vary of the degree to which different governments can be expected to adhere to legal standards, whether domestic or international. But to the extent that existing administrative agencies and courts are available, they should be used. These domestic institutions, which are generally acceptable and often respected, should be called upon in the first instance to deal with most questions of alleged illegal conduct by a government or its officers. The International Court of Justice and other international tribunals and administrative agencies should be thought of primarily as appellate facilities that should become increasingly available to review decisions made by national institutions.[1]

---

[1] The idea of international courts and administrative agencies reviewing decisions made by national institutions has increasingly been advocated. As early as 1920, the Secretariat of the League of Nations proposed in its memorandum on different operations arising in connection with the establishment of the Permanent Court of International Justice: "Apart from those questions of competence which have been mentioned already,

In considering the desirability of using national institutions to
decide an international question and the ways by which to expand their use, it is helpful to divide them into the following
categories: those of the defendant country, whose conduct is
being questioned; those of the plaintiff country, whose government or national is raising the questions; and those of third
states, which, more or less, are neutral with respect to the question raised. Although some third states may, in fact, be deeply
involved in the question, these categories should be adequate for
purposes of preliminary analysis. Each of these three kinds of
domestic courts and administrative agencies will be discussed in
turn.

1. *Remedies of the defendant country*. There are strong arguments
for expanding the use of the courts and other institutions of the
very government whose conduct is in question. They are the primary institutions that cause a government to respect legal limits
on its authority. A government regularly finds its own courts acceptable and generally, if not always, is willing to comply with
their decisions. A government would rather be told what to do
by its own courts than by a foreign or international court.

Not only are the courts of a defendant country acceptable to
the defendant government; they are often acceptable to a foreign plaintiff. There are innumerable cases in which foreign
plaintiffs not only were willing to resort to the United States
Court of Claims but recovered substantial amounts. Foreign
governments also have been willing to use American courts to
settle what would otherwise be thought of as an international

it might be found desirable that the Court should be made a Court of Appeal from national Courts in matters of International Private Law, and that appeals might be taken to
it from minor international Courts such as the Danube Commission Court" (P.C.I.J. Advisory Committee of Jurists: documents presented to the Committee relating to existing
plans for the establishment of a Permanent Court of International Justice, at 109). In his
letter dated May 3, 1934, and addressed to the President of the Permanent Court of
International Justice, Judge Anzilotti pointed out that " . . . en ce qui concerne la question
dite de l'appel, je n'ai le moindre doute que la Cour peut fonctionner comme instance
d'appel; et j'ajoute aussi: comme instance de cassation ou de revision" *(P.C.I.J. Ser. D. Acts
and Documents Concerning the Organization of the Court. Third Addendum to No. 2, at 915).*
More recently, a number of states answered the questionnaire on *Review of the Role of the
International Court of Justice* and suggested, in general, that the Court should be granted
the review function in an appellate procedure. *See* U.N. Doc. A / 8382, Sept. 15, 1971:
Switzerland (at 54); Cyprus (at 86 and 91); the United Kingdom (addendum 1, at 5 and
7); and Turkey (addendum 3 at 4).

case. For example, the Swiss Confederation sued the United States in the Court of Claims and recovered 80 percent of the amount claimed.[2] The Republic of Peru used American courts to recover on a bond it had posted to obtain the release of a ship for which it had claimed immunity.[3] Monaco unsuccessfully tried to recover damages from Mississippi in the Supreme Court.[4] In 1948 the Government of Norway by a special claims convention[5] agreed that the claim of a Norwegian citizen, Hannevig, for some $68 million would be submitted to the United States Court of Claims for final adjudication.[6] On maritime matters, governments that own ships frequently resort to the local courts of a foreign country. For example, following the Texas City disaster, France, seeking to limit its liability, initiated an action in a United States District Court leading to the domestic litigation of a multimillion-dollar claim directly between the United States and France.[7] The Cuban Government from 1960 to 1964 brought many cases in United States courts despite the precarious relations between the two governments.[8]

To the extent that both a defendant government, whose active compliance we seek, and a plaintiff government would find the legal institutions of the defendant country acceptable in a given case, it would seem highly desirable to increase their availability and use. A number of possibilities appear worthy of consideration.

a. *Opening courts and administrative remedies to foreigners.* In those countries where there are limitations on suits by foreigners or foreign governments, the local government should be encouraged to adopt whatever legislation may be necessary to ensure that foreigners and foreign governments may use the local courts to challenge the legality of the conduct in which govern-

[2]Swiss Confederation v. United States, 70 F. Supp. 235 (Ct. Cl. 1947)

[3]*Ex parte* Republic of Peru, 318 U.S. 578 (1943).

[4]Principality of Monaco v. Miss., 292 U.S. 313 (1934).

[5]Convention for the Settlement of the Claims of Christoffer Hannevig and George R. Jones, March 28, 1940, United States – Norway, 62 Stat. 1798, T.I.A.S. No. 1865.

[6]*See* Hannevig v. United States, 84 F. Supp. 743 (Ct. Cl. 1949).

[7]Republic of France v. United States, 290 F.2d 395 (5th Cir. 1961), *cert. denied*, 369 U.S. 804 (1962).

[8]*See* Banco Nacional de Cuba v. Sabbatino, 376 U.S. 398 (1964); Republic of Cuba v. Mayan Lines, S.A., 145 So. 2d 679 (La. App. 1962); Banco Para el Comercio Exterior de Cuba v. S.S. *Ruth Ann*, 228 F. Supp. 501 (D.C.P.R. 1964).

ment officers are engaged. If the *Kukatush Mining* case, referred to above,[9] is the law in the United States, then that law should be changed. We should not only make our courts available to foreign citizens and governments, we should encourage them to make use of the courts when they wish to question particular conduct.

The Federal Tort Claims Act, which allows both aliens and citizens to recover damages for negligent injury caused them by government officers or employees in the scope of their employment, excludes torts committed in foreign countries.[10] It would seem wise to remove this limitation. By doing so, the extent of the government's liability could be determined by legal, rather than political, techniques and by a domestic, rather than an international, court.

Administrative remedies might also be made available to foreign governments and their citizens. Here, the problem is more one of practice than one of law. The Inspector General in the Army, the Comptroller General, and the FBI, for example, should encourage aliens and foreign governments to call to their attention conduct whose legality is being questioned. The State Department might try to get itself in the habit of thanking someone for informing it of some alleged violation of international law, rather than issuing a flat denial that no such violation had occurred. The Legal Adviser on the request of a foreign government could prepare a legal opinion setting forth the guidelines for future action that international law would seem to require with respect to a particular situation. Such a set of opinions, specifying the legal restrictions that the State Department's top lawyer considered applicable, should constitute over time a significant restraint on the conduct of government officials. As long as both the requests and the opinions were focused on the legal standards applicable to future conduct, even an office as political as that of the Legal Adviser might be expected to produce determinations that adhered to professional standards of legal reasoning and interpretation.

b. *Making international law the law of the land.* A fundamental

---

[9]Kukatush Mining Corp. v. SEC, 309 F.2d 647 (D.C. Cir. 1962). *See also* Chapter VIII n.17 and accompanying text.
[10]28 U.S.C. § 2680(k) (1970).

limitation on the use of domestic institutions to enforce international law is the degree to which the domestic courts consider international legal obligations as legally binding and effective in their courts. This is not an either/or question. In the United States, for example, by virtue of article VI, clause 2 of the Constitution, treaties are part of the law of the land and supersede any prior inconsistent legislation.[11] On the other hand, subsequent legislation inconsistent with a prior treaty is considered as a governmental decision which repudiates at least that part of the treaty in conflict with the legislation.[12] Subsequent domestic statutes are treated as superior to the prior international obligation so far as litigation in domestic United States courts is concerned. Customary international law is also the law of the land,[13] at least for some purposes, but generally is treated as superseded by domestic legislation, state or federal.

In some other countries the legal supremacy of international obligations is explicitly recognized.[14] Under the Philippine,[15]

[11] U.S. CONST. art. VI, cl. 2. As early as 1829, however, the Supreme Court distinguished between "self-executing" treaties and those which required legislation in order to have effect as United States law: "Our constitution declares a treaty to be the law of the land. It is, consequently, to be regarded in courts of justice as equivalent to an act of the legislature, whenever it operates of itself without the aid of any legislative provision. But when the terms of the stipulation import a contract, when either of the parties engages to perform a particular act, the treaty addresses itself to the political, not the judicial department; and the legislature must execute the contract before it can become a rule for the court." Foster v. Neilson, 27 U.S. (2 Pet.) 108, 121 (1829).

[12] See, e.g., Reid v. Covert, 354 U.S. 1 (1956) in which the Court states: "This Court has also repeatedly taken the position that an Act of Congress, which must comply with the Constitution, is on a full parity with a treaty, and that when a statute which is subsequent in time is inconsistent with a treaty, the statute to the extent of conflict renders the treaty null." Id. at 18.

"But state law must yield when it is inconsistent with, or impairs the policy or provisions of, a treaty or of an international compact or agreement." United States v. Pink, 315 U.S. 203, 230–31 (1941).

[13] "International law is part of our law, and must be ascertained and administered by the courts of justice of appropriate jurisdiction, as often as questions of right depending upon it are duly presented for their determination." The Paquete Habana, 175 U.S. 677, 700 (1899). More recently the New York State Court of Appeals stated: "It is settled that, where there is neither a treaty, statute nor controlling judicial precedent, all domestic courts must give effect to customary international law." Argentina v. City of New York, 25 N.Y.2d 252, 259; 250 N.E.2d 698, 700; 303 N.Y.S.2d 644, 648 (Ct. App. 1969).

[14] See, e.g., Wilson, International Law in New National Constitutions, 58 AM. J. INT'L L. 432 (1964); van Panhuys, The Netherlands Constitution and International Law, 58 AM. J. INT'L L. 88 (1964).

[15] PHIL. CONST. art. II, § 3.

Italian,[16] German,[17] Japanese,[18] and Dutch[19] constitutions, legislation that is contrary to international law is without legal effect. In order to make domestic institutions more effective in enforcing international law, the legal supremacy of international law ought to be more widely recognized. The United States could amend its Constitution so that it would correspond with the Dutch and German constitutions. In that event, subsequent legislation inconsistent with international legal obligations, like law inconsistent with the Constitution itself, would be treated as invalid by the courts. Such an amendment would not be so drastic as it might seem at first. The government, in most cases, still would have the de facto power to act contrary to international law. The executive would simply have to be prepared to defy a clear judicial decision, where presently it need defy only an ambiguous obligation.

A number of other steps might be taken to improve the status of international law in domestic courts, and thereby further encourage foreigners and foreign governments to make use of these courts to resolve international questions. The United States, for example, might provide by a constitutional amendment that international legal obligations should be treated as binding by the courts and that no official should have the right to act contrary to those obligations, except pursuant to a special resolution submitted by the President and receiving the advice and consent of two-thirds of the Senate, or some other such limitation. A more simple but nonetheless valuable step would be to enact a statute which provided that customary international law was the law of the land and should be so treated by the courts in the absence of a contrary statute by Congress. Just as the courts, where possible, construe domestic laws so as to make them constitutional, so they similarly, when possible, should construe domestic laws so as to make them consistent with international legal obligations. To some extent, courts might adopt this position on their own without waiting for such legislation.[20]

[16] CONSTITUZIONE art. 10 (Italy).
[17] GRUNDGESETZ arts. 25, 100 (W. Ger.)
[18] KENPO (Constitution) art. 98 (Japan).
[19] GRONDWET art. 63 (Neth.)
[20] See Dickinson, *The Law of Nations as National Law: "Political Questions,"* 104 PA. L. REV. 451 (1956).

Also, national courts, in the absence of domestic legislation, might reexamine their fundamental doctrines with respect to international law and find that nationalist or positivist trends had caused them to depart from wiser and more valid conceptions of the nature of law and the appropriate role of courts. If Congress passed a statute saying that Canada was part of the United States, the American courts certainly ought to recognize that just because Congress says this is so does not make it so. In cases before it, a court should continue to treat Canada as a foreign country and treat the statute as invalid. The statute would be invalid because it would be contrary to international law — a system of law which makes the Constitution valid for the United States — not because the statute would be contrary to the Constitution. Certainly, judicial ingenuity and wisdom could go far in devising appropriate means for allowing domestic courts to decide more questions of international law, whether raised by domestic citizens, by foreigners, or by foreign governments.

c. *Greater use by foreign plaintiffs of available remedies.* Often, one government that is concerned with the conduct of another government fails to consider the advantages of proceeding through the latter government's administrative or judicial channels. As contrasted with exclusive reliance on political pressure, using a defendant government's own courts and agencies might provide it with both an easier way of backing down and additional reasons for doing so. If, for example, an American citizen charged with spying is detained incommunicado in violation of treaty provisions, it might be well for the United States to apply through the detaining government's appropriate judicial or administrative channels for the correction of legal error in addition to whatever hue and cry may be deemed appropriate at the international political level.

Similarly, Cuba might have been well advised prior to the Bay of Pigs attack, at a time when there was substantial evidence of United States governmental activity in support of a possible invasion, to have sought an injunction in a federal district court against designated American officials on the ground that the conduct in question was in violation not only of international law but of the Neutrality act[21] as well. Finding a domestic forum in

---

[21] The Neutrality Act, 22 U.S.C. § 441 (1970).

which the legal question could be focused and discussed can serve to stimulate greater action from domestic forces in favor of compliance with international law.

The less military and explosive an issue, the greater the chance that the use of a country's own courts and procedures might be effective to resolve it. For example, if Mexico objected to the use of a harsh practice by state police in dealing with Mexicans who had improperly entered the United States, one might guess that a suit by the Mexican Government in a United States federal court would lead to a satisfactory decree concerning such practice for the future. Using a domestic forum might be both quicker and more successful than an exchange of diplomatic notes looking toward possible arbitration or adjudication of the disputed conduct.

d. *Insisting upon exhaustion of local remedies by governments.* There is a well-established rule of international law that a government may not espouse the private claim of one of its nationals against a foreign state unless that individual has exhausted all local remedies there which might reasonably be expected to afford him relief. If a plaintiff government, on behalf of one of its nationals, raises a question at the diplomatic level, the defendant government may properly refuse to discuss the question until the individual claimant has first pursued every avenue available to him, unless to do so would obviously be fruitless. An international court[22] or arbitral tribunal[23] with jurisdiction will normally refuse to consider a case at that stage. When, however, the original claim is that of one government against another, the rule of exhaustion of local remedies has not been thought to apply. Here, the practice has been for one government to proceed diplomatically against the other or to bring the claim directly to an international tribunal, despite the fact that it might have been able to obtain satisfaction through the courts or administrative agencies of the defendant country. There are several ways by which this practice might be altered so as to increase the use of the courts and procedures of the defendant country to deal with what otherwise would be an international dispute.

A defendant government could adopt a policy of asking other governments to make maximum use of its available legal or

[22]*E.g.*, The Interhandel Case, [1959] I.C.J. 5.
[23]*E.g.*, Ambatielos Claim, 23 I.L.R. 306, 340 (Arb. Comm'n 1956).

other formal procedural means of seeking relief before pressing the matter diplomatically. When the claim is for a financial amount, other governments could be invited to follow the example of the Swiss Government and sue the United States in the Court of Claims.[24] Such a suit, of course, would be without theoretical prejudice to the foreign government's eventual right to proceed on the international level. The plaintiff government would thus have two chances to recover rather than one: the United States would be bound conclusively by a decision in the Court of Claims, but the foreign government would not be so bound. On the other hand, the United States would have the matter tried in its own court, and an international tribunal would be likely to give great weight to the findings of fact and conclusions of an eminently fair court which had heard the case.

More significant than cases involving financial compensation would be those cases in which one government is concerned about the continuing conduct of another government. In extradition cases, foreign governments routinely appear in the domestic courts of this country to present evidence justifying the extradition of an accused person for trial abroad. The Soviet Union, seeking to build a new chancery for its embassy personnel in Washington, not only raised the matter diplomatically but also litigated the matter before the local zoning board. The Republic of Argentina went before the courts of New York State concerning the taxation of its diplomatic premises.[25]

In 1958 Corporal Girard, while in Japan, brought a suit against the Secretary of Defense in Washington seeking to enjoin the Secretary from turning him over to the Japanese Government for trial.[26] It so happened that the executive branch of the United States Government was on the same side of the issue in that case as was the government of Japan and handled the litigation here. If, however, pressure from nationalist elements within the United States had been successful and had made the executive reluctant to turn Girard over for a foreign trial, it

---

[24] Swiss Confederation v. United States, note 2 *supra*.

[25] *See* Argentina v. City of New York, 25 N.Y.2d 252; 250 N.E.2d 698; 303 N.Y.S.2d 644 (Ct. App. 1969). *See also* the letter dated Jan. 27, 1969, addressed to a local authority by the Legal Adviser of the State Department, 63 Am. J. Int'l L. 559 (1969).

[26] Wilson v. Girard, 354 U.S. 524 (1957).

might well have been an appropriate occasion for the Japanese Government to have sought mandamus in the United States courts to require the Secretary of Defense to hand over Girard pursuant to the treaty. In such cases, the issues would have been almost identical to those issues that actually were litigated. The court might have decided the case the same way, and its decision could have relieved the executive of responsibility for an action which was unpopular in many quarters. Furthermore, in circumstances where foreign citizens or foreign governments believe that they are being deprived of their legal rights by action of a government officer, they should be encouraged to seek an injunction or mandamus in the domestic courts so as to have that question decided. The adoption of a policy that disputes are not ripe for international attention until such an effort has been made could increase significantly the use of the courts and procedures of a defendant country.

Such a policy might be reinforced if a government were to provide that the International Court of Justice would have jurisdiction over a dispute only after a plaintiff government had exhausted available domestic remedies. Governments that have not yet accepted the compulsory jurisdiction of the International Court of Justice might be persuaded to do so subject to such a condition. This would assure these governments that their own courts would first have an opportunity to hear the entire case, reach a decision on it, and write an opinion justifying their decision. One could expect that the International Court would give weight to such a decision.

A government might go further and provide that it would accept the compulsory jurisdiction of the International Court of Justice for the limited purpose of reviewing denials of justice by its local courts, but not for reviewing cases on their merits. A government which was not willing to accept the general jurisdiction of the International Court of Justice might nonetheless be willing to have that Court determine whether local judicial decisions, involving foreign governments or foreign nationals, had been so arbitrary or unreasonable as to constitute a denial of justice. In short, such a government might accept the power of the Court to review only those questions which, in American terminology, involve procedural due process. Such a measure, a partial, yet desirable, step toward the realization of full international judicial review, would tend to increase the willingness of governments to use the local courts of defendant countries and also would tend to cause those courts to follow fair procedures.

A defendant government can thus deal with the exhaustion of local remedies rule so as to increase the extent of usage of its courts and its administrative procedures. The International Court of Justice, on its own, might develop the rule so that it would apply to direct governmental cases as well as to those cases which governments were espousing on behalf of their nationals. There are both logic and precedent to support such a development. There is little reason for government-to-government litigation in the International Court if the defendant government has not finally denied the requested relief; and as long as it is offering a reasonable opportunity for relief in its own courts, the defendant government can hardly be said to have finally rejected the claim. The same considerations that support the application of the local remedies rule to a claim originating with an individual also support the rule's application to a claim originating with a government: saving international remedies for situatons when no other course is available and allowing a government the maximum opportunity to correct its own mistakes.

e. *Applying the exhaustion of remedies rule abroad.* There is some disagreement about whether the rule of customary international law requiring an individual to exhaust local remedies available to him against a foreign government before his own government may press his claim at an international level applies to claims arising outside of the territorial limits of the defendant government. For example, if the Japanese fishermen who were injured by fallout from one of the American nuclear tests in the Pacific could have brought suit in an American court under the Federal Tort Claims Act,[27] then could the United States properly have insisted that they would have to do so before it would discuss the matter diplomatically with the Government of Japan? When the Canadian smelter produced fumes that damaged farms in the United States, the farmers could argue that they did not have to seek relief in Canadian courts because such remedies were not "local" in so far as they were concerned.

[27] Federal Tort Claims Act, note 10 *supra*.

Whatever might be the proper construction today of the rule requiring the exhaustion of local remedies, it would seem desirable to have the rule apply broadly with respect to fact situations arising within or without the territorial limits of a defendant state. To be sure, for a Pakistani farmer whose cow has been killed by a piece of falling American satellite, the Court of Claims in Washington might not be readily "available" in practical terms. But the ingenuity of governments should make it possible to have remedies reasonably available. Perhaps local embassies or consulates could provide assistance in filing claims or in raising other challenges to the legality of a government's own behavior. Whether or not judicial remedies within a country could be made readily available to individuals abroad, such remedies would be sufficiently available to their governments. Once the exhaustion of local remedies rule were applied to governments,[28] it could be applied readily to events arising outside the territorial limits. In terms of geography, the United States Court of Claims is as available to the Embassy of Pakistan in Washington as is the Department of State.

2. *Remedies of the plaintiff country.* The desirability of making greater use of existing legal institutions applies not only to those of the country whose government's conduct is in question but also to those institutions of the country whose government or national is raising the question. A defendant government is, on the whole, more likely to comply with a determination by one of its own courts or administrative bodies than with a determination by a foreign court. Yet, to a large degree, compliance will be a function of the perceived legitimacy of the determination. The use of a plaintiff's own courts and procedures should not be dismissed out of hand. They may be useful both for screening out bad claims and for strengthening good ones.

If an American citizen is complaining that Taiwan is violating international law by reprinting a copyrighted book without his permission, it might be useful to have an American court consider the claim and conclude, as it almost certainly would, that no violation of international law was involved. (Copyright is gov-

[28] For a proposal to apply the local remedies rule to governments and some objections to it, see Mummery, *Increasing the Use of Local Remedies*, 57. AM. SOC'Y INT'L L. PROC. 107 (1964).

erned exclusively by treaty and Taiwan is not a party to the Universal Copyright Convention.)[29] Such a decision would serve to focus concern more precisely on the action that is needed. Similarly, if an American citizen is claiming vast amounts from a foreign government, it might be better for international relations if his claim were whittled down to size by an American court rather than by a comparable decision reached by either a foreign or an international court.

The courts or administrative procedures of a plaintiff country can also serve to strengthen a case. To the extent that there is a reasonable basis for considering the question, the procedures followed are demonstratively fair, and the conclusion appears impartial rather than partisan, the kind of forces that tend to cause a government to comply with an international determination will also tend to cause it to comply with a determination by a plaintiff's court. Such a determination need not be a final one; international review might also be available here. But, such a determination can nonetheless be a desirable step toward fostering second-order compliance.

Several different ways of increasing the extent to which a plaintiff country's courts and other institutions could and would take up international legal questions deserve exploration. We are concerned here with giving such courts *jurisdiction* to make a determination. For a determination to be at all effective, it must be legitimate; that is, the rules of law must permit the court or other agency to make the kind of determination it is making. We therefore need to consider ways of increasing the jurisdiction of the courts and agencies of one country to hear suits involving alleged violations of law by the government or officers of another country.

In considering what might be done to broaden existing jurisdictional rules, we are again limited to those measures which governments ought to find acceptable. This may mean that we should confine any suggested changes to marginal development in notions of jurisdiction that are currently accepted as fair. Obviously, a country could amend its own jurisdictional statutues to provide that its courts would have jurisdiction over all foreign

<hr/>

[29] Universal Copyright Convention with Three Protocols Annexed Thereto, Sept. 6, 1952, 6 U.S.T. 2731, T.I.A.S. No. 3324, 216 U.N.T.S. 132.

governments and that suits against such governments could commence by sending them notice by mail. At the present time, however, such a statute would not be considered legitimate, and the determinations reached by such courts would be accorded little respect. On the other hand, some states within the United States have enacted laws providing that any out-of-state corporation which does business within the state or has a general agent there submits itself to the jurisdiction of its courts and that suit may be begun by serving the agent. Under the Federal Constitution, other states give full faith and credit to a determination reached on that jurisdictional basis. In due course, it might not be unreasonable for a country to adopt a comparable approach internationally and to say that a foreign government which engages in activities within its territory or has an ambassador there submits itself to the jurisdiction of its courts and that suit may be begun by service of process on the ambassador. There are, however, more modest measures that would be somewhat more consistent with traditional limits on national jurisdiction and that therefore should be more acceptable to nation-states.

a. *Authority to make nonbinding decisions.* Just as the International Court of Justice may render an advisory opinion on a question of international law at the request of the United Nations General Assembly, so the highest court of a country might render a similar opinion at the request of its own government. Although the federal courts of the United States have found that the Constitution precludes them from issuing advisory opinions, Thomas Jefferson apparently thought otherwise. As Secretary of State, he requested the opinion of the Supreme Court on several questions of international law in 1793 — questions that the Court declined to answer. Many American state courts as well as the courts of other countries do give advisory opinions. Since it is recognized that such decisions theoretically are not "binding," the right of a court to make such decisions is accepted. They are given less weight than a "binding" decision in which the court had "real" jurisdiction over the defendant. (The advantages and disadvantages of advisory opinions are considered in Chapter XIV.) We are simply noting here that a plaintiff country can give its own courts that kind of jurisdiction over the conduct of another government. And, it is not meaningless to do so. If the

Supreme Court had answered Jefferson's twenty-nine questions about America's duties under international law as a neutral in the contemporary European wars, it might well have strengthened the hand of the United States in its efforts to keep French privateers away from its shores.[30]

A plaintiff government may use its own institutions to decide not only questions of international law but also questions of fact that are involved in an international dispute. An interesting example in point is the authority that has been given to the Foreign Claims Settlement Commission of the United States to determine the validity and amount of claims of American citizens against Canada. Unlike many other international settlements in which the Claims Commission has simply divided among American claimants a lump sum previously agreed upon between the United States and a defendant government, here the Commission adjudicates the amount of the individual claims in advance of international negotiation.[31] Thus, when the United States takes up the matter with a foreign government, here seeking compensation for damage to United States property from flooding for which Canada is responsible, its facts are surer and its claim is stronger by virtue of the prior domestic adjudication of the individual claims by the Commission. Although the Commission's determinations in theory are not binding on Canada, they will be to some extent. If Canada accepted an invitation to participate in such proceedings and in fact had resisted and argued about each claim, the Commission's determinations would have a significant practical effect in any subsequent negotiation or international adjudication, whatever might be the theory.

b. *Abolish the Act of State Doctrine.* Before considering how a plaintiff country might increase its lawful jurisdiction to make binding determinations with respect to alleged noncompliance with international law by another country, it should be noted that there is one way by which a plaintiff country could make better use of the existing jurisdiction of its courts. In the United States and in some other countries, there has developed what is

---

[30] 1 C. WARREN, THE SUPREME COURT IN UNITED STATES HISTORY 107 (rev. ed. 1964).

[31] For discussion of the Lake Ontario program, see Re, *Domestic Adjudication and Lump-Sum Settlement as an Enforcement Technique,* 58 AM. SOC'Y INT'L L.PROC. 39, 44 (1964).

called the Act of State Doctrine. Under this doctrine, an American court will decline to consider a case between two parties, over whom it has unquestioned jurisdiction, if to decide the merits of the case would require the court to pass on the validity under international law of the actions of another government taken within its own territorial limits.[32] That doctrine, which was restated by the Supreme Court in the case of *Banco Nacional de Cuba v. Sabbatino*,[33] runs counter to the position here being urged, namely that compliance with international law would be furthered by greater use of the domestic courts of a plaintiff country on questions of international law.

The *Sabbatino* case involved a great many questions both of substance and procedure.[34] For our purposes the following points seem most relevant. The development of international law and of respect for law as a system applicable to governments is more likely to take place if decisions on questions of international law are made not by the political branch of a government but by the judicial branch. In the United States, the State Department is much more subject to short-run national pressures than are the courts. Although the judiciary in other countries may not be as independent as it is here, as a general rule, it is certainly no more biased than is the executive branch which has been carrying on the disputes. As each country effectively submits its views of international law for general acceptance by the international community, there is a somewhat greater chance of

[32] The doctrine was announced by the Supreme Court of the United States in the case of Underhill v. Hernandez, 168 U.S. 250 (1897). Justice Fuller, speaking for the Court, held: "Every sovereign State is bound to respect the independence of every other sovereign State, and the courts of one country will not sit in judgment on the acts of the government of another done within its own territory. Redress of grievances by reason of such acts must be obtained through the means open to be availed of by sovereign powers as between themselves." *Id.* at 252. For a restatement of the conditions for the applicability of the doctrine see Menzel v. List, 49 Misc. 2d 300, 267 N.Y.S.2d 804 (1966) and 60 Am J. Int'l L. 851 (1966).

[33] 376 U.S. 398 (1964). *See also* 58 Am. J. Int'l L. 779 (1964).

[34] *See* Falk, *The Complexity of Sabbatino,* 58 Am. J. Int'l L. 935 (1964); Stevenson, *The State Department and Sabbatino — Ev'n Victors are by Victories Undone,* 58 Am. J. Int'l L. 707 (1964); Wright, *Reflections on the Sabbatino Case,* 59 Am. J. Int'l L. 304 (1965); Metzger, *The State Department's Role in the Judicial Administration of the Act of State Doctrine,* 66 Am. J. Int'l L. 94 (1972); Delson, *The Act of State Doctrine — Judicial Deference or Abstention?,* 66 Am. J. Int'l L. 82 (1972).

global acceptance of those views submitted by a court than of those views advanced by the very officials who are most involved in a dispute.

More fundamentally, if international law is to be treated as law affecting the legal rights and duties of people, it should be subject to judicial scrutiny as are other laws. Questions of international law necessarily come up in many cases; they are routinely dealt with by domestic courts as required to reach a decision. The Act of State Doctrine is a nonlegal notion which suggests that it is inappropriate for the courts of one state to sit in judgment upon the acts of the government of another state. But courts regularly do just that and should. In the war crimes trials that followed Nuremberg, the national military courts of the United States and of other countries, consistent with a long legal tradition, sat in judgment of the legality under international law of the conduct of officers of the German, Italian, and Japanese governments.[35] Prize courts for centuries have ruled on the legality of ship seizures by their own government and of the legality of the conduct of the ship seized.

Apparently, a major consideration supporting the Act of State Doctrine was concern over the consequence, in cases such as *Sabbatino*, of a court's finding that the foreign government's seizure of an alien's property violated international law. The State Department, as well as the private defendants in that case, apparently assumed that if the seizure of the sugar by the Cuban Government was contrary to international law, then title to the sugar remained in the former owners. This position assumes a substantive rule of international law which provides greater respect for private property than that which is guaranteed by the Constitution of the United States. If the United States takes property by eminent domain, title under American law immediately passes to the government. The former owner is left with an unliquidated claim against the United States for cash. Within its territorial limits, the government has the sovereign power effectively to take title to property, whether it pays just compensation now or whether it leaves the former owner with a long-unsettled claim for payment. We would hardly expect an alien

[35] For reports of these trials, see INTERNATIONAL MILITARY TRIBUNAL, TRIAL OF THE MAJOR WAR CRIMINALS (1948).

owner of a ship seized during war or the owner of land underlying a proposed dam to be able to keep possession of his property until its value had been determined and he had been assured full payment. Unless international law provides greater protection to private property than the fifth amendment, Cuba had the legal power to take the sugar and leave the owners with an unliquidated claim against the Cuban Government.

With such an appreciation of the substantive law, there is no need for an Act of State Doctrine. Although the former owners of sugar and other expropriated property might not be content, domestic courts could face up to the legal questions and decide them.[36] Without the Act of State Doctrine, courts with jurisdiction could decide legal cases in a lawyerlike way, rather than deferring to some vague notion that, in some cases, they should not do so. The long history of the law suggests that both better decisions and better respect for the law are produced if courts articulate their conduct in terms of rules of law, rather than fashioning vague and variable "doctrines" which constitute neither legal rules nor limits on jurisdiction.

c. *Removing sovereign immunity from categories of property.* One way of increasing the jurisdiction of the courts of a plaintiff country to decide the legality under international law of the conduct of another government is to limit further the property of foreign governments that is accorded sovereign immunity. There has always been a question of how much foreign property should be considered as partaking of the immunity of the sovereign. The United States long followed the classical or virtually absolute theory of sovereign immunity under which one government could not, without its consent, be made a respondent in the courts of another government.[37] In 1952, in the famous Tate Letter from the acting Legal Adviser of the State Department to

---

[36] In some cases, such as takings by the Nazis in violation of basic human rights, the courts might find that a government did not have the legal power to change the status. *See* Bernstein v. Nederlandsche — Amerikaansche Stoomvaart Maatschappij, 210 F.2d 375 (2d Cir. 1954), where the court reversed its earlier holding, 173 F.2d 71 (2d Cir. 1949). *See also* the citation of that case in 58 AM. J. INT'L L. 505 (1964), and the case of Banco Nacional de Cuba v. First National City Bank of New York, 442 F.2d 350 (2d Cir. 1971).

[37] The doctrine was introduced in American practice in 1812, in the decision of the Supreme Court in The Schooner *Exchange* v. McFadden. Speaking for the Court, Justice John Marshall stated that a sovereign is "bound by obligations of the highest character

the Acting Attorney General, the United States switched to a restrictive view of sovereign immunity under which "the immunity of the sovereign is recognized with regard to sovereign or public acts (*jure imperii*) of a state, but not with respect to private acts (*jure gestionis*)."[38] In particular, sovereign immunity was no longer recognized by the executive branch with respect to commercial property owned by a foreign government, state-owned trading vessels, and so forth. The State Department recognized that the matter was governed by international law, that there were two views of international law, and that it was as a matter of discretion adopting the more restrictive theory of immunity.

Since then Congress has enacted the Foreign Sovereign Immunities Act of 1976, adopting the restrictive theory and, consistent with views suggested here, making immunity a legal rather than a political question. The statute adopts the view that "[u]nder international law, states are not immune from the jurisdiction of foreign courts insofar as their commercial activities are concerned, and their commercial property may be levied upon for the satisfaction of judgments rendered against them in connection with their commercial activities."[39] In view of the blending of public and private activity both in countries that are nominally socialist and in those that are nominally free enterprise, courts will find it difficult to draw the line between "commercial" activities and "commercial" property that is subject to attachment and governmental activities and property that are protected by sovereign immunity.

d. *Holding nonimmune property for governmental activities.* Under

---

not to degrade the dignity of his nation, by placing himself or its sovereign rights within the jurisdiction of another." 10 U.S. (7 Cranch) 478, 481 (1812). As later explained by the Court in *Ex parte* Republic of Peru, this principle requires "that courts may not so exercise their jurisdiction, by the seizure and detention of the property of a friendly sovereign, as to embarrass the executive arm of the Government in conducting foreign relations." 318 U.S. 578, 588 (1943).

[38] Tate Letter, 26 DEP'T STATE BULL. 984, 984 (1952). American courts have applied the restrictive theory of sovereign immunity in many cases. *See, e.g.,* Victory Transport v. Comisaria General de Abastecimientos y Transportes, 336 F.2d 354 (2d Cir. 1964); 2nd Ocean Transport Co. v. Government of Republic of Ivory Coast, 269 F. Supp. 703 (E.D. La. 1967). For a detailed expression, in a legal text, of the restrictive theory of sovereign immunity, see European Convention on State Immunity and Additional Protocol, May 16, 1972, Europ. T.S. 74.

[39] Pub. L. No. 94–583, 90 Stat. 2891 (1976).

current international law, the property of a foreign government involved in commercial or trading activities can be attached and held by court order as security for a judicial determination only if that determination is with respect to a financial obligation arising from such nonimmune activities. There seems no necessary reason for thus distinguishing between governmental and commercial financial obligations of a foreign government, even if one continues to respect a distinction between the immunity from judicial execution of different categories of governmental property.

For example, would it be reasonable to change the domestic law of the United States to permit the United Nations, while seeking to collect the unpaid assessment of the Soviet Union, to attach two Soviet merchant ships in New York harbor and then to seek a determination by a New York court that the assessment was, in fact, a legal obligation of the Soviet Union and that the ships could be sold to meet that obligation? If the United States were to alter its domestic view of sovereign immunity in such a way, one could expect other governments to follow suit. There is a potential danger that foreign courts might be even more partisan than our own courts, and the result of such domestic legislation restricting sovereign immunity might be more chaos, rather than more law. However, it should be possible to lay the groundwork for a legitimate assertion of jurisdiction. The United States, for example, might assert such jurisdiction only in connection with an acceptance of the jurisdiction of the International Court of Justice to review the correctness of the determination of the legal obligation thus being enforced. Further, it might well be possible to prepare and to get adopted in advance by the General Assembly an appropriate resolution recommending that governments make their courts available for this purpose, provided that they made their decisions subject to review by the International Court. Such a resolution, framed not in terms of international legislation but rather in terms of clarifying the law of sovereign immunity might well legitimate such a reduction in the role of sovereign immunity and, consequently, broaden the use of the domestic courts of a plaintiff country for making determinations on international law questions.

e. *Distinguishing between immunity from decision and immunity from*

execution. The Government of the United States, in many respects, has removed its immunity from suit without having removed its sovereign immunity from execution to satisfy an
adverse judgment. For example, one may sue the Federal Housing Authority, but if the Authority declines or fails to pay a judgment against it, one may not levy execution on its funds in the
hands of the Treasury.[40] It might be possible to use such a distinction to reduce the immunity of foreign sovereigns without
risking that the courts might go too far.

For example, a domestic statute might provide that public
government property remain immune from seizure by judicial
decree and that foreign ambassadors and other diplomats remain free from arrest or detention of any kind. However, the
statute might provide that suits seeking recovery out of such
property or suits against such foreign officers physically within
the jurisdiction could be brought and tried. The defendant government or individual should be accorded full opportunity to be
heard directly or through counsel without waiving immunity
from execution. If a defendant did not appear, the court should
appoint counsel to present his side of the case. The theory would
be that such a judicial determination, like the one against the
Federal Housing Authority, was legally binding, even though
the court would be legally unable to enforce it with a levy of execution or with a contempt order.

The problem of dealing with parking violations by diplomats
in New York and Washington suggests that such formal judicial
determinations might have some effect in causing compliance.
Rather than assuming that an ambassador's diplomatic immunity protects him from any official reaction to his parking in a
no-parking area, the city of New York might well ticket his car
and notify him that at a given time there would be a hearing, to
which he was invited to appear by counsel, on whether the law
permitted him to park in that place. A determination might then
be made by a magistrate or police official that the ambassador
had parked his car in a no-parking area, that the car was not
allowed to be so parked, and that his diplomatic immunity from
arrest did not legally entitle him to park in no-parking areas.
The determination could be accompanied by an order that in

[40] FHA v. Burr, 309 U.S. 242, 250 (1940).

the future he should not so park. This order could be given appropriate publicity in the press, and copies sent to the ambassador's government.[41] A similar procedure might be followed in civil cases, whether they involved the nonpayment of a charge account, the regular holding of noisy parties disturbing the neighbors, known abuse of the diplomatic pouch for smuggling purposes, or the nonsupport of a diplomat's illegitimate child. In each case, the ultimate immunity from execution could be recognized, while giving domestic institutions a chance to consider both the facts and the law and to reach a determination.

A comparable result might be reached by a single procedural rule which provided that courts should first consider the merits of a case and then turn to the question of possible immunity. Such a rule might be justified (plausibly, if somewhat inadequately) on the ground that a question of diplomatic immunity is a touchy international matter upon which a domestic court should not pass if the question can be avoided. If it should turn out that the plaintiff had no case on the merits, it would be unfortunate that the court first had to conclude that the defendant was without immunity, a holding which might upset his government, which would be irritating to him, and which — it turned out — was not essential to a disposition of the case. By reserving for later consideration all questions of immunity, a domestic court could reach a determination with regard to questions of law and fact even though it might later conclude that it could not issue an order to implement that decision because of the immunity of the property or individual involved.

f. *Holding nonimmune property as security for compliance with an ultimate decree.* To the extent that our primary goal in seeking second-order compliance is not compensation for past illegality but rather affecting future governmental conduct, a typical determination we would like to have made will not be a financial judgment but an order instructing some government official to

[41] In 1964 the State Department adopted a policy of treating parking tickets as an authoritative determination of a fine owed and announced that it would not issue diplomatic license plates to officials against whom charges for parking violations were outstanding. The Department stated: "This policy does not in any way infringe upon the diplomatic immunity of foreign diplomats stationed in Washington. Under no circumstances will diplomatic officials be subject to arrest or detention for failure to pay charges incurred for parking violations." Dep't of State Press Release No. 140 (April 1, 1964).

stop doing some specific thing. Since the relief requested is not money, jurisdiction over some property held by a foreign government appears irrelevant. On the other hand, one of the standard means of causing compliance with an equitable decree is the imposition of a cumulative fine for every day of noncompliance, for which the availability of assets within the jurisdiction is relevant.

In domestic law, we recognize that an individual's property within a jurisdiction may be attached and thereby provide an adequate basis for adjudicating claims unconnected with that property, provided only that the property may be sold to carry out the judgment if it is not otherwise paid. By analogy, property within a country might strike the international community as an appropriate basis for jurisdiction to issue injunctive type relief — the injunction being subject to enforcement by the imposition of a cumulative fine (to be realized from sale of the property) for each day's noncompliance with the injunction. The jurisdictional basis and the chance of compliance would be stronger if the injunction related to conduct that occurred within the state or at least had an impact there.

An example of the exercise of this jurisdictional basis might be the attachment by a German court of a commercial ship owned by the Soviet Government within a German harbor in connection with a suit by a German radio station seeking to enjoin deliberate jamming of its local broadcasts by a Soviet transmitter. Pending litigation, the ship itself might be released in exchange for a bond.[42] If the German court should find that the Soviet Government was improperly interfering with the German station's local broadcasts, it might order the Soviet Government to stop such interference. Upon finding that the government was not complying with that order, the German court might decree the imposition of a fine of DM2,000 a day for each day thereafter in which the interference continued, such fine to be realized from the sale of the Soviet commercial ship or from the bond, as the case might be. Where the injury is occurring within Germany, even if the action originates elsewhere, such a method of obtaining jurisdiction does not seem outrageous. The legitimacy of the determination here, as elsewhere, would be greatly

[42] *Cf. Ex parte* Republic of Peru, 318 U.S. 578 (1943).

strengthened by the German Government's acceptance of the jurisdiction of the International Court of Justice to review the merits of its own court's decision in such a case, even if the general compulsory jurisdiction of the International Court of Justice was not accepted.

g. *Remedies of third countries.* We have considered above the desirability of greater use of the domestic legal institutions in the country in which someone is seeking relief and in the country whose government's conduct is in question, and what might be done to promote those goals. In many instances, the most appropriate forum may be in some third country, either because the action is taking place there or because some property or an official relevant to the action is within that country. Moreover, because of the greater likelihood of their being less partisan, the courts of a third state may be even more appropriate than the courts of one of the parties to the dispute.

The general techniques discussed above with respect to the courts and institutions of a plaintiff country would seem equally applicable. With a large number of countries making their courts available for such litigation, the chances of being able to get a legitimate determination would increase significantly. Just as the widespread use of extradition treaties makes it difficult for a criminal to avoid his responsibility by fleeing the jurisdiction, so the widespread acceptance of the notion that a government's commercial property could be attached would make it increasingly difficult for a government to avoid its international obligations.

CHAPTER X

Blending International Institutions into Domestic Law

Although domestic courts should be used as much as possible to determine whether a government is not complying with international law, it is clear that the International Court of Justice and other international institutions should also be available if the final judicial determination is to have maximum legitimacy and, hence, produce maximum compliance. National courts are undoubtedly influenced by national considerations. For many decisions, national courts may be acceptable. The long history behind the International Court of Justice reflects the deeply felt necessity for an impartial body that is institutionally independent of the participating states. The desirability — the practical necessity — of an International Court of Justice is here taken for granted. The question for consideration in this chapter is how that Court and other international institutions should be related to the domestic legal systems within each country.

1. *Giving domestic effect to international administrative decisions.* Continuing the general policy of lessening the sharp distinction that historically has been made between international law and "real" law, it would seem wise to study and to extend the practice of giving international agencies the power to make determinations to which legal effect is routinely given by domestic law. By the various treaties establishing and conferring powers on international agencies, it could be provided that within their respective areas of competence, their decisions should be legally effective without the necessity of further governmental action. Where possible, the action of an international agency dealing with a particular question should be in the form of a decision binding on people, rather than a decision which is either binding upon governments or recommendatory to them.

Some international agencies now have the power to issue regulations to which legal effect is automatically given by national law. An early example is that of the 1930 convention designed to preserve sockeye salmon fisheries.[1] The treaty establishes an international commission which has the power to issue regulations from time to time. Statutes of Canada[2] and the United States[3] give these international regulations the force of domestic law, providing that persons who fail to comply with orders or regulations of the commission shall be subject to punishment. Similarly, the quotas of the European Coal and Steel Community carry automatic domestic legal sanctions.[4] Such built-in domestication obviously increases the chance that people will go along with the international decision.

The Sockeye Salmon Commission's[5] regulations are orders of general applicability. There is no reason why international agencies should not issue specific orders dealing with particular instances of alleged noncompliance that clarify the rule for the future and indicate what ought not to be done. Problems come up before the International Civil Aviation Organization, the Universal Postal Union, or the agencies that oversee international control of narcotics. These and other international agencies dealing with specific problems where disputes might arise should have the right to issue decisions that have legal effect under the domestic law of the countries concerned.[6] Although, as discussed in the next chapter, such decisions need not be conclusive, they should be binding unless affirmative action of some kind is taken to set them aside.

2. *Domestic effect of foreign legal decisions.* As the international legal system is pulled more closely together, it would seem wise to have the courts of one country respect the decisions of the courts of other countries.[7] In considering how international de-

[1] Sockeye Salmon Fisheries Agreement, May 26, 1930, United States–Canada, 59 Stat. 1614, E.A.S. No. 479.

[2] Sockeye Salmon Fish Convention, 20–21 George 5, c. 10, 130 Can. Stat. 143.

[3] Sockeye Salmon Fishery Act of 1947, c. 345, 61 Stat. 511.

[4] Treaty establishing the European Coal and Steel Community, Apr. 18, 1951, art. 58.

[5] *See* Sockeye Salmon Fisheries Agreement, *supra* note 1, at arts. II and IV.

[6] For a survey of international organizations with power to adopt mandatory resolutions, see Skubiszewski, *A New Source of the Law of Nations: Resolutions of International Organisations*, RECUEIL D'ETUDES DE DROIT INTERNATIONAL, EN HOMMAGE À PAUL GUGGENHEIM 508 (1968).

[7] Present international practice is still largely based on the legal philosophy expressed by Justice Gray in the case of Hilton v. Guyot, 159 U.S. 113 (1895): "No law has any effect, of its own force, beyond the limits of the sovereignty from which its authority is derived. The extent to which the law of one nation, as put in force within its territory,

cisions should be made effective, it is apparent that the general theory must be that legal decisions are legal decisions.[8] In order to have the judgment of a court of one country enforceable in the courts of another, it should not be necessary to have to go to an international tribunal unless there is some question about the legality under international law of the first judgment.

Within the United States, the courts of one state are compelled by the Federal Constitution to accord full faith and credit to the judgments of a sister state.[9] By statute, federal courts must also respect the decisions of the state courts.[10] However, the situation is quite different with respect to recognition and enforcement of the judgments of foreign courts. The generally understood law in this regard is that one nation, if it chooses, may allow a plaintiff who obtained a judgment in a foreign court to sue on that judgment in a domestic court without the need to prove again the merits of his case. But this is a matter of comity only — a matter of being obliging, rather than obliged.[11] Each country and, within the United States apparently, each judge is free to issue a new judgment based solely on the foreign judgment or to ignore the foreign judgments completely.

It is rather ironic that under the Act of State Doctrine the courts of a second country will consider a hasty administrative act of a foreign country as conclusively settling a legal question over which that foreign country then had jurisdiction but will decline to give comparable weight to an orderly decision of a court of that foreign country reached in a case where that court concededly had full jurisdiction over the parties.

---

whether by executive order, by legislative act, or by judicial decree, shall be allowed to operate within the dominion of another nation, depends upon what our greatest jurists have been content to call 'the comity of nations.'" *Id.* at 163.

[8] As Chief Justice Fuller stressed, "[T]he doctrine of *res judicata* applicable to domestic judgments should be applied to foreign judgments as well, and rests on the same general ground of public policy that there should be an end of litigation." *Id.* at 229 (dissenting opinion).

[9] U.S. CONST. art. IV, § 4.

[10] 28 U.S.C. § 1738 (1948).

[11] Speaking for the Court in Hilton v. Guyot, Justice Gray stated: "'Comity,' in the legal sense, is neither a matter of absolute obligation, on the one hand, nor of mere courtesy and good will, upon the other. But it is the recognition which one nation allows within its territory to the legislative, executive or judicial acts of another nation, having due regard both to international duty and convenience, and to the rights of its own citizens or of other persons who are under the protection of the laws." *Supra* note 7, at 163–64.

Within the United States, the judgments of the courts of one state have not been given automatic effect by the courts of sister states. It has been necessary for the successful party to go to a local court and obtain a fresh judgment. He need not prove again his case. The first judgment itself provides him with a cause of action on which he can now sue. Recently, steps have been taken by some states to permit the judgment of a sister state to be recorded in the second jurisdiction and thereby given immediate effect without the necessity of a second lawsuit. Whatever might be eventually desirable in the international community, it is likely that for the foreseeable future local judicial scrutiny of the first judgment will be in order if the losing party is not complying with it. It would seem sufficient if the judicial decisions of one country were to be given automatic effect by *judges* in other countries and not necessarily by sheriffs or others seeking to follow up such decisions.

Extradition is a current example of where, by treaty, the courts of one country cooperate with the judicial proceedings of another. Normally, a person convicted by the courts of one country who has escaped to another country will be held and, by court order, turned over to officials of the first country for his return thereto.

Obviously, there are limits on the extent to which the courts of one country should give legal effect to the decisions of the courts of another. Two basic limitations are that the foreign court had jurisdiction and that the court proceeded lawfully. Each of these limitations is a matter both of international and domestic law. Thus, a foreign court judgment will not be entitled to legal effect in another country unless:

1. the country's assertion of jurisdiction was consistent with international law (*e.g.*, the defendant was within its territorial limits);

2. its national law authorized the courts to exercise jurisdiction in such a case;

3. the procedures followed did not violate notions of internationally protected human rights; and

4. the court acted lawfully according to its national law.[12]

It would seem appropriate that once the courts of a second coun-

[12] *See also* H. STEINER & D. VAGTS, TRANSNATIONAL LEGAL PROBLEMS 702 (1968).

try found that these four conditions had been met, it should treat the foreign decision as legally binding and as having decided what it purports to decide.

A question can be raised whether such a decision should be binding if a court of the second country concludes that the decision is wrong as a matter of international law. It is somehow easier to give finality to decisions on questions of fact than it is to those decisions on questions of law. But if decisions are to be accorded weight, it is because they are final. Something has in fact happened, conclusively. To say that a decision will be respected unless it is "wrong" is to leave every case open for redetermination. To do so leaves the defendant and others feeling that the defendant is free not to comply with a determination because he can continue to argue that the decision is wrong and, if wrong, is without legal effect. Issues of substantive error should be taken up on appeal to an international court; if there is no appeal, both parties should be as bound by the decision abroad as they would be within the country whose court rendered the decision.

It could be that issues of procedural fairness, if not taken up on appeal to an international forum, also should be foreclosed. It can well be argued that as long as the defendant had an opportunity to raise in an international forum any claims he might have had that the procedure by which the national decision was reached was unfair, then there was no unfairness in the total procedure. As a step toward increasing the international effectiveness of national decisions, however, it seems wisest to start with the finality of those judgments which were fairly reached. In due course, it might be possible to extend on the international level the doctrine of full faith and credit until that doctrine is as broadly applied as it is now among the states of the United States.

The problem of finality is not likely to be so great in the area with which we are primarily concerned — judicial decisions telling officials not to engage in specified conduct — as it is in the area of criminal conduct and civil judgments for compensation. Courts within a country generally have the power to modify their own decrees relating to ongoing conduct. If a court could lawfully modify its own decision in light of later circumstances, there would be nothing improper in having the courts of another country do likewise.

3. *International review of national decisions.* Whenever a national decision fails to respect what is alleged to be an internationally protected right, there should be an international forum available to resolve that question. When a decision by a national administrative agency appears to be contrary to a decision which an international administrative agency might rightfully reach within its limited area of competence, it should be possible to "appeal" the decision of the national administrative agency to the international agency. For example, if a national agency should restrict the range of a radio station on the ground that it was required to do so by virtue of the international allocation of frequencies, the aggrieved station should be able to appeal that decision to the international agency that administers radio frequency allocation.[13] The same should be true if, for example, the plaintiff were a Canadian station asking the Federal Communications Commission to rule that a Detroit station was using more power than that permitted by international agreement.

The more frequent situation would be when a party was dissatisfied with a determination made by a national court — a determination which he believed to be contrary to international law. For example, the Czech Government might seek in a West German court an injunction against the officers of an American-financed venture seeking to restrain them from releasing balloons carrying propaganda east into Czech airspace. If the German court should deny any relief, finding that the conduct was not contrary to any international rule, the Czech government might want to appeal that decision to the International Court of Justice. Ideally, the International Court should have broad enough jurisdiction to review at the international level all those cases which, as discussed in Chapter IX, we wanted to have ini-

[13] United States v. McIntire, 365 F. Supp. 618 (D.C.N.J. 1973) illustrates the practical interest in establishment of forms of appeals to international agencies against decisions of national agencies operating under international conventions. In that case, the defendant, contesting the power of the United States to regulate broadcasting originating beyond its territorial limits, argued that the authority of the Federal Communications Commission to license broadcasting from vessels pursuant to § 301(e) had been superseded by the terms of article 7, § 1(1) of the 1959 International Telecommunications Convention, Dec. 21, 1959, 12 U.S.T. 1761, T.I.A.S. No. 4892.

tiated. There are a number of problems in expanding the present jurisdiction of the International Court of Justice to include review of domestic court decisions. This chapter just identifies some of the steps that could be taken to broaden the Court's jurisdiction. The next chapter is concerned with ways of making such steps acceptable to governments.

It has been suggested that for the United States and, perhaps, for other countries, it is contrary to basic constitutional law to have an international court review and possibly reverse the decisions of the highest national court. In the criminal law area, the United States would certainly have a problem with allowing an international court to reverse what purported to be a final acquittal. Notions of double jeopardy would stand in the way of such action, at least unless there was some procedural error in the trial. (On the other hand, the dual jurisdiction theory, as harsh and erroneous as it may be, that permits the United States to try a bank robber acquitted by a state court, could be used to permit an international trial of a man acquitted by a national court.) If the procedure of the first trial were fair even if the result "wrong," there would seem to be no need for a second trial.

The argument that international review would be inconsistent with the necessary finality of Supreme Court decisions seems clearly wrong. On many occasions, decisions of United States courts, including those of the Supreme Court, have been subjected to review in international arbitration.[14] Also, the doctrine of exhaustion of local remedies, long asserted by the United States and most other countries, rests on the assumption that only after a national court has reached a final decision is the matter ripe for international consideration.

More serious than problems of domestic constitutionality, which, in any event, could be removed by amending those constitutions that might be deemed to require it, are jurisdictional problems that would arise for the International Court of Justice when either the plaintiff or the defendant was not a government.

[14]See, e.g., The Betsey, Furlong (United States v. Great Britain) (Nov. 19, 1794) 3 Moore's Arb. 3160 (1898); The Hiawatha (1871), 2 Black 635, 4 Moore's Arb. 3902 (1898); and The Circassian (1871), 2 Wall. 155, 4 Moore's Arb. 3911 (1898) (containing a dissent contending that the Supreme Court should be upheld in doubtful cases.)

As suggested above, the concept of automatic espousal might handle those cases where an individual was the plaintiff. A government could adopt willingly a regular practice of formally espousing international claims at the request of its nationals. The government could take whatever action was deemed by the International Court of Justice sufficient to demonstrate that the state was in law if not in fact a party. (This should not involve much more than form.)

Where a national was proceeding against his own government for an allegedly continuing violation of international law, it is difficult to see how any international review would be possible, at least if the case were in the courts of the government concerned. And here, perhaps, no international review is needed. It may be useful to have a citizen free to ask his courts to order his government or one of its officers to stop doing something which may violate international law. But if that court concludes that the government is behaving lawfully, and if no foreign government or national and no international agency wishes to pursue the matter, then the international community might as well let the matter rest.

When the action is against a government officer as an individual, there is also a jurisdictional problem for the International Court of Justice since only states may be parties to cases before it. In most circumstances, it should be possible to consider the international wrong that is being brought to the International Court as the allegedly erroneous action of the national court. The government whose court rendered the decision being appealed would be the defendant in the international case brought to the International Court of Justice. Alternatively, when the action is against an officer, his government could be the defendant. The theory here would be that the government was committing an international wrong by allowing its officer to continue to engage in the conduct in question. As discussed in Chapter XIV *infra*, there are many advantages to proceeding against an officer as an individual, rather than proceeding against his government. Therefore, it might seem preferable to involve the government as defendant only on the ground of its being responsible for the judicial decision, and not as being the active defendant whose action led to the original case. This difference in theory would bring a different defendant before the Court if, as in the hypothetical case noted above about balloons over Czechoslavakia, the initial action were brought in the courts of a third state.

4. *Domestic effectiveness of international judicial decisions.* A final feature of the integration of international and domestic legal systems would be the existence of a domestic legal duty on all public officials to comply with the decisions of the International Court of Justice. Just as there is an immediate obligation on the part of state officials within the United States to comply with decisions of the Supreme Court, so there should be an analogous obligation on all national officials to comply with a decision of the International Court. Further, such prompt compliance should not be dependent on the necessity of a subsequent domestic political decision to comply. In the absence of an effective political decision *not* to comply, domestic law should give effect to the international decision.

International decisions might be better carried out if they were in the form of a remand, sending the case back to a national court to issue a decree in accordance with the opinion of the International Court. Domestic courts would be legally bound to follow up the international decision and to take whatever supplemental action might be required.

With domestic law arranged to give legal effect to international determinations, a case might go back and forth from one forum to another. A hypothetical scenario, illustrating the kind of legal procedures that ought to be available, might run along the following lines: A Mexican fishing company applies to the United States Nuclear Regulatory Commission (NRC) alleging that a California corporation engaged in the disposal of radioactive waste materials is dumping these materials in the ocean, inadequately packaged and in a part of the high seas where currents tend to take that waste into territorial waters of Mexico and elsewhere on the high seas where the company fishes. The Mexican company asks the NRC to issue an administrative order to the California corporation requiring it to package the waste in more durable containers and to dump it much farther out in the ocean.

The NRC holds hearings. It finds that one container of radioactive waste is known to have burst, but that there is no evidence that the waste reached Mexican territorial waters. It thus finds the current refusal of Mexican citizens to buy fish caught off Lower California to be wholly unjustified. It nonetheless designates a somewhat smaller area within which the waste products may be dumped and orders the company to adhere closely to the specifications for containers previously issued.

The Mexican plaintiff, still not satisfied, applies to the International Atomic Energy Agency (IAEA) in Vienna. The IAEA notes that not enough countries have ratified the "International Convention on the Disposal of Radioactive Waste Products" to bring it into effect and concludes that until that Convention is in effect the IAEA does not have jurisdiction over the present type of dispute.

The Mexican plaintiff then applies to the federal district court in California seeking to enjoin the California company from further disposing of these radioactive waste products at sea, pending the establishment of international standards and proof that no fish are being contaminated. The district court and, on appeal, the court of appeals deny the requested relief. The Supreme Court thereafter denies certiorari, declining to take the case.

The Mexican plaintiff, with the standing permission of his government to act for all Mexican citizens with comparable grievances, files a case in the name of the Government of Mexico against the United States in the International Court of Justice. After proceedings in which the principal work is handled by the Mexican company and the California corporation and in which the governments of Mexico and the United States play only a modest role, the International Court of Justice decides that when the risk of contamination, if rupture of the containers occurs, is great and the period of contamination is extremely long-lived, it is the duty of those using the high seas to "take every reasonable precaution to see that their use of the high seas does not prejudice reasonable use by others." The Court further finds that the one known rupture of a container demonstrates that every reasonable precaution was not being taken and decrees that the United States must take greater care in this kind of waste disposal.

On motion and after a hearing on the International Court of Justice's findings, the federal district court of California orders the California company to use every reasonable precaution in its waste disposal and finds that this requires that such waste materials should be disposed of in reinforced concrete barrels of a specified strength and should not be so disposed less than 200 miles off the coast. By ordering such remedial action, the district court recognizes its duty to comply with and execute an authoritative and, thus, legally binding determination of the International Court of Justice.

Chapter XI

Making International Institutions Acceptable

1. *The problem of reducing institutional power.* I have suggested in Chapters VIII-X that obtaining a legitimate and authoritative determination with respect to future conduct is essential to the entire concept of second-order compliance with international law. I also have recommended that the major effort to improve compliance with international law should be directed toward having governments and government officials comply with particular determinations of what they ought or ought not to do in the future. In order to realize this objective, there must be institutional means of producing such determinations. As I argued in Chapter IX, domestic legal institutions can be used far more than they have been to resolve international law questions. However, the possibility of international review, as described in Chapter X, appears essential as a way of legitimating national determinations and as a way of resolving authoritatively and acceptably challenges to the fairness of these determinations.

The critical role of such an impartial or third-party decision with respect to disputes over questions of international conduct has long been recognized. It has also been recognized that institutions for reaching such legitimate determinations cannot successfully be imposed upon the governments of the world. The very authoritative and legitimate nature of the decisions desired appears to require that the institutions be acceptable to the international community. Although it is not necessary that every government accept every international agency and tribunal, it would appear necessary that the great majority of governments find international institutions acceptable if they are to survive.

A government which is being asked to accept a scheme designed to cause compliance with international rules is subject to two basic concerns, often at the same time. It fears that the scheme will be too weak and too strong — too weak when it is dealing with other governments and too strong when it is dealing with the government in question. Attacks within the United States on the International Court of Justice illustrate the problem. One is told that the International Court of Justice is useless because it lacks the power to enforce its decisions. One is also told, often by the same critic, that to accept the jurisdiction of the International Court would deprive the United States of its sovereign power and would place the country at the mercy of a handful of foreign judges.[1]

Most of this book is devoted to exploring the question of how an international legal system might overcome the problem of its being too weak. This chapter considers ways of overcoming a government's fear that the international system would be too strong — that the international institutions a government is asked to accept would have too much power.

The gap between existing or proposed international institutions and existing attitudes of governments can be reduced either by devising more acceptable institutional arrangements or by altering the views of governments about such institutions. Both parts of this task are important. It is highly useful to point out to governments where their true interests lie. Such an effort would help governments to understand why they should find the International Court of Justice and other international institutions acceptable and why they should formally accept the legal right of such institutions to make authoritative determinations. At the same time, it is valuable to examine the reluctance of governments to reach that conclusion. By so doing, we can consider what might be done to modify existing institutions to make them more acceptable but still capable of making useful determinations. If political attitudes are taken as more or less fixed for the short range, then the most relevant problem is to design acceptable international institutions that could contribute toward the objective of second-order compliance. I shall not try to propose a particular scheme which would fall just on the right side of the

[1] That kind of fear produced the Connally Amendment to the declaration of acceptance of the complusory jurisdiction of the International Court of Justice by the United States. The declaration denies the jurisdiction of the Court in all "disputes with regard to matters which are essentially within the domestic jurisdiction of the United States of America *as determined by the United States of America*," United States Recognition of Compulsory Jurisdiction of The International Court of Justice (Declaration by President of United States), *done* Aug. 14, 1946, 61 Stat. 1218, T.I.A.S. No. 1598 (emphasis added).

line of political acceptability. Instead, it seems more useful to identify variables that might be adjusted in order to make a scheme sufficiently acceptable.

2. *Staffing the international institutions.* Acceptability may be defined for present purposes as the willingness of a government to agree in advance that an institution has the power to make authoritative determinations on questions of international law. One critical element of such acceptability is the composition of the particular institution — the people who will in fact be making the decisions. Acceptability might be greater if the names of these people were known in advance. Since such prior notification is not possible in an ongoing institution, we need acceptable rules for choosing the people who will make decisions. These rules include substantive provisions fixing eligibility criteria, such as nationality, age, and so forth, as well as procedural requirements governing the selection process. In the past, a great deal of attention has been given to this problem.[2] The manner of selecting judges for the International Court of Justice illustrates both the problem and the kind of solution that can be expected.

The Statute of the International Court of Justice provides for fifteen judges, each serving for nine years.[3] Five judges are elected every three years by a majority vote both in the General Assembly and in the Security Council. The judges are nominated not by governments as such but by "national groups" consisting of four persons "of known competency in questions of international law" and "of the highest moral reputation."[4] The members of the "national group" are selected by their govern-

---

[2]The proposal for the establishment of a permanent Court of Arbitral Justice was defeated at the Second Peace Conference of the Hague mainly because of disagreement on the Court's composition. For a comprehensive examination of the issues raised by the composition of the International Court of Justice, see Rosenne, *The Composition of the Court,* 1 THE FUTURE OF THE INTERNATIONAL COURT OF JUSTICE 377 (L. Gross ed. 1976). *Also see* the recommendations of the Institut de Droit International in its resolutions *The Composition of the International Court of Justice,* 44/2 ANNUAIRE DE L'INSTITUT DE DROIT INTERNATIONAL 474–75 (Sienne, 1952) and *Study of the Amendments to be made in the Statute of the International Court of Justice,* 45/2 ANNUAIRE DE L'INSTITUT DE DROIT INTERNATIONAL 296–97 (Aix-en-Provence, 1954).

[3]I.C.J. STAT. art. 3, para. 1; art. 13, para. 1.

[4]*Id.* at art. 4, para. 1. *See also* Convention of the Hague of 1907 at art. 44, 36 Stat. 2199, T.S. No. 536.

ments.[5] In the case of the United States and other countries who adhere to the Convention establishing the Permanent Court of Arbitration, the members of the "national group" are those persons nominated to serve on the Arbitration Court's permanent panel of members.[6] President Kennedy chose two well-known professors of international law for this country's members of the Permanent Court of Arbitration and of our "national group" — Louis Henkin of Columbia and Myres S. McDougal of Yale. On the other hand, President Johnson selected two practicing lawyers — Edwin Weisl of New York and Leon Jaworski of Houston, Texas. The national groups each nominate up to four persons for the International Court of Justice, but no more than two of their nominations can be of the nationality of the group.[7] When the United States Group met in August 1960, it nominated only one American, Professor Philip C. Jessup, who was subsequently elected,[8] and several foreign judges and legal scholars, most of whom were ultimately chosen by the General Assembly and the Security Council.

The process by which the national groups select their nominations for the International Court helps to assure that the final choices will be more acceptable to that group's government and to other governments. Before making its nominations, the national group "is recommended to consult its highest court of justice, its legal faculties and schools of law, and its national academies and national section of international academies devoted to the study of law."[9] In 1960 the United States National Group sent a circular letter soliciting "advice and suggestions" to a number of leading international lawyers and scholars in this country, including the Chief Justice, the presidents of several organizations concerned with international law, and the deans of sixteen principal American law schools. The National Group received responses to this circular letter after some of the re-

---

[5] I.C.J. Stat. art. 4, para. 2.

[6] *Id.* at art. 5.

[7] *Id.*

[8] At the end of Judge Jessup's term, the national group designated Professor Hardy Dillard, a former president of the American Society of International Law, as American candidate. He was elected and became a member of the Court on Feb. 6, 1970. [1973–74] I.C.J.Y.B. 21.

[9] I.C.J. Stat. art. 6.

cipients, such as the American Society of International Law, conducted an extensive process of internal consultation.[10] Article 9 of the Statute of the International Court of Justice also provides:

> At every election, the electors shall bear in mind not only that the persons to be elected should individually possess the qualifications required, but also that in the body as a whole the representation of the main forms of civilization and of the principal legal systems of the world should be assured.[11]

Procedures have been established to resolve possible deadlocks between the General Assembly and the Security Council.[12] It is also provided that if for any case the Court includes no judge of the nationality of one or more of the parties, such a country may choose a person to sit as judge on that case[13] "preferably from among those persons who have been nominated as candidates."[14]

These rules for selection of judges of the International Court of Justice illustrate two problems involved in creating institutions acceptable to governments. First, they raise the question of how many persons should be involved in reaching a decision. The efficiency of having a single judge is offset by the greater confidence one has in a decision reached by a larger number. This consideration is a familiar one. It was articulated by Senator Lee S. Overman of North Carolina in urging Congress in 1908 that only a three-judge court should have power to enjoin an officer of a state government:

> The point is, this amendment is for peace and good order in the State. Whenever one judge stands up in a State and enjoins the governor and the attorney-general, the people resent it, and public sentiment is stirred, as it was in my State, when there was almost a rebellion, whereas if three judges declare that a state statute is unconstitutional the people would rest easy under it.

[10] *See* Baxter, *Editorial Comment: The Procedures Employed in Connection with the United States Nominations for the International Court in 1960*, 55 AM. J. INT'L L. 445 (1961). Professor Richard Baxter was himself later elected a judge of the International Court, beginning his term of office in 1979.

[11] I.C.J. STAT. art. 9.

[12] *See* I.C.J. STAT. arts, 11 & 12.

[13] *See* I.C.J. STAT. art. 31, paras. 2 & 3. Almost invariably states make use of this provision. For a list of national (or ad hoc) judges on the bench of the International Court of Justice since its institution, see [1973–74] I.C.J.Y.B. 11–12.

[14] I.C.J. STAT. art. 31, para. 2.

But let one little judge stand up against the whole State, and you find the people of the State rising up in rebellion.[15]

In an international setting, this argument has a special significance. Frequently, two governments will decide to submit a dispute to a tribunal for final determination. In claims cases, for example, each side will often name one member of a commission, and they in turn will pick a third member to serve as chairman. By assuring that no single person representing only one nationality has to decide the case, both sides are more willing to accept the process leading to a determination and ultimately to comply with the result. Thus, in the *I'm Alone* case,[16] the United States was encouraged to agree to the creation of a two-member commission and to comply with the result because it was able to name Associate Justice Van Devanter as a commissioner, who joined his Canadian counterpart in a single decision.

With more than one decider, it becomes possible to vary the kind of majority vote needed for different types of decisions. Until it was amended in May 1968, the Ohio Constitution provided that the state supreme court could reverse an appellate court and hold a statute unconstitutional only with the consent of six of the seven justices of that court.[17] This use of a special majority for important decisions might be valuable, for example, as a means of getting countries to make greater use of the Permanent Court of Arbitration. Under the Convention establishing the Permanent Court, all decisions are by simple majority vote of the members chosen for an arbitration panel.[18] A revised provision might allow the parties to agree that a particular decision required a special majority, *e.g.*, four of the five members who usually serve on a panel of the Permanent Court of Arbitration.

The Soviet "troika" proposal of 1961 is another example of these principles. The requirement of unanimity and the question of the veto overshadowed the equally significant contention

[15] 45 CONG. REC. 7256 (1910).
[16] The *I'm Alone*, 7 Am. Dig. 203 (Anglo-Am. Liquor Commission 1935). *See also* Convention for the Prevention of Smuggling of Intoxicating Liquors, Jan. 23, 1924, United States – Great Britain, 43 Stat. 1761, T.S. No. 685.
[17] OHIO CONST. art. IV, § 2 (amended 1968).
[18] Art. 78 of the Convention for the Pacific Settlement of International Disputes, Oct. 18, 1907, 36 Stat. 2199, T.S. 536.

that decisions should be made by several people, rather than by one person. For the proposed comprehensive nuclear test ban, the Soviet Union recommended that there should be "an administrative council of three equal representatives, one each from the principal groups of states — the socialist states, the countries belonging to western military blocs and the neutralist states."[19] The theory underlying this proposal was summarized in a Soviet memorandum given President Kennedy in Vienna in 1961, reading, in part:

> The control commission, on which all principal groups of states will be represented, can adopt sound, just decisions, taking into consideration the interests of all states. However, it is not enough to take such decisions. It is imperative to guarantee their impartial implementation. Impartiality cannot be guaranteed if the implementation of the decisions is entrusted to one man alone.[20]

In suggesting that important decisions should be made by a group rather than by an individual, Khruschev said nothing new or controversial. Americans are familiar with the device of giving a group rather than an individual responsibility both for formulating and for executing policy. After Congress has decided what a particular policy should be and has adopted appropriate legislation, it is often reluctant to leave its implementation to a single person, as is illustrated by the establishment of the Federal Communication Commission, the Federal Trade Commission, and other regulatory agencies. Policy decisions in private corporations normally are made by boards of directors, and even at the level of execution an executive committee is common. Military policy in the Defense Department is implemented by the Joint Chiefs of Staff. Of course, even though most domestic government agencies and private corporations do act by collective agreement, they do not require what Khruschev was demanding — a unanimous decision in favor of any new action. Although unanimity is rarely a formal requirement, there is, however, often a working rule that various kinds of important action will not be taken against the views of a strong minority.

No clear line can be drawn between big decisions, where it is

[19] Soviet Aide-mémoire of Mr. Khrushchev to President Kennedy, 1961 Doc. on Int'l Aff. 434.
[20] Id.

generally recognized that joint wisdom is best, and little decisions, where the efficiency of a single responsible officer is usually desired. If the decision is big enough to cause substantial concern on the part of one country, it may be big enough to deserve a collective judgment. If we in this country, with our common bonds, interests, and law, are unwilling to trust a single official, we should have understood better than we did the concern that the Soviet "troika" proposal reflected.

Where the views of different representatives in a group are sharply divided, as might be the case between representatives of East and West or of "have" and "have-not" countries, the product of a group will tend to be less a collective judgment and more a collective bargain. But even where interests sharply conflict, the group process can nonetheless be a useful means of arriving at an acceptable accommodation. In an international institution, how petty must the determinations be before the drawbacks of a collective decision process outweigh its benefits? This is a question about which one should hesitate to be dogmatic.

The rules about staffing the International Court of Justice illustrate a second problem involved in creating institutions acceptable to governments. More significant than the number of persons selected to reach a determination is the question of how independent these persons will be. The method of selection and of possible removal, the terms of office, and the requirements for being chosen all affect the independence of the deciders. These are problems about which there is a good deal of knowledge and experience in the fields of public administration and political science. It would be a mistake to think that there is a single wise answer. Techniques of producing political control or independence are available. The question is rather one of producing a satisfactory balance between independence and responsibility.

The traditional virtue of a court is independence. We like to think that a judge should be selected for his personal integrity, learning, and judgment, rather than as a spokesman for a particular group or constituency. Yet, in this country we also have a tradition of judges who must be elected and reelected by the people. Appointments on our Supreme Court are often made with greater attention to a judge's representational role than to his personal ability. It is deemed important that the Court include a Jew, a Catholic, a Republican, a Southerner, a Westerner, a state judge, and so forth. With this domestic experience we can understand why an international court, if it is to be accepted and able to make decisions that will be accepted, must be staffed with an eye to nationality as well as to judicial ability. Just as it became important in this country to have a black on the Supreme Court, so it was desirable for the International Court of Justice to include an African judge. The election of two African judges to the Court in recent years was, in part, a result of the desire to make the Court's process of decision more acceptable to African countries.[21]

The range of possible solutions between independence and representation tends to be far broader for administrative agencies. In some circumstances we may want a man to decide a question as he personally would decide it, paying a minimum of attention to the views of others. In other circumstances we may wish him accurately to reflect the views of his government, just as the personal views of an ambassador or of a delegate to a conference are often of little or no importance.

Techniques for giving each official of an international agency more or less autonomy are well known. A man may be considered as an official of the agency or of his government. He may have life tenure, serve for a term of years, or be removable for cause or at will. Here again, there is little basis for being dogmatic. We have had experience, both good and bad, with political appointees and with a civil service, with bodies like juries that require unanimity, and with bodies like congressional committees, where an energetic minority has effective power to do what it wants. The state of Virginia has discovered that one of the most effective means of maintaining political control over a government is to have a small commission with the power both to raise and to lower the pay of individual state officials at any time.[22]

As we have seen, international institutions can be staffed in a sufficiently partisan manner so as to be acceptable to govern-

---

[21] Judge Isaac Forster of Senegal became a member of the Court on Feb. 6, 1964, and Judge Charles D. Onyeama of Nigeria became a member of the Court on Feb. 6, 1967.

[22] VA. CODE § 14.1, art. 7 (1950).

ments. But, in addition, governments can be persuaded that they stand to gain more from having the institution impartial than from having it under their control. Two examples, one from the United States and one from the Soviet Union, illustrate how a government may become convinced that the tribunal which serves it best is not the one which is most biased in its favor.

In the United States the practice developed of inserting in government contracts a clause which gave administrative officials of the government the legal power to determine authoritatively all factual disputes and all questions of legal obligation arising under the contract. The validity of such a clause was upheld no matter how arbitrary or capricious the decision of the administrative official might have been.[23] In fact, the Supreme Court decided that the only ground for review of an administrative decision concerning a contract with such a finality clause was fraud — "conscious wrongdoing, an intention to cheat or be dishonest."[24] As a result, the government found itself winning a lot of cases that it probably would have lost before an impartial body.

Rather than being pleased, the government adopted a statute which precluded the use of such clauses in the future and assured those who did business with the government of a more impartial tribunal to resolve disputes of law and fact.[25] In its report on the proposed statute, the House Judiciary Committee explained why the legislation was desirable:

> After extensive hearings it has been concluded that it is neither to the interests of the Government nor to the interests of any of the industry groups that are engaged in the performance of Government contracts to repose in Government officials such unbridled power of finally determining either disputed questions of law or disputed questions of fact arising under Government contracts. . . . A continuation of this situation will render the performance of Government work less attractive to the responsible industries upon whom the Government must rely for the performance of such work, and will adversely affect the free and competitive nature of such work. It will discourage the more re-

[23] United States v. Wunderlich, 342 U.S. 98 (1951).
[24] Id. at 100.
[25] 41 U.S.C. §§ 321, 322 (1970).

sponsible element of every industry from engaging in Government work and will attract more speculative elements whose bids will contain contingent allowances intended to protect them from unconscionable decisions of Government officials rendered during the performance of their contracts.[26]

We saw in Chapter VI that a government's desire for a good "credit rating" may cause it to respect clear obligations. Here we find that this same desire to preserve its reputation may cause a government to accept an impartial, as contrasted with a partisan, institution for interpreting a disputed obligation.

The arbitral tribunals that the Soviet Union insists be used to settle disputes arising under foreign trade contracts illustrate an interesting balance between a government's desire for partiality and for impartiality. On the one hand, the Soviet Government insists that such disputes be heard in Moscow before a Russian arbitration tribunal. On the other hand, the Soviet Government experiences the same kind of pressures that caused the United States Government to favor impartial rather than partisan decisions on disputes about government contracts. Professor Harold Berman has described these Soviet tribunals:

> There is much evidence that the Foreign Trade Arbitration Commission has striven to achieve a reputation for impartiality (without which, indeed, it would be difficult to secure consent of foreign parties to its jurisdiction). It has shown a thorough familiarity with the commercial law and commercial custom of many countries; its fifteen-member panel of arbitrators are, for the most part, prominent professors of law or economics who are experts in international trade; its procedure is fair; it gives reasoned opinions in connection with its awards; and it has decided many cases in favor of the non-Soviet party.[27]

In explaining this impartiality, Professor Berman points out that "Soviet domestic state-trading and industrial enterprises have had a long experience of impartial adjudication of disputes arising out of their contracts with each other."[28] The Soviet leaders

[26] HOUSE COMM. ON THE JUDICIARY, FINALITY CLAUSES IN GOVERNMENT CONTRACTS, H.R. Doc. No. 1380, 83d Cong., 2d Sess. 4 (1954).
[27] Berman, *The Legal Framework Of Trade Between Planned And Market Economies: The Soviet-American Example*, 24 LAW & CONTEMP. PROB. 482, 493 (1959).
[28] *Id.*

expect a similarly impartial tribunal to operate in international trade disputes involving foreign trade combines.

3. *Reducing the problem of delay.* One serious problem that presently deters governments from seeking an authoritative determination by international institutions is delay. International procedures are notoriously cumbersome. If they are superimposed on national legal procedures, the total elapsed time between the initiation of a case and the final authoritative determination could well run several years. In the meantime, the damage may have been done. Goa may have been swallowed up by India; the Suez Canal may have been blocked; the Abadan refinery may be operating under new control; eggs may have been smashed that cannot be put back together again. One can well ask how the ponderous pace of the law can be expected to cope with the hurly-burly of international conflict. If we want to make international institutions acceptable to governments, we must address ourselves to this problem.

a. *Lowering our sights.* The first and most important way of adjusting international institutions to meet the problem of delay is to recognize that the problem cannot be eliminated.[29] Here again, our sights must be lowered so that we are designing and seeking to establish enforcement techniques that are within the realm of the attainable.

It is striking that both international optimists and cynics seem to judge international machinery by its ability to produce a trouble-free utopia. The goal of making war impossible is not an appropriate guide to practical legal institutions any more than the goal of "making disease impossible" would be an appropriate guide to practical medical institutions. In the medical field such a goal would presumably require vast inspection techniques to check daily on the health of all people. Existing medical practices would be dismissed as unacceptable because they failed to make disease impossible for a number of reasons. One of those reasons would be the great delay that is likely to occur between the development of the first symptom and the final diagnosis and

[29] *See, e.g.,* Jully, *Arbitration and Judicial Settlement: Recent Trends,* 48 AM. J. INT'L L. 380, 396–97 (1954); Gross, *The Time Element in the Contentious Proceedings of the International Court of Justice,* 63 AM. J. INT'L L. 74 (1969).

prescription. Such delay is unfortunate. People die because of it. Yet this delay does not deter doctors from doing the best that can be done.

We are familiar with the delays attending domestic litigation. A litigant frequently suffers irremedial damage during the interval between the time that a question is first raised and the time that a court renders a final decree. Further delays may occur thereafter. A man may serve months and even years in prison before an appellate court finds that he should be free. A child may grow up before a court finally holds that he had a right to attend a particular school. Although effort should be made to reduce the delays that occur in both domestic and international procedures, we should recognize that such delay is inevitable. To the extent that the rules originally broken are precautionary in nature, the harmful consequences of delay will be reduced. Nevertheless, adopting an objective of second-order compliance means that, in many circumstances, damage will occur which cannot be undone by obtaining compliance with a subsequent determination.

b. *Interim decisions.* Probably the best way to limit the problem of delay in judicial proceedings is to authorize and to facilitate the issuance by courts of interim determinations of various kinds. What we have been calling a single authoritative determination can in fact consist of a number of partial determinations, each one being limited to a particular subject matter or for a period of time. As with domestic litigation, one might expect a sequence of decisions.

The first decision need not await final adjudication of all problems involved in a dispute. Even an international body can quickly issue an interim order designed to maintain the status quo or otherwise to lessen the harm that might be caused while other measures are being considered. The International Court of Justice, for example, has the power under article 41(1) of its Statute "to indicate, if it considers that circumstances so require, any provisional measures which ought to be taken to preserve the respective rights of either party." The Court's rules provide that a request for such measures has "priority over all other cases" and that the decision will "be treated as a matter of urgency."[30] Thus, in *The Anglo-Iranian Oil Company Case*, the full bench of the International Court of Justice issued on July 5, 1951, an interim order after receiving on June 22 a request for such relief from the United Kingdom and holding a hearing on June 30.[31] Iran contended that the Court lacked jurisdiction in the case and refused to participate in the proceedings on the request for interim measures.[32] The Court heard the case ex parte and held that the United Kingdom's complaint did raise a question of whether Iran had violated an international agreement.[33] In such circumstances the Court should perhaps ask a reputable international lawyer from a third country to present the absent government's side of the case or explicitly permit a party challenging the Court's jurisdiction to appear specially and argue the point without submitting generally to the jurisdiction of the Court.[34] Such action would serve to demonstrate the International Court of Justice's impartiality and desire to hear all relevant arguments. It also might encourage a country to argue its own case rather than to abstain and later to attack the interim relief order as one-sided. Iran refused to comply with the Court's order, and its contention that the Court lacked jurisdiction ultimately was upheld.[35] Nevertheless, the case demonstrates the kind of speed and interim relief that could be expected from the International Court of Justice and the techniques that the Court could use in determining the desirability of maintaining the status quo without having to decide the merits of a controversy.

[30] I.C.J., Rules of Court, Rule 66(2).

[31] [1951] I.C.J. 89.

[32] *Id.* at 92. Iceland adopted the same attitude in the Fisheries Jurisdiction Case ([1972] I.C.J. 11, 32) as France did in the Nuclear Tests Case ([1973] I.C.J. 98, 136) and India in the Case Concerning Trial of Pakistani Prisoners of War ([1973] I.C.J. 327, 329).

[33] [1951] I.C.J. 89, 93.

[34] *See* Gross, *The International Court of Justice*, 65 AM. J. INT'L L. 253, 307 (1971).

[35] [1952] I.C.J. 91, 114. Before the decision of the Court that it lacked jurisdiction in that case, the British Government had turned to the Security Council for the enforcement of the Court's interim order of July 5, 1951, on the basis of the U.N. CHARTER art. 94, para. 2, 6 U.N. SCOR (559th mtg.) 4, U.N. Doc. S / p.v. 559 (1951). It was the only instance when a state requested the application of that Charter provision, and the request raised the legal question whether, in addition to judgments, the Charter was applicable to interim orders. The question was not solved, because the Council decided, by 8 votes to 1, with 2 abstentions, to adjourn its debate until the Court had ruled on its own competence in the matter. 6 U.N. SCOR (565th mtg.) 12, U.N. Doc. S / p.v. 565 (1951).

In many cases it may be possible to reach a forward-looking order which effectively resolves a case without ever deciding the rightness or wrongness of past conduct. The Soviet underground nuclear test of January 15, 1965, raised a question about a possible violation of the Moscow Test Ban Treaty of 1963 in which each party undertook "to prohibit, to prevent, and not to carry out any . . . nuclear explosion, at any place under its jurisdiction or control . . . if such explosion causes radioactive debris to be present outside the territorial limits of the State under whose jurisdiction or control such explosion is conducted."[36] The January 1965 test resulted in radioactive debris outside the Soviet Union.[37] If a court had had to consider this problem, it might have spent a great deal of time and effort in seeking the facts about the test to determine whether the Soviet Union had either carelessly or deliberately conducted a test contrary to the Treaty. On the other hand, by looking forward a court readily might have found that the Treaty permitted underground tests as long as a party took all reasonable precautions to prevent radioactive debris from leaving the State. The court could then have issued an order to the Soviet Union, or even to all parties to the Treaty, to take such precautions in the future. So long as other parties did not wish to terminate the Treaty, there was no necessity of spending a lot of time trying to determine whether or not in the past Soviet precautions had met the standard required by the Treaty. Regardless of who committed an alleged violation in the past, the court's order could have directed conduct expected from all parties to the Treaty in the future. A process of deliberation which produces an "impersonal" decision — one directed to all concerned parties — should encourage an alleged violator to accept and to participate in the proceedings.

c. *Accelerated adjudication.* The problem of delay can be further reduced by giving priority to those cases that require it. Not every problem is in need of urgent attention. Constitutional litigation in this country usually requires years to work its way through the courts. Nevertheless, when the situation is deemed to require it, our courts can act far more rapidly. In *Youngstown*

[36] Moscow Nuclear Test Ban Treaty, Aug. 5, 1963, 14 U.S.T. 1313, 1316–17, T.I.A.S. No. 5433, 480 U.N.T.S. 43.
[37] N.Y. Times, Jan. 20, 1965, at 1, col. 1.

Co. v. Sawyer,[38] the Supreme Court issued its final decision on June 2, reviewing action which the President had taken on April 8. The pace of litigation is suggested by the fact that the district court decided the case on April 30, the court of appeals stayed its decision the same day, the Supreme Court granted certiorari on May 3 and heard argument on May 12 and 13.[39]

There seems nothing inevitable about the currently leisurely pace of international litigation. Parkinson's law (that work expands to fill the time allotted to it) has its converse in that many of the time-consuming aspects of the procedure of the International Court of Justice could be dispensed with in a case demanding rapid action, or in all cases on a more crowded calendar. In *The Anglo-Iranian Oil Company Case*, the Court was able to hear the United Kingdom's request for interim relief eight days after it was submitted and to issue a decision five days after the hearing.[40] The Court routinely could pressure the parties to adhere to deadlines for the submission of memorials. In the *Case Concerning the Barcelona Traction, Light and Power Company, Ltd.*, the Court granted the Spanish Government a one-month extension for submitting its memorial. But the Court made it clear in its order that it was not content with having deadlines disregarded.[41] Other steps that the Court might take include having simultaneous instead of sequential translations and limiting issues by pretrial conferences. The United States Supreme Court used to allow almost unlimited time for oral argument; now each side is routinely limited to thirty minutes.[42] Oral proceedings before the International Court of Justice presently go on for days; a substantial reduction in the time allowed should prove possible.[43]

[38] 343 U.S. 579 (1952).

[39] *Id.*

[40] *See* note 31 and accompanying text *supra*.

[41] [1968] I.C.J. 13, 14.

[42] Sup. Ct. R. 44, paras. 3 and 4.

[43] In their responses to a questionnaire prepared by the Secretary-General, Cyprus, the United States, Sweden, Canada, and Turkey suggested that the Court should speed up its procedure (U.N. Doc. A / 8382, at 112, 114–15 (1971), and A / 8382 / Add. 3, at 3, 4 (1971)). The United States observed that in the contentious procedure the Court might dispose of the oral phase (U.N. Doc. A / 8382, at 112). *See also* a similar proposal by Madagascar (U.N. Doc. A / 8382, at 115) and the speech by the representative of Guyana in

Finally, delay in international litigation may not be the fault of the institution being asked to make a determination. Examining in detail the amount of time consumed in reaching a decision in cases that have been heard before the International Court of Justice, Professor Leo Gross concluded that his study and the accompanying statistics should

> dispose once and for all of the criticism that proceedings before the Court are so slow as to discourage governments from submitting cases to it. They are as slow or as expeditious as the parties choose to make them. The Court, there can be no doubt about it, would like them to be expeditious and it has indicated this strongly, though with the usual restraint, in the Order [in the *Barcelona Traction, Light and Power Company Case*].[44]

As for the advisory opinions of the Court, Professor Gross shows that these cases "were invariably completed in less than one year and in time for the advisory opinion to be considered by the requesting body at its session following that in the course of which the request was made."[45] Efforts should be made to reduce delay in international litigation in order to make institutions more acceptable to governments. At the same time, one must bear in mind that the factor of delay may on some occasions prove to be a convenient excuse rather than a valid reason for a government's avoiding an authoritative determination.

4. *Making the process less expensive.* Governments might more readily accept a process leading to determinations by international institutions if the cost of litigation was reduced.[46] In the *South West Africa Cases* decided in 1966, the legal fees for the plaintiff governments, Ethiopia and Liberia, were reportedly in

---

the Sixth Committee (U.N. Doc. A / C. / SR. 1284, at 8 (1971)). Switzerland and Turkey thought it advisable to limit the length of oral statements and the number of speakers for each party (U.N. Doc. A / 8382, at 144 and U.N. Doc. A / 8382 / Add. at 3 and 4).

[44] Gross, *supra* note 29, at 78.

[45] *Id.* at 82.

[46] In their responses to the aforementioned questionnaire, Norway, Argentina, the United States, Cyprus, Denmark, and Canada observed that the expenses of litigation before the Court were onerous for states (U.N. Doc. A / 8382, at 28, 47, 102–03), and the United States, Sweden, Turkey, and New Zealand made the proposal that certain litigant states might be assisted from the budget of the United Nations (U.N. Doc. A / 8382, at 115–16, U.N. Doc. A / 8382 / Add. 3, at 5, and U.N. Doc. A / 8382 / Add. 4, at 4).

excess of $500,000.[47] If a government knows that submitting a dispute to an international tribunal will result in great expense, it may prefer to seek a "cheaper" political settlement, however unwise that course of action may be. On the other hand, some oppose opening up international courts because they fear that adjudication will not be sufficiently expensive. They fear that people with frivolous claims who are certain to lose will tie up both governments and courts with useless litigation. Surely it should be possible to avoid both unnecessary expense and frivolous litigation.

Simplifying litigation can reduce its total cost. In many cases, a ready administrative procedure can avoid the necessity of more formal legal proceedings. As noted in Chapter IX, the use of domestic administrative procedures could eliminate some expense. If an international administrative agency were required in a dispute, inexpensive procedures could be established for cases brought by individual claimants and even by governments. For example, the European Commission of Human Rights has received hundreds of complaints from individuals. To avoid the expense of having the full Commission conduct hearings on the admissibility of each complaint from an individual, the Commission's rules of procedure provide that individual complaints are sent to a screening board composed of three of the fourteen members of the Commission. If all three find the complaint admissible, the case is referred by the Commission to the defendant government for comments on whether it is admissible. If the three members are not unanimous, the Commission can either declare the petition inadmissible or request comments from the defendant government.[48] In this way, the Commission avoids being overwhelmed with the consideration of frivolous complaints by individuals located in the fourteen countries adhering to the Convention for the Protection of Human Rights and Fundamental Freedoms. At the same time, the Commission assures that complaints which may have merit receive further consideration. To regulate their work and protect their proce-

---

[47] N.Y. Times, July 19, 1966, at 17, col. 2.

[48] Rule 45 of the Rules of Procedure of the Commission on Human Rights of the Council of Europe, *reprinted in* EUR. COMM. ON HUMAN RIGHTS DOCUMENTS AND DECISIONS 58, 76 (1955–1956–1957).

dures, other international tribunals — not necessarily the International Court of Justice — could employ some analogous device, at least in regard to certain categories of claims.

Even with existing international institutions and procedures, less expensive litigation is readily available to those who may desire it. The International Court of Justice already has the means of conducting litigation on a less cumbersome basis. Article 26 of the Court's Statute authorizes it to establish chambers of three or more judges to hear particular categories of cases. With the consent of the parties the Court may form a chamber of any number of judges to hear a particular case. To further reduce expense, such chambers may sit and exercise their functions away from the Hague. In addition, the Court has a standing chamber of five judges who, at the request of the parties, may hear and determine cases by summary procedure.[49]

The inherent costs of international adjudication might operate to deter people or governments from seeking determinations that ought to be obtained. If so, the costs of such litigation could be spread. At the present time, the allocation of the costs of domestic litigation is quite arbitrary. Some of the costs, such as a judge's salary and the cost of the courthouse, are met by the taxpayers in general. Other costs are met by the party who loses; and some are met by each litigant independent of the outcome of the case. In Britain the losing party pays heavy costs, including the attorneys' fees of the successful litigant. In the United States even a successful party pays his own attorneys' fees. On the other hand, a criminal defendant who cannot afford a lawyer will have one provided, sometimes at the expense of the lawyer himself. In some jurisdictions the taxpayers support not only the public prosecutors but public defenders as well.

However expensive international litigation may be, few would doubt that, in total terms, the expense is justified. Indeed, the costs of other ways of dealing with conflict are likely to be even more expensive. The problem is largely one of allocating the costs so that they will not act as an impediment to appropriate use of the institutions. Many techniques are available. Either national or international officials can serve as counsel for indi-

[49] I.C.J. STAT. art. 29.

vidual litigants, or fees can be met with public funds. Briefs and records can be provided at nominal cost. Even with respect to administrative agencies, an "ombudsman" can be appointed to investigate individual grievances.

Subsidizing litigation in this fashion might result in suits by individuals or even by governments that are obviously frivolous. A measure introduced to make international institutions less expensive and more acceptable to governments would risk producing an opposite effect. But the solution would not be to cut off the subsidy. Instead, we should seek to develop techniques to avoid abuse of the system and to assure that clearly unmeritorious cases are dismissed at the outset. The procedures of the European Commission of Human Rights, discussed above, suggest one method of coping with this problem.[50] An alternative approach would be to assess heavy costs against a losing litigant if the tribunal finds that the action was either frivolous or brought in bad faith to harass the defendant. The procedural rules of international courts might allow defendants to move for early dismissal of a suit on grounds analogous to summary judgment or "failure to state a claim"[51] under rule 12(b)(6) of the Federal Rules of Civil Procedure. We have had little difficulty in limiting access to international institutions. Our problem is the opposite — opening them up in a manner acceptable to governments.

5. *Increasing acceptability by limiting jurisdiction.* One of the easiest and best ways of making an international institution acceptable to a government is to limit its jurisdiction to make authoritative determinations on questions of international legal right. There are an infinite number of ways to define the scope of an international institution's jurisdiction. The right of an institution to consider and resolve questions may be limited to those arising under a particular treaty, or to those concerning a certain subject matter, or to those between certain countries, or to those arising after a certain date. The International North Pacific Fisheries Commission, for example, may consider only issues arising from the need to conserve the stock of halibut, herring, and salmon in "waters, other than territorial waters, of the

[50] *See* note 48 and accompanying text *supra.*
[51] FED. R. CIV. P. 12(b) (6).

North Pacific Ocean . . . [including] the adjacent seas."[52] Similarly, the International Boundary and Water Commission, established by the United States and Mexico, may pass only on questions and differences concerning the two countries' boundary line formed by the Rio Grande and the Colorado River.[53] New international tribunals could be created with analogous limitations on their jurisdictional grants.

Particular categories of issues could be specifically excluded from the jurisdiction of an international tribunal. In domestic law, the Federal Tort Claims Act contains an intriguing variety of grants and exclusions of jurisdiction, including special prohibitions on the exercise of jurisdiction over any claim for damages caused by the imposition or establishment of a quarantine by the United States or concerned with a claim arising in a foreign country.[54] The convention establishing the United States–Mexican Claims Commission excepted from the tribunal's jurisdiction claims "arising from acts incident to the recent [Mexican] revolutions."[55]

Greater use could and should be made of jurisdictional limiting techniques with respect to the kind of *relief* that an institution may order. A government might, for example, accept the jurisdiction of the International Court of Justice to issue, with respect to any legal dispute, a forward-looking decree which defined conduct in which the government could not lawfully engage in the future, but deny to the Court jurisdiction either to award financial damages for past conduct or to order affirmative conduct in the future. Alternatively, the Court might accept jurisdiction to award compensatory damages, but only up to a designated amount in any one case. Or it might allow compensatory damages for actual injury suffered by either another gov-

[52] International Convention for the High Seas Fisheries of the North Pacific Ocean, May 9, 1952, art. 1(1), 4 U.S.T. 380, T.I.A.S. No. 2786, 205 U.N.T.S. 65. *See* Selak, *The Proposed International Convention for the High Seas Fisheries of the North Pacific Ocean*, 46 AM J. INT'L L. 323, 326 (1952).

[53] Convention to Avoid the Difficulties Occasioned by reason of the Changes which take Place in the beds of the Rio Grande and Colorado River, March 1, 1889, United States–Mexico, art. 1, 26 Stat. 1512, T.S. No. 232.

[54] 28 U.S.C. § 2680(f) and (k) (1970).

[55] General Claims Convention with Mexico, Sept. 8, 1923, United States–Mexico, art. 1, 43 Stat. 1730, T.S. No. 678.

ernment or individual, but exclude exemplary or punitive damages.

Professor Sohn has suggested an important and practical result of making the jurisdiction of the International Court and of other international institutions more acceptable.[56] He has pointed out that limited grants of jurisdiction to the Court, such as those discussed above and a number of others, might be regarded as incremental steps to be taken over a period of time. In this process leading to increasing jurisdiction for the Court, Professor Sohn foresees the possibility of gaining the participation of more states on more issues:

> Such rampant gradualism should permit even the most recalcitrant state to accept something and in this manner to take the first hesitating step toward broader acceptance in the future. Once states find that the first steps did not prove disastrous, they might become more venturesome and start taking several steps in quick succession. Slowly, but surely, the jurisdiction of the Court would expand and, hopefully, the number of cases presented to the Court would increase, and one day we might discover that the problem which seems to be so intractable today has been solved by the process of gradual accretion.[57]

6. *Coping with jurisdiction to decide jurisdiction.* I have suggested that one means to increase the acceptability of international institutions is to limit their jurisdiction. But, however limited an international institution's jurisdiction might be to make an authoritative determination on a matter of international legal right, it seems highly desirable that each such body be given the legal right to decide whether or not it has jurisdiction. The authoritative nature and legitimacy of a decision within an institution's area of legal competence is greater if a losing party is precluded by law from contending that the decision is ineffective because the institution acted beyond its jurisdiction.

There is a subtle relationship between the powers lawfully conferred upon an international institution and those which

[56] Sohn, *Step-By-Step Acceptance of the Jurisdiction of the International Court of Justice*, 57 Am. Soc'y Int'l L. Proc. 131 (1964).

[57] *Id.* at 131–32. For a less optimistic view on this proposal, see Fitzmaurice, *Enlargement of the Contentious Jurisdiction of the Court*, 2 The Future of the International Court of Justice, (L. Gross ed. 1976).

that institution then as a practical matter becomes able to exercise. In the preceding section on the jurisdictional limitations of an international institution and in the succeeding section of this chapter on how an institution should act, we are discussing a kind of international law — special rules regulating the functioning of international institutions. Logically, we come to the problem of how *these* rules are going to be enforced. What mechanism shall we use to get international institutions to comply with their own rules? A rule may state that an international institution is to act only with respect to certain categories of questions. Nonetheless, the International North Pacific Fisheries Commission might hear a complaint concerning excessive salmon catches in the Atlantic Ocean and issue a decision in the dispute. A treaty may provide that an international institution is to act only in accordance with stated procedures, as in the case, for example, of the European Convention on Human Rights, which permits the European Court of Human Rights to hear a case only after the European Commission of Human Rights has studied the facts and issued a report. But, the institution may have a will of its own — the Human Rights Court might hold hearings on a petition which the Commission had never considered. If a court is to be the only judge of its own competence, some would argue that it may run amuck, deciding that it has far greater legal powers than it was intended to have. As a result, governments may be unwilling to accept international institutions that have the lawful right to decide the extent of their own powers.

Any such gap between the power an institution needs to be effective and that which it needs to be acceptable should be closed by governmental persuasion or by other limitations herein suggested, and not by eliminating the institution's jurisdiction to decide its jurisdiction. Where appropriate, appeal of jurisdictional questions to the International Court of Justice could lessen fears of a runaway institution without giving each government the right to decide the jurisdictional question itself. The failure to give an international institution the right to decide its jurisdiction would undercut the authoritative nature of its determinations, even when it was acting well within its apparent authority. If the international institution does not have the right to decide this question, then every government may decide that question for itself. The "authoritative" determination becomes far from authoritative since a recalcitrant government may argue plausibly that the institution acted improperly, and that therefore the determination is not binding.[58] It was for this reason that the drafters of the Statute of the International Court of Justice included article 36(6), which provides that "[i]n the event of a dispute as to whether the Court has jurisdiction, the matter shall be settled by the decision of the Court."[59]

On the other hand, granting an institution the legal right to decide the extent of its own jurisdiction does not empower that body to make an effective determination which clearly exceeds the scope of its lawful jurisdiction. The International North Pacific Fisheries Commission, even if it had full legal authority to interpret the extent of its jurisdiction, would not have much power to issue orders concerning salmon fishing in the Atlantic, or narcotics production in Turkey, or radio frequency allocations to Japan. Similarly, the European Court of Human Rights would be unable to gain compliance with its order in a case which the Commission had not considered before the reference to the court. A determination by an international institution derives a large measure of its power from its apparent legitimacy. A determination which patently exceeds the lawful authority of an institution or is made in obvious disregard of that institution's procedural rules will have little power indeed. Paper rights are important. But the paper right to define the edges of one's paper rights does not carry with it the effective power to extend one's rights very far. If international institutions are to remain acceptable to governments and if their decisions are to have some effect, the institutions will have to act substantially within their granted authority and in compliance with their procedural rules.

7. *Rules which an institution applies.* The acceptability of an international institution to governments can be increased by

---

[58] For a discussion of the determination by the political organs of the United Nations of their own jurisdiction, see D. CIOBANU, PRELIMINARY OBJECTIONS RELATED TO THE JURISDICTION OF THE UNITED NATIONS POLITICAL ORGANS 163 (1975).

[59] For a comprehensive discussion of this question, see I. SHIHATA, THE POWER OF THE INTERNATIONAL COURT OF JUSTICE TO DETERMINE ITS OWN JURISDICTION (1965).

elaborating rules that specify both the substantive standards to be applied and the procedures to be followed by that institution. Such rules, like jurisdictional limitations, are enforced by checks and balances within the institution and by the general lack of regard that others will accord to determinations reached in open disregard of the rules.

A court is instructed, implicitly if not explicitly, to decide questions according to "the law." An institution which is to decide matters according to preexisting rules will generally be more acceptable to governments than one which is to decide matters according to new rules that it is free to promulgate on the spot. The more that officials from different governments work together on common problems, the greater is the likelihood that they will develop common perceptions of the generally understood rules of the game. To be sure, some new countries believe that they would like to be freed from the "old" international law. In a particular dispute being submitted to arbitration, these countries might prefer the arbitrators to have a free hand. However, it is most unlikely that any government would be willing to give an international institution, with continuing jurisdiction over such matters as might be referred to it, the right to make authoritative determinations on whatever basis seemed fair to its members. Unless the particular dispute has been narrowly defined in advance and is submitted ad hoc to arbitration, the broad standard *ex aequo et bono* is probably too loose.[60]

Special international institutions can be made to follow closely confined substantive standards. The International Whaling Commission, for example, has the power to limit whale catches by issuing regulations protecting certain species, closing certain waters, limiting the size of catches, and taking other actions of this nature.[61] But these regulations, according to the Convention, may be issued only if they meet a number of specified criteria, including the findings of scientific studies.[62] Other institutions, like the Universal Postal Union and the Interna-

[60] During the fifty-six years of their existence, neither the International Court of Justice nor the Permanent Court of International Justice received any case submitted *ex aequo et bono* as permitted by the I.C.J. STAT. art. 38, para. 2.

[61] International Whaling Convention, Dec. 2, 1946, art. V(1), 62 Stat. 1716, T.I.A.S. No. 1849, 161 U.N.T.S. 72.

[62] *Id.* at art. V(2).

tional Monetary Fund, are permitted to determine international debts on the basis of strict accounting standards.

Although the lack of fair procedural rules would make an international institution unacceptable to governments, there is usually no great difficulty in devising rules that strike most governments as fair. As we have seen, there is much room for reducing the delay and expense of adjudication before the International Court of Justice. But, in general, once an international institution gains governmental acceptance by adopting any number of the techniques considered here, its procedural rules will usually not pose a critical problem.

8. *Acceptability also depends on the decision and its consequences.* The various techniques discussed above should tend to make international institutions more acceptable to governments as a forum for reaching binding determinations with respect to international legal rights. But a government considering submission of a dispute to an international institution will want to know what that body is likely to decide and how that body is going to follow up its decision. The remaining three chapters of Part II consider the problems of who should be the object of a determination by an international institution (Chapter XII), what should be the content of its decision (Chapter XIII) and how the institution, governments, and international organizations can follow up such decisions (Chapter XIV). In each of these chapters, we shall be attempting to devise a system for reaching decisions which governments will accept and with which they will comply. Acceptability remains a problem throughout our analysis of second-order compliance.

Chapter XII

Determinations Against Whom?

Beyond the problems of finding a "plaintiff" to raise a question of noncompliance with international law and of finding an appropriate and acceptable tribunal to hear that question, there is the problem of the defendant. If we are to produce a determination with which there will be second-order compliance, it is important to think about the parties toward whom that determination should be directed. There are three possibilities. First, a determination may be directed at no one in particular; rather than ordering someone to engage or not to engage in certain conduct, the decision constitutes advice or a declaration of legal rights. Second, a determination may be directed against a government; this kind of decision raises questions about the appropriate role of sovereign immunity. Finally, a determination may be directed against individuals; rather than threatening the sovereignty of a government, the court rules on the legality of a particular officer's actions. This chapter considers each possibility in turn.

1. *Determinations in the abstract.* This section is concerned with international determinations, such as advisory opinions and declaratory judgments, that are not in the form of a decision directed against a particular defendant. The questions for consideration are the advantages and disadvantages of this kind of decision and the opportunities it offers for improving the international law enforcement system.

It may be useful to consider first what the rules ought to be in order to maximize compliance with such decisions and then to consider what would constitute wise practices by the various parties concerned.

a. *What should the rules about advisory and declaratory judgments be?* The International Court of Justice,[1] like its predecessor, the Permanent Court of International Justice,[2] has the power to is-

---

[1] *See* I.C.J. STAT. art. 65.
[2] *See* LEAGUE OF NATIONS COVENANT art. 14.

sue advisory opinions and has repeatedly exercised that power.[3] In the United States, the federal courts have the power to issue declaratory judgments but not to give advisory opinions. Some state courts, though, such as the Supreme Judicial Court of Massachusetts, regularly do issue advisory opinions. How promising for the international community are these forms of determination?

(1) *Advisory jurisdiction of international tribunals.*

(a) *Non binding advice as a way of getting jurisdiction.* The one great advantage of allowing the International Court of Justice to give an advisory opinion is that it enables the Court to consider questions that might not otherwise come before it. The following kinds of questions may fall into that category.

1. *Disputes with an international organization.* Since only states may be parties before the International Court of Justice, the Court's advisory jurisdiction permits it to resolve a question which primarily involves an international organization. For other international tribunals a better approach might be to accord sufficient standing to selected international organizations so that they could bring contentious cases in their own right.[4]

2. *Preventive adjudication.* Judge Hudson thought it wise to give an international court advisory jurisdiction so that it could deal with situations before they had ripened into conflicts.[5] This position seems questionable. A matter is not likely to be referred to the court unless disagreement on the point has developed. The possible advantages of "preventive adjudication" seem out-

---

[3]The International Court of Justice has given some fourteen advisory opinions through the one on the Western (Spanish) Sahara in 1975. It has since 1975 issued one additional "judgment," The Aegean Sea Continental Shelf Case (Judgment of 19 Dec. 1978) (looseleaf).

[4]A number of states have suggested that intergovernmental organizations should have access to the Court in contentious proceedings. *See* Review of the Role of the International Court of Justice, U.N. Doc. A / 8382 (1971) : Cyprus (at 70), Denmark, Guatemala, and the United States (at 71); Argentina, Finland, and Mexico (at 72); Switzerland (at 73–75); Sweden, Canada, and Madagascar (at 76); Iraq (at 77); United Kingdom, U.N. Doc. A / 8382 / Add. 1, at 6; Ivory Coast, U.N. Doc. A / 8382 / Add. 2, at 4; Turkey, U.N. Doc. A / 8382 / Add. 3, at 4; New Zealand, U.N. Doc. A / 8382 / Add. 4, at 3–4; Ethiopia, U.N. Doc. A / C.6 / SR. 1271, at 4 (1971); Brazil, U.N. Doc. A / C.6 / SR. 1277, at 11 (1971); Uruguay, U.N. Doc. A / C.6 / SR. 1278, at 3 (1971); Greece, U.N. Doc. A / C.6 / SR. 1281, at 14 (1971); El Salvador, *id.* at 13; Colombia, U.N. Doc. A / C.6 / SR. 1283, at 13 (1971); and Guyana, U.N. Doc. A / C.6 / SR. 1284, at 7 (1971).

[5]Hudson, *Advisory Opinions of National and International Courts*, 37 HARV. L. REV. 970 (1924).

weighed by the increased strain that such a case is likely to place upon the court and by the inherent difficulty that any court has in reaching a wise decision before events crucial to the controversy have taken place. Frankfurter expressed this view in arguing that "advisory opinions are bound to move in an unreal atmosphere. The impact of actuality and the intensities of immediacy are wanting . . . . Advisory opinions are rendered upon sterilized and mutilated issues."[6] To the extent that a court is seeking to decide a legal question in advance of a dispute, this criticism is certainly true.

3. *Disputes where no compulsory jurisdiction exists.* The advisory jurisdiction of the International Court has made it possible for the Court to consider and to announce its views on questions of international law raised by disputes between governments over which the Court would not have had jurisdiction on the application of either government. The fact that governments which are still unwilling to accept the compulsory jurisdiction of the International Court have agreed to empower that Court to render advisory opinions has opened the door for many additional judicial determinations.

A question may be raised whether advisory jurisdiction does in fact confer upon the Court the lawful power to render an advisory opinion with respect to an ongoing international dispute between two states where one of them does not want the Court to do so. In the *Status of Eastern Carelia* cases, the Permanant Court of International Justice declined to express an opinion on the questions put to it by the Council of the League of Nations. The Soviet Government had denied that the Court had jurisdiction to render even an advisory opinion and had refused to participate in the proceedings.[7] In these circumstances the Court thought it inexpedient to attempt to deal with the question, and stated:

> The question whether Finland and Russia contracted on the terms of the Declaration as to the nature of the autonomy of East-

---

[6]Frankfurter, *A Note on Advisory Opinions*, 37 HARV. L. REV. 1002, 1006 (1924).

[7]In a telegram dated June 13, 1923, and addressed to the Registrar of the Court, Tchitcherin, the Commissar of Russian Peoples for Foreign Affairs, made it unmistakably clear that "the Russian Government categorically refuses to take any part in the examination of this question by the League of Nations or by the Permanent Court." Status of Eastern Carelia, [1923] P.C.I.J., ser. C, No. 3, at 70.

ern Carelia is really one of fact. To answer it would involve the duty of ascertaining what evidence might throw light upon the contentions which have been put forward on this subject by Finland and Russia respectively, and of securing the attendance of such witnesses as might be necessary. The Court would, of course, be at a very great disadvantage in such an enquiry, owing to the fact that Russia refuses to take part in it. It appears now to be very doubtful whether there would be available to the Court materials sufficient to enable it to arrive at any judicial conclusion upon the question of fact: What did the parties agree to?

. . . .

The Court is aware of the fact that it is not requested to decide a dispute, but to give an advisory opinion. This circumstance, however, does not essentially modify the above considerations. . . . Answering the question would be substantially equivalent to deciding the dispute between the parties. The Court, being a Court of Justice, cannot, even in giving advisory opinions, depart from the essential rules guiding their activity as a Court.[8]

Despite the view expressed in the final sentence quoted above, it seems that the Court was treating its refusal to accept jurisdiction as a question of discretion rather than as one of a legal limitation upon its power. That position has been supported by the Court's subsequent practice.

The Court's view is most clearly stated in the case of *Interpretation of Peace Treaties with Bulgaria, Hungary and Romania* in 1950:

The consent of states, parties to a dispute, is the basis of the Court's jurisdiction in contentious cases. This situation is different in regard to advisory proceedings even where the Request for an Opinion relates to a legal question actually pending between states. The Court's reply is only of an advisory character: as such it has no binding force. It follows that no state, whether a Member of the United Nations or not, can prevent the giving of an Advisory Opinion which the United Nations considers to be desirable in order to obtain enlightenment as to the course of action it should take.[9]

Since the International Court of Justice has the legal right to

[8] Status Of Eastern Carelia, [1923] P.C.I.J., ser. B, No. 5, at 28–29.

[9] [1950] I.C.J. 71. Similarly, in the case of Legal Consequences for States of the Continued Presence of South Africa in Namibia (South West Africa) Notwithstanding Security Council Resolution 276 (1970), the Court, overruling the objection based on the

give advisory opinions with respect to disputes over which it has no compulsory jurisdiction, there is presently no need to expand or to contract its powers in this regard. Advisory jurisdiction of a comparable type would seem desirable for other international tribunals, such as commissions or special boards established by treaty to deal with particular problems.

(b) *The status of nonbinding advice.* Although the International Court, upon request, may render an advisory opinion, such an opinion is understood to be "not binding." Exactly what is meant by the concept of nonbinding advice is unclear.[10] It may or may not be desirable to have some clarification of the theoretical basis for the nonbinding character of advisory opinions.

At one end of the scale is the notion that advice of the International Court has no more inherent authority than the advice which might be given by an international lawyer. The advice should be accorded only such weight as the reputation and the persuasiveness of those giving it can muster in its support.

Another position may be that it is open to the recipient of the advice of the International Court, for example, the General Assembly, to "accept" the advice, thereby resolving the question at issue. Some of the arguments of the United States on the United Nations payments matter suggest that once the Court has spoken, and the General Assembly has accepted its advisory opinion, members became legally obliged to follow that advice. A

---

precedent of Eastern Carelia, observed that "[i]t is not the purpose of the request to obtain the assistance of the Court in the exercise of the Security Council's functions relating to the pacific settlement of a dispute pending before it between two or more States. The request is put forward by a United Nations organ with reference to its own decisions and it seeks legal advice from the Court on the consequences and implications of these decisions." [1971] I.C.J. 24.

[10] Sir Gerald Fitzmaurice has made a distinction between the nonbinding and the authoritative character of advisory opinions. In his view, there are two cases in which the advisory opinions are in practice negatively binding, *i.e.*, have prohibiting force. The first case would be when the opinion indicates that a certain course of action would be contrary to international law or to the Charter or to some other international instrument. In such an instance, it would be virtually impossible for the requesting organ to follow that course, and difficult for any individual member state to do so. The second exception would be where the opinion indicates that, of various possible courses, only one is legally correct. Fitzmaurice, *The Law and Procedures of the International Court of Justice: International Organizations and Tribunals*, 29 BRIT. Y.B. INT'L L. 1, 54–55 (1952). *See also* Secretary of State Rusk's comments on the World Court's advisory opinion in the U.N. payments case: *The Role of International Law in World Affairs*, 51 DEP'T STATE BULL. 802 (1964).

narrower position is that countries which in the General Assembly voted to accept the advisory opinion are legally obliged to recognize its conclusions as correct.

The concept of stare decisis provides another analogy. An advisory opinion can be looked upon as comparable to a decision in a case in which each party may raise the defense that it was not a party. Alternatively, such an opinion might be considered as deciding the abstract legal question but leaving it open to each country to raise a defense comparable to that of sovereign immunity. It also might be thought of as being like a judgment of the Court of Claims; the legal questions have been dealt with, but the government is not "bound" to appropriate the money.

Outside arrangements may give an advisory opinion the force of a conclusive judgment. That possibility was contemplated by the French and the British governments in the case of *Nationality Decrees Issued in Tunis and Morocco* when they decided to ask the Council of the League of Nations to request an advisory opinion on the matter from the Permanent Court of International Justice.[11] Subsequently, Albert Geouffre de Lapradelle and Démètre Negulesco, in their several reports on *La nature juridique des Avis Consultatifs de la Cour permanente de Justice internationale, leur valeur et leur portée positive en droit international*, advanced the idea of what they called "advisory arbitration" as a convenient means for peaceful settlement of international disputes in those cases where the contentious procedure of the Court or of any other international arbitral tribunal could not be set in motion.[12]

The "advisory arbitration" of the International Court of Justice, or any other international court or tribunal, may be organized not only on an ad hoc basis but also by statute or by treaty.

[11]Speaking before the Court, de Lapradelle, the representative of the French Government, stated: "In reality this procedure for furnishing advisory opinions to the Council is—and if one goes to the root of the matter this statement applies with its full force today for the first time—fundamentally a procedure by arbitration. No doubt politics have their niceties; the law sometimes resorts to indirect methods, and language sometimes strikes upon particularly convenient expressions. But, though, on the face of it, we are here simply to give you information to enable you to reply to the Council's request for an opinion, we have before us—and I think that after hearing the Attorney-General's speech yesterday, no one will have any doubt on the matter—what in reality amounts to an arbitration." [1923] P.C.I.J., ser. C., No. 2, at 52–53.

[12]*See, e.g.*, their first report on the subject, 34 ANNUAIRE DE L'INSTITUT DE DROIT INTERNATIONAL 409 (Stockholm, 1928).

Thus, article 11, paragraph 1 of the Statute of the United Nations Administrative Tribunal provides that if a member state, the Secretary General, or a party to a judgment objects to the judgment on certain grounds, then they may apply to the Committee on Applications for Review of Administrative Tribunal Judgments asking it to request an advisory opinion of the International Court of Justice on the matter.[13] Paragraph 3 of the same rule provides that if not requested to convene specially, the Tribunal at its next session shall confirm its judgment or bring it into conformity with the opinion of the Court.[14]

The Convention on Privileges and Immunities of the United Nations went further by making the "advisory arbitration" of the International Court of Justice not optional (as in the case above), but binding. Article 30 of the Convention provides that an advisory opinion shall be requested if there is a difference between a member and the United Nations and that "the opinion of the Court shall be accepted as decisive by the parties."[15] The best example of such a provision in a treaty remains article XII of the Administrative Tribunal of the International Labour Organization, which provides that if a question is raised about the validity of one of its judgments, an advisory opinion of the International Court of Justice will be binding.[16] As the International Court itself observed in the case of *Judgments of the Administrative Tribunal of the International Labour Organisation upon Complaints made against the United Nations Education, Scientific and Cultural Organization*:

> Such effect of the Opinion goes beyond the scope attributed by the Charter and by the Statute of the Court to an Advisory Opinion. However, the provision in question is nothing but a rule of conduct for the Executive Board, a rule determining the action to be taken by it on the Opinion of the Court. It in no wise affects the way in which the Court functions; that continues to be determined by its Statute and its Rules. Nor does it affect the reasoning

[13] Procedure for review of United Nations Administrative Tribunal judgements: amendments to the Statute of the Administrative Tribunal, G.A. Res. 957, 10 U.N. GAOR, Supp. (NO. 19) 30, U.N. Doc. A / 3116 (1955).

[14] *Id.*

[15] Convention on the privileges and immunities of the United Nations, *opened for signature* Feb. 13, 1946, 21 U.S.T. 1418, T.I.A.S. No. 6900, 1 U.N.T.S. 16.

[16] [1956] I.C.J. 80–81, 84.

by which the Court forms its Opinion or the content of the Opinion itself. Accordingly, the fact that the Opinion of the Court is accepted as binding provides no reason why the Request for an Opinion should not be complied with.[17]

Even in the absence of outside arrangements, determinations of an advisory nature are not meaningless. Some political weight can and should be rallied in their support. Their status is uncertain, as Judge Lauterpacht pointed out in the case *Admissibility of Hearings of Petitioners by the Committee on South West Africa*:

> For it may not be easy to characterize precisely in legal terms a situation in which South Africa declines to act on an Advisory Opinion which it was not legally bound to accept but which gave expression to the legal position as ascertained by the Court and as accepted by the General Assembly.[18]

Yet failure of states to comply with advisory opinions does not necessarily amount to outright defiance of the Court.

(c) *Power to declare the law without ordering relief.* The debate over declaratory judgments that has occurred within the constitutional framework of the United States has not taken place in the international context. In this country, the federal courts may consider only "cases" and "controversies" and may not declare the law, even when they otherwise have complete jurisdiction over the parties.[19] The jurisdiction of the International Court of Justice, as defined by its Statute, includes the power to grant declaratory judgments or, to state the same point differently, the power to declare the law authoritatively without ordering relief.[20] Any doubt in this regard was dissipated by the Permanent Court of International Justice in the *Case Concerning Certain German Interests in Polish Upper Silesia*. There the Court stated:

> Article 59 of the Statute, which has been cited by Poland, does not exclude purely declaratory judgments. The object of this article is simply to prevent legal principles accepted by the Court in a particular case from being binding upon other States or in other disputes. It should also be noted that the possibility of a

[17] *Id.* at 84.
[18] [1956] I.C.J. 47.
[19] U.S. CONST. art. III.
[20] I.C.J. STAT. arts. 65–68.

judgment having a purely declaratory effect has been foreseen in Article 63 of the Statute, as well as in Article 36.[21]

This does not mean, of course, that the status of a declaratory judgment is similar to that of an advisory opinion. And, as Judge Hudson pointed out in the case of *The Diversion of Water from the Meuse*, "a declaratory judgment will frequently have the same compulsive force as a mandatory judgment; States are disposed to respect the one not less than the other."[22] A declaratory judgment is normally concerned with the future, rather than the past, conduct of states; it is sought mainly for the purpose of obliging the respondent state to adopt that course of action which the Court decides is required by general international law or by treaty.

(2) *Advisory jurisdiction of national tribunals.* From the point of view of compliance with international law, would it be desirable for national courts to have jurisdiction to give advisory opinions on questions of international law? With the general blending of domestic and international litigation suggested in Chapter XI, it might be thought that the same kind of jurisdiction ought to exist in both systems.

The first decision of the United States Supreme Court which determined that the Court lacked the power to give advisory opinions came in response to a request in 1793 from Secretary of State Thomas Jefferson, at the behest of President Washington, for advice on questions of international law.[23] The questions on which the executive wished advice demonstrate the inherent difficulty in answering general legal questions apart from a specific case and explain the Court's reluctance to embark on such a course. The following are illustrative of the twenty-nine questions submitted by the President to the Justices of the Supreme Court.

1. Do the treaties between the United States and France give to France or her citizens a *right*, when at war with a power with whom the United States are at peace, to fit out originally in and from the ports of the United States vessels armed for war, with or without commission?

---

[21] [1926] P.C.I.J., ser. A, No. 7, at 19.
[22] [1937] P.C.I.J., ser. A / B, No. 70, at 79.
[23] 3 PUBLIC PAPERS OF JOHN JAY 486–89 (H. Johnston ed. 1890).

. . . .

2. If they give such a *right*, does it extend to all manner of armed vessels, or to particular kinds only? If the latter, to what kinds does it extend?

. . . .

16. Does it make any difference in point of principle, whether a vessel be armed for war, or the force of an armed vessel be augmented, in the ports of the United States, with *means* procured in the United States, or with means brought into them by the party, who shall so arm or augment the force of such vessel? If the first be unlawful, is the last lawful?

. . . .

20. To what distance, by the laws and usages of nations, may the United States exercise the right of prohibiting the hostilities of foreign powers at war with each other within rivers, bays, and arms of the sea, and upon the sea along the coasts of the United States?

. . . .

22. What are the articles, by name, to be prohibited to both or either party?

. . . .

29. May an armed vessel belonging to any of the belligerent powers follow *immediately* merchant vessels, enemies, departing from our ports, for the purpose of making prizes of them? If not, how long ought the former to remain, after the latter have sailed? And what shall be considered as the place of departure from which the time is to be counted? And how are the facts to be ascertained?[24]

Such a list of questions should be enough to convince any court that it should find some basis for not answering them.

It might well be, however, that the existence of jurisdiction in national courts, as in the case of the International Court of Justice, to render advisory opinions could provide them an opportunity to reach a determination where they would otherwise be without jurisdiction. A national court might play a useful role on a narrow and specific question. For example, following the Chamizal arbitration between the United States and Mexico, there was a question whether the award was binding or whether the arbitrators had exceeded their authority.[25] It might have

[24] 10 J. SPARKS, WRITINGS OF WASHINGTON 542–45 (1836).
[25] *See, e.g.,* 1 G. HACKWORTH, DIGEST OF INTERNATIONAL LAW 411–17 (1940).

been both appropriate and useful for the United States Government to have submitted to the Supreme Court the question whether it was legally bound by that arbitral award. There is at least a fair chance that the Court would have found the United States to be bound, and thus, the dispute might have been finally settled fifty years sooner than it was and at much less political cost to the United States.

To the extent that other forms of relief might be available from national courts (such as the possibility of an action by Mexico in United States courts to enforce the award), there would be less justification for trying to establish advisory jurisdiction.

(3) *Standing to request advisory opinions.* In Chapter IX it was suggested that the power to initiate an international proceeding should be scattered broadly. Apparently, a different approach is required when one considers advisory opinions. Why? Although the International Court of Justice has jurisdiction to render advisory opinions, it may not do so simply at the request of any state.[26] Presumably, to allow a single state to request, whenever it pleased, an advisory opinion would run the risk of further weakening respect for the decisions of the International Court of Justice.

On the other hand, the possibility of an international office which could render legal opinions on questions of international law should not be dismissed out of hand. One can contemplate the establishment of an "opinion office" within the Office of Legal Affairs of the United Nations which would be prepared, in appropriate circumstances, to give advisory opinions on questions of international law at the request of any member. This occasionally is done now, at least with respect to questions directly affecting the United Nations.[27] It also might be desirable

---

[26] U.N. CHARTER art. 96 provides: "1) The General Assembly or the Security Council may request the International Court of Justice to give an advisory opinion on any legal question. 2) Other organs of the United Nations and specialized agencies, which may at any time be so authorized by the General Assembly, may also request advisory opinions of the Court on legal questions arising within the scope of their activities."

[27] In the case of Legal Consequences for States of the Continued Presence of South Africa in Namibia (South West Africa) Notwithstanding Security Council Resolution 276 (1970), Vickers, the representative of the Secretary-General of the United Nations answered a question by Judge Gros on the competence of the Secretary-General to inter-

to establish a special office of distinguished lawyers, retired justices from the International Court, and outstanding international scholars to render such opinions. Any such office should certainly have the discretion to decline to issue an opinion. An opinion from such a body might well serve, on occasion, as a semiauthoritative, impartial determination carrying some political weight. Although a state might request and receive an opinion from such an office, it is doubtful that individuals should have similar access.

b. *What should the practice be?* Perhaps more critical than the formal jurisdictional rules are the practices that are followed by those who deal with advisory opinions. Even though the International Court of Justice has jurisdiction to render advisory opinions, the General Assembly and others empowered to request advisory opinions would be wise to avoid referring to the Court a list of questions such as that sent by Thomas Jefferson to the United States Supreme Court.[28]

(1) *Those seeking an opinion.* When the General Assembly, for example, is considering requesting an advisory opinion of the International Court of Justice, what are the general guidelines that the Assembly should keep in mind? Certainly one guideline should be a presumption against requesting the opinion if there is substantial chance that the matter can be adequately dealt with by political accommodation. We in the United States are particularly prone to turn political questions into legal ones. Instead of

---

pret the Charter. He explained: "The Secretary-General, however, himself offers interpretations of the powers of these organs when it becomes necessary to do so in the discharge of his own functions either as Chief Administrative Officer of the Organization, or as Secretary-General of the Security Council and of the General Assembly. Furthermore he also offers interpretations for the assistance of the organ concerned, either on his own initiative or at the request of that organ." Legal Consequences for States of the Continued Presence of South Africa in Namibia (South West Africa) Notwithstanding Security Council Resolution 276 (1970), I.C.J. Pleadings, Oral Arguments, Documents, vol. II, at 477. Such interpretations are usually prepared for the Secretary-General and on many occasions directly provided by his legal counsel. Thus, in 1968, the counsel interpreted article 12 of the Charter at the request of Peru. [1968] U.N. JURID-ICAL Y.B. 185. More recently, the counsel interpreted the meaning of the word *credentials* in rule 27 of the Rules of Procedure of the General Assembly (25 U.N. GAOR, Annexes a.i. 3, at 3, U.N. Doc. A / 8160 (1970)). *See also* Schachter, *The Development of International Law through the Legal Opinions of the United Nations Secretariat*, 25 BRIT Y.B. INT'L L. 91 (1948).

[28]*See* notes 23 & 24 and accompanying text *supra.*

asking, for example, what arrangements would best accommodate differing views about the role of religion in public school education, we tend to ask for a legal definition of the rights of children, the rights of parents, and the rights of the state. Rather than seeking to avoid a problem or to work out a solution to a particular situation, we tend to welcome a "test case" which will define legal rights and duties. The drawbacks that this tendency has within a national legal system are multiplied when it results in converting ordinary problems into controversial questions of international law. Edvard Hambro is no doubt correct when he states:

> It can do nothing but harm to the cause of international law and to the Court itself to try to saddle it with important political questions. Political questions should be settled by political means in the political organs of the United Nations and it is believed that very little good can be achieved by trying to solve these questions by legal procedures, dressing them out as legal questions and referring them to the Court. This can do immense harm by creating political division in the Court. The strongest warning ought to be given on this score, although the problem is not new.[29]

Although one can question the assumption apparently implicit in the above quotation that there is a clear distinction between political questions and legal questions, a distinction undoubtedly exists between pursuing a solution through political and legal avenues. In the last analysis, a solution is going to be political. A legal determination can play a useful role in realigning political forces. Those with the power to request an advisory opinion should exercise self-restraint.

Once it is decided to ask a question of the Court, there is great scope in formulating the question on which an advisory opinion is sought. Perhaps a study of advisory opinions should be made with the objective of developing guidelines for the drafting of such questions. Generally, the more narrowly drawn the question, the more easily the Court will be able to answer it while operating within the bounds of normal judicial techniques. A question which can be answered "yes" or "no" will not require as

---

[29] Hambro, *The Authority of the Advisory Opinions of the International Court of Justice*, 3 INT'L & COMP. L. Q. 2, 19 (1954) (citations omitted).

much of a legislative or an administrative task as will an open-ended question asking for a definition of rights or of duties. For instance, in the *International Status of South-West Africa Cases* the General Assembly asked: "What is the international status of the Territory of South-West Africa and what are the international obligations of the Union of South Africa arising therefrom?"[30] It is true that subsidiary questions clarified this matter to some extent, but the Court was asked to define general obligations. To avoid needless division on the Court and to avoid asking for broad decisions that might prove unwise in the light of subsequent facts, questions should usually be phrased as specifically as possible and should have reference to facts that have already occurred.

Also, in looking ahead to the compliance problem, those seeking an advisory opinion should consider whether it would be better to phrase the question in terms of the rights of those who may wish to exercise them, rather than in terms of the affirmative duties of those who will be reluctant to carry them out. An advisory opinion can add enormous legitimacy to self-help or to remedial action that might be taken by the United Nations or by a single state. Looked at from this point of view, the General Assembly's third request for an advisory opinion on South-West Africa was phrased in such a way as to minimize the problem of noncompliance. Rather than again inquiring about the obligations incumbent upon the Union of South Africa, the General Assembly asked the Court whether it was consistent with its first advisory opinion for the General Assembly's Committee "to grant oral hearings to petitioners on matters relating to the Territory of South-West Africa."[31] Although an advisory opinion may not be sufficient to compel action by a reluctant state, it may well serve to authorize action that states are able and, but for doubts as to its legality, willing to take.[32]

(2) *Guidelines for the tribunal.* In considering the practices that

[30][1950] I.C.J. 128, 131.

[31] Admissibility of Hearings of Petitioners by the Committee on South West Africa, [1956] I.C.J. 24.

[32] This seems to have been the objective of the Security Council when it requested the Court to give an advisory opinion on Legal Consequences for States of the Continued Presence of South Africa in Namibia (South West Africa) Notwithstanding Security Council Resolution 276 (1970).

should be followed by the International Court of Justice and by other tribunals in the rendering of advisory opinions, we are concerned with those practices which will maximize second-order compliance. How should a court behave in order to play its optimum role in causing compliance with international law?

The first question is how a court should exercise its discretion to decline to give an advisory opinion. Should a court decline to render an advisory opinion simply because it is satisfied that its views will not be accepted by one or more states whose legal rights are involved? Are there categories of questions that it should decline to answer because of the problem of subsequent noncompliance?

A related issue is whether a court should decline to deal with a question when one of the states concerned refuses to participate in the proceedings. This happened with the Soviet Union in the *Status of Eastern Carelia* case,[33] with Turkey in two cases, *Expulsion of the Ecumenical Patriarch*[34] and *Interpretation of Article 3, Paragraph 2 of the Treaty of Lausanne*,[35] and with three countries in the case of *Interpretation of Peace Treaties with Bulgaria, Hungary and Rumania.*[36]

As a general matter, such nonparticipation should not disqualify a court from going ahead. If the court does hear the question, it may wish to assure itself that all points of view are heard by appointing counsel to present positions which would not otherwise be heard. Since dissenting opinions undercut the force of an advisory opinion, members of a court might well wish to adopt even greater self-restraint when giving advice than when rendering a decision in a contentious proceeding.[37] Hambro emphasized the distinction in this respect between a judgment and an advisory opinion:

[33] Status of Eastern Carelia, note 7 *supra*.

[34] *See* the telegram dated May 16, 1925, and addressed to the Registrar of the Court by Dr. Tewfik Rouchdy, the Minister for Foreign Affairs of Turkey, [1925] P.C.I.J., ser. C, No. 9–II, at 108.

[35] *See* the telegram dated Oct. 8, 1925, and addressed to the Registrar of the Court by Dr. Tewfik Rouchdy, the Minister for Foreign Affairs of Turkey, [1925] P.C.I.J., ser. C, No. 10, at 17.

[36] Interpretation of Peace Treaties, note 9 *supra*.

[37] Calls to this effect were made by President Percy Spender in the South West Africa Cases, [1966] I.C.J. 51–57 and by Judge Sture Petrén in the Nuclear Tests Case, [1974] I.C.J. 306–07.

A judgment of the Court, even if it is not perfect and even if the reasoning can be criticised, can serve a useful purpose because it will put an end to a dispute between two or more States. An Advisory Opinion, on the other hand, does not serve this purpose. It stands or falls with the legal arguments that can be deduced from the reasoning of the majority and it is very much to be feared that a Court seriously split on any legal question submitted to it for Advisory Opinion will not contribute anything useful to the solution of that question.[38]

The greatest scope for influencing compliance may well be in the scope of the opinion rendered. Although, to some extent, this will be determined by the question that is posed, a court in forming its answer may be able to deal narrowly and wisely with the matter before it despite the breadth or form of the question presented.[39] As Judge Lauterpacht emphasized in the case of *Admissibility of Hearings of Petitions by the Committee on South West Africa*, "the absence of the requisite degree of precision or elaboration in the wording of the request does not absolve the Court of the duty to give an effective and accurate answer in conformity with the true purpose of its advisory jurisdiction."[40] Having the discretion to decline to answer a question at all, the court should feel free to exercise its discretion to answer only a portion of a question presented if that seems the wise course.[41]

[38] Hambro, *supra* note 29, at 21.

[39] *But see* the view expressed by Judge Anzilotti in the case of Free City of Danzig and International Labour Organization. He considered it inadmissible "for the Court to modify the request in order to bring it into harmony with what the Court holds to be the law in force." [1930] P.C.I.J., ser. B, No. 18, at 20.

[40] [1956] I.C.J. 38.

[41] The practice of the International Court of Justice and of the Permanent Court of International Justice, its predecessor, points to the conclusion that both courts did not hesitate either to reformulate the questions submitted to them or to leave unanswered parts of those questions. Thus, in the case of Free City of Danzig and International Labour Organization the Permanent Court refrained from answering the question. [1930] P.C.I.J., ser. B, No. 18, at 9. In the case of Judgments of the Administrative Tribunal of the International Labour Organization upon Complaints Made against the United Nations Educational, Scientific and Cultural Organization, the International Court of Justice observed that "[i]n the Request for an Advisory Opinion, Question II has been placed within the orbit of Article XII. Actually, it is outside that Article. Accordingly, it cannot be considered by the Court for the purpose of acting upon the request made to it." [1956] I.C.J. 99. In the case of Reparation for Injuries Suffered in the Service of the United Nations the Court left practically unanswered the question of priority between diplomatic and functional protection. *See* [1949] I.C.J. 174.

The general question of formulating determinations so as to maximize second-order compliance is dealt with in Chapter XIV.

(3) *Guidelines for those affected by the advisory opinion.* Obviously, a state faced with an advisory opinion which is contrary to the position that it has advocated can increase second-order compliance by accepting the opinion and by governing its behavior accordingly. Before doing otherwise, a state should consider the general benefits of such a practice. Although one state's acceptance of a particular advisory opinion will in no way guarantee that other states will accept other advisory opinions, its refusal to do so will tend to facilitate comparable refusal by other states.

Where a state is faced with an advisory opinion with which it concludes that it should not comply, even taking an enlightened and long-range view of its self-interest, it should justify its non-compliance on the narrowest possible legitimate grounds. For the interest of the community and its own future interest in the court, that state should look for grounds that do not constitute a frontal assault on the competence or integrity of the court or on the authority of its opinions. It may be possible, for example, for the state to distinguish the opinion, construe it narrowly, or find that subsequent events, not considered by the court, have changed conditions so as to make the opinion inapplicable or have altered the particular conduct which might otherwise be required of it. As unfortunate as it may be to have a state fail to comply with the good faith meaning of an advisory opinion, it is probably better to have it continue to "play the legal game" than to engage in a frontal assault on the court and its legal conclusions.

c. *Conclusion.* In 1954 Hambro took the following skeptical view of the impact of advisory opinions: "One must look behind the legal forms and investigate the political realities. It will then be seen that the real effect of the opinions on political issues has not been very great."[42] However, in view of the reluctance of states to accept the compulsory jurisdiction of the International Court and at the same time of the willingness of both the General

[42] Hambro, *supra* note 29, at 19. *See also* 2 S. ROSENNE, THE LAW AND PRACTICE OF THE INTERNATIONAL COURT 747–54 (1965); Gross, *The International Court of Justice and the United Nations*, 120 RECUEIL DES COURS (Hague Academy of International Law) 312, 411 (1967).

Assembly and the Security Council to request advisory opinions, there is a substantial opportunity to make constructive use of such opinions. The maximum opportunity appears to be in areas where the Court would be legitimating collective or individual self-help, rather than in compelling action from a reluctant state.

2. *Determinations against governments.* In deciding what rules and practices should govern national and international tribunals that make authoritative determinations of questions of international law with respect to defendant governments, we must confront the long-established doctrine of "sovereign immunity."

A frequent suggestion is that all governments should accept, without reservation, the compulsory jurisdiction of the International Court of Justice. Yet the United States itself, for example, has been unwilling for over 190 years to allow all suits against the government, even in its own courts. Furthermore, under the eleventh amendment each of the fifty states of the Union preserves the defense of sovereign immunity against most plaintiffs.[43]

This section considers whether it is reasonable to expect a general abandonment of sovereign immunity in the international arena in light of the experience and methods by which law has been used in the domestic arena to control governmental behavior.

a. *Purposes of sovereign immunity.* Existing immunities of governments can be explained by historical accident, but what functions do these immunities now serve? Of the rationales that have been advanced to support the idea that courts should not have jurisdiction over governments three appear to have no merit.

1. To save busy officials from wasting time in court. The immunity of a government, it can be argued, is like that of a diplomat. To permit public officials to carry on their important duties the government is freed from having to go to court to justify its conduct. This is nonsense. Most officials are not personally immune from suit. Furthermore, they can be represented by counsel. Judicial appearances, like appearances before congressional committees, can be arranged to accommodate their schedules.

---

[43]U.S. CONST. amend. XI.

2. To save public funds for proper purposes. One theory supporting governmental immunity is the same as that which supports the doctrine that charitable institutions (such as Harvard) should be immune from liability for their torts. The immunity of such enterprises, where it exists, has been widely criticized. It would seem proper that a government should be fair before it is generous, and that the costs of government should not fall in random fashion upon those who happen to get hurt by its unlawful conduct.

3. To make government illegality less destructive of law and order. Where government officials have decided to violate a statutory or constitutional restriction upon what the government may lawfully do, the illegality can often be obscured if the government is able to stay out of court. In these circumstances, it can be argued, the example for others is not so bad. On the other hand, after a court has spoken, governmental illegality stands naked and sets an example for others which is likely to induce further illegality. To allow a court to take jurisdiction and to determine that a government is acting unlawfully can thus be said to increase the risk that some violation of the law which the government concludes is politically necessary will undercut general respect for law.

The need that governments have to act with substantial freedom and flexibility is not, however, best met by leaving governments free to break the law. Laws can be enacted that provide for governmental discretion. Judicial consideration of the lawfulness of governmental action is far more likely to prevent governmental abuse than it is to stimulate lawlessness by others.

4. Another and far more persuasive justification for sovereign immunity is that it provides needed support for the doctrine of the separation of powers: It serves to keep the courts from deciding questions that they ought not to decide.

Within a domestic law system sovereign immunity helps implement the notion of separation of powers. Some questions are for the political branches of the government to decide. The immunity of the government from direct suit prevents the courts from reviewing matters that are beyond their competence; it holds the courts at a distance.

This appears to be the sound basis for making a government immune from suit in its own courts. Despite that immunity, governments, such as that of the United States, have been brought substantially under a rule of law and their actions subject to judicial review. To a large extent, this has been accomplished through the device of suing individual officers, as discussed below.

b. *How much immunity from international tribunals?* What does this domestic doctrine of sovereign immunity say about the two related questions with which we are most directly concerned — the extent to which it should be possible to seek a determination against a government in the courts of a foreign nation and in an international tribunal? Do the considerations of keeping the courts at a distance in order to avoid intruding on questions best decided by nonjudicial bodies still hold?

It would appear that all the reasons for sovereign immunity that would keep a court from accepting suit against its own sovereign would be applicable to preclude that court from accepting a suit against a foreign sovereign. In addition to the fear of judicial intrusion into matters best resolved by legislative or executive discretion, there is the fear of judicial intrusion by the courts of one state into matters best resolved by the decisions of another state.

After years of study and debate, the United States enacted the Foreign Sovereign Immunities Act of 1976,[44] which came into effect on January 19, 1977. This law clarifies and codifies the extent to which foreign states may be sued in United States courts. In the course of the deliberations preceding the enactment of this statute, a great deal was written and said about sovereign immunity.[45] There is no intention to provide here a general treatment of the subject or to review the many ways in which the line may be drawn between what is immune from judicial scrutiny and what is not; rather, let me simply advance a few propositions.

There should be some possibility of reaching authoritative determinations against governments as such. A government, like a corporation, should have the competence to sue and to be sued. Some duties, such as financial obligations, are clearly those

[44] Pub. L. No. 94–583, 90 Stat. 2891 (codified at 28 U.S.C. § 1330 (1976)).

[45] *See, e.g.,* articles cited in footnote 8 of Note, *Sovereign Immunity — Limits of Judicial Control,* 18 HARV. INT'L L.J. 429, 430 (1977).

of the government as an entity and cannot readily be dealt with by suits against officers.

Sovereign immunity has served as a precautionary rule to maintain the separation of powers. In theory, the elimination of sovereign immunity should not reduce the area of a government's lawful powers but should only shift the determination of that legal question from a political body to a court. In practice, giving courts the right to tell governments, as such, what they may and may not do leads courts to decide matters that are lawfully and properly decided by political organs.

When a court tells a government to do something — particularly where the court is requiring affirmative action — it is extremely difficult to define what ought to be done without making a decision as to how it should be done. This usually means a court's deciding some aspect of the conduct where the political branch of the government should, by law, be free to do it differently. For example, if a court orders a government to issue "a passport," the substantive law might, in fact, give the government discretion to issue identity cards, or to issue no passports to anyone, or to change the form of the passport. If a court orders a government to integrate schools or to reapportion its election districts, the court is in a quandary as far as producing a decision which will lead to second-order compliance. If the order is detailed and explicit as to what should be done, the court will necessarily have decided on one of several legal ways of taking the action. It will have exercised discretion that normally would have been left to the executive. Ordering anything more than the most routine ministerial acts encroaches upon the sovereign discretion of the government and is likely to encounter a feeling of legitimate resistance. A sense that a court has gone beyond its normal role is not conducive to compliance.

If, to avoid this problem, a court issues a broad decision identifying the result that the law requires but leaving it up to executive officials to determine the appropriate means of accomplishing that result, the chances of compliance may be no better. As is discussed in Chapter XIV, a vague order as to what ought to be done leaves considerable room for plausibly justified noncompliance.

An example of this dilemma in domestic American law is

where the Supreme Court decides a case brought by one state against another over the fair allocation of irrigation water from a common river. If the judges seek to specify the exact amount of water that each state may withdraw during designated hours and days at different river conditions, then the decision is likely to create resentment; the judges are deciding upon one of many equally lawful solutions in an area where they are not experts. On the other hand, if the Court simply orders the states to divide the waters fairly, then the decision is not likely to produce much real compliance.

The best solution in such cases may be to give the parties time in which to produce an agreed decree which can then be incorporated in a judicial order. Or, a master may be appointed to work out a decree in consultation with the parties. Sovereign immunity tends to avoid this kind of dilemma in that its application normally will avoid a court's reaching a determination in a form where second-order compliance will be difficult.

Reaching determinations against a government is not necessary in order to subject governments to legal restraint. As the experience of the United States has shown, it is possible for courts to reach determinations as to the illegality of government conduct in proceedings brought against officers rather than against the government as such. This, however, is not true in all cases. In particular, it seems not to be true where the desired relief is the payment of money, such as in actions for contract or tort damages.

Accepting international judicial review of the decisions of a national *court* does not seem to involve the same dangers of judicial excess (and judicially ineffective action) as are involved in permitting original international proceedings against a government as such, that is, proceedings which seek executive or legislative action.

A broad waiver of sovereign immunity, permitting international courts to reach determinations against governments, would greatly increase the probability that such determinations would be in a form less likely to produce compliance than if the determinations were more narrowly directed against specific officers.

3. *Determinations against officers.* This section considers the advantages (and disadvantages, to the extent they exist) of having an issue of alleged noncompliance with international law determined in a proceeding brought against an individual officer, rather than against a government. Domestic experience suggests that suits against officers are more acceptable to governments, lead to better legal decisions, and lead to decisions with which compliance will be easier to bring about.

a. *Suits against officers are more acceptable.* Examples from United States legal history suggest how readily the concept of sovereign immunity can be reconciled with permitting a suit involving a governmental question against a government officer.

In *Osborn v. Bank of United States*, the Bank brought suit against officers of the state government of Ohio.[46] After the state of Ohio levied a tax on the Bank, some $100,000 was seized from the Bank's vaults by Osborn, the State Auditor, and turned over to Sullivan, the State Treasurer. Since the state of Ohio was immune from suit, an action was brought against these two officers. Chief Justice Marshall concluded that "it would be subversive of the best-established principles to say that the laws could not afford the same remedies against the agent employed in doing the wrong which they would afford against him could his principal be joined in the suit."[47] The circuit court's decision ordering restitution of the money was affirmed.

Some time after the Civil War, George Washington Custis Lee, son of Robert E. Lee, sought to recover the Arlington estate, which had been acquired by the United States Government in 1864 through a public sale of doubtful validity for an alleged failure to pay property taxes. For more than ten years the Arlington estate had been used by the United States Government as a national cemetery and a military station. Lee brought an action of ejectment against Frederick Kaufman and Richard P. Strong, who were the officers in charge of the cemetery and the balance of the estate, respectively. In a five-to-four decision the Supreme Court affirmed the circuit court's decision for Lee.[48]

[46] 22 U.S. (9 Wheat.) 738 (1824).
[47] *Id.* at 843.
[48] United States v. Lee, 106 U.S. 196 (1882).

Writing for the majority, Mr. Justice Miller said:

> While by the Constitution the judicial department is recognized as one of the three great branches among which all the powers and functions of the government are distributed, it is inherently the weakest of them all.
>
> Dependent as its courts are for the enforcement of their judgments upon officers appointed by the executive and removable at his pleasure, with no patronage and no control of the purse or the sword, their power and influence rest solely upon the public sense of the necessity for the existence of a tribunal to which all may appeal for the assertion and protection of rights guaranteed by the Constitution and by the laws of the land, and on the confidence reposed in the soundness of their decisions and the purity of their motives.
>
> From such a tribunal no well-founded fear can be entertained of injustice to the government, or of a purpose to obstruct or diminish its just authority.[49]

The same arguments would presumably apply to suits directly against the government.

Under United States law, suits against officers on governmental issues are permitted on one of two different theories. The first is that of ordering a legally prescribed task:

> It is clear that if an executive official refuses to perform an act which Congress has directed him to perform and as to which he has been left by the Congress with no discretionary choice, or if he refuses to perform a purely ministerial act, the court can compel him to act.[50]

The second theory is that the courts may restrict an officer to his statutory authority. If he steps outside the scope of his lawful authority, he may be told to get back within it.

Suggestive of the international possibilities of this latter theory is the case of *Bigelow v. Princess Zizianoff* from the Court of Appeals of Paris in 1928.[51] Princess Zizianoff had applied for

[49]*Id.* at 223.

[50]Chapman v. El Paso Natural Gas Company, 204 F.2d 46, 54 (D.C. Cir. 1953) (Prettyman, J., concurring in part).

[51]Bigelow v. Princess Zizianoff, Cour d'Appel de Paris, Gazette du Palais, May 4, 1928, *reprinted in* M. HUDSON, CASES ON INTERNATIONAL LAW 432 (3d ed. 1951).

a visa to the United States and had been turned down by United States Consul Bigelow. She protested the denial. Bigelow, in the course of explaining to the press the reasons for the decision, stated that the Princess was an international spy who had been sent to the United States to engage in espionage. The Princess instigated a proceeding against Bigelow in a French court. The court found that it was competent to consider those acts that went beyond Bigelow's proper duties.[52] If, instead of being a quasi-criminal action, the Princess had sought, in advance, an injunction against Bigelow's disclosing the allegedly false and defamatory report as being contrary to some international rule, we would have an example of the kind of international case here being considered. The example suggests how the United States might be more willing to have a case brought against Bigelow than it would against the United States Government as such.

When an action is brought against an officer, there is less basis for the mystical concern with "sovereignty." The abstract nature of the concept of government tends to reinforce the vagueness that exists in most people's minds about sovereignty. Rather than undertake the difficult educational task of developing public understanding of the legal concepts of sovereignty (an area of lawful discretion; a status equal to that of other governments; the right to have no one else decide on the extent of one's rights; etc.) and the political concepts of sovereignty (effective political power, and so on), it will probably prove easier to duck the question. People know that individuals are not "sovereign" and that they can be sued. From the point of view of the international community, there seems no necessity for having determinations sought against governments as such. If all individuals can be caused to respect international decisions, there will be no problem of governmental defiance.

On a purely practical basis, there are good reasons for a government's being more willing to have its officer sued than to have a judicial determination against itself. There is likely to be less at stake in any one case. The probabilities are that the worst outcome of a given judicial proceeding would be less serious for the government if the action were against an individual officer

[52] *Id.*

rather than if it were against the government as a whole. Since the risks are fewer, the procedure is more acceptable.

b. *Suits against officers produce better decisions.* The quality of a judicial decision is likely to be higher in a case where the plaintiff is seeking an injunction or other forward-looking decree if the case is against an individual officer rather than against the government as such. This would seem to be true for two reasons.

(1) *Specificity.* If the court is framing a determination as to the future conduct of a given individual officer, it is likely to be looking at real facts and to be influenced by them. The decision is less subject to the ills of declaratory relief.

(2) *Less judicial encroachment.* When dealing with the question of formulating an order to an individual officer, a court is not so likely to take upon itself executive duties of deciding how something ought to be done. The two theories permitting suits against officers limit the problem: a court may affirmatively order a ministerial task or prohibit an officer from acting illegally. A court can thus order an individual officer not to block the schoolhouse door or not to install a radar station on someone else's property. When speaking to a single individual, the court is unlikely to tell him how to set up a school district or where to install a radar station; it is not within the lawful authority of that given individual to produce the affirmative governmental result. The fact of his limited authority tends to preserve the area of discretion to be exercised by the executive. If, however, a court is talking to a government, it may be tempted to avoid delay and just tell the government how to do what it ought to do, since the government as a whole does have the lawful authority to carry out almost any instructions that the court might make.

c. *Suits against officers produce decisions that are more likely to be complied with.* Where a judicial determination results in a decision that a *government* should behave in the future differently than it has behaved in the past, compliance is likely to require a governmental decision. Someone will have to call a meeting; a group of officials will have to consult about what to do. Unless and until they agree on a new course of action and issue appropriate instructions to those who will execute it, the government is unlikely to comply with the determination.

Where a judicial determination results in a decree which tells a particular *officer* exactly what he is or is not to do, the situation is quite different. The officer is likely to find himself faced with conflicting views as to his obligation. Faced with such a conflict, he is likely to defer to the view that is most recent and most explicit. A general obligation to carry out the laws of the state is likely to seem less persuasive than an order stating that "you, John Jones, from and after ten A.M. Monday morning next shall stop intercepting messages on Smith's telephone line."

In such a case, governmental inertia is on the side of compliance. Unless and until a group of officials gets together, consults about what to do, agrees upon a course of organized defiance of the decision, and issues appropriate instructions, the individual officer is likely to comply with the judicial determination.

Where a decision runs against a government, it is often possible that each officer who would be involved in compliance will not regard it as his responsibility to take the initiative necessary to bring about compliance. For example, if the United States Government is ordered to stop polluting an international river, no single official may know exactly what he is supposed to do. Legislative officials may regard the matter as one for executive action. On the other hand, legislative authorization and appropriations may be required. State and federal officials may each regard the primary duty for taking action as resting with others and may have sound considerations supporting that position. Noncompliance may result not from any desire for defiance but from institutional buck-passing. The risk of this problem is greatly reduced if the determination is a decision about what one or more designated officers ought to do.

In following up a decision against a *government*, it turns out that sooner or later the legal system must deal with the conduct in which *people* ought to engage. An abstraction, like a government, or a corporation, or a town, can act only through people. It is the conduct of individual officers that must finally be affected. The chances of initial noncompliance can often be reduced if the stage of telling an abstraction what to do can be bypassed.

Reaching a determination against an individual officer often succeeds in producing compliance through a process of "divide and conquer." Unless his colleagues all rally around, the individual may decide to go along with that decision this time. Why should he stick his neck out? His colleagues, on the other hand, are not directly involved in this case. Why should they stick their necks out?

This domestic experience with suits against individual officers has particular relevance to improving compliance with international law. Enforcing international obligations by bringing the judicial process to bear on individual officials will be most successful where the court is asked to enjoin conduct found to be illegal — conduct in which the officer has no legal right to engage. Such enforcement also has a good chance of success where an officer is being ordered to take affirmative action that is clearly defined and routine — action of a ministerial sort. It will be least likely to succeed if the court must order large-scale affirmative action. Here, as the litigation involving the racial integration of public school systems in the United States has demonstrated, courts become involved in administration. They find themselves selecting one scheme (that they believe best) among numerous alternatives, each of which would be lawful. Judicial decisions of that kind tend to be the least acceptable and to command the least respect.

CHAPTER XIII

The Content of a Decision[1]

So far, we have considered the problems of an appropriate plaintiff's finding a suitable forum in which to seek an authoritative determination about an alleged violation of international law by either a government or its officials. We now consider the content of the decision that such a tribunal should render in order to maximize compliance with its findings. First, we review the general role that the decision plays in the process of causing second-order compliance with international law. Second, we examine ways of maximizing the legitimacy of a decision. Finally, we consider the kinds of decisions that a tribunal can produce and the techniques that it can use in framing decisions so as to secure maximum compliance therewith.

1. *Changing the question.* Before looking in detail at the content of a decision by a domestic or international tribunal, it may be helpful to review the general theory of how we hope to produce second-order compliance. By hypothesis, there has been a failure to achieve first-order compliance. A government has concluded that it was in its interest to engage in certain conduct that violated a standing rule of international law. What, if anything, should we do about that violation, and how can we persuade that government not to take similar action in the future? This problem is frequently stated in terms of making a government do something that it does not want to do.

In some cases, our task may not be too difficult. An individual or a government may have made a mistake through ignorance or miscalculation. The captain of a pelagic fur-sealing vessel, or even a State Department official, might think that a Russian official may be denied the right to board and to search the fur-sealing ship on the high seas when there is reasonable cause to believe that the ship is violating the Interim Convention on Conservation of North Pacific Fur Seals.[1] In these situations, it

---

[1] *Signed* Feb. 9, 1957, 2 U.S.T. 2283, T.I.A.S. No. 3948, 314 U.N.T.S. 105.

should be possible to educate private parties and officials into seeing the error of their ways. The captain or State Department official can be told that article VI of the Fur Seal Convention allows the Russian in these circumstances to board and to search the sealing vessel.[2] But for the typical violation this is hardly a promising approach. As we have already observed, most governmental violations of international law are the results of conscious choice, not inadvertence. Even in these instances of deliberate violations, it may be possible to change a government's values or desire. Perhaps the Government of North Korea could be persuaded to provide better treatment to the captured crew of a ship alleged to have violated North Korea's territorial waters. In a domestic setting we have attempted to change southern attitudes towards blacks by education and persuasion. (And, we sometimes try this on our children: "Now, Junior, you really *like* rice pudding.") But domestic and personal experience suggests that that approach is not very promising.

The basic hope lies not in persuading governments to change their minds about a given issue. Instead, governments should be presented with a decision which poses a different issue from the one which was previously decided. We should seek to revise the original question so that existing attitudes and forces will produce a different result. The task can be looked at not as increasing the weight on one side of a balance but rather as shifting the fulcrum. As a result, some of the weight that came out on one side of the question of first-order compliance would now press toward compliance with the decision of a domestic or international tribunal.

A question has many dimensions; an authoritative determination may change them all. For purposes of analysis we can consider (*a*) the parties, (*b*) the demand (that is, the conduct that is required), (*c*) the offer (that is, the anticipated consequences of engaging in the required conduct) and (*d*) the threat (that is, the anticipated consequences of noncompliance). Second-order compliance is likely to depend upon the extent to which a determination alters each of these factors. To make these factors more concrete, let us consider a hypothetical case. In international law

[2]*Id.* at art. VI.

there is a general obligation that governments which share an international river should divide its waters equitably, giving appropriate priority to established irrigation. Assume that a river runs across the territory of two countries. The government of the upstream country has just completed a new dam which will divert waters from the international river and will reduce supplies to long-established canals in the downstream country.[3] What role can an authoritative decision play in resolving the dispute that occurs when the downstream country's government accuses the upstream country of violating the international rule on the division of the waters of a river?

a. *Parties.*

(1) *Defendant.* The government whose conduct is in question presumably considered the diversion of the upstream waters as an institutional decision. The first-order "violation" of the obligation was decided upon by a group of officials or, perhaps, by an individual government officer acting in his official capacity for the good of his country.

An authoritative determination might effectively change the person who must decide. By pointing the finger at a single official who participated in the decision, we would force him to decide, even if the original violation was approved by a broader group. In many cases, however, there may be no change in the defendant. In our hypothetical situation, an official may have decided to go along with superior orders based on a governmental decision to divert the waters. As a result, he opened the gate letting the water into the new canal. If we want him (and perhaps his government superiors) to reach a different decision, we will have to present them with a different question.

(2) *Plaintiff.* The opposing party in a river dispute is fairly well identified. In some cases, such as pollution of the high seas, there is no identified opposing party until a dispute arises. A decision to engage in conduct that does not impinge upon any defined party is probably easier to reach than is one to engage in conduct that does impinge upon a particular plaintiff. Before a case reaches the tribunal, therefore, one change may already have taken place: there may be a plaintiff where there had been none

[3] For a similar situation arising between India and Pakistan, see Laylin, *Indus River System — Comments*, 54 AM. SOC'Y INT'L L. PROC. 144 (1960).

before. In criminal cases, the party plaintiff is represented in a persuasive manner as the entire community.

Although the existence of an adversary in cases where there would not otherwise be one adds some weight on the side of compliance, the nature of the parties will be further changed in this direction after a determination has been made. If the International Court of Justice decides that the upstream country should not divert waters from the international river to the new canal, the demand for restraint comes not from an opponent but from an institution above the conflict. This makes it easier for the government of the upstream country to go along with the request. Giving in to the demands of the downstream country runs the risk of whetting its appetite to make more demands. It may be appeasement to yield to an opponent. It is not appeasement to comply with the reasoned decision of a fairly constituted international tribunal.

The form and content of a decision should reflect this shift in parties in order to get the maximum benefit from the change as it will appear to the country whose compliance is desired. The request for action or restraint should now come from the tribunal or some impartial official, not from the plaintiff country. It would seem less desirable simply to decide that the plaintiff was right and that *he* could now continue to press *his* demand. In the water dispute, the International Court should not limit itself to telling the upstream country that its intended action violates an international obligation with the downstream country. With such a decision, the downstream country's government would still be the party demanding restraint by the government of the upstream country. Instead, the Court should itself enjoin the upstream country from proceeding with its diversion of the waters of the international river. In any event, the upstream country need only comply with the decision of an impartial tribunal — not yield to its downstream adversary.

b. *Demand.* In a particular case, an authoritative determination can confront a government official with a dramatically different request from the one which he appeared to face when he considered the question of first-order compliance with a standing international rule. The standing rule is likely to be both broad and vague. Our canal official and his superiors were faced with a general obligation of international law that governments which share an international river should divide its waters equitably, giving appropriate priority to established irrigation. Consider how the government of the upstream country would regard a broad demand to restrict the opening of any new canals until permission is obtained from the downstream riparian. To the upstream country, the decision appears to be one requiring a choice between going ahead with the canal program or stopping it. If the upstream country is told that international law requires this choice, the government is likely to feel that the law is asking it not to open any new canals.

An authoritative determination could narrow the question facing the upstream riparian a great deal. What looked like a broad demand can now be made an extremely narrow one. Instead of being asked to stop the canal program, a tribunal would say: "Do not open this one canal at this time." The character of such a request could be further changed if there were a handful of international officials available to "enforce" the decision. For example, the tribunal might send a marshal to shut the canal gate. In that event, the request facing the local official at the canal has been changed from one concerning the gates to one asking him not to assault the international official in the blue uniform.

A tribunal's decision can change the character of the demand on a government in other respects as well. For instance, what was previously ambiguous can now be made extremely clear. The requirement to divide the waters of the international river equitably may now appear as a request to the upstream country not to draw off more than X gallons of water each day. This clarity may exist not only with respect to the content of the action demanded or prohibited but also with respect to its timing. Further, the restraint can be temporary. If the order is of short duration, the upstream country will probably be more willing to comply with it. Complying with a temporary restraining order, which is effective for only a few days, is far less difficult for a government than accepting a permanent injunction. Although the temporary order may be extended, the initial threat is considerably reduced. In our example, the upstream country would not have to give up its position in the event of a temporary order.

It would simply have to defer its action pending what might be a more favorable settlement of the dispute.

Compliance in the first instance with a determination is easier when the decision is subject to being reviewed and upset on appeal. The question previously presented to the government being asked to comply was whether to go along "forever" with the restriction implicit in the adversary's view of international law. Now the question is whether to go along in the short run with the decision. Most governments, like most people, tend to see a situation from their own point of view and to believe that they are in the right. They are usually so confident that they are in the right that they become convinced that fair and right-minded people will agree with them. The new canal can remain closed for a few months so that the upstream country's government has a chance to show that its diversion does not constitute an inequitable division of the river's waters. Appellate litigation in domestic courts attests to the optimism with which each side views the outcome of an appeal. This optimistic view that one's position will eventually be vindicated is extremely helpful for compliance at the early stages of law enforcement. Knowing that it has a right of review, a government will tend to accept a determination for the time being.

c. *Offer.* Not only is the question presented to a government changed by altering both the character and the content of the request addressed to it by a tribunal, but the consequences which a government anticipates may also be drastically affected by that request. There are not many rewards for good behavior in the international community. Whatever rewards do exist are likely to be greater for deferring to an international determination than they are for deferring to standing rules. Although the troublemaker may gain some respect by being feared, there may on occasion be a comparable or even greater advantage flowing to the now friendly cooperator who, on a small issue, is prepared to acquiesce. There is almost no reward for quietly being good and obeying a primary rule. But there may be some political rewards for belated improvement. Before placing Soviet missiles in Cuba, Khrushchev received little mention for refraining from that action, just as the upstream country got no praise for not diverting the international river before the construction of the new canal. But the Soviet leader did receive some favorable recognition for removing the missiles from Cuba, and the upstream country would probably benefit from a similar reaction if it followed an order from a tribunal limiting diversion of the river.

Building up the prestige of an international legal system by yielding to it and complying with its decisions brings with it the possible future gain that may result from a general improvement in international order. There were no real advantages to the United States in not permitting the use of nauseating gas in South Vietnam. On the other hand, to have deferred to a resolution of the General Assembly that such gas should not be used would have strengthened the prestige of the United Nations and made it slightly more potent for the future.

d. *Threat.* Although a determination can alter the favorable consequences resulting from compliance, it can more effectively alter the consequences that will flow from *not* respecting what a tribunal decides. In the first place, it may be possible to reduce the gains that the government may have foreseen as resulting from noncompliance. The international community may find it hard to compel affirmative action on the part of the wrongdoer. Nonetheless, it should not prove too difficult to devise decisions that make it unlikely that a government will reap as great benefits from its illegality in violating a decision as it may have anticipated.

In our example, the upstream country expected a number of benefits from diverting waters to the new canal — perhaps increased irrigation for crops or perhaps a new transportation facility. But, a decision that either no water or only a certain amount of water can be diverted from the international river for the new canal might incorporate provisions which make violating it considerably less attractive than was violating the standing rule of international law. For example, if the water was for irrigating export crops, the decision might ask traditional importers of these crops to refrain from purchasing any crops produced with illegally diverted water. Or, the decision might authorize seizure of the exported crops and their sale for the benefit of the downstream country's citizens who suffered from an excessive diversion. If the canal was to irrigate internally consumed crops or for local transportation needs, we might want a decision legitimizing destruction of this property if it is used contrary to an authoritative international decision. Perhaps we would want an international official with authority to enter the country and turn off the machinery diverting water to the new canal. In any event, our extensive experience with framing decrees in domestic litigation should help us in preparing a decision which decreases the benefits that the wrongdoer would gain by ignoring the determination.

A determination not only can decrease the gains expected from noncompliance, it also can increase the possible costs. An authoritative determination can affect the action that other countries will feel justified in taking and the action that international institutions may take. Defiance of an international determination is far more destructive of the international system than is a simple first-order violation of some rule of law. When a first-order rule is ambiguous, as in our international river case, the costs of permitting defiance are not very great. But once a tribunal has interpreted the rule and issued an order based on its decision, permitting noncompliance undercuts the entire international system of settling disputes by reaching fair determinations based on reasoned judgments. An international determination thus constitutes a form of escalation by the international community against the individual defendant or the defendant government. Changing the question, if well done, structures the issue so that the community has far more to lose from successful defiance than the defendant country stands to gain. If all countries see the question this way, and if they behave rationally, they will do what they can to ensure that successful defiance does not take place.

The individual defendant or defendant government is likely to take a similar view of the costs of noncompliance, even without anticipating what other countries will say. For the upstream country, the decision from a tribunal in the river dispute might allow less water diversion for the new canal than it would have liked. But the loss must be measured against the even greater loss that would result from its refusal to obey the determination. The upstream defendant also has an interest in the ongoing international community and in the continued respect for some kind of orderly system of settling disputes. After all, the government of the upstream country may find itself as the plaintiff in the next case. For these reasons, the costs to the defendant from defying the determination, if it is well conceived, are likely to be sufficiently great to outweigh whatever benefits might be obtained through noncompliance. As a result, the defendant should be led to second-order compliance.

2. *Maximizing the legitimacy of a decision.* There is a marked difference between the political impact of a naked request for relief coming from an individual plaintiff and the rendition of a judicial decree for the same relief coming from an admittedly competent court. Because of legal and institutional arrangements made in advance and because of the way the court conducts itself, the community believes that greater deference should be given to the judicial decision. As a result of this belief, members of the community who had been indifferent or opposed to the plaintiff's having his way will now believe that the judicial decision should be complied with. The content of the determination may be identical. The decision differs from the request only in the degree of its legitimacy.

This difference in legitimacy is not a simple either/or choice between having it or not having it. There are degrees of legitimacy. Obtaining an authoritative determination is the primary way suggested for resolving conflicting views as to what ought to happen and for causing most of the effective political community to throw their weight behind one view rather than the other. But the degree of support that a community is likely to give to a determination is a function of far more than the fact of a determination. In general, a judicial determination will appear more legitimate than a partisan demand, but some judicial determinations will appear far more legitimate than others and will have a correspondingly greater inherent force toward compliance. The very vocabulary we often use suggests the close relationship between the esteem or "respect" with which a decision is held and the chance of its being "respected" in the sense of being complied with. (And, some demands can be legitimated so that even without an authoritative determination they will be accorded more respect than others.) Here, as elsewhere, there is a whole spectrum. A determination may run from the highly dubious, with which few will wish to comply, to the weighty, authoritative, necessary, and obvious decision that will commend itself to all.

In seeking to produce second-order compliance we will wish to maximize the legitimacy of determinations. This can be accomplished by procedural arrangements made in advance, by substantive legal rules adopted in advance to authorize or to prescribe certain kinds of determinations, and by the way in which the tribunal making the determination performs its task.

a. *Advance establishment of procedural arrangements.*

(1) *Legal authority to make determination.* In the discussion of the problem of making tribunals acceptable, it was generally assumed that we wanted or needed bodies which had an admitted right to make determinations. Even where the body is not a court, with the authority to decide questions conclusively, but is rather a commission or other organization which simply makes recommendations, we will want it specified in advance that this body has the explicit legal right to make such recommendations. The more explicit the lawful right of that body is to make a determination, the less that determination will be subject to being undercut by a "jurisdictional" attack.

(2) *Maximum status of determinations.* Clarification in advance, by treaty or otherwise, of the status of a type of determination may reduce the risk of its being undercut later. If agreement can be reached that decisions of a given kind will be "binding," such agreement will be helpful later on. On the other hand, where such agreement may not be possible, it may be better to have a determination of ambiguous status than one that is known to be wholly advisory and without legal effect.

(3) *Composition of the body making the determination.* The same kinds of considerations which are likely to make an international body acceptable to governments are also likely to make that body's decisions more acceptable after they have been made. One can quickly list such respect-inducing qualities in judges as age (but not too old); prior judicial experience (but not necessarily a requirement); appropriate distribution among races, geographical regions, and ideologies; selected by a fair procedure, etc.

(4) *Procedural rules of the body.* Again, advance agreement on

the procedure to be followed by a tribunal or other body is likely to be important, both for the acceptability of the institution and for the deference that will be accorded to its determinations. At a minimum, those who are going to be told what to do should have a fair opportunity to be heard. Efforts should be made to make the procedure of the body familiar to those who use it. A bilateral British-American tribunal may use common-law procedures, but Ethiopia should not have to find an American lawyer when it argues in the International Court of Justice.

b. *Advance establishment of substantive rules about remedies.* In the drafting of treaties and domestic legislation that implements international rules, attention should be given to the kind of determinations that ought to be reached in cases of alleged noncompliance. The tendency will be to focus on deciding the question of whether or not there has been a violation. Such a decision is far less important than a decision as to what ought to be done next. There is no compliance problem with respect to decisions about past guilt or innocence. The critical question for decision is: "What ought to be done now?" That is true, whatever the evidence of prior conduct.

The legitimacy of a decision about what ought to be done next will be greatly increased if there was prior agreement that a particular kind of relief was authorized and appropriate for cases of the kind being litigated. The talent of the law to deal with disorder in an orderly way depends, in large part, upon the existence of a law of remedies — rules about what should happen when the rules are broken. If a government has agreed about what should happen in the event of a breach of a rule, it has thereby weakened any basis it may have had for complaining if that particular result is imposed.

Although the fact of agreement helps, prior agreement cannot legitimate any and every kind of determination. The authorized relief should conform as closely as possible to commonsense notions of what kind of relief would be appropriate. For example, a treaty might provide that a ship found to have been engaged in illegal whaling should be subject to forfeiture to any government which captured it and established the illegality of the whaling to the satisfaction of an international whaling commission. Without such a prior rule, turning the boat over to another country would seem far from legitimate. However, with the preestablished rule, the decision would seem fair and tolerable. A prior agreement that nuclear material wrongfully diverted from a peaceful reactor to a military program was subject to being retaken or destroyed by force would make an international decision ordering the destruction of a given quantity of material far more legitimate than it would be if the prior agreement were silent about remedies and simply provided that the nuclear material should not be diverted to military use.

Rules about the appropriate determination in the event of a breach of international law can be established by practice, as well as by formal agreement. One reason that espionage is not so destructive of international order as one might suppose is that there exists a common practice about what should result when it is found that one government has been spying on another. The aggrieved government does not proceed against the offending government. Rather, it submits the spy case to a national tribunal for decision. Decisions that limit the relief to the imposition of punishment upon the individual spy are understood to be legitimate and are accepted as fair by other governments. Other kinds of relief, equally within the power of the aggrieved government, would be deemed inappropriate and are not engaged in.

c. *Action by the tribunal to maximize legitimacy.* Much of what a tribunal can do to maximize the legitimacy of its decisions lies in the formulation of the relief that it orders, as discussed below. In addition, the procedure the tribunal follows, its general approach toward its job, and the justification it provides in support of its decision can all help increase the legitimacy of its determinations.

(1) *Procedures.* Obviously, a body which wants to have its determinations respected should abide by the procedural rules that are supposed to govern its conduct. Beyond that, within the area of its discretion it should act with the problem of subsequent compliance in mind. It should consider not only the standards of fairness of the community in general but the standards of fairness that are most likely to influence the parties before it. As previously noted, if a defendant is unwilling to participate in the proceedings, the tribunal may wish to appoint counsel

to represent that point of view. If the agent of one of the parties has difficulty speaking the language used before the court, he should be given extra time or a translator. If a procedural rule operates to the prejudice of one of the parties, the tribunal should reexamine the rule as it applies in the particular case.[4]

(2) *General approach.* A court, commission, or comparable body which makes a determination as to what ought to be done in a given case cannot avoid the fundamental dilemma of a legal system. There is a fairness which comes from looking in detail at all the facts in a particular case and from reaching a human decision as to what should happen. On the other hand, there is a fairness that comes from deciding cases according to preestablished rules by which one ignores, for example, the race, creed, color, and wealth of the particular parties before the court. This constant tension between the ideal of flexibility and the ideal of a rule has been reflected in the age-old conflict between equity and law, in the conflict between executive discretion and the rule of law, and in the conflict between activist and conservative judges. The respect that will be accorded a determination is not unrelated to the way in which this problem is handled.

From the point of view of noncompliance, the dangers in reaching an activist "reform" type of determination seem greater than are the dangers in reaching a wooden, conservative, old-fashioned determination. Most tribunals are not thought of as legislative bodies. A large part of their power depends upon the community's accepting the notion that it is being governed according to "law." Judges who "find" the law are likely to be accorded greater deference than are judges who "make" the law. Our Supreme Court has a great deal of power as long as it acts within certain bounds. The area within which it may act effec-

[4]This seems to have been the point made by Judge Gros in the Nuclear Tests Case. He was dissatisfied with the way in which article 53 of the Statute of the International Court of Justice had been applied during the proceedings. In his opinion, the policy of the Court to maintain a formal equality between the applicant and the respondent had actually created in that particular case an advantage for the applicant. This is because the latter benefited from the long time limit fixed by the Court for the production of a memorial by the defaulting respondent, which had clearly notified the Court of its unwillingness to participate in the proceedings. [1974] I.C.J. 290–91. *See also* the separate opinion of Judge Petren, *id.* at 298–301.

tively has no doubt increased over the years. In contrast, the power of an international tribunal today is less, and so is the area within which it may act with reasonable hope of effectiveness. An awareness of the limits on judicial power is important to maintaining the legitimacy of a determination.

When a determination is admittedly recommendatory, rather than binding, comparable considerations apply. The resolutions of the United Nations General Assembly, for instance, could have greater impact if the Assembly was to distinguish more clearly between those resolutions which embody standards with which it could reasonably ask the countries of the world to comply now and those which embody what are merely hopes and political goals for the future.

(3) *Justification for determinations.* Most judicial determinations are accompanied by an opinion which explains how and why the decision was reached. A good written statement of reasons can add weight to a decision and can explain what might otherwise seem to be arbitrary or unreasonable. Opinions, however, are not infrequently used as a vehicle for carrying on an argument with a fellow judge or with unsuccessful counsel. So used, opinions can often do more to damage than to augment the legitimacy of a determination. A tribunal should devote a larger proportion of its opinion to presenting its decisions in a way which will commend them to those who are supposed to be governed by them and less to attacking the losing party or to criticizing the reasoning of fellow judges.

A recitation of precedent will often enhance the legitimacy of a decision. An indication that a given decision follows previously adjudicated cases can be a critical factor in establishing the authoritative nature of that decision.

3. *Compliance as a function of the relief ordered.*

a. *The all-important variable.* Even within a legal system that is functioning tolerably well, compliance with a decision is not assured. Whether there will or will not be compliance with a decision is likely to depend upon what is decided.

It is frequently assumed that a tribunal makes a simple choice between the position taken by the plaintiff and that taken by the defendant and that its decision is either for the plaintiff or for the defendant. That approach omits consideration of what is, perhaps, the single most critical variable in causing compliance, namely, the character of the relief ordered by the tribunal. A denial of relief — that is, a decision for the defendant — usually raises no significant compliance problem. The defendant is presumably satisfied with the status quo or else he himself would have come to the tribunal. (In some cases each party will be asserting claims against the other and demanding affirmative relief.) Whenever a tribunal decides that it must make some kind of affirmative decision rather than leaving the litigants in the position where they stood before the case began, the tribunal has a choice. The success of the adjudicatory process as a way of enforcing international law will often depend upon how wisely the tribunal makes that choice. The tribunal should look ahead to the problems of compliance as well as backward to the incidents that created the dispute.

b. *A choice for the tribunal and others.* Although the formulation of the relief is largely a question for the tribunal, the same considerations that guide a tribunal in fashioning such relief should guide others as well. These considerations should be taken into account particularly by those who establish the tribunal and give it authority, by those who draft treaties, agreements, and statutes that may specify appropriate remedies for their breach, and by those who come before the tribunal. A wise plaintiff will seek the kind of relief with which compliance is likely. By so doing he may improve both his chance of persuading the tribunal to decide in his favor and his chance for concrete results.

c. *General guidelines.* The following points suggest elements that are likely to maximize the chance of compliance with a determination.

(1) *Designated individual.* The determination should deal with the conduct of one or more designated individuals. The individuals, preferably identified by name as well as by position, should have no doubt about who is affected by the decision. Further, the tribunal should speak directly to them. Such specificity eliminates the possibility of tacit noncompliance, while each of a number of people justifies doing nothing on the ground that the responsibility lies elsewhere.

(2) *Timing.*

(a) *Immediacy.* The decision should probably speak to the immediate future and specify conduct that should be taken beginning almost at once. The more remote the scheduled date for compliance is, the more opportunity there is to develop enthusiasm and legitimacy for the status quo ante compliance. The original school desegration decisions were weakened by the fact that compliance with the standard of integration was postponed to a future date. If the Supreme Court had considered immediate integration to be impossible, it might have been well advised to have formulated for those particular cases some relief that could have begun immediately, such as to invite proposals for ways to achieve racial integration.

(b) *Specificity of time.* The forces for compliance are likely to be strengthened by a tribunal's being explicit about the exact date on which given conduct is to take place. Such ambiguous phrases as "with all deliberate speed" make it possible for those who do not wish to comply with an order to justify their noncompliance. A judicial determination has more bite if it states the exact time and date on which given conduct is to begin or take place. If such specificity does not appear possible in view of the kind of relief contemplated, it might be wise to reexamine the question of relief and to consider what kind of relief might appropriately be ordered to begin on a date certain.

(c) *Short range.* Relief ordered for a specified period of time may be more acceptable than that ordered on a permanent basis. Whether or not a tribunal at the time of rendition contemplates modifying its order in light of changed circumstances, it may often find it desirable to leave open the possibility of change. A reluctant loser may be more willing to go along with a decision for the time being if he sees some prospect for its modification in the future.

(3) *Narrow vs. broad decisions.* The critical question to an officer or a government in considering whether to comply with a determination is likely to be: "How much does it hurt?" The less it hurts, the more likely is compliance. A tribunal concerned with compliance should thus try to draft the narrowest possible decision consistent with justice in the case before it. The virtues of laying down a broad decision, which might serve as a guide to others in the future, should be weighed against the risks of immediate noncompliance.

(4) *Limited precedent.* One of the costs of going along with a decision, even with one that has been narrowly drafted to deal with a specific case, is the degree to which such compliance may establish a binding precedent.

(a) *Substantive precedent.* Each decision is a bit of a rule which gets strengthened when the decision is complied with. The scope of the rule depends in part upon objective facts and in part upon what is said by the tribunal in deciding a case. To maximize the chance of compliance, a tribunal should bear in mind the possibility of narrowing the decision both in terms of the immediate physical conduct called for and in terms of the precedent that the decision will tend to establish.

(b) *Procedural precedent.* Complying with one decision sets a precedent for complying with subsequent decisions. This consideration may cut either way. A losing party may be persuaded that an additional reason for complying with this decision is to set a precedent which will tend to cause other losing parties to comply with future decisions. Or, a losing party may fear that by complying with this decision he will increase the pressure on himself to comply with future decisions that may be even less palatable.

(5) *Specificity.* To minimize the risk of noncompliance, a decision should not only be narrow and immediately effective, it should also be specific. If one wants action, an ambiguous request is counterproductive.

For example, an international tribunal might decide that a given country must make a "substantial payment" toward its United Nations budget obligation before 10 A.M. the following Wednesday or be deprived of its vote for the ensuing year. Although such a decision would have the advantage of being explicit as to time, it would still have the great drawback of being vague about exactly what conduct the tribunal required. The defendant, confronted with the order to make a "substantial payment," does not know how much he should pay. On the one hand, he runs the great risk of paying more than what, in fact, would be necessary to retain his vote. On the other hand, if he underpays, he runs the risk of making the payment and of still falling short of what is deemed required. Thus, there are strong arguments against making any payment — arguments that would disappear if the order specified the exact amount required.

(6) *Determination of status.* In some circumstances it is possible to formulate a decision as a simple determination of status which does not immediately require action or inaction by anyone. A decision which determines that title has passed so that property belongs to B rather than to A may well resolve a dispute and be respected even though there is no specific conduct ordered of anyone. Such a decision essentially authorizes action rather than requesting it. People and governments are affected by notions of property and can be expected to be influenced by them. A determination of a boundary or of citizenship, for example, lays a foundation for their subsequent activity.

(7) *Inaction vs. action.* The chances of compliance are, in general, greatly increased if a decision is negative in form, that is when it tells somebody what he should not do rather than ordering him to take affirmative action. (In some cases of routine activity, "inaction" may not mean a complete absence of action but rather to refrain from making any change in the way things are being done.)

A negative injunction runs less risk than does an affirmative order of impinging upon governmental discretion. It is also much easier to comply with an order not to do something than with one that requires action, and much more difficult to justify noncompliance. If a judicial decision demands action from an individual, the community will be prepared to admit that some excuses would justify noncompliance. The defendant may have become sick, he may have been prevented from carrying out his task by superior force, or, for one reason or another, performance may have been physically impossible. Excuses that may not be legally adequate may nonetheless undercut community support for compliance; for example, the defendant may have been deterred from compliance by threats of personal violence. To ask for affirmative action is by definition to ask for more than simply to do nothing. The more one asks for, the more one increases the weight of the considerations operating to persuade a defendant toward noncompliance.

(8) *Stopping further injury vs. compensatory relief.* A tribunal concerned with enforcing international law should first direct its at-

tention to the task of preventing or limiting future wrongs rather than that of providing redress for past wrongs. The problem of extracting money from a government for a past wrong is particularly difficult and far less central to the task of developing an orderly international community. The early adoption of the eleventh amendment to the United States Constitution (which precludes the federal courts from hearing most cases asserting a claim against a state government) and the long time that passed before the United States Government subjected itself to judicial decisions on contract and tort claims suggest that in the international arena compensatory relief should not be the area of primary effort. Even where an international tribunal has jurisdiction to grant such relief, as did the International Court of Justice in *The Corfu Channel Case*, compliance with its order cannot be assumed. Indeed, Albania has never paid the International Court's judgment against it in that case.

Some measures can be taken to alleviate the problem of non-compliance with compensatory relief. A maximum limit on the amount of a judgement in any one case might make governments both more willing to subject themselves to suits seeking compensatory relief and more willing to comply with such a judgment. Where the compensation desired is in the form of an apology or "satisfaction," it should prove possible to devise some kind of declaratory decision which, in itself, constitutes sufficient vindication for the prevailing party.

(9) *Ways of producing affirmative action.* In some cases, however, affirmative judicial relief may be the only way to stop further injury to a government or private complainant. A court may have no choice other than to order that dangerous property should be removed or destroyed, that a nuisance should be abated, or that a canal should be closed, etc. In such cases one technique will be to legitimate self-help. If there is someone who is both able and desirous of taking the needed action, the court decision might specifically authorize him to do so.

If action will be required within the territory of a potentially recalcitrant government, it would be highly useful to have a few international marshals available who could be authorized and ordered to take the action. By shifting the burden of affirmative activity to those who will be willing to undertake it, the action required of reluctant parties has been reduced. Without international marshals, compliance requires reluctant parties to undertake affirmative action contrary to their desires. With international marshals it simply requires them to do nothing. In the absence of marshals, noncompliance can easily be accomplished by doing nothing. With international marshals, noncompliance requires the organization of an effort to frustrate them.

(10) *Compulsory bargaining.* In some instances a tribunal may find a problem so complex and so involved with governmental decisions that it is reluctant to reach a decision, but on the other hand the parties seem unwilling to reach one by themselves. There is little international law which would support the proposition that a government has a duty to negotiate with another government, although some material can be found in such areas as the sharing of an international river.

A tribunal would be reluctant to issue a final decision ordering two governments to negotiate.[5] Yet it might accomplish the same objective if it asked the parties to present an agreed decree, embodying some general conclusions which the tribunal had reached. Alternatively, a tribunal might issue a rough draft and ask the parties to work out, perhaps with the help of a mediator or "master," improvements in it.

---

[5] Apparently the only case in international judicial practice is the Fisheries Jurisdiction Case, in which, by a vote of ten to four, the International Court of Justice held "that the Government of Iceland and the Government of the United Kingdom are under mutual obligations to undertake negotiations in good faith for the equitable solution of their differences concerning their respective fishery rights." [1974] I.C.J. 34. The Court also imposed the same obligation upon the Government of Iceland and the Government of the Federal Republic of Germany. [1974] I.C.J. 205. This part of the judgment produced strong dissent on the bench of the Court. Judge Dillard observed that the Court "should have stopped short of imposing on the parties a *duty* to negotiate. In other words, it should have merely indicated the *basis* for negotiations without including a *duty* to engage in them." [1974] *I.C.J.* 67 (italics in the text). *See also* the remarks by Judge Gros (*id.* at 143, 146) and Judge Petren (*id.* at 160).

CHAPTER XIV

Following Up a Determination

A judicial determination that there has been a violation of international law and that certain remedial action or nonaction is required will not always be sufficient to produce compliance. This will be true no matter how legitimate the tribunal and no matter how ably drafted is its decree. This chapter deals with strategies for following up a determination and for improving the chance that reluctant parties will comply with it.

1. *Removing justifications for noncompliance.* There is something about a government which causes it to justify conduct in which it is openly engaged. A government may choose to keep some matters secret. Other matters, though known to the public, may remain dormant because no one is vigorously or seriously questioning the government's conduct. But when a government's handling of a particular matter is both publicly known and controversial, its officials run the risk of losing political backing unless they can give reasons that support and justify the conduct in question.

If an authoritative determination concludes that a government's given conduct is illegal and specifies the conduct that the government ought to undertake in the future, there will be some political pressure on that government to comply with that determination. If other considerations appear to outweigh that pressure, the government may decide not to comply with the determination. But, if history is any guide, the government will state publicly its reasons for not complying with the decision. These reasons will suggest why it is "right" for the government to pursue the course on which it has embarked.

The essential process in following up a determination and in enforcing compliance with it is to whittle away these justifications. If the procedure works well, such justifications will be brought to the attention of a competent tribunal, which will consider them and, if it finds them without merit, will issue a further determination to that effect. As, one by one, the reasons which have been advanced to justify noncompliance are found authoritatively to be invalid, the political pressure on the government to comply with the decision will increase. And as these reasons, which the government advanced in order to maintain political support for its conduct, are found to be insufficient, the political support they were designed to produce should be weakened. Ultimately, if all goes well, the government will find itself in an untenable position. It will find that further noncompliance will leave it standing in naked defiance of a system which it purports to accept. Perceiving that its course of action commands less political support than it did before, the government will shift its position to one which will command more political support.

An interesting example of such pressure on a government to justify noncompliance with a legal determination is found in a case where the problem never materialized. In 1935 President Roosevelt feared that the Supreme Court was about to decide that all bonds which contained a gold clause had to be paid in dollars in an amount calculated on the prior gold standard, that is, some $1,690 for every $1,000 bond. In anticipation of an adverse decision he prepared a radio address explaining that the government was not going to abide by the Court's decision. The text of this address, which was never given because the Court did not reach the decision the President feared, shows an attempt both to obscure the fact of defiance and to advance a number of reasons which made it "right" for the President to do what he proposed.[1] After stating that he did "not seek to enter into any controversy with the distinguished members of the Supreme Court," who had "decided these cases in accordance with the letter of the law as they read it," the President went on to say that "the legislative and executive officers of the Government must look beyond the narrow letter of contractual obligations so that they may sustain the substance of the promise originally made in accord with the actual intention of the parties." He went on to refer to the Golden Rule, the precepts of the Scriptures, and the dictates of common sense.[2]

If a legal system is to deal with this kind of noncompliance — noncompliance by a government which has the physical power to engage in it — the legal system needs to have jurisdiction to

[1]3 FDR, His Personal Letters, 1928–1945, at 456–60 (E. Roosevelt ed. 1949).
[2]*Id.* at 459–60.

consider and to deal with the justifications advanced. It must not let the resisting government get outside the system. In the case of the *Chamizal Arbitration*, for example, the United States refused to go along with the award on the ground that the tribunal, which had the authority to decide whether the disputed land belonged to Mexico or the United States, had exceeded its authority by ordering the land divided.[3] There was no other tribunal available to consider the legitimacy of this excuse for noncompliance. Again, when the arbitral tribunal that had been set up to deal with questions arising from the partition of Pakistan and India dissolved itself, there was no court available to consider disputes arising from the implementation of its prior decisions. The first and essential requirement of post-decision enforcement is to have a tribunal available to deal with and to resolve authoritatively claims of rightful noncompliance.

An apt illustration of the strong, but not unlimited, power of a court with such jurisdiction is found in the history of the litigation over the stock of the Dollar Steamship Line. That litigation also suggests the general style of law enforcement that might be hoped for in the international community. In that case, the United States Court of Appeals of the District of Columbia held that Dollar and other individual plaintiffs were entitled to the contested stock of the Dollar Line and ordered the Secretary of Commerce to deliver the stock to them.[4] For a number of reasons, the Secretary of Commerce declined to do so. He acted pursuant to the advice of the Attorney General and, finally, pursuant to the explicit written instructions of the President that "you are directed to continue to hold this stock on behalf of the United States."[5]

The court did not turn this presidential order into a head-on confrontation. On the contrary, it wisely chose to treat the President's order as a legal argument advanced to justify noncompliance and, upon due consideration, decided that "whoever advised the President misconstrued the legal posture of the controversy."[6] The court concluded that the argument was a legally insufficient defense and issued a further decree, finding the Sec-

[3] *See* Chapter XI *supra*.
[4] Sawyer v. Dollar, 190 F.2d 623 (D.C. Cir. 1951).
[5] *Id.* at 639.
[6] *Id.*

retary (and the Solicitor General and a number of other government lawyers) in civil contempt and again ordering them to deliver the stock certificates. The long opinion of the court of appeals considered each justification advanced for noncompliance and found each wanting. The court's findings of fact, conclusions of law, order, and opinion are well worth reading in any consideration of the problem of enforcing a judicial determination against a reluctant government.

The court's decision had some effect. The *New York Times* commented editorially: "The real problem here is whether or not the Government in fighting this case has shown an excess of zeal that amounts to actual defiance of the courts. This is an even more important issue than the question of who actually owns the steamship line."[7] The settlement of the case (selling the stock and dividing the proceeds 50–50) probably reflects both the power of the court's decision and the residual power of the government.

Dealing with noncompliance thus appears to require a tribunal with both the lawful competence to consider all justifications for noncompliance and the willingness to treat every such justification as an appropriate matter for its determination.

2. *Following up against objects.* Once there has been a determination that given conduct is contrary to international law, it may be possible for the tribunal to enforce that decision by issuing orders that deal with inanimate objects, rather than with the future conduct of a government or its officers.

To the extent that the implementing decision would be made by a national court, that court could look to its own marshals, sheriffs, or other officials to take the required action with respect to the objects. In some cases, such decisions might be made by the International Court of Justice or by some other international tribunal or commission. In order to make it possible for international bodies to take direct action against objects, it would be desirable that there be some international constabulary whose size should be not so large as to make it appear to threaten the national security of any state. Such a force might be wholly effective in many cases, even if it were to consist of no more than a dozen unarmed persons.

[7] N.Y. Times, Nov. 18, 1951, part IV, at 10.

Dealing directly with objects has several advantages. One advantage is that such an approach tends to keep the dispute — now identified as being one between the tribunal and a reluctant defendant — narrowly focused. Another advantage is that action against an object may limit the reaction of the defendant and, thus, avoid escalation of the dispute. Further, this approach also is consistent with an intuitive sense of fairness that has been reflected in many provisions of law, both domestic and international. For example, under English common law, an object which was the immediate cause of a person's death was a "deodand" that was forfeited to the crown. Today, weapons used in the commission of a crime are similarly forfeited, and other objects involved in a crime may be deemed contraband and subject to destruction.

In considering the possibilities of following up an authoritative determination by acting toward objects rather than toward governments or officers, we should consider the alternative purposes for which we might be acting. Such purposes may be: (a) as a deterrent to future violations; (b) as a way of obtaining compensation; (c) as leverage to induce compliance; and (d) as compliance itself.

a. *As a deterrent.* Although here we are concerned with following up a determination as a way of bringing about second-order compliance, it may be well to note that follow-up action against objects can often be justified solely as a deterrent. And, as a deterrent, the seizure or destruction of objects may not suffer as seriously from the drawbacks discussed in Chapters III and IV that are applicable to most forms of punishing officers or governments.

Examples from domestic law of deterrent action against objects include the provision of 49 U.S.C. 781–84 authorizing the forfeiture not only of such items as contraband drugs, firearms, and counterfeit obligations but also of any vehicle in which they were being transported.[8] The loss of the vehicle must be justified primarily as a deterrent penalty. Massachusetts has a comparable provision authorizing the forfeiture of any motor vehicle found to be an implement in the illegal sale of alcoholic beverages.[9]

[8] 49 U.S.C. §§ 781–84 (1970).
[9] MASS. ANN. LAWS ch. 138, § 50 (Michie / Law Co-op 1933).

Presumably much of the international law of prize, in particular the rule that a neutral engaged in running cargo through a blockade forfeits not only the cargo but the vessel itself, operates to create a deterrent. To the extent that the seizure of the vessel is designed physically to prevent future violations, then the rule has the additional purpose of producing compliance, as discussed in section *d* below. Similarly, Professor Louis Sohn has suggested that in implementing arms control or disarmament agreements it might be wise to authorize the destruction not only of any arms that are illegally manufactured but also of the factory in which they are made.[10] This added penalty, which might credibly be threatened, would operate as a deterrent.

b. *As compensation.* Probably the most commonly considered reason for having a legal system go against tangible property is to obtain the value of that property as compensation for an injured plaintiff. We think of seizing property or of attaching a bank account as ways of assuring the plaintiff some money, even if the defendant skips town or otherwise fails to pay a judgment which may be entered against him.

This rationale underlying the seizure of property in domestic law raises the following questions concerning a possible similar practice in the international context.

To what extent should an international legal system seek to provide compensatory relief? A great deal of past effort has been directed toward providing compensation and, in particular, just compensation for property that has been taken. I would suggest that the greatest opportunity for improvement lies in the development of injunctive-type relief rather than in improving the means of assuring that a government makes amends for past conduct which, after litigation, proves to have been illegal. Proposals for schemes of international attachment may be necessary if money is to be collected, but not too much attention should be spent on the collection problem. International collection proposals are likely to scare off countries whose interested participation is desirable.

Should the property seized be related to the wrong? If so, how closely? Treaties might, for example, provide that ships or aircraft which are wrongfully used can be forfeited to provide com-

---

[10]G. CLARK & L. SOHN, WORLD PEACE THROUGH WORLD LAW 309 (2d ed. 1960).

pensation to an injured government. Being related to the offense somehow makes the forfeiture easier. This is true as long as one is thinking of a legislative, *i.e.*, treaty, solution. Under customary international law, it is difficult to consider most kinds of attachment as consistent with sovereign immunity.

If there is to be international attachment of nonimmune property, should such property be subject to seizure for "political" debts as well as for commercial ones? Under such circumstances, for example, the commercial, nonexempt property of France would be subject to attachment in New York by the Secretary General to collect France's "debt" to the United Nations. Such a rule might well lead to retaliatory attachment by France. Similarly, in cases where the claimant was not the United Nations but a private party, internationally authorized seizure of France's assets might lead to retaliatory seizures directed either against the private claimant or against the international authority. Under the present state of international law, the matter of attachment is particularly difficult to solve, as the *Case of the Monetary Gold Removed from Rome in 1943* makes abundantly clear.[11] This problem is considered in Part 3 of this chapter.

c. *Objects as leverage.* Rather than going after objects as valuable property which can be liquidated to produce a fund as a substitute for that which the defendant ought to have paid, objects may be held as means of inducing a reluctant defendant to comply with an authoritative determination. In such a case, the action desired is less likely to be the payment of funds than it is to alter some course of conduct. The property is held as a kind of hostage; if compliance takes place, the hostage will be released.

The critical fact underlying any such theory of going after objects is that one is seeking to influence a human decision. The objects, which possibly can be controlled physically, are simply the means to an end. The end is a decision — of a government or of an individual — which, it is hoped, will be induced by fear or by hope.

This general approach is discussed in Parts 3 and 4 of this chapter, which are concerned with follow-up action designed to secure the compliance of governments and of officers.

d. *Dealing with objects as compliance itself.* In some circumstances,

[11][1954] I.C.J. 19.

one can deal with an object as the direct means of producing the compliance desired. This category of cases would appear to hold great promise. Domestic law examples of such cases include towing away an illegally parked car, removing an illegally located billboard, abating a nuisance, and seizing and returning stolen property to the owner. On the international level, one can consider the destruction of illegal arms, the recapture of stolen property, the impounding of illegal narcotics, and the destruction or jamming of an illegal radio transmitter as comparable examples of compliance through dealing directly with objects.

In some circumstances, such as towing away an illegally parked car from a highway during a rush hour, the purpose of the enforcement action is identical to the purpose of the rule. In other cases, such as the forfeiture of game illegally killed, there is no possibility of restoring the situation of the status quo ante. We are confiscating the game in order to deprive the hunter from benefiting from his illegal conduct. Whether or not there are other penalties which might operate as a deterrent, the community rests easier if the illegal venture has been frustrated.

3. *Following up against governments.* At this point, we consider the problem of "making" a government comply with a determination which authoritatively decided what that government should do. If the legal system were operating at all well, in most cases the decision would have been so legitimate, it would have asked so little, and the probable consequences of compliance would have looked to the government so much more attractive than the possible consequences of defiance, that the government would have gone along with the decision. We would have achieved second-order compliance. In some instances, however, this will not prove to be the case. If instances of second-order defiance were common, the political repercussions would undercut the system itself. Nonetheless, we must expect some noncompliance with decisions. Moreover, the frequency of such noncompliance may well depend upon how the international system operates when noncompliance actually occurs.

When the international system is faced with a recalcitrant government which has been authoritatively told what it ought or ought not do but fails to comply, two appraoches are possible. The first is directed at influencing a governmental decision to comply. The second approach is directed at producing compliance by physical force. These two approaches also can be combined.

a. *Influencing a decision to comply.* If a defendant government was not persuaded to comply with a tribunal's decision by the apparent choice with which it was then confronted, it will almost certainly be necessary to alter some aspect of that choice. We are again faced with the necessity of changing the issue. It will probably not be possible at this stage to increase the perceived legitimacy of the decision. We then have three basic variables: (1) the demand (the action or inaction called for by the decision); (2) the consequences of compliance; and (3) the consequences of defiance.

It would also appear difficult at this stage to provide larger rewards for compliance than those which existed at the time the determination was made. This leaves two basic elements that might be further shifted to influence a government to comply when it had previously declined to do so: the demand and the consequences of further defiance.

(1) *Changing the demand.* As was apparent from the discussion in Part 1 of this chapter on the process of removing justifications for noncompliance, wherever there is resistance, we should anticipate not a single decision but rather a sequence of decisions. Not only would such a sequence of decisions deal with arguments advanced to justify noncompliance, but the sequence of decisions might alter the relief required. This alternation could make compliance with the latest decision easier than it was with the earlier decisions.

Just as our original determination changed the question with which the government was confronted so as to make the demand more explicit and narrower than the demand that appeared to be required by the standing rule, so subsequent determinations can continue to sharpen the demand.

Perhaps the most effective way by which a demand can be changed is to convert it from one that calls for action into one that calls for inaction. It is almost invariably easier to cause compliance with a negative decision than it is with a decision which calls upon a government to undertake affirmative action. If, for instance, the Government of South Africa had failed to comply with an international decision requiring it to submit reports on the mandated territory, a subsequent decision might simply order the Government of South Africa not to interfere with a helicopter inspection trip by two United Nations observers. Having a small international staff who could take affirmative action should make it possible to convert most demands for governmental action into demands for governmental inaction.[12]

One difficult case is that of a money judgment. Money is usually thought of as something which can be manufactured only by a government. Even in this particular case, it might be possible to shift a decision to one that called for governmental inaction. For example, a treaty establishing a particular commission or tribunal with limited competence could conceivably authorize that body (within designated limits) to print currency in an amount sufficient to meet any judgment against a defendant government that remained unpaid for a given length of time. What would otherwise be counterfeiting would then become an authorized issuance of supplemental currency. Such a proposal might be practical in particular cases where small amounts of moeny would be involved. For example, governments might be willing to authorize the Universal Postal Union to print enough of a government's stamps to cover any unmet charges owing to the Union. Under such circumstances, international marshals would be ordered to carry out the desired result, and the tribunal's order to the reluctant government would simply be an order to refrain from interfering.

(2) *Increasing the threatened consequences of defiance.* The major attention in an "enforcement" action designed to influence a defendant to comply is usually directed at the nature of the threatened consequences of a failure to comply. The effectiveness of such a threat may be increased (1) by increasing the magnitude of the losses which would be suffered by the defendant, (2) by

---

[12] To some extent this technique is applied in the current peacekeeping operations that are ordered by the Security Council of the United Nations, such as those carried on by the United Nations Emergency Force for the Middle East. The Report of the Secretary-General on the Implementation of Security Council Resolution 340, U.N. Doc. S / 11052 / Rev. 1 (1973) approved by the Security Council on Oct. 26, 1973, makes it clear that the use of force in self-defense "would include resistance to attempts by forceful means to prevent it from discharging its duties under the mandate of the Security Council." *Id.* at 4(d).

making those losses appear more likely than they appeared heretofore, and (3) by making the anticipated losses more immediate than they had been previously.

(a) *Magnitude.* To the extent that the major consequence of defiance of an international determination lies in the damage done to the international community from which each country benefits, the losses will be magnified by the degree to which a given decision puts the interests of the community at stake. When confronted with such a situation, a tribunal will be engaged, to some degree, in a form of brinkmanship with the defiant government. To maximize the pressures toward compliance the tribunal commits itself and its reputation to a given decision. The more it commits itself to a particular decision, the greater the damage done to its authority and prestige in the event of defiance. An attempt to increase the magnitude of this kind of loss may not in fact increase the effectiveness of the threat. Since forcing an issue is a two-edged sword which can create as much risk for the tribunal as for the recalcitrant government, the threat may lose in credibility what it gains in content. The 1964–65 United Nations payments crisis suggests that the threat that the Soviet and French governments' nonpayment of peacekeeping funds would completely wreck the United Nations was offset by a Soviet belief that the United Nations would not in fact want to destroy itself.[13] In cases where the primary threat is of national action by the plaintiff government or other governments, a determination by the tribunal might increase the magnitude of the threat by legitimating or authorizing heavier action.

(b) *Credibility.* Subsequent decisions can increase the likelihood of follow-up action. Possible consequences can become increasingly probable.

(c) *Immediacy.* In many instances a government may not be impressed with the threatened consequences of defiance because those consequences seem remote. As time passes, and as subsequent decisions bring closer the day on which the losses will be

[13] *See generally* Yost, *The United Nations: Crisis of Confidence and Will*, 45 FOREIGN AFF. 19 (1966); Stoessinger, *Financing the United Nations*, 535 INT'L CONCILIATION 61; Claude, *Implications and Questions for the Future*, 19 INT'L ORGANIZATIONS 841–42 (1965); D. CIOBANU, FINANCIAL OBLIGATIONS OF STATES UNDER ARTICLE 13 OF U.N. CHARTER 72–73 (1974).

sustained, the threat of such losses will have greater impact. Without any increase in magnitude, a threat of loss tomorrow is more influential than is a threat of the same loss a year or two hence. Thus, a government may be induced to comply simply by bringing closer the day of loss.

(3) *Shifting the threat to an individual.* Although we speak of a determination against a government and of threats to a government, it is people who make decisions. Domestic legal experience suggests that the most effective change in a threat is one which shifts it from a threat against a government to threats against specific officers of that government. If a state or a town fails to comply with a court decision, that court is likely to turn to individual officers responsible for the noncompliance and to issue new orders to them. These orders will be backed up expressly or implicitly with new threats directed to those individuals.

An illustrative case is that of *Commonwealth v. Hudson*[14] which involved the town of Hudson's refusal to comply with an administrative order, made pursuant to a statute, which directed the town to chlorinate its water supply. The state Attorney General brought an action against the town to enforce the order, and the Supreme Judicial Court of Massachusetts sustained the order. The town of Hudson, in town meeting, had twice voted not to install chlorinating equipment as ordered by the state. Town counsel had suggested that a decree against the town would be futile and unenforceable and, hence, that the court should not issue such a decree. The following excerpts from the court's opinion indicate the way in which a judgment against a government can be enforced by shifting the demand to individuals:

> Now that the town has exhausted its legal remedies in opposing the order, and its duty to obey the order has been established in the courts, no lawful course remains open for the town, its officers and its voters, except prompt and complete obedience to the legislative mandate and to a judicial decree establishing the duty to obey that mandate. With the ordering of such a decree, our function normally would end. We do not ordinarily find it necessary to detail the measures that may be taken for the execution of a judgment or decree, or to point out the path that leads to the jail door. We commonly assume that municipalities and public officers will do their duty when disputed questions have been fi-

[14] 315 Mass. 335 (1943).

nally adjudicated and the rights and liabilities of the parties have been finally determined. When a decree runs against a municipality, a subordinate agency of government, to which have been delegated certain law-making functions, and which itself expects and may require obedience from individuals to its by-laws and regulations, it may rightly be expected to set an example of obedience to law.

We say more in the present case only because of a contention made by counsel for the defendant town which is without precedent in our experience.

. . . .

That argument is so full of dangerous errors, and if relied on by the town and its officers and inhabitants might lead to such serious consequences to them, that we are unwilling by silence to permit counsel or his clients to remain under the delusion that a town may thus safely defy the Commonwealth and its courts. . . .

. . . .

Of course attachment of the person is impossible in the case of a municipality or other corporation. But like other corporations, a town or city may be fined for contempt in disobeying a decree. For the satisfaction of a judgment or decree for payment of money by a town, the property of any inhabitant may be taken.

Any person, whether lawyer or layman, though not a party to the cause, who counsels or aids a party in disobeying a decree, is himself punishable.

Officers of a town or city may be required to do all acts within their power to cause the municipality to obey a decree against it, and may be punished for failure to do so. It is not at all clear that compliance with the decree, to say nothing of penalties, could be escaped as suggested in the brief for the defendants by having the officers "resign from office before they could be held in contempt."

. . . .

Moreover, we are by no means prepared to concede that the voters, to whom the law has entrusted the duty to make appropriations, stand any differently from officers with respect to their duty to use their power so as to cause the town to obey the order and decree in this case.[15]

The judicial rule that a judgment against a town may be enforced by acting against individuals is incorporated in the statutes of some states. Chapter 530 of the New Hampshire Revised

[15]*Id.* at 343–44, 347–49.

Statutes, for example, provides that if a town does not pay a judgment within sixty days, execution may be levied against the goods or estates of the selectmen; or, if they are insufficient, against the goods or estates of any inhabitant of the town, and, if they are insufficient, against the property in the town belonging to any nonresident.[16]

(4) *Action designed to influence compliance in later cases.* One form of following up against a government — namely punishment for defiance — may be considered either as action to influence compliance or as action to produce compliance. If a government is punished for defying a determination, the punishment can serve to close the case. The matter will be considered concluded, and in the public's view, a form of compliance will have occurred in the sense that the government did not "get away with it."

Punishment of a government, such as for criminal contempt, may also be viewed primarily as a measure to induce future compliance with future decisions. In addition, it may be desirable to carry out threats actually made, so that subsequent threats will be credible.

b. *Producing results by physical means.* Follow-up action can be designed not only to influence a recalcitrant defendant to change his mind but also to bring about the desired result by physical means. It is extremely difficult to cause a government to undertake affirmative action by physical means. Thus, when we want to use force to bring about the desired result, we will first want the decision to call for inaction, rather than for action.

(1) *Action against a country.* The most likely kind of action intended to prevent a country from continuing in some wrongful conduct is either military or economic. Economic measures are usually intended to influence a government's decision. But economic embargoes may also be applied against a country in an attempt physically to preclude that country's being able to carry on some illegal activity, such as an aggressive war. The League of Nations' sanctions against Italy, for instance, were justified largely on the theory that they would physically incapacitate Italy from conquering Ethiopia.[17]

[16] N.H. REV. STAT. ANN. ch. 530, § 1–3 (1974).
[17] *See* Taubenfeld & Taubenfeld, *The "Economic Weapon": The League and the United Nations*, 58 AM. SOC'Y INT'L L. PROC. 183 (1964).

(2) *Action against individuals.* Action designed to prevent defiance, just as action designed to influence a defendant not to continue defiance, can be more effective if the object of that action is shifted from the government to individuals. Physical measures must either affect objects or people. When enforcement measures are directed at people it is preferable to treat them individually as lawbreakers rather than to treat them collectively as soldiers doing their duty for a government that is the "real" culprit.

4. *Following up against individuals.* Assuming that a tribunal has issued an order to a particular officer that he cease a specific activity and that officer fails to comply with the order, what should the tribunal do?

When faced with such a second-order enforcement problem, the tribunal might authorize some follow-up action against the officer, designed either to induce his compliance or to prevent by physical means his continuing defiance. To one or the other of those ends, the tribunal could devise and subject the offending officer to various threats, punishments, or preventive measures. The effectiveness of such measures, however, depends far less upon their content than it does upon the likelihood that they will in fact be implemented. If the tribunal's initial order is being defied, it will do little good to authorize the tribunal to issue a follow-up order which will similarly be defied. Ensuring, to the greatest extent possible, that the court's second order will be actually obeyed is more important than the kind of sanction it calls for. The most important requirement is that the new order not be ignored.

a. *Sanctions from abroad.* One suggested solution to this problem is to devise sanctions that can be imposed from abroad. This approach assumes that if the officer's own government had been opposed to the conduct in question, that conduct would not have taken place, and that if his own government favors the conduct, the only sanctions that can be imposed against the officer are those imposed from other countries. Suggested sanctions have included various kinds of moral condemnation, a prohibition on travel, and refusal by other governments to deal in any way with the officer in question. Another approach is the idea of eventual punishment, as at Nuremberg, of a particular individual when conditions have so changed as to permit international authorities to capture him. Leo Szilard suggested the possibility that an international tribunal, after appropriate procedures and factual determinations, might declare as an outlaw an officer who could have appeared before the court but refused to do so (perhaps going so far as to declare that anyone could thereafter lawfully execute the man at any time.)[18] It also might be physically possible to organize international kidnapping ventures from abroad analogous to that organized by Israel to apprehend Eichmann in Argentina.

Conceivably, such threats in support of an international tribunal's orders might cause obedience that would not otherwise occur. It is also possible that the pressure of such sanctions would coerce an official into altering his ongoing conduct. But the success of these actions seems unlikely. Moral condemnation by foreigners is less persuasive than moral support by one's own community. In addition, as indicated above, threats of personal hardship are not a reliable way of causing a public official to abandon what he sees as his duty. This is particularly true where the threats are modest, remote, or subject to frustration by one's own government. Also, if one's own government is actively resisting the international decision, a threat in support of the decision can be more than offset by counterthreats of punishment that are equally serious and more certain. One can probably say that any system of sanctions that does not have at least the passive acceptance of the community within which the officer is acting will be ineffective.

In this situation, rather than asking what sanctions can be imposed upon an officer over the resistance of his community, it seems wiser to ask what can be done to increase the chances of a community's acceptance of a sanction. The problem of designing sanctions in support of orders to government officers is one of designing a system that is acceptable and that will produce orders, which in turn, are both acceptable and effective. The dilemma posed is similar to the problem of trying to catch a bird by putting salt on its tail. The difficult part is arranging matters so that one is in a position to impose the salt. If that can be done,

---

[18]Conversation with the author.

one's objective can be accomplished without actually putting the salt on the bird's tail. The same holds true for the government officer: if one could so arrange matters that sanctions could be imposed upon the officer, then rarely, if ever, would it be necessary to do so.

b. *Limits upon a sanction scheme.* The imposition of sanctions for second-order violations by government officers requires designing a system which meets three different criteria of acceptability. Although interrelated, these criteria can be considered separately:

1. The sanction scheme must be acceptable to governments so that it will in fact be adopted by treaty, or statute, or both.

2. The sanctions authorized must be acceptable to the tribunal that is supposed to prescribe them so that they will in fact be ordered.

3. The sanctions ordered must be acceptable to other government officers so that the community around the officer will give effect to them.

Finally, the sanctions should be "efficient" — that is, if ordered and put into effect, they should bring about the desired result.

The first of these problems — that of making the international institutions and their authority initially acceptable to governments — has been discussed in Chapter 11. We now consider the other limits that acceptability imposes on the sanction scheme and the kind of follow-up orders that might be effective within those limits.

(1) *Sanctions must be acceptable to the tribunal.* As previously indicated, tribunals are reluctant to punish an officer for attempting to do his duty as he saw it, no matter how mistaken he may have been. Even when there is continued defiance of a cease-and-desist order and a tribunal must issue further orders designed to coerce or incapacitate the offending official, the tribunal will probably be unwilling to issue orders that seem unduly harsh. Orders imposing the death penalty or torture could be expected to encounter judicial reluctance. A tribunal undoubtedly would consider other decisions that might have a devastating effect on the resisting officer to be so unfair that it would not issue them. In this category of unacceptable judicial action would fall decisions based on illusory evidence, such as

orders that the officer be confined for observation as a dangerous sexual psychopath, or that he be arrested for treason for
allegedly being in the pay of a hostile foreign government.

A national or international tribunal is unlikely to be willing to
order any sanction that does not seem fair, honest, and appropriate. False charges or other clever gimmicks that might in fact
incapacitate a resisting officer cannot be relied upon. The orders
authorized and desired must be ones that seem fair and reasonably appropriate to the factual circumstances.

(2) *Sanctions must be acceptable to other officers and to the community.*
An order of an international or a national tribunal probably will
not be given effect unless the order is one that the community
generally accepts as legitimate. An order to arrest or to impose
consequences upon an official will not be effective unless the
other officials in that government are prepared to go along, at
least passively, with the order. This requirement of general community acceptance is, perhaps, the most critical limitation upon
possible sanctioning schemes.

The following factors can be suggested as ones which tend to
increase the likelihood and the degree of acceptance by other
government officers of an international decision imposing consequences on one of their colleagues.

(a) *There should be a previously established domestic duty to obey an
international order.* When a sanction scheme is adopted, each
country might establish by domestic legislation, executive order,
or otherwise, a legal duty to comply with the subsequent decisions of the international tribunal. As discussed in Chapter X,
such built-in domestication obviously increases the chance that
the community in general will go along with the international
decision.

(b) *The order should not create unique or unusual duties.* An international order would seem to have a good chance of general acceptability if it were identical in effect or closely comparable to
orders and decisions frequently issued for internal reasons by
domestic governments. An extremely novel order, such as one
prohibiting the officer from eating so long as he remained in
defiance of the court order and enjoining all persons from providing him with any food, would lack popular support because
of its very novelty. On the other hand, an order which simply
shifted a person from one well-established and known status to

another would seem to have the best chance of public support. Such an order, for example, might be one suspending a particular officer from government service.

(c) *The order should prohibit action rather than demand it.* Another element in a sanction order that could increase its acceptability to the community lies in the degree to which acceptance requires inaction rather than action. If an international decision can be put into effect through the inaction of third parties, then the chances for its effectiveness are increased. When confronted with conflicting demands, a third party will prefer to do nothing until the issue is resolved. If it is the international decision that calls for inaction and the officer who is resisting it who is calling for action, the tendency of the community will be to do nothing and hence to support the international decision.

It is well recognized that a court has an easier time prohibiting action than requiring it. The history of the efforts by equity courts to bring about affirmative action suggests that in those cases where some affirmative action is required it is more easily accomplished by the court's designating and authorizing a particular court officer to take the action than it is by ordering the defendant to do it. If a government officer were to resist a court order requiring action, the court might be authorized not only to suspend him but to designate another to take the action on his behalf, much as a court designee will sign a deed on behalf of a defendant who has refused to comply with a grant of specific performance.

(d) *If affirmative action is required, it should be stated with great clarity.* The impact of an order depends, to some extent, upon its specificity. The following extract of the court of appeal's follow-up order in *Land v. Dollar*[19] illustrates this nicely.

> 18. It is considered and adjudged that, because of their acts and omissions described in the foregoing findings of fact, the respondents, Charles Sawyer, Peyton Ford, Newell A. Clapp, Edward H. Hickey, Donald B. MacGuineas, Philip B. Perlman, Philip B. Fleming, George L. Killion, Philip Angell and Paul D. Page, Jr., are, and each of them, is, guilty of civil contempt of this court.
>
> 19. Respondent Perlman may purge himself by rescinding his

[19] Sawyer v. Dollar 190 F.2d 623 (D.C. Cir. 1951).

advice to the Secretary of Commerce to disobey this court's decree and the implementing order of the District Court, and by advising the Secretary of Commerce to comply forthwith, fully and effectively, with the decree.

20. The other Department of Justice respondents may purge themselves by withdrawing the contemptuous advice and instructions which they have given to respondents Sawyer, Killion and Page, and to American President Lines, Ltd., its secretary, directors and transfer agents, and by advising and instructing that the decree of this court be complied with immediately, fully and effectively; and by taking whatever steps are necessary to relieve American President Lines, Ltd., and its stock transfer agents of the preliminary injunction issued by the District Court in California which prohibits American President Lines, Ltd., and its stock transfer agents from transferring on the corporate records the shares represented by the certificates presented by the Dollar interest.

The respondents will not be heard to say it is beyond their power to accomplish this. If it is necessary to do so in order to remove the restraint of the preliminary injunction, the Department of Justice respondents can dismiss without prejudice the suit to try title which they instituted in the name of the United States in the California District Court, and can then immediately re-file it.

21. Respondent Sawyer may purge himself by endorsing on the certificates "United States Maritime Commission, by Charles Sawyer, Secretary of Commerce," and by causing respondent Killion, American President Lines, Ltd., and its transfer agents to transfer the shares to the Dollar interests on the corporate books and to issue certificates to them.

. . . . .

24. The respondents will be given until 3:00 P.M., E.D.T., May 24, 1951, to purge themselves of the civil contempt of which they are guilty. They are hereby ordered to present themselves before this court in the courtroom of the United States Court of Appeals Building, 5th and E Streets, Northwest, Washington, D.C., at that hour and day, unless prior to that time they shall have presented to the court evidence that they have fully and effectively obeyed the decree and the court has found such evidence to be adequate. Or they may present at the time of their appearance evidence that they have fully and effectively obeyed the decree, which evidence the court will immediately examine for adequacy. If evidence of compliance is not presented to the court at or before the time thus fixed or, it presented, the evidence shall be found by

the court to be inadequate, respondents will then be committed to custody to remain in confinement until they have fully and effectively complied with the decree.

Proof of compliance which does not show that American President Lines, Ltd., has issued and delivered to the Dollar interests certificates evidencing the shares in question will not be regarded as adequate.[20]

(e) *Any authority for deciding to reject an international decision should be narrowly confined.* In some situations it is possible that in order to make an international institution acceptable to governments it may be desirable to give each government some legal procedure by which it can, in effect, veto the decisions of that institution. By authorizing the head of state or other designated official or officials to set aside a decision such a provision should also help increase the chance of compliance with that decision by the individual defendant and by other officers in general. If there were no such escape clause, each officer might feel a conflict between his duty to the nation and his duty to uphold the international decision — a conflict which he would have to resolve. But if a treaty grants someone, such as the President, a right to suspend a decision and provides that unless so suspended everyone else shall obey it, then officers in general need not decide for themselves where the national interest lies. Although they may advise the President, until he acts they can be expected to comply.

c. *Effective sanctions within the above limitations.* The limitations that acceptability imposes upon a follow-up scheme designed to produce second-order compliance are thus serious. At every stage, the question is not only what order would be most effective against the defendant if carried out but also what order is most likely to be carried out. In these circumstances, it seems wise to design an enforcement scheme that would have the maximum chance of accomplishing the minimum objective. If it turns out that more can be done, well and good; but the primary focus should be on the minimum task of law enforcement: successfully coping with continued defiance of a tribunal's explicit command.

In some cases, a tribunal might successfully cope with defiance

[20]*Id.* at 634–35.

of its order by granting a petition for rehearing, reconsidering its decision, and concluding that it had been mistaken. In the typical case, however, its minimal goal should undoubtedly be to prevent the defiance from continuing. Although a threat might be used to obtain compliance with a court's order, as is done in this country by the threat of criminal contempt, the requirement that the threat be supported and carried out by other government officers around the defendant suggests that preventive as well as deterrent action should be contemplated. Rather than trying to make noncompliance unreasonable by making it appear more painful than compliance, the prevention method attempts to make noncompliance difficult.

This method's objective is to have the court issue an order which will incapacitate the officer from further defying the court's decision. This apparently requires that the officer be separated from the other officers who constitute the government. It is frequently assumed either that an officer is acting contrary to government policy, in which case there will be no enforcement problem once the matter is brought to light, or that he is acting pursuant to government policy, in which case the government will back him up. In fact, no such dichotomy exists. Even when an officer's government strongly supports the policy underlying his conduct, it may be possible to so narrowly focus a particular order that the government will not back up the officer in resisting it. An illustrative example is state resistance to racial integration of public schools. Some state governments, as a matter of strongly held governmental policy, were opposed to integration. School principals and other individual officials who were resisting integration had been carrying out that governmental policy. This situation did not mean, however, that the best way for the federal authorities to secure compliance with court orders was to proceed against the state governments as such. Instead, narrowly drawn decrees were directed at recalcitrant individual officers. Although supporting the officers in principle, the state governments, to the extent that any collective decision was reached, often chose not to join issue. The officer in such cases, finding himself alone, yielded to the decree.

The most critical single element in accomplishing such isolation would appear to be legitimacy: the order must appear to be legitimate and the conduct of the resisting officer somehow tainted or illegitimate. In this respect, the enforcement problem is not unlike the problem of controlling mutinous troops or the problem in Algeria when General de Gaulle and General Salan were issuing conflicting orders. Force is on whichever side is able to persuade the officers that right is on its side. To isolate a re-sisting officer requires that an order appear to be fair and le-gitimate to most other officers. If similarly perceived by people generally, the order will be one that will effectively incapacitate the resisting officer from continued defiance.

Apparently the quickest way to isolate an individual from the support of others is to identify him, in a plausible manner, as belonging to some "contaminated" group. A government offi-cial who has been publicly identified as being a communist or mentally unstable may have difficulty in obtaining support from others. During the Oxford, Mississippi, incident in the fall of 1962, when a court committed Major General Edwin Walker, one of the leaders of those politically opposed to the Adminis-tration, for mental observation to determine whether he was suf-ficiently sane to answer criminal charges, General Walker's ability to lead an effective political force was badly shattered. The damaging effect of Senator Joseph McCarthy's unsubstan-tiated charges indicates how politically effective even unofficial assertions of an untrustworthy status can be. No one would sug-gest reviving McCarthyism. But revulsion with smear tactics, like revulsion with nuclear warfare, is hardly a reason for refusing to examine such weapons. At this point, we are seeking to un-derstand the power of these weapons, not proposing their use. Could a comparable effect be legitimately obtained in situations involving a government officer's noncompliance with a court de-cision to respect an international treaty?

A statute might provide that an officer who was found by a court, after hearing, to be in continuing defiance of a federal court order of which he had knowledge, could be held, if the judge thought the circumstances so warranted, for sixty days of mental observation at St. Elizabeth's to determine his mental sta-bility or sanity. It might be legitimate to infer that defiance of the federal court order on an important matter at least raised a ques-tion about the mental fitness of an individual. Not only would such a statute act as a deterrent, an order issued under it would tend to incapacitate those who once defied the court from further effective defiance. The critical question would arise when other government officials had to decide their reaction to a court order that, for example, required that a Deputy Assistant Secretary of the Air Force, who had refused to comply with a court order, be given a mental examination. Resisting a judicial order to determine whether a government official is sufficiently stable to carry on his important work might not commend itself to many officials. It is difficult to see how research could establish such reactions in advance, but experience suggests that such an order would have at least some impact. In fact, an instinctive revulsion to the idea of charging a dedicated public official with insanity as a means of forcing him to conform tends to confirm the intellectual judgment that such a statute and such a court order would indeed have a coercive effect if a court were willing to issue it.

Alternatively, a statute might provide that an officer's defiance of a court order raised a question not of that officer's sanity but rather of his possible adherence to the views of a foreign government, authorizing the court to suspend the officer temporarily pending a hearing on his loyalty.

If, rather than seeking to incapacitate the officer from continuing or repeating a violation, the court tries to coerce him into changing his mind, then the degree of pressure exerted against that officer would depend upon the degree to which the court was able to muster at least the passive cooperation of other officers of the government. As judicial experience with confinement for civil contempt shows, the most effective pressure exists when the defendant voluntarily can stop the pressure at any time by yielding. The more closely related the pressure is to the result desired, the more likely others will perceive the use of that pressure as fair and thus lend it their support. A statute providing that a government employee should not receive pay for any day in which he was in contempt of court would be expected to receive far more widespread support than would a statute that barred his traveling across state lines or that tripled his income tax.

The most successful sanctioning orders would be ones that

were nonpunitive in nature and designed to incapacitate the officer by altering his status in some way. The simplest means to accomplish this objective would appear to be for a court to issue an order suspending that person from office. Domestic legislation might give an international tribunal the power to suspend any domestic officer for, say, sixty days. Such suspension would, of course, be subject to being overridden should the government actively veto the decision. In the meantime, however, the suspension would be legally effective. A statute which explicitly spelled out the consequences of suspension might help to give the suspension practical effect. The statute could provide, for example, that the defiant official's security clearance be automatically withdrawn and that any other person who thereafter disclosed classified information to him would be guilty of a security violation. It also could stipulate that all documents or orders issued by him thereafter would be without legal effect and that the government (including a subsequent administration) could recover any amounts disbursed or authorized by him, would not be obliged to pay for any work he ordered, and so forth.

The effectiveness of a government official depends largely on the fact that other people treat him as an official. They recognize that he has certain legal authority. If a statute provided that on the happening of certain contingencies — as found by a court — the official's authority in certain respects would terminate, an official might well find that in those respects a court order effectively limited his power to act. He would be restrained from repeating a violation, not because he was deterred, but because he no longer had the actual power to continue to act contrary to the court order due to doubts about his legal power. In the United States, weapons procurement is an elaborate process involving enormous expenditures, some part of which it should be possible to stop with a well-planned legal monkey wrench. If a court found a particular military procurement to be contrary to a disarmament treaty and, therefore, illegal, it should be possible through a combination of prior legislation and a carefully drawn decree to cast such doubt upon the legal validity of the future acts of a designated official that most officials and others would not do business with him. The example suggests that it is both more effective and safer to have enforcement take place through paper orders than through physical action by international or opposing national forces.

5. *Evasive compliance.* It may be useful to consider instances where formal compliance leaves some members of the community dissatisfied. What should we expect of the legal system in such cases? Should these instances be considered as failures or successes of the system?

a. *Victory for the defendant.* One can guess that there might not be any compliance problem in roughly one half of the cases brought. In such cases the plaintiff may believe or allege that the defendant is violating international law, but the tribunal finds to the contrary. In many cases the unhappy plaintiff will remain unhappy; however, he has had his day in court, and that is probably the best that the system should try for.

b. *An erroneous victory for the defendant.* It must be assumed that at times a tribunal will make a mistake. In many instances there will be no objective criterion for determining that the tribunal erred. If the tribunal has authority to interpret the rule and to determine the facts, how can it be mistaken? Yet the tribunal, in certain cases, may find the facts to be contrary to what they physically are. A country in fact has engaged in some illegal conduct which the tribunal then finds did not take place. Such a finding could be thought of as a judicial whitewash. Rules and conduct are reconciled by a process of mistaken interpretation of conduct. It should be noted that so long as the whitewash is accomplished by an honest, respected, and competent body, one of the objectives of compliance will have been achieved. No noncompliance will have occurred that would tend to cause disrespect for the system.

If the dispute was solely concerned with past facts and possible compensatory action, then the matter will be closed. Although it is regrettable that the tribunal made a mistake, one cannot expect perfection. If, however, the matter involved continuing conduct, then one could start over again by initiating some sort of new case.

c. *Pyrrhic victories for the plaintiff.* In many circumstances the plaintiff might win his case, yet will find that he has already been deprived of a meaningful victory.

(1) *Gain not worth the cost.* As with Pyrrhus (who is supposed to
have said: "One more such victory over the Romans, and we are
utterly undone"), the costs incurred in gaining a desired decision will in some instances outweigh any benefits to be derived
from that decision. The hollowness of the determination in such
a case, however, does not present the legal community with any
problem of noncompliance.

(2) *The decision comes too late.* In other instances the delay involved in reaching a determination could rob the plaintiff of the
substance of the relief sought. For example, the farmer who
seeks an equitable sharing of the drought-time supplies of an
international river may not get a decision until it is too late to
save his crops. As unsatisfactory as this result may be for the
people concerned, it does not pose any problem of defiance.

d. *Postdecisional "avoidance."* As more than one litigant has discovered, a good deal of slippage can occur between obtaining
the paper victory of a judicial determination and obtaining the
substantive results that appear to have been won. The law makes
a distinction between avoidance and evasion. A taxpayer who
"avoids" a tax has found a lawful way of not subjecting himself
to the tax that would otherwise be required. A taxpayer who
"evades" a tax has adopted what turns out to be an unlawful way
of attempting to obtain the same substantive result. From the
point of view of the legal system, avoidance of legal obligations
if far preferable to evasion. It is in the community interest that
the energies of those who are unwilling to pay taxes be expended
in looking for tax loopholes and other avoidance schemes. It is
less destructive of the legal system to have people act lawfully
than to have them defy the law.

For purposes of the government's revenue collection, tax
avoidance is just as bad as tax evasion. In fact, it may be worse.
Some tax evaders may be caught eventually and required to pay
some of the taxes; by hypothesis, the tax avoiders have lawfully
ducked the obligation, at least until the law is changed.

Similar considerations are involved in the conduct of a defendant with respect to an adverse determination. He can frustrate much of the plain purpose of the determination and yet
still comply with the letter of the law. In a section entitled "Cir-
cumventing Judicial Decision," J. W. Peltason points out a num-

ber of ways by which a party who was unsuccessful in appellate litigation finally came out quite well indeed.[21] He notes that a party can win his case on another ground in the lower court upon remand, or he may prevail by obtaining a legislative change of the rule or by an amendment to the Constitution, which occurred after *Chisholm v. Georgia*.[22] In addition, a decision can be reversed on rehearing or overruled in a subsequent case.

A reluctant and resisting defendant will continue to fight even after he has "lost." He will stall for time; he will seek to affect the form of the judgment; he can raise questions of changed circumstance or newly discovered evidence. He can engage in legal maneuvers outside the context of the particular case, shifting to new legal grounds. He may comply with one decision, only to drag his feet in complying with another. In addition, officials may resign, and property be transferred to other hands. The history of resistance to legal decisions requiring racial integration in public institutions is filled with examples of such judgment avoidance.

Another example of compliance with the letter of a decision but not with its substance is found where a "test" case is limited to its particular facts. For instance, the Internal Revenue Service has developed a procedure of "nonacquiescence" in some decisions of the tax court. The Bureau complies with the immediate mandate in the particular case but continues in other cases to raise identical questions and to pursue the same policy. When the Supreme Court decided a case prohibiting a particular prayer in a public school, a number of other schools, not directly involved in the case, continued to conduct prayers that could not be distinguished from that involved in the litigated case.

For the legal system, the important point is that such tactics are preferable to outright defiance. The possibilities of avoidance should be sufficient to encourage a reluctant defendant to "play the game" within the legal rules. We should not expect a determination to provide a final solution to every problem. Our objective is less to cope with an ultimate problem than to avoid reaching such ultimate problems. When a conflict takes place

[21] J. PELTASON, FEDERAL COURTS IN THE POLITICAL PROCESS 58–62 (1955).
[22] 1 U.S. (2 Dall.) 16 (1793).

within a legal framework, it is less dangerous and less destructive than it would otherwise be. We should not expect to achieve an orderly world, but rather one in which we cope with disorder in an orderly way.

CHAPTER XV

Where Do We Go from Here?

If there is any one conclusion to be drawn from this book, it is that something can be done. There is an opportunity to improve compliance with international law. There appear to be dozens upon dozens of ways in which to strengthen the ability of the international legal sysem to deal with the compliance problem.

There is no one panacea. In fact, thinking about utopian solutions may divert us from practical steps that can be taken. Nor is there any one person who by himself can do what should be done. If the ideas scattered throughout this volume are correct, a great many people have roles to play in improving the international legal system. In every country, in the government and in the private sector, there are things that can be done. Members of United Nations delegations, judges, writers, foreign service officers, Justice Department officials, corporate counsel, legislators, advisers, teachers, and others — each can do something to make the international system function a bit better. Why don't we?

To some extent it is because we do not know which way to go. This book is an attempt to suggest a desirable direction in which to proceed. To a greater extent we do not spend our time trying to improve the way in which the world responds to international disputes and violations because we do not see that as our job. We are busy doing other things. Apparently nobody in the world has the full-time job of improving the functioning of the international legal system. What might that job involve?

It would involve diagnosing the international legal system in order to sort the various painful symptoms into useful categories and within each category to suggest causes. It would involve identifying alternative approaches, such as that suggested in this book, for reducing the problems, and selecting those that seemed most promising. More importantly, it would involve converting each idea into a suggestion of a specific action which a given individual could take, and then getting that suggestion effectively onto the agenda of that individual. Most people, most of the time, react and respond. The needed ingredient is initiative. Our hypothetical person whose job is to improve the functioning of the international legal system would be an activist, not a spectator. Would look forward, not back. Would respond to bad ideas by coming up with better ones. Would spend less time criticizing and more time solving problems. Would place less emphasis on constraints and more on choice. Would have the goal of improving the game of nations, not winning it.

Each of us caught up in some aspect of the international legal system need not pass the buck to such a hypothetical improver of the system. The best way to improve a game is to play the game in ways that make it a better game to play. Any reader has the opportunity to make a difference. To the extent that he or she gives greater weight to the concern of improving the functioning of the international legal system, some choice will be affected. To the extent that the ideas herein expressed have merit, they suggest what might be done. To the extent that they do not have merit, it is because other ideas and other approaches are better. Either way, if we want to improve compliance with international law, it is up to us.

Analytical Table of Contents

Improving Compliance with International Law

Index